■ BROADCAST/ CABLE COPYWRITING

Fifth Edition BROADCAST/ CABLE COPYWRITING

Peter B. Orlik

CENTRAL MICHIGAN UNIVERSITY

Allyn and Bacon Boston/London/Toronto/Sydney/Tokyo/Singapore

Senior Editor: Steve Hull
Editorial Assistant: Brenda Conaway
Cover Administrator: Suzanne Harbison
Composition Buyer: Linda Cox
Manufacturing Buyer: Louise Richardson
Editorial-Production Service: Grace Sheldrick, Wordsworth Associates
Production Administrator: Ann Greenberger

Library of Congress Cataloging-in-Publication Data

Orlik, Peter B.
  Broadcast/cable copywriting / Peter B. Orlik.—5th ed.
    p. cm.
  Includes bibliographical references and index.
  ISBN 0–205–15082–9
    1. Broadcasting—Authorship. 2. Broadcast advertising.
I. Title.
PN1990.9.A8807 1994
808′.066791—dc20   93–27113
                                                           CIP

Printed in the United States of America
10 9 8 7 6 5 4 3 2 1   98 97 96 95 94 93

To
Chris, Darcy, and Blaine
my patient Color Tour trio

CONTENTS

LIST OF ILLUSTRATIONS

PREFACE

Some writers are motivated by their profession's artistic challenges. Others are energized by its financial incentives. Broadcast/cable copywriting offers the stimulating opportunity to have it both ways: to experience constantly evolving tests of your verbal artistry while enjoying significant monetary rewards for successfully passing those tests. Whether you are an experienced media professional seeking to hone your writing ability further or a novice wordsmith striving to gain employment in radio and television, this book is designed for you.

Broadcast/Cable Copywriting, Fifth Edition, introduces you to the special requirements and pitfalls of creating the continuity, commercials, and off-air presentations that are the life's blood of electronic communication. Unlike the limited-access world of full-length entertainment and documentary script creation, broadcast/cable copywriting is a widespread enterprise that requires thousands of practitioners. It is a function that every local outlet must perform; an activity in which every advertising, public relations, and other corporate entity communicating via radio/television must engage. And despite their comparative brevity, commercial continuity pieces exemplify all the requisites of media form and content that electronic journalism and feature-length fiction demand. Thus, guided exposure to these short, standard elements of the copywriter's repertoire also will acquaint you with the stylistic techniques you'll need to master long-form projects.

On the other hand, like many wordsmiths before you, you may discover that the opportunity, the compensation, and the challenging diversity of *copywriting* are difficult to abandon in favor of the more sober environment of the newsroom or the much less stable world of program script creation. Do not be surprised if you decide to spend your *entire career* as a copywriter and/or continuity supervisor, marketing services manager, or agency creative director.

Over the years, electronic media copywriting has become much more than the audio/visual hawking of goods. Audiences now view the best commercials as entertainment in their own right, with entire television specials built to showcase the copywriter's art. And like any art, copywriting requires continuous training. "Writing," Professor Dennis Brown reminds us, "is not like riding a bicycle, a skill which if learned once is not forgotten. It is more like music—we must practice constantly not just to improve but to maintain our competence."[1] *Broadcast/Cable Copywriting*, Fifth Edition, strives to assist in such productive practice.

As in the previous edition, this volume is divided into four main parts. After an appraisal of the copywriting marketplace (Chapter 1) and how our jobs reflect communication process considerations (Chapter 2), Part One continues with an inventory of the tools (Chapter 3), human motivations (Chapter 4), and audience characteristics (Chapter 5) that the writer must learn to manage. Part One concludes by examining copy creativity, definition, and validation as well as prominent regulatory and stylistic constraints (Chapter 6). This first section thereby sets the stage for Part Two, which probes radio's key elements (Chapter 7), commercials (Chapter 8), and additional endeavors (Chapter 9). The parallel Part Three then uses a similar chapter trio (Chapters 10, 11, and 12) in the exploration of television. Finally, Part Four delves into the interlocking process of campaign construction: first, for the conventional radio/television campaign (Chapter 13); next, for the more specialized creation of public service appeals (Chapter 14); and last, for the hazardous practice of political, controversy, and crisis advertising (Chapter 15).

For teachers using *Broadcast/Cable Copywriting* as a class text, a separate Instructor's Manual provides a model syllabus, a selection of industry copy acceptance guidelines, and a series of Suggested Exercises to facilitate application of the techniques this Fifth Edition explores.

Throughout the book, a great many rules and precepts are advanced. Even though each has been tested time and time again in the intensely competitive electronic media, each (except for those ordained by government or industry regulations) can also be broken, given a specific and unique set of circumstances. Knowing the general rules, however, ensures that when you do decide to ignore one, your decision is not inadvertent but is based on a careful, conscious, and calculated appraisal of why this proven principle does not apply to the assignment at hand.

You are cautioned not to view the separate chapters of this book as independent and self-standing wholes. Do not, for example, think that you will acquire all of the information pertinent to writing *radio commercials* simply by reading the chapter bearing that title. Instead, the fifteen chapters in this Fifth Edition are mutually supportive. Each contributes additional perspectives to what is covered in others. Thus, guidelines introduced in conjunction with television *commercials* are at least partially applicable to *public service announcement* writing, and vice versa. In the constantly mutating world of electronic copy, nothing remains totally discrete for very long.

Like the four previous editions, this latest version of *Broadcast/Cable Copywriting* deepens your comprehension of the subject through numerous examples and illustrations. Many of these models are quite current. Others are more historic and are featured because they have made enduring contributions to the practice of effective radio/television communication. It is especially gratifying to be able to include samples contributed by many of my former students (in order of appearance): Andrew Schmittdiel, Christopher Conn, Sheila O'Donnell, Paul Boscarino, Dan Nelson, Jerry Downey, Susan Montgomery, John Schroeder, and Stephen Serkaian. These people are true professionals who have established themselves in the communications business and who continue to excel there as they did in the classroom we once shared.

One final bit of housekeeping before we begin. In an effort to increase the number of examples while still keeping the length of the book manageable, we have condensed the format of the sample scripts. IN ACTUAL PRACTICE, ALL COPY SEGMENTS THAT ARE SINGLE-SPACED IN THIS BOOK NORMALLY WOULD BE DOUBLE-SPACED, AND ALL COPY HEREIN DOUBLE-SPACED WOULD BE TRIPLE-SPACED.

Now, lets proceed, in the words of creative director Curvin O'Reilly, to "*Have some fun.* Despite all signs to the contrary, advertising is still the toy department of the business world. Enjoy."[2]

ACKNOWLEDGEMENTS

First and foremost, the author wishes to thank his wife, Chris, for her eternal belief in this project and its author, as well as for her patience, understanding, and continuous encouragement during *Broadcast/Cable Copywriting*'s five-edition evolution.

Appreciation is expressed to the many professionals in the electronic media and publishing industries who collectively provided the wealth of script and other illustrative material for this Fifth Edition. Many of their names appear in the text following the copy or other creative achievements they made available. The multiple quotes from *ADWEEK* and *Winners* have been reprinted with the permission of *ADWEEK*.

Further thanks are due to the following respected colleagues who reviewed the manuscript for this book: Robert Habermas, Liberty University; Anthony J. Miceli, Gannon University; Patton B. Reighard, Appalachian State University; and Joe Richie, Ohio University.

Allyn and Bacon's communications editor Stephen Hull and Grace Sheldrick of Wordsworth Associates continue to provide the editorial support and productional expertise that are essential in the publishing of a very complicated manuscript package. Thanks, too, to Dr. B. R. Smith, chairman of Central Michigan University's Broadcast & Cinematic Arts Department, and Patti Hohlbein, its administrative secretary, for the resource and service support associated with the compilation of this book and its exhibits.

Finally, gratitude goes to our two children, Darcy and Blaine, who have grown up with this seventeen-year project and put up with all of its distractions.

Thank *you*, the reader, for your company as we now explore together the specific components and techniques of copywriting for the broadcast and cable media.

Endnotes

1. Dennis Brown, "Students Need More Writing Instruction, Not Less," *Chronicle of Higher Education* (October 19, 1988), B 3.
2. Curvin O'Reilly, "Why Some People Have More Ideas," *ADWEEK* (February 15, 1988), 57.

■ *Chapter 1*

The Copywriting Marketplace

In order to understand the prerequisites and pressures of radio and television copywriting, we must, at the outset, find out something about the employment situations into which the copywriter is thrust. When we refer to copy jobs, we are not talking about the singular and largely inaccessible world of the entertainment scriptwriter, a world that regularly employs only a few hundred people. Nor are we referring to the discrete reportorial world of the media journalist. Instead, our focus encompasses that multitude of situations in which nonnews *copy*, the life's blood of all electronic media activities, is created.

Copy is the short piece of written craftsmanship that propels, promotes, defines, and ultimately helps to pay the bills for every carrier of radio and television programming. Unlike full-length (long-form) program scripts, which are the exclusive province of a handful of East or West Coast specialists, pieces of copy must be created by writers at virtually every station, cable system, and other local electronic medium. Copy must also be generated by the many agencies, corporations, and institutions that seek to make an impact on and through those telecommunications delivery vehicles.

The typical piece of copy is ten, fifteen, thirty, or sixty seconds long. Nevertheless, like the full-length script, it must tell a tale or reveal a truth within the time allotted. This is why some writers view copy creation experience as invaluable preparation for a career in news or long-form program writing. As Guy McCann points out, "A copywriter practices a disciplined form of creativity which requires study of a subject, identification of benefits and the generation of useful ideas that achieve precisely defined objectives. A copywriter, it might be said, must have a pragmatic inspiration when required and on schedule."[1]

Some wordsmiths aspire to media management and realize that success both in media *and* in management depends on the deft supervision of written words. They quite rightly view copywriting experience as a valuable preparation for later administrative roles. Other writers, however, see copywriting as a complete career in itself. Along the way, these folks learn that, although job contexts differ, traditional writers and *copy* writers share several key traits. As author and ad agency owner Lois Wyse puts it, both novels and pieces of

1

copy "require the ability to express ideas in succinct, powerful and caring terms."[2] But merely "having the urge to write doesn't necessarily make you a writer," adds Professor Howard Good. "Writing requires attention, discipline, and a strong backside."[3]

Assuming *your* backside is hardy, study and practice in the contexts and techniques of copywriting can pay significant professional dividends whatever your own long-term expressive goals may be. Most of this book is about techniques. But for a few pages, let's look first at the major employment contexts from which copy springs.

Freelance

This term has a decidedly mercenary origin. It was first applied to warriors too poor or unaccomplished to have their own land or liege lord. They hired themselves and their lances out to anyone who would employ them in order to establish a reputation and accumulate a little wealth. Set designer Dane Krogman recounts that the Duke of Argyll organized freelancers when he unified the Scots against the English. "But it didn't do any good. They got beaten and went back to being lances for hire. It's the same thing for anybody who's a freelancer today—you're true and loyal to whoever's paying you the most money for that particular day."[4]

Freelancing is one way for young copywriters to test, even on a part-time basis, their ability to create marketplace material that successfully serves a commissioned need. Initially, this might be constructing anything from public service spots for the local YMCA to commercials promoting a home-town merchant. Ultimately, if such small assignments are successfully dispatched, the freelancer may move beyond writing to become a one-person advertising agency: "pitching" area business folk on the need for radio and television exposure, creating the commercials, supervising their production, and even handling the actual time buys on stations and cable systems.

Part-time freelancing is a prudent way for the fledgling writer, like the obscure warrior, to fashion a reputation and make a little money before attempting to slay the fiercer dragons lurking in full-time employment and comprehensive media campaigns. For seasoned writers, too, freelancing on a full- or part-time basis can be professionally, psychologically, and economically satisfying. As veteran writer Susie Burtch testifies: "You don't have to hold the client's hand or be on the phone all day. I earn a full-time salary, there's no overhead, I'm my own boss and set my own hours. And as far as I'm concerned, you just can't get a better deal."[5] Tom Tawa, one of advertising's most successful freelancers, adds, "You are totally in control of your own time. There's none of that guilt if you want to go skiing or running. I have time for doing things I never had the time to do—like my taxes."[6]

On the other hand, if a freelancer is unsuccessful in soliciting assignments, there may be no taxes to do because there is no income. Therefore, observes industry commentator Alison Rogers, "the personality traits common among the most successful freelancers are quick-wittedness for the busy times and optimism for the slow times."[7] Even under the best of conditions, cash flow and work flow are uneven; and this problem can be compounded by clients who are quick to issue deadlines but slow to pay your invoice. In addition, because freelancers are usually retained for individual assignments, they are seldom able to participate in campaign planning or development for a major client. This also means that they are much more likely to be assigned the stand-alone radio commercial than the glamorous flight (series) of television spots. "If you look through the [awards] books," laments award-winning freelancer Luke Sullivan, "you won't find a freelancer keeping a high profile over any length of time. Probably because they can't get a hold of the big projects."[8]

To lessen these difficulties, some freelancers choose to specialize in a given product or media category. They become experts in agricultural or high-tech or health-care accounts. They learn how to use radio to promote financial services. Or they develop skill in fashioning industrial slide shows or video training tapes.

Still, despite such precautions, freelancing may end up as full-time anxiety for part-time pay. For this reason, many copywriters who have the choice either do not freelance or freelance exclusively on a moonlighting basis outside of salaried work hours. In the latter case, Luke Sullivan warns, freelancing might be viewed as "the F-Word because there are those who will argue that people who hold jobs in the creative staff of ad agencies and then go off to do freelance work after hours are nothing but a bunch of Marketing Slimebuckets, carpet-bagging fly-by-night Glory Hogs who cheat on their agency wives, who take their agency paychecks and then go sleezing around town with some bimbo of a client—and all for cheap thrills, quick cash, and One Show Pencils."[9]

Whether on a full-time or part-time basis, freelancing clearly has its pitfalls as well as its prizes. Therefore, given the option, many copywriters do not freelance. They conclude that they acquire fewer bruises when they fight today's creative battles as a full-fledged member of the corporate team. Still, a number of agencies and client in-house advertising departments continue to rely on freelancers who must be paid only when needed and who don't consume expensive fringe benefits. And, points out Alison Rogers, "when staff positions are eliminated to save money, freelancers get more work."[10]

Advertising Agency

At the opposite end of the spectrum from solitary freelancing is a copywriting slot in a large, multifaceted advertising agency. Here, you need not worry about soliciting assignments, procuring artwork, paying the phone bill, or finding a photocopy machine. Here, account executives attend to clients, art directors help with layouts and storyboards, creative directors provide a steady stream of assignments, and a variety of support staff assist with word processing and overall project execution.

Agency life is what most people visualize when they think of copywriting. Much popular sociology, and not a few theatrical movies, are fixated on the foibles of the slickly dressed agency scribe who spouts catchy clichés and snappy slogans that would sour in the mouth of a backwoods con artist. Contrary to this stereotype, asserts Ketchum Advertising's Jim Colasurdo, "In reality, copywriters are the ones in threadbare clothing or stylishly self-conscious 'I'm OK, you're OK' garb that can only be classified as 'Early Earth Shoe.' Nothing fits right, and sometimes even socks don't match. Many have the confidence of baby seals just before the hunters close in."[11]

Nevertheless, whatever their demeanor, agency copywriters tend to be among the top professionals in their field from the twin standpoints of talent and take-home pay. In most cases, they have had to prove themselves in one or more other media jobs before an advertising agency would even consider hiring them as wordsmiths. During 1991, for instance, the average salary for advertising agency copywriters in the United States was $41,700[12]— well over twice as much as copywriters who worked for radio stations. As this figure suggests, clients, and consequently the advertising agencies themselves, have come to demand that each writer on board perform as a seasoned professional.

Assuming that you do make it into an agency creative department either directly or, more probably, via the freelance, in-station or other apprenticeship route, you will encounter one of two main types of structures. You may be working in a department in which all copywriters serve the total media needs of the clients to whom they are assigned. In this case, you might be helping to create newspaper and magazine layouts, direct-mail pieces, and even point-of-purchase (POP) displays and billboards—all in addition to radio and television copy. This diversity forces the copywriter to be much more of a generalist and to be equally familiar with the distinct requirements of print and electronic communication.

Alternatively, you may find yourself in one of the far fewer number of agencies that segregate their radio/television writers from wordsmiths servicing print media. This pattern goes back at least to the 1950s, when the new medium of television caused many clients to demand advertising that reflected the talents of video specialists (or, at least, of writers who were striving mightily to become such specialists). Later, when integrated, cross-media campaigns came to the fore, most agencies abandoned this dual pool organization. Nonetheless, so. full-service shops continue to believe that specialists are the only way to maximize the impact of their radio and television messages. These agencies share this attitude with the small *boutique* shops that devote most of their attention to the creative aspect of advertising—especially messages that are designed for the broadcast and cable media.

The differences in working climates between such small firms and the giant agencies can be substantial. As small-agency executive Tony Benjamin argues, "Because small agencies generally (though not always) work with small budgets, they can't afford to allow execution to overshadow content. As a result, *ideas* have to work uncamouflaged by excessive production values. This means goodbye to the useless helicopter shots, the unnecessary high-tech visuals, the mandatory Jamaican locations, the mega-dollar celebrity endorsers and the overpriced models. Instead, small shops unglamorously create advertising that stands or falls on ideas alone."[13]

In the small organization, there are fewer people standing between the copywriter and the client, and the client companies themselves tend to be smaller. Because there are fewer decision makers to appease, and because the budgetary stakes are lower, the urge to pioneer new creative techniques can be fed more easily. If these techniques succeed, the small agency acquires notoriety and starts to grow. However, warns small shop owner Jerry Fields, "As soon as a small or mid-size agency starts developing a highly visible image based on its creative work and/or successful new-business track record, it's not long before some mega-agency with deep pockets makes them an offer they can't refuse. Swallowed up in the many-splendored layers of the conglomerate agency management and politics, all the creative and entrepreneurial elements that destined the small agency for greatness disappear."[14]

For the copywriter, this change might not be all bad because larger agencies offer more back-up support, which helps compensate for the interference from added layers of managerial overseers. Still, says creative Vice-President Barry Rosenthal, "There are people above you, beside you, and below you who all chime in with their opinions and directives. Your job is to somehow satisfy all the people who count and still create an effective spot or campaign."[15] In addition, large agencies frequently pit their creative teams against each other for the privilege of producing a television spot. As award-winning large-shop creative Sharon Occhipinti admits, "I understand the television medium very well. But I also know that you have to be lucky to get something produced."[16]

In the small agency, conversely, you do not encounter several other copywriters working on competing versions of the same project. "There are four of us in the creative department," reveals Joe Sweet of Pedone & Partners. "There's really nowhere to hide when you have a job to do. It's small here. You can feel the four walls at the agency."[17]

But no matter what particular structure and bulk a given advertising agency exhibits, and no matter how few or how many functions it serves besides actual message creation, the prime function of copywriters is still to *write*. As creative director Steven Penchina describes the agency scene, "You hole up in your office with your art director . . . and sweat it out. Trying out an idea, honing it, refining it, loving it, throwing up on it, starting over again and again, killing yourself and praying that by 2 o'clock in the morning of the presentation, you'll get that last 10 percent of inspiration that gets you over the hump. It's torture. It always was and always will be. But when you succeed, you'll cherish it. And your client will cherish it."[18]

Corporate In-House

Certain types of firms prefer to fashion their own advertising rather than to contract it out to a separate agency. They therefore set up units within their own organization—often in conjunction with their public relations division—to plan and execute the advertising effort. This pattern is especially popular with utility companies, financial institutions, retail chains, and some packaged goods manufacturers. Their managements feel that corporate policy, image, and attitude can best be communicated by writers who thoroughly understand the business. And what better way to stimulate understanding than by making the writer a full-time employee of the organization and dependent on it for that weekly paycheck?

This rationale exposes the greatest weakness of the in-house system: *lack of objectivity.* Writers who are part of the enterprise they are publicizing are leery of criticizing its marketing plans and reluctant to question a defective campaign or outmoded corporate slogan. In-house writers come to know their company's sacred cows so well that a whole system of preferred or untouchable subjects can, by accretion, clog the entire creative process and strangle the universal need for constant creative evolution. "The in-house agency," reveals advertising executive Lynne Seid, "generally forgets what drives the brand in the market and gets more involved in what will sell the campaign inside the company."[19] What's more, the in-house pattern can be stifling to the writer who is forced to deal exclusively with the same product or service year after year without the opportunity to grow through exposure to new and different assignments and clients.

Giving it its due, the in-house system generally does offer writers a greater chance of job stability and a heightened opportunity to analyze fully the products and services their copy will promote. Such in-depth knowledge can result in clearer and more accurate messages because of the writer's continuous familiarity with the subject. Inadvertent deception arising from writer misunderstanding of client data is minimized, and corporate decision makers can be kept more closely in touch with consumer opinions about both the advertising and the product or service being marketed.

In-house (also known as *client-side*) copywriting can offer excellent preparation for a career at an outside agency as well. Further, the competition for entry-level in-house jobs generally is less intense. Writers who wish to make the jump from client-side to agency work, however, must not wait too long.

For whatever reason, many agencies conclude that people who have spent more than two or three years on the client-side must be second-rate talent. There is little rational justification for this prejudice, but it persists nonetheless. Many copywriters—skilled ones—have spent entire careers happily and lucratively at corporate in-house billets. You may do likewise. Just be sure that such a setting is where you want to be before you lose your mobility.

Government/Institutional In-House

Much of what has been said about the corporate in-house situation carries over to the government/institutional environment. Working for a nonprofit organization does not make the writer's problems significantly different from those an in-house counterpart faces at a profit-making enterprise. The lack of objectivity is still a real danger and is perhaps heightened by the fact that an allegedly praiseworthy public or charitable institution is doing the communicating. In their haste to promote a worthy cause, writers may distort or exaggerate that cause's actual mission.

Still, the in-house setting is the only practical organizational pattern for many small charities, institutions, and foundations that cannot afford outside talent but must rely on the work of regular employees who often perform other functions as well. The municipality, the college, the religious organization, and several like establishments need people who thoroughly understand their institution's role and philosophy and can explain them in a consistent manner whatever the specific issue involved.

This is another generalist environment to which the copywriter trained only in radio/television (or only in print, for that matter) may have difficulty adapting. But if you have a strong commitment to that church, charity, or civic organization, such a setting can be personally gratifying and, given the breadth of jobs you may have to perform, professionally stimulating as well. Just remember to reserve a place in your pencil box for well-sharpened objectivity. Mayors and bishops can be just as shortsighted as marketing vice-presidents.

In-Station

Copywriters within a station or cable system experience a more varied brand of in-house work. Despite the prevalence of canned (preproduced) video and audio material from outside suppliers, all radio and television stations and most cable systems must generate some aired copy of their own. These self-created writing efforts include such items as station/system identifications (known as "IDs"), program promotions, public service copy, and, most lucratively, commercial messages (spots) to serve the needs of local advertisers. Outlet employees who turn out such writing may or may not be called copywriters, but they draw the scripting assignments nonetheless.

The paradox has been that those major-market stations/systems with the largest staffs have needed in-station writers least. Virtually all their "spot load" (schedule of commercials) accrues from substantial national or regional advertisers whose agencies deliver the commercials prepackaged and ready for airing. Large outlets, in short, have had the greatest capability to hire advertising copywriters but the least need for them. Thus, in their recent study of 210 midwestern radio stations, David MacFarland and Brian Cooper found that "Medium market stations appeared to offer the best chance for a prospective full-time copywriter. This was the only category in the survey in which the majority of stations hired a writer fulltime. Medium markets are typically large enough to establish a substantial amount of competition for clients, but are not large enough to support more than a few advertising agencies."[20]

But with cable systems now bolstering their local advertising efforts and with the competition for fragmenting audiences accelerating in broadcast television as well as in radio, even major market facilities are starting to invest in copywriter positions to handle promotions if not commercial assignments. The burgeoning options available to listeners and viewers require not only greater efforts by existing stations to hold the audience but also aggressive marketing by new delivery systems to establish a niche in the consumer's listening/viewing patterns.

At many stations, the old promotions unit (which used to consist of a secretary sending out bumper stickers) has been upgraded into a Creative Services or Marketing Department that handles everything from on-air promotion, to client and press information packets, to the overall design of the outlet's programming. Some facilities have even abolished the program director's position and placed that responsibility in the hands of the marketing director. Such fundamental changes in emphasis have meant new prestige and job opportunities for copywriting professionals. (On the downside, promotion-based positions are also the most unstable. John Miller, NBC's executive vice-president for marketing, laments that nearly 40 percent of the promotion/creative service director positions at NBC affiliates turn over every year.[21])

For both advertising and promotion tasks, small operators are also becoming increasingly aware that copywriting slots can pay for themselves. These stations and cable systems have either scraped together enough money to hire one person for full-time writing chores or have retained only those time salespeople and air personalities who can be counted on to generate effective copy in conjunction with their other duties. This trend demonstrates that good writing skills are important to electronic media employability regardless of whether you see yourself as a copywriter.

As is often the case with freelancers, even full-time in-station/system copywriters may discover that writing duties also encompass at least some responsibility for producing, announcing, and actually pitching spots to clients or their representatives. In the case of outlet promotion materials, this selling job is directed to one's own bosses; but it makes the work-load no less demanding. Whether freelancing or in-station, if you are the only real writer around, be prepared to shepherd your concept from the keyboard right through its placement on the program log and ultimate projection to consumers.

In-station writers also face two conditions not present in the agency setting: (1) extremely short deadlines and (2) the need to serve competing clients. At an advertising agency, assignments are usually time-lined over a number of days. At a local station/cable office, they may be required within the hour! A retail client wants to change his or her 11 o'clock commercial to reflect a spur-of-the-moment sale, or a station salesperson demands a sample (spec) spot to impress a potential client over lunch. Both of these demands must be attended to immediately while still keeping up with the normal flow of writing assignments.

There is also the problem of competing clients. Most electronic media outlets number several different banks, eateries, gas stations, grocery stores, auto dealers, and other local businesses among their continuing clientele. Because these enterprises are often too small to hire ad agencies, the station/system copywriter must create commercials for each of them. No advertising agency ever handles more than one account in a given product category. But in-station/system writers must service competing clients all the time—keeping each one satisfied and differentiated from its rivals.

Other Employment Options

The previous five categories encompass the majority of electronic media copywriting positions, but a number of other options also may be available. Both broadcast and cable networks employ their own promotions writers to craft promos and the other brief material used between program segments. This type of writing can be an especially high-stakes adventure. If it actually had to pay for the airtime it uses, the promotions department of any of the networks would be that network's own biggest client. With such multimillion-dollar time investments at stake, network promotion writers must be especially clever.

Similarly, specialty service firms such as FirstCom, JAM and Film House use high-talent writers to create jingle, promotion, and image packages that enhance programming flow and appeal on behalf of local outlets around the country. Station slogans, comedy bits, musical sell lines, and 'concept' channel identifications may all be a part of the specialty service's highly attractive output.

Finally, mention must be made of commercial, industrial, and educational production houses. Although much of their activity revolves around the creation of full-length projects, many of these projects are of ten to twenty minutes' duration. Such audio, video, and tape/slide presentations are, in fact, copy extensions that copywriters therefore are uniquely qualified to prepare.

Continuity—the Copywriter's Main Product

In most of the employment contexts we have just explored, the electronic media copywriter is engaged in the task of creating *continuity*. This term, which is so central to the writer's role, has both a broad and a narrow definition. To understand our writing responsibilities, we must be aware of each definition's parameters.

In the broad sense, *continuity* encompasses all short, nonprogrammatic aired material. Thus, within this use of the term, everything that is not an integral part of a self-contained information or entertainment show can be called continuity. This definition therefore excludes news copy, but it does include commercials and public service announcements as well as promos, station/channel IDs, time/weather blurbs, and similar between-program matter.

Commercials and PSAs (public service announcements) are *excluded* under continuity's narrow designation. This much more restrictive use of the term defines continuity as *brief, nonprogrammatic and nonspot aired material designed to promote, interlock, and increase attention to the aired features and commercials.* This definition, therefore, primarily embraces the role of promotion writers. Commercial copywriters, conversely, exercise the wider responsibilities that are reflected in continuity's broad definition.

Many outlets maintain a traffic and continuity department or person charged with the task of preparing program logs and the associated scheduling of all material segments to be aired. Under such an arrangement, a natural relationship exists between the scheduling function, which sets down all the programs and announcements in sequence, and the writing function, which seeks to make the flow between all those disparate parts as smooth as possible. The traffic and continuity staffer thus is often both organizer and writer. In each of these contexts, the emphasis is on the *segue*. Originally borrowed from music, the term *segue* is now used in the electronic media as verb and noun—both to describe the process of one sound merging without a break into another and to denote the result of this process.

The radio/television industry places a high premium on these segues in order to give the listener or viewer as little excuse as possible to tune out mentally, as little time as possible to flip the dial or push the button. The writer who constructs stimulating and informative copy is just as important to segue achievement as is the technical director or on-air talent. Conversely, dead air and dead copy can be equally lethal to the maintenance of program and audience flow. The aim, of course, is to give the audience the feeling that pleasing and interesting stimuli are proceeding in an unbroken stream that deserves the continuing investment of their time as well as the more or less constant devotion of their attention.

The fashioning of meaningful, listener-holding transitions is a vital part of the copywriter's craft and a core duty whether you deal with continuity in the broad or narrow sense. What is more, transitions are as essential within a full-length entertainment or information program as they are to the interlocking of a newscast with the game show that follows it. Skill-honing in constructing between-program transitions improves your ability to sculpt the unified full-length scripts that you might later be called on to write. Even in its most limited sense, continuity writing is therefore both a valuable training ground for more expansive writing efforts and a means of gainful employment in its own right.

It is not necessary to justify continuity writing as a mere preliminary to 'bigger' things. Indeed, it might be argued that the writer who can surmount the immense time problems inherent in a 30-second spot and still create an attention holding and memorable vignette possesses and exhibits a cogent talent that few novelists or playwrights ever attain.

Portfolio Creation

Just as the novelist or playwright collects scenario ideas and character sketches for possible use in some future project, continuity writers should be gathering, preserving, and upgrading the copy assignments on which they have worked in order to advance to better accounts or jobs in the months and years ahead. This means developing a professional portfolio. Unlike playwrights and novelists, copywriters' names do not adorn each spot or promo they've penned. In fact, the writer of commercials and other continuity remains anonymous to all but the supervisor or client. This absence of attribution is the price we pay for the relative security of a salaried job and a regular paycheck. To secure that first and subsequent media job, therefore, copywriters must compile their own tangible record of what they have done to serve as a promise of what they will do.

"For us," states The Martin Agency's creative director Mike Hughes, "the portfolio is 95 percent of getting a job. We put so much emphasis on it that people get very competitive in putting the portfolio together."[22] "The book is everything," reveals agency head David Suissa. "The book tells you what kind of attitude they have. It's all there in the work."[23] And senior copywriter Tom Puckett chimes in, "I don't think creatives have to worry about their resume. Your portfolio is your resume."[24]

Thus, to give yourself every advantage, it is strongly recommended that you begin your portfolio NOW. A promo or a 30-second spot need not have been actually aired in order to demonstrate your wordsmith's skill any more than a novelist's character sketch must be actually published before it has merit. The important thing is that the spot or the sketch exposes a true writer's insight and execution.

You will find that portfolio development is easier if you do not have to think up both the market problem and the copy solution. Whenever possible, use and improve exercises encountered in class or stimulated by this book. Such exercises will helpfully determine the limitations within which you must work. Dreaming up your own assignments for portfolio exhibits, on the other hand, can be not only tedious but also misleading. It is much too easy to create a problem for a solution you have already conceived or to avoid instructive pitfalls by bending the task around them. As opposed to the playwright or novelist, the continuity writer can seldom choose the subject and can virtually never determine the length of time expended in addressing it. So get your assignments from somewhere or someone else as your new portfolio begins to take shape. Learn to work within the unyielding time and subject constraints that are an intrinsic part of the continuity writer's world—and let your portfolio reflect this reality.

Bad advertising is another source for portfolio exhibits. The next time you encounter an ad that you think is a failure, jot down its essence and then show how you would improve it. When the portfolio sets the original and your enhanced version side-by-side, your marketing and creative abilities are graphically revealed. If the portfolio leads to a job interview, these kinds of exhibits are also very potent discussion starters.

Just make certain that such comparative displays are the only bad advertising in your book! Successful freelancer Yvonne Smith reveals that "It says something about the judgment of the person who ruined an entire portfolio by including that one bad thing. Judge the person on the worst thing in the book. You [the perspective employer] may get something equally bad."[25] Similarly, counsels creative director David Butler, "If a book is really up and down, it's almost like the person can't tell a good ad from a bad ad, and you form an opinion, justly or unjustly, that they can't edit themselves."[26]

Once you are certain your creations are uniformly good ones, you are ready to compile them. Portfolio cases constitute the vehicles through which copywriters arrange and display their creations. These cases come in a variety of sizes and are available at many art and office supply stores. Copywriters can usually make do with smaller sizes than can art directors, but if your samples include full-page newspaper layouts or oversize brochure pages or storyboards, a larger case may be required. These cases are similar to a zippered vinyl or leather briefcase with paired handles, but they open flat to expose a binder arrangement of three or more rings to which mounting pages are fastened. Individual exhibits are set on these pages, which are then held in place and protected by attached plastic covers (see Figure 1–1).

Including from fifteen to twenty copy samples is considered the norm. Dozens of exhibits are too cumbersome for you to carry and too time-consuming for a prospective employer to wade through. The portfolio's binder design makes it easy to remove old exhibits and replace them with newer, improved examples. It is also a good idea to have one or more spare portfolios so your job seeking is not brought to a halt if one executive asks to keep your book for a while.

The ultimate test of a portfolio, maintains Dave Butler, is "the quality of the work. Can we look through a book and find a significant number of ads that make us say, 'Gee, I wish I'd done that.'"[27] Roger Proulz of Ogilvy & Mather adds, "A book tells me whether or not a person is excited and eager about advertising and *really* wants to go into it and take it seriously. So it's a good exercise, a good discipline. A lot of these kids look at advertising and think it looks easy. They don't have any idea how difficult this business is, what hard work it is, how competitive it is, until they struggle to put a book together."[28]

Above all, do not wait until you are actually in the job market to get your portfolio started. Under the pressure of finding immediate employment, the

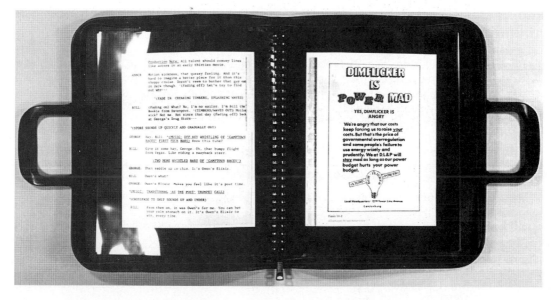

Figure 1-1
A Typical Copywriting Portfolio

range of your work will be too limited and the scope of your talent too blurred. Granted, the stress of fulfilling assignments is a constant part of the copywriter's lot. But pressure to come up with what those assignments *should be* is not. Further, no writer—novice or veteran—can create, in a short period of time, a copy catalog sufficient to demonstrate either versatility or breadth of experience.

Writing style and character are in a continuous process of evolution. They exist, as composer Aaron Copland said about music, "in a continual state of becoming."[29] Not even a hint of this growth can be captured in a portfolio created within a single month. So begin your portfolio now. Improve it gradually throughout your career. Keep thinning it out so that only the hardiest hybrids from each copy species remain. Then, let that portfolio help propel you toward whatever sector of the copywriting marketplace best suits your own aims, goals, and documented abilities.

"Creating advertising is a never-ending thing," cautions BBDO chairman Phil Dusenberry. "The difficulty is trying to top yourself. What do you do for an encore to all those commercials? Advertising is very much a what-have-you-done-for-me-lately business. You always have to be sharpening your sword, trying to be better tomorrow than you were yesterday."[30] Being 'better' requires surmounting both your own past limitations and the constraints imposed by the characteristics of the electronic media. These constraints are explored in the following chapter.

Endnotes

1. Guy McCann, "The Relationship between Psychological Type and Performance in a Copywriting Course" Paper presented to the Association for Education in Journalism and Mass Communication 1989 Convention (Washington, DC), 1.
2. James Baker, "Creative Moonlighting," *ADWEEK* (June 2, 1986), S.S. 12.
3. Howard Good, "Teaching Writing as a Beautiful and Bleak Passion," *The Chronicle of Higher Education* (July 17, 1991), B3.
4. Alison Rogers, "Lancers for Hire," *Winners* (August 1989), 4.
5. Kandy Kramer, "The Freelance Life: Nice Work and Susie Burtch Has It," *ADWEEK* (October 28, 1985), 38.
6. Maryanne McNellis and Kim Foltz, "The Ups (and Downs) of Freelancing," *ADWEEK* (February 3, 1986), C.R. 36.
7. Alison Rogers, "The Freelance Life," *Winners* (August 1989), 54.
8. Ibid., 53.
9. Luke Sullivan, writing in "Viewpoint," *Winners* (October 1987), 3.
10. Rogers, "Freelance Life," 55.
11. Jim Colasurdo, "Life as a Copywriter: It Ain't Easy," *ADWEEK* (March 24, 1986), 22.
12. Meryl Davids, "Flatliners: The New Reality," *ADWEEK* (June 3, 1991), 28.

13. Tony Benjamin, "10 Reasons to Think Small," *ADWEEK* (July 31, 1989), 24.
14. Jerry Fields, letter to the editor, *ADWEEK* (February 24, 1992), 30.
15. Barry Rosenthal, "What Drives the Creative," *BPME Image* (December 1990), 12.
16. "The New Avant-Garde," *Winners* (February, 1989), 30.
17. Mary Huhn, "The Art of Job-Hopping, '88 Style," *ADWEEK* (May 9, 1988), S.S. 28.
18. Steven Penchina, "Gone Are the Glory Days," *ADWEEK* (March 4, 1991), 32.
19. Richard Morgan, "Separation of Church and State: Can Tarlow Be Both Agency and Client?" *ADWEEK* (August 14, 1989), 2.
20. David MacFarland and Brian Cooper, "The Job Market for Fulltime Copywriters," *Feedback* (Winter 1991), 21, 28.
21. Robert Rimes, "John Miller," *BPME Image* (March 1987), 6.
22. Susan Korones, "War of Wits," *Winners* (November 1987), 13.
23. "Perusing the Portfolios," *ASAP* (May/June, 1989), 27.
24. Huhn, 28.
25. "Perusing," *ASAP,* 28.
26. Ibid,
27. Ibid,, 27.
28. Whit Hobbs, "Hiring by the Book," *ADWEEK* (July 1, 1985), 32.
29. Aaron Copland, *Music and Imagination* (Cambridge, MA: Harvard University Press, 1952), 2.
30. Michael Kaplan, "The Last Temptation of Phil Dusenberry," *Winners* (October 1988), 11.

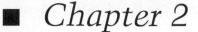

■ *Chapter 2*

Copywriting and the Communication Process

Like anyone professionally engaged in reaching large and diverse groups of people, the broadcast/cable copywriter must be acutely aware of the dynamics of the communication process. The fact that your messages employ exotic electronic media does not lessen the need for you to appreciate the most basic components of human communication. Broadcast/cable writers who concentrate only on the electronic implements of their delivery system tend to construct messages attuned to media agencies rather than to the audiences those agencies are attempting to impact.

In the final analysis, copywriters are paid, not to reach 'media,' but to reach *people through* those media. Therefore, there must be no misconception as to the primacy of individual consumers, grouped into masses of various sizes and types, in determining what we write and how we write it. The unemployment lines continue to be fed by practitioners who write "for" radio and television rather than for other human beings.

Communication Fundamentals

No matter how simple or sophisticated its delivery system, all communication aimed at people includes and activates the four components pictured in Figure 2–1. Any or all of these components can exist in multiple form and still not change the fundamental functioning of the process.

1. Originator

Limiting our discussion to *human* communication (this is not, after all, a text on computer programming or animal husbandry), we assume the *originator* to be a human being with some desire to communicate with another human being or beings. In our business, this desire is most often stimulated by money. The originator's task is to establish a temporary linkage with another person in order that they both will focus on the same object, event, or idea.

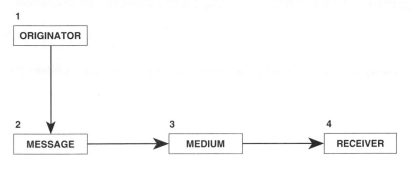

Figure 2-1
The Basic Communication Process

The duration of this linkage and the clarity of this focus are influenced by every component of the process but initially depend on the originator's overt and covert behavior. We have all experienced situations in which an originator's overt action clashes so strikingly with his or her covert (underlying) behavior that real doubt is cast on that originator's motives. The man who shakes your hand warmly but studiously avoids eye contact becomes as suspect as the woman whose warm vocal "hello" is accompanied by physically backing away. Links have been established, of course, but with much different impacts than the originators intended—or thought they intended.

In certain instances, originators might fool *themselves* as to the fundamental factors influencing their communications. (More than one inadvertently bad peanut butter advertisement can be traced back to some poor copywriter who never could stand the stuff.) Every originator has some financial, social, or professional stake in the results of every communication he or she initiates. The most successful people are those who have learned to probe their own motivations before seeking to influence others.

This influencing may consist of nothing more than attaining attention (which, in the cacophonous environment of radio/television, is no small task). Once such attention/linkage has been established, the originator has satisfied the basic mechanical requirements of the communication process. Whether the outcome of this linkage is favorable or unfavorable to the originator is a more long-range and often subjective judgment. As we discover in later chapters, it is not too difficult to secure momentary attention. Holding and parlaying such attention toward ends acceptable or advantageous to the originator, however, are much more extensive and intensive tasks.

2. Message

A *message* is the commodity one must possess in order to be justifiably labeled an originator. It is a commodity one must also *transmit* in order

17

actually to *function* as an originator. This does not mean that originators are always aware of the content they are transmitting—or even that they are transmitting at all. Human beings, in sensory proximity to each other, can receive messages that are products of that proximity rather than of any conscious desire on the part of the alleged originator to communicate. What is interpreted as a "come hither" look on the part of that handsome male across the dance floor may result only from a slippage of his contact lens. Similarly, though she is not aware of the fact, the dozing student in the back of the classroom is originating a distinctly unpleasant message as far as her instructor is concerned—and one that will not have its impact diminished merely because it was inadvert.

Except in total isolation from other people, it is very difficult if not impossible for us to avoid assuming the more or less continuous role of originators transmitting a steady stream of intended and unintended messages to people with whom we come into contact. When the situation instills in us an *active* desire to transmit, we tend to make special efforts to avoid the simultaneous sending of seemingly conflicting messages.

3. Medium

The vehicle through which originators project their messages can be simple or complex. It can emanate exclusively from the originator's own body or use external mechanisms. In fact, some authorities divide media into two broad categories: *communication* and *communications* vehicles. The first category consists of intrabody devices. Thus, oral behavior using the human vocal apparatus as well as physical gestures and other visible body movements (nonverbals) constitute *communication.* Writing on a blackboard, typing a letter, or marking a forest trail with piled rocks, on the other hand, are all considered *communications* because they rely on message-carrying instruments external to the human anatomy.

A key advantage of communications media is that they extend our ability to communicate in time and/or space. A note left on the refrigerator or on the dining room table will convey the originator's message even though it may have been written hours or days ago and the originator might be miles away when that note is discovered.

Mass communications vehicles constitute a special subgroup of communications media because their extreme efficiency not only extends our ability to communicate in time and space but also makes it possible to reach large and diversified audiences quickly, if not instantaneously. As the radio/television copywriter soon learns, however, the optimum use of mass communications requires that each person within the 'mass' audience is led to feel that he or she is being addressed directly and singly. In fact, the electronic media in particular are at their most effective when they simulate a *communication* rather than *communications* experience. The script that assists an announcer in seeming to talk "across the table" to you (a communication setting) has a much greater chance of success than one that bellows at "all you folks out there in TV-land" and thereby calls more attention to the medium than to the message it carries.

4. Receiver

The receiver is the *detector* of the message the originator has transmitted via some medium. We say detector, rather than target, because receivers spend much of their time picking up messages that are not really aimed at them. In the most alarming sense, this occurs in bugging and other forms of electronic eavesdropping, where a conscious and technologically sophisticated effort is made to intercept messages intended for others. Usually, however, detection of messages by unintended receivers is simply a case of sensory proximity. We have all overheard conversations of people at adjoining restaurant tables or in nearby bus seats. We have all glanced over others' bulletin board notes and postings. In doing so, we became receivers even though the originator of the message sent via the communication or communications vehicle was not seeking to establish a link with us.

Straightforward originators usually do not worry about whether people other than those at whom they aim have, in fact, become receivers of the message. Their only concern is whether they have made receivers of the people they have actively tried to reach. For truly successful communication is more than accidental or mechanical meshing of originator, message, medium and receiver. Instead, this success requires:

AN ORIGINATOR (with a conscious desire to communicate)
  A MESSAGE (of significance)
    through A MEDIUM (that is appropriate)
      to A RECEIVER (attaching like significance)
        who RESPONDS *in an originator-advantageous manner.*

The Radio/Television Communication Process

Keep in mind that the originator, message, medium, and receiver are components basic to any and every application of the communication process. When we move beyond simple one-to-one interchanges, additional subelements come into play. Thus, in the copywriter's electronic media world, we encounter the system represented in Figure 2–2.

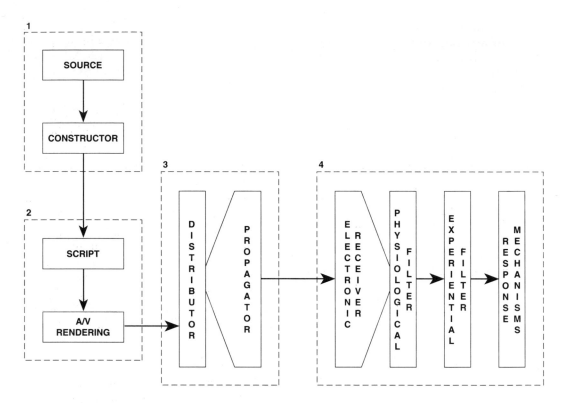

Figure 2-2
The Radio/Television Copywriter's Communication Process

1. Originator

Unless the same person owns, operates, and prepares all the advertising for an enterprise, the origination function in the electronic media is shared by a SOURCE working in cooperation with a message CONSTRUCTOR. This source is usually referred to as the client. It may be a bank, cereal manufacturer, or fast-food palace. In noncommercial assignments (resulting in *public service announcements*, or PSAs), the source may be the United Way, CARE, even the local Society for the Preservation of Hibernating Chipmunks. It is the source whose aims drive the process and set the agenda for what is to be communicated.

The other half of the originator function, the constructor, then strives to further this agenda by putting together a message that is appropriate to the task and maximally adapted to take advantage of the unique capabilities of radio or television. Presumably, you are reading this book as a means of preparing yourself to be, or assist, such a constructor. Electronic media constructors work within media outlets, at advertising agencies, or in any of the other contexts discussed in Chapter 1. Whatever the environment, however, you must recognize that a radio/television message constructor seldom has the last (or even the first) word as to what will be communicated. To a general or specific degree, it is the source who pays the bills—the constructor's salary included—and who therefore calls the shots.

Shaller Rubin Associates' Executive Vice-President Paul Goldsmith illustrates this inevitability by observing that

> the greatest hype a copywriter has is at the moment the "final" version of the copy comes out of the typewriter. It's all downhill from that moment. My ideal copywriter is fully aware of the downhill realities of the advertising process—recognizing that his work will go through more sieves, more review than any other piece of work in the agency. After it's submitted to the scrutiny of his supervisor, it goes to the creative director. On to the account group for its suggestions and changes before it reaches the client who will surely incorporate his ideas and alterations. This tedious trip through a creative person's chamber of horrors unfortunately comes with the territory.[1]

An appropriate secret motto for copywriters is therefore one articulated a quarter-century ago by American Association of Advertising Agencies chairman James McCaffrey: *Illegitimis Non Carborundum Est* (a loose Latin translation for "Don't Let the [boneheads] Grind You Down.")[2]

2. Message

When people think of the electronic media message, they understandably focus on the audio and/or video form in which that message reaches them. Yet, that communication first had to be set down in more traditional written form to constitute a SCRIPT. Granted, on some occasions, the message is extemporized, entirely ad-libbed, or edited down from taped actualities and interviews. In these instances, a script is either unnecessary or becomes a *transcript* for contractual or record-keeping purposes. In most copywriting situations, however, the script constitutes the motivating creative blueprint.

After approval by the appropriate sources (and supervisory constructors), this blueprint is translated into "live" on-air readings, or audio, video, or film recordings for easy playback by electronic outlets. As we subsequently explore in Chapters 7 and 10, the effectiveness of the script depends almost as much on its form as on its content. The best-laid concepts can be maimed, if not murdered, when the scripts that convey them are confusing or disorganized.

Assuming that the script is cast into the industry-recognized pattern, it must then be transformed into one of the just-mentioned audio or video formats. This transformation (or A/V RENDERING as Figure 2–2 labels it) should be as true to the original script as possible. Nevertheless, copywriters must understand that the printed word is only a partial representation of actuality. A picture, a snatch of music, or a vocal inflection can be generally indicated in the script, but their final on-air rendering will have a distinct and much more specific dimension. This same principle applies to the radio/television message as a whole, which can include all of these elements. Thus, although the printed script is both a creative chronicle and a contractual promise, its final result in sight and/or sound is a discrete phenomenon unto itself. This is a maddening fact of life for both sources and constructors. But it is the price gladly paid for the potential dynamism of the electronic media communication.

In the final analysis, the script is like a composer's musical score. It must set down the writer's intentions in as precise a manner as the format allows—with the realization that these intentions will be conveyed through the expressive interpretations of other people.

3. Medium

As with the message component, the *medium* (transmission) function of radio/television communication also proceeds through two stages. Even though it is often no more than clerical processing, an off-air DISTRIBU-TOR operation precedes the actual airing of the pre-constructed message. If the project begins and culminates entirely within a single station or system, this distributor function may involve nothing more than placing copies of the completed script in the appropriate continuity books for voicing by on-air talent. If the message has been put on tape or is destined for use by other enterprises, distribution takes on more varied forms. Today, in fact, commercials are regularly disseminated by satellite to individual stations and cable system interconnects for later insertion in their program schedules.

Generally speaking, the larger the number of outlets and the more major the source, the more comprehensive the distributor function becomes. Scripts engendered by the creative departments of national advertising agencies and produced by their contracted production houses result in the dubbing and dissemination of multiple copies of the air-ready message to scores of media outlets (or to satellite uplinks). Copies may also be sent to network continuity acceptance departments and to the headquarters of media groups in order to ensure that the message does not violate these organizations' self-policing standards.

After this behind-the-scenes activity, the message is finally transmitted by each participating outlet as per its own schedule, or it is simultaneously aired as part of a network feed. This transmission or PROPAGATOR function is the factor that gives the message potential access to thousands, even millions, of people. It is not our purpose here to inventory the immense variety of electromagnetic equipment that plays a part in this dissemination operation. Nor do we have the space to isolate all the technical malfunctions beyond the writer's control that may interfere with optimal message transmission. Suffice it to say that at this point in the process, science takes over from art, and the copywriter must rely on the specialized expertise of engineers and the highly improved reliability of their solid-state technology.

4. Receiver

This same reliance must be accorded the first (ELECTRONIC RECEIVER) stage of the overall receiver function. Electronic transmitters do not talk directly to people;—they talk to people's radio/TV sets, which translate the electromagnetic impulses so that human beings can apprehend them. These electronic receiving sets vary widely in cost, age, sensitivity, and ability of their owners to adjust them properly. Stressing the particular color of a product on television through the visual alone, for instance, may be a risky venture on home sets that make Peter Jennings look like the Jolly Green Giant. Similarly, immersing your key selling point in an audio kaleidoscope may not be the wisest strategy when filtered through pocket radios operating on six-month-old batteries. Despite today's digital sophistication, there are a lot of malfunctioning and misadjusted receiving sets in use by consumers. The less you, the writer, take for granted as to these units' performance, the more care you will come to exercise in safeguarding the clarity of your message's content.

The final three stages of the receiver function are internal to each human being in our audience. The first of these, the PHYSIOLOGICAL FILTER, refers to the various sensory limitations inherent in each of us. People with hearing loss obviously encounter greater difficulty in picking up the radio transmission or television soundtrack than do folks with unimpaired auditory mechanisms. Individuals with sight problems will experience trouble in perceiving certain elements of the television picture (but may acquire greater auditory sensitivity as a partial compensation).

As in the case of the electronic receiver, the copywriter cannot assume too much about the functioning level of the physiological components within our human receptors. Even people who hear or see fairly well may have problems discerning a brand name read over a "heavy" music backdrop or a television "where-to-call" graphic projected in small, indistinct numerals. Remember also that some individuals with well-functioning eyes and ears take longer to process this sensory information through their brain. Say it or show it too quickly or obscurely and they, too, will miss the main point of your message.

Assuming that these sensory barriers are successfully penetrated, our message must then encounter the much more varied and sometimes down-right bizarre hurdles presented by the EXPERIENTIAL FILTER. This is the sum total of all the events, episodes, and situations through which audience members have acquired knowledge of their world and of themselves. Because no two people have experienced exactly the same things, each of us sees the world through different eyes, or, as media theorist Marshall McLuhan put it, through different "goggles." Our preconceptions, preferences, fears, and preju-dices are all part of this experiential filter, which acts to guarantee that each of us behaves as a unique individual.

Fortunately for the mass communicator, even though each person is a one-of-a-kind item, individuals can be grouped into broad categories deline-ated by such factors as age, sex, education, geography, income, and national origin. Labeled *demographic characteristics,* these factors are used by market researchers and other social scientists to predict the programs we will watch, the products we will use, and the candidates we will vote for (or against). Because radio and television, like all mass communications institutions, are unable to monitor audience feedback until well after the message has been sent, they must rely on these demographic assumptions in formulating the structure and content of everything from 10-second station IDs to multipart entertainment programs.

In short, the electronic media industry engages in a giant guessing game that tries to predict not only the demographic composition of a likely audience, but also the words and images that best appeal to that assem-blage. Through even more in-depth *psychographic research,* media strate-gists further attempt to probe lifestyle and other psychological preference patterns that can cut across, or subdivide, individual demographic clusters. But however the population pie is sliced, its constituent parts remain relatively large.

Somewhat standardized or "common-denominator" message construc-tion is therefore inevitable as we try to reach those research-targeted phan-toms without boring them, on the one hand, or confusing and overloading them on the other. Two common expressions graphically illustrate these two undesirable communication extremes: (1) talking *down to;* and (2) talking *over* the intended audience.

The dulling, oversimplified message that seems to assail us with kinder-garten concepts is diagrammed in Figure 2–3. The message gets through our sensory system without difficulty. But it is so blandly basic that it seems deliberately to insult our intelligence. "They're *talking down* to me," is our reaction; and our attention either is diminished or is entirely diverted to more stimulating things.

How would most women react to the following 60-second radio spot?

ANNCR: The yucky bathroom soap dish. You've probably got
         one in your home right now. That's because you don't
         know how to drain the water out of it. You should
         realize that standing water dissolves a bar of soap.
         That means it turns the solid soap to liquid. In
         other words--yucky. Acme's Tidy Housewife Soap Dish
         can help. The Tidy Housewife Soap Dish features a
         porous--that means full of little holes--top. This
         top lets the water drain into the dish's
         round-shaped bottom. With the Tidy Housewife Soap
         Dish, you can protect your precious soap. Get a
         fashionable Tidy Housewife Soap Dish today. Your
         husband will think you're really smart. Ask the nice
         people at a store near you for an Acme Tidy
         Housewife Soap Dish. It will brighten your life and
         give you more time for your favorite soaps--the
         one's on TV. Write down the name so you won't
         forget. Acme Tidy Housewife Soap Dish.

At the other extreme is the fulsomely esoteric message that is so cabalistic or recondite that almost no one understands it. The course of such a communication is charted out in Figure 2–4. Here again, the message successfully passed through the sensory system, but then was acutely deflected by the individual's lack of experience with the terms or concepts used. "They're *talking over* my head" is the conclusion, and attempted message decoding ceases. Now, look back to the terms *fulsomely, esoteric, cabalistic,* and *recondite.* Did these words and the sentence that contains them turn you off?

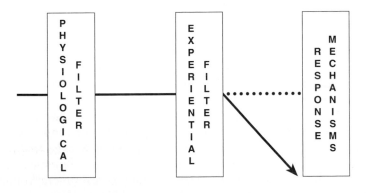

Figure 2-3
Talking Down

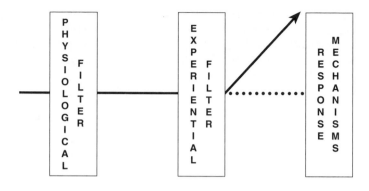

Figure 2-4
Talking Over

If so, you've experienced this "over-my-head" conundrum (or, should we say, *problem*) first hand.

Let us assume, however, that the copywriter has fashioned a message capable of passing through both the physiological and experiential filters with minimal perceptual 'bending.' This means that (1) key words and concepts are easy to hear or see and (2) the spot offers understandable and interesting rewards to the people at whom it is aimed. Now, the target consumer's RESPONSE MECHANISMS can be fully engaged. Perhaps our audience members will buy it, vote for it, donate to it, or mix it with the cat's food once a week. At the very least, the copywriter strives to have them *remember* it so that a gradual familiarity with and favorable disposition toward the product or idea will be built up in the weeks and months ahead.

The appropriateness or inappropriateness of audience responses in terms of the originator's expectations for the message are stringently evaluated after the fact by ratings points, sales curves, votes cast, or similar measuring devices. If possible, field trials and other test marketing have been undertaken to sample results on a limited basis as a preliminary to the costly, full-scale campaign. In any event, if the responses are found deficient in character or quantity, the message must be changed. Worse, if the responses are adjudged *negative* in nature, it may be that the constructor must be changed. For unlike the dog in Pavlov's famous psychology experiment, it is not the subject audience that is "punished" for deviant responses. Instead, punishment is administered to the experimenter/constructor—in other words, to the copywriter!

What makes all of this even more dicey is audience members' tendencies to interpret things in ways we never anticipated. Despite the misleading orderliness of our communication process diagram, message meanings accrue not only from what copywriters put into them but also from what audience members take out of them. Meanings, in other words, are not ultimately in messages but in the people who decode those messages. As British communication theorist John Fiske points out, an aired electronic media "text can no longer be seen as a self-sufficient entity that bears its own meaning and exerts a similar influence on all its readers. Rather, it is seen as a potential of meanings that can be activated in a number of ways."[3]

Thus, the broadcast/cable copywriter's messages are unavoidably *polysemic*—they possess multiple significances because of the contexts in which individual listeners/viewers receive and decode them. Granted, the possibilities for receiver-constructed meanings of a piece of copy are not limitless. We can narrow meaning options through what we put into our spot, what we leave out, and how we arrange the elements we *do* choose to include. Nevertheless, we can never be completely certain of what consumers will make of our message.

Even though process diagrams are helpful in freeze-framing for us the essential components of communication, we should not over-estimate their applicability. Like any static model, they are incapable of accurately conveying the dynamic process of one person interacting with another, let alone the method whereby radio/television creators attempt to interact with unseen millions.

If all of this unpredictability fails to diminish your interest in electronic media copywriting—congratulations!

You obviously possess two ingredients essential for work on the creative side of radio and television: an uncommon appetite for stress and a thirst for constant challenge. As advertising placement executive Dany Lennon advises, when it comes to copywriters, "If they're not hungry, if they're not totally driven, we have no tolerance for them. The industry is not carrying anybody today."[4] DDB Needham's chairman, Keith Reinhard, adds: "If security, tranquility and peace are your goals, you're in the wrong business."[5]

The remaining chapters in this book strive further to analyze your commitment to copywriting. They also provide opportunities to probe the outer limits of your talent. Whether you see yourself as a radio/television copywriter or as an interdependent colleague of such writers, good luck! As premier radio communicators Bob (Elliott) and Ray (Goulding) used to say, *write when you get work.*

Endnotes

1. Paul Goldsmith, writing in "Monday Memo," *Broadcasting* (September 22, 1980), 12.
2. Richard Morgan, "Illegitimis Non Carborundum Est," *ADWEEK* (April 6, 1992), 38.
3. John Fiske, "British Cultural Studies and Television," in Robert Allen (ed.) *Channels of Discourse* (Chapel Hill: University of North Carolina Press, 1987), 269.
4. Betsy Sharkey, "Across the Great Divide," *ADWEEK* (February 1, 1988), C.R. 8.
5. "Quips, Quotes, Gripes, Swipes," *Winners* (November 1988), 48.

Chapter 3

Tools of Our Trade

Now that we have surveyed the various work environments in which electronic media copywriters operate and have explored the communication complexities to which they are subjected, we can proceed to inventory the writing implements that they typically employ. Broadcast/cable copywriters rely on many of the same devices as other worksmiths to accomplish their tasks. They also work in situations in which clarity, conciseness, and speed are of paramount importance.

Excess is the radio/television writer's greatest enemy—whether it is an excess of ideas that muddles a PSA, an excess of words that forces a commercial into a longer and more expensive format, or an excess of time in completing an assignment that puts an entire campaign off schedule. The writing tools most important to us, therefore, are those that replace excess with *functional frugality*, helping us communicate on target, on budget, and on time. "The thing that makes you a good copywriter is compression," affirms Ketchum Advertising creative director John Lyons. "Michelangelo had a whole ceiling. We have a matchbook cover."[1]

In achieving such compression, punctuation is a vital instrument because it provides the mechanism for grouping words into their most cogent and quickly understandable patterns. It is no exaggeration to say that punctuation is a major, perhaps even the prime, tool for successful electronic copywriting.

Print Punctuation Versus Radio/Television Punctuation

Both print and electronic media writers use words set to paper as a means of initially snaring their thoughts. But the role played by this paper prototype varies significantly between the two media categories. In print vehicles, the writer's arrangement is in fundamentally the same form in which the intended audience will ingest it. Certainly, some editor or typesetter may perform minor alternations, but we still have a message the writer affixes to the page that the audience will pick up and read from the page. In other words, print punctuation symbols serve as *direct communication* between originator and receiver.

For the electronic writer, on the other hand, the copy is only a linguistic halfway house in the communication journey. As we see in Chapter 2, the written radio/television message comes to life for the audience only after it has been translated into aural or visual form. Broadcast/cable consumers do not *read* the script but *hear* and, in the case of television, also *see* the translation of that script as a real-time happening. They can neither go back and reread it nor scan ahead to preview it. Thus, radio/television punctuation strives to interpret the writer's message to and through announcers and technicians in order to reach the audience as natural sounding *speech.* In the final analysis, electronic punctuation serves as systematic stage directions to intermediaries rather than as direct communications with the target audience.

Unfortunately for broadcast/cable copywriters, any punctuation system, no matter how modified, remains somewhat print-bound. No written symbology can ever specify completely all the nuances of a spoken message any more than a musical score is a total blueprint for a heard composition. Both the score and our script require the services of competent performer/interpreters. What composers or copywriters must do is make certain that their notation or punctuation is as systematic and standardized as possible so that, at least, it does not convey something fundamentally different from what they intended.

Even though no system of radio/television punctuation is universally accepted, the following guidelines serve to keep the various punctuation marks mutually discrete so each fulfills its specific function as unequivocally as possible. As a general rule, remember that for electronic media copy, your *ear* rather than print-oriented grammatical commandments should be the final judge of what constitutes proper punctuation. The grammatical structure of spoken prose is more fluid than that of written prose. Therefore, broadcast/cable copywriters must write for *speech*—and must punctuate accordingly.

Period

As in print media, the period indicates that a whole thought, complete in itself, has been concluded. Moreover, the period in electronic copy tells the performer to insert a pause before beginning the next thought. (The duration of this pause depends on the overall pacing of the copy.) At their option, radio/television writers may decide to put a period after a sentence that is *grammatically* incomplete, if the sense, flow, and memorability of the copy will thereby be enhanced:

<u>Visit Lou's.</u> For shoes.

Thirteen thousand sympathetic towtrucks. Your Acme Auto Club.

Radio. Red hot because it works.

<u>Your best deserves the best.</u> Butter. Real Butter.

Notice that there are nine aurally effective *idea units* in these four examples even though only the two underlined segments happen to be grammatically proper sentences.

Because the period denotes a discernible pause, it is wise to avoid its use in abbreviations, since a performer may not know whether a pause is desired after "Dept." or not. Abbreviations are undesirable anyway because announcers, reading an extended piece of copy, have been known to draw a temporary blank as to the full pronunciation of the term represented by such shortcuts as "Corp.," "Capt.," "lb.," or "GA." Imagine yourself stumbling across the following sentence in the middle of a long on-air stint:

The Brockett Corp., Capt. Foster charged, dumped its contaminants by the lb. in GA.

Even a single abbreviation can trip up an announcer on a bad day—and announcers, like copywriters, are never immune to bad days. Take every precaution to use periods only at the end of sense-complete thought units. Whether the thought unit is also *grammatically* complete is largely irrelevant.

The only exception to this singular use of the period should be in abbreviations that are virtually never written out and that, in fact, are much more commonly used than the words they might stand for. Basically, there are six of these:

Dr. Mr. Mrs. Ms. A.M. P.M.

As four of these words are always followed by a proper noun (Ms. Hanson), and the remaining two are preceded by numerals (11 A.M.), the use of the period with them cannot, by itself, be easily mistaken for the end of a thought unit. The acceptable indication for doctor (Dr.) does, however, make it doubly important that we never write

Lakeside Dr. or Clive Dr.

when we mean

```
Lakeside Drive and Clive Drive.
```

Comma

Just as in print, the comma generally indicates a separation of words, phrases, or clauses from others that are part of the same thought unit and of a similar or like type:

```
Bertha's Breakfast Grotto for the tummy yummyist waffles,
pancakes, omelets, and sweet rolls.

Rain, snow, sleet, and fog. Channel 10 weather keeps track
of them all.
```

In a like manner, commas are used to set off the name of a person addressed from the rest of the sentence:

```
But golly, Mr. Whipple, I can't help squeezing.
```

More important to radio/television performers, the comma also provides a short breathing space that can be used as necessary to keep the tone round and the head clear. We thus insert commas wherever needed to facilitate announcer breathing and to gather words more clearly into effective rhythmic groupings without the period's imposed finality. As Pico Iyer observes, "A comma, by comparison, catches the general drift of the mind in thought, turning in on itself and back on itself, reversing, redoubling and returning along the course of its own sweet river music."[2]

In using commas to promote copy flow, the electronic writer may find it necessary to employ them in some places not called for by conventional grammatical rules.

```
Taco Heaven, it's the place, where real sour cream, drips
down, your face.
```

In other instances, aural copy may omit commas where a grammar book would demand their placement.

```
At the Deli and the Baker and the Ice Cream Maker. Howard
Johnson's.
```

Here again, the resultant *sound* of the message rather than the strictures of print-oriented grammar must be the decisive factor.

Semicolon

The semicolon, too, is a helpful tool in promoting copy rhythm. It is used between main clauses within a single thought unit and takes the place of such drab, time-wasting connectives as *and, for, but,* and *or.* Notice how the pace and forward motion of the following sentence,

```
Something had happened but she didn't know what.
```

is enhanced by replacing the connective with a semicolon:

```
Something had happened; she didn't know what.
```

To the announcer, the semicolon indicates a short vocal pause between two closely related thoughts. This contrasts with the proportionately longer pause that the period deserves, coming as it does at the end of a self-sufficient thought unit. For Iyer, "A period has the unblinking finality of a red light; the comma is a flashing yellow light that asks us only to slow down; and the semicolon is a stop sign that tells us to ease gradually to a halt, before gradually starting up again."[3]

In addition, the semicolon imparts a pleasing sense of balance to the two subparts of its thought unit while still keeping them in close temporal proximity. Finally, semicolon patterns like the following provide more extensive breathing options for the speaker than do those ordained by a comma:

```
                         (that)
Radio 93's Midday News;           brings you the action in
time for lunch.
```

```
                                        (and)
The Norseman blanket saves you cash today;      keeps you
cozy tonight.
```

Question Mark

A question mark comes after a direct query in electronic copy just as it does in print copy. The radio/television writer further must realize that, in our culture, most spoken questions end with an upward inflection. We thus must be especially careful to keep questions in our copy short so the performer can easily perceive that the thought unit is indeed a question and prepare the upward inflection in a smooth and gradual manner. Otherwise, the poor announcer may realize it's a question only after most of the sentence has passed. The sudden ascending inflection that results may be humorous to listen to but hardly contributes to meaningful communication of the message. Even if the talent detects a long question early, it is almost impossible to sustain the proper rising modulation for very many words. Try reading the following copy segment aloud in such a way that it continuously sounds like a question:

```
Doesn't there have to be a reason why Sims' Fruit Emporium
has been the best place for pears, apples, oranges,
peaches, and plums since Grampa Sims put up his first
striped awning back in the quiet Clintondale summer of
nineteen-ought-six?
```

For better clarity, and unstretched vocal cords, the essence of the question should be isolated like this:

```
Why is Sim's the best place in Clintondale for fruit? Well,
since 1906 when, etc.
```

Keep queries short and to the point so the question mark can be easily seen and accommodated by the announcer as well as easily "heard" and felt by the audience.

Exclamation Mark

Both print and radio/television punctuation use the exclamation mark (!) after complete thought units that demand special emphasis. Comic strip characters seem to talk in nothing but exclamation marks, and this fact should not be lost on us. Since we strive for copy that sounds natural and believable, the constant use of exclamation marks is at best an irritant to the listener and at worst an indication that Daffy Duck was the writer. In most cases, emphasis should be built naturally into the copy through your choice of words and the arrangement of the words you've chosen. A piece of continuity permeated with exclamation marks can do nothing but cast doubt on your wordsmith's ability. Wield this punctuation symbol with extreme reluctance. If you've already developed an exclamation problem, make a pact with yourself to donate a dollar to your favorite charity each time you end up using an exclamation mark in your copy creation. In the long run, this practice will either make you a much better writer or lower your income tax. (Note the absence of an exclamation mark after that last sentence.)

Quotation Marks

For the commercial and continuity writer, quotation marks also are more to be avoided than embraced. Their main legitimate use is to set off direct quotations that must be read exactly as written. Occasionally, the testimonial spot or PSA will use such word-for-word statements, but it is in news copy that these punctuation symbols are primarily employed. In most cases, then, if your writing job keeps you out of the newsroom, keep away from quotation marks. Because each set of quotation marks consists of four printed strokes on which eye/tongue coordination can stumble, they clutter copy appearance and inhibit smooth message delivery by announcers who are reading the copy "cold." (Notice how those just-used quotation marks caused a brief hesitation in the flow of even your silent reading.)

Apostrophe

Because this symbol makes use of only one ' instead of two ", it has only half the potential for script clutter that quotation marks entail. The apostrophe is more practical, therefore, for setting off sarcastic or ironic comments that, in print communication, depend on quotation marks.

You can't call this black gunk 'coffee' and get away with it.

Why can't my 'big strong man' remember to pick up more Hefty Bags?

The apostrophe also identifies a part of a larger word. The apostrophe pair indicates the subunit, and underlining identifies the work as a whole:

We now hear 'Let Me Say Just One Word' from Puccini's <u>The Girl of the Golden West</u>.

That was 'Big D,' a salute to the home of the Cowboys from the hit musical revival <u>The Most Happy Fella</u>.

From Bill Cosby's hilarious album <u>To Russell, My Brother, Whom I Slept With</u>, here's a tribute to 'The Apple.'

Colon

This symbol, too, performs a task in radio/television broadcast copy that quotation marks would otherwise be called on to serve. The colon is used to set up each line of dialogue in a spot, PSA, or other continuity writing that calls for speeches by separate characters. When combined with proper spacing, the colon ensures that the copy will be definitive and easy to read without the necessity for a jungle of quotation marks. Imagine the copy clutter in the following 60-second spot if pairs of quotation marks had to be used in place of each colon.

BRUCE: So that's when she starched my shorts. You'd think I drove the car into the ditch.

ED: How'd she get out?

BRUCE: Oh, she finally found a phone booth about a mile up the road.

ED: Called you from there?

BRUCE: No. Called her mother. That was my bowling night.

ED: Swell. So then what happened?

BRUCE: They got this gas station guy to pull her out. Cost her mother sixty bucks.

ED: Why didn't your wife pay for it?

BRUCE: I borrowed her last five for beer money.

ED: You're lucky she only starched your shorts.

BRUCE: Maybe you're right. So then she gets this idea to join that Acme Auto Club thing so we could get free road service.

ED: Your wife said this?

BRUCE: Yeah. But I think it came from her mother.

ED: Why don't you?

BRUCE: Join Acme Auto Club? I've already got car insurance.

ED: So what? Acme Auto Club only sells insurance as an extra service. The important thing is the membership.

BRUCE: You belong?

```
ED:       You bet. Costs me fifty bucks but it's worth it. I
          get road aid and notary service and all the help I
          want in trip planning. Acme even taught my kid to
          drive.

BRUCE:    Cost you just fifty bucks for Acme membership?

ED:       Right. Sit down and I'll tell you about it.

BRUCE:    Can't.

ED:       Why not?

BRUCE:    My shorts.

ED:       Oh.
```

In addition to dialogue clarification, the colon also paves the way for any direct quotations called for in the message. It puts the performer on notice that a distinct and generally extensive passage is to follow.

```
TV 22 is helping you. Bob Lane of the Stoltz City United
Fund says: "We have exceeded our pledge goal for this
year's campaign. And much of the credit goes to the folks
at TV 22 in helping to publicize how the United Fund helps
us all." TV 22. Serving Stoltz City; serving you.
```

In a similar vein, the colon can prepare the announcer for a long list of items that are to follow as component parts of the same thought unit.

```
Today, the Sharkville Diner and Car Wash is featuring: veal
surprise, chicken over-easy, potted pork pie, and ham hock
delight.
```

Dash

The dash serves functions similar to, but more exaggerated than, those accommodated by certain of the other punctuation symbols. Like the semicolon, it can be used to improve copy rhythm and flow by replacing drab words. It is preferred over the semicolon if more than one word is being omitted.

```
                        (when you)
Keep a garden in your kitchen---keep a cupboard full of cans.
```

```
        (it has)
Radio 97---the greatest tunes this side of Boston.
```

In both of these examples, the dash creates a longer pause than that indicated by the semicolon while still helping to convey that the phrases on either side of it are both component parts of the same thought unit.

Like paired commas, paired dashes can be called on to segregate a single word or phrase from the rest of the sentence. But whereas commas serve to underplay that isolated segment, a duo of dashes strives to heighten and emphasize it. In our previous example:

```
But golly, Mr. Whipple, I can't help squeezing.
```

we want the listener to focus, not on Mr. Whipple, but on what you can't help doing to the product. Paired commas are thus appropriate. The following specimen, on the other hand, features the product name (always our most important information) within the separated segment. Because we wish to accent that product name, paired dashes are mandated.

```
The smoothest way---the Finster way---to blend the best in
tea.
```

As an experiment, let's reverse our punctuation use in these two instances. Read the two lines aloud in the manner the punctuation decrees.

```
But golly---Mr. Whipple---I can't help squeezing.
```

```
The smoothest way, the Finster way, to blend the best in
tea.
```

Note the difference in effect and impact? So would your listener. Appropriate words must go hand in hand with appropriate punctuation.

In a more specialized way, a dash can be used to denote a sudden breaking off of a thought either because of hesitancy on the part of the speak,

```
All of a sudden I want to---
```

or because that speaker was interrupted by another.

```
SAM: Florida grapefruit is---
```

```
ANN: Great fruit.
```

Underlining

An underlined word, which is placed in italics if set in type, is another way of requesting special emphasis from the performer. As in the case of the "great fruit" line above, underlining is especially helpful at directing attention to words on which we normally don't focus or that occur at a place in the sentence that prohibits the use of alternative punctuation.

```
I don't know why my wash is grayer than yours.
```

Any of the other means of directing attention via emphasis would only inject an unwanted pause or pauses into this thought unit and, consequently, inhibit copy flow. Note how the following punctuation marks either misdirect or hobble the thought.

```
I don't know why. My wash is grayer than yours.

I don't know, why my wash is grayer than yours.

I don't know why, my wash is grayer than yours.

I don't know; why my wash is grayer than yours.

I don't know why; my wash is grayer than yours.

I don't know---why---my wash is grayer than yours.
```

As discussed in conjunction with the apostrophe, underlining is also used to denote the titles of complete literary works, programs, albums, or complete musical compositions. Because we normally wish to direct attention to these titles anyway, underlining in such instances serves two mutually compatible functions.

Ellipsis

The ellipsis is a series of three dots that, when used more than once, can make your copy appear to have contracted the pox. It can also make for choppy copy voicing.

Use of the ellipsis . . . should therefore . . . be avoided . . . like the plague.

Its sole recognized function in electronic writing is to indicate clearly that words have been omitted from a direct quote so that the announcer can make that fact clear in how the copy is read. Yet, for some reason, lazy copywriters blissfully substitute the ellipsis for commas, dashes, semicolons, and even periods. They therefore deprive their copy of the subtle but effective shadings that the discrete and specialized use of each punctuation mark can help bring to their writing. Furthermore, because each ellipsis consists of three individual dots, it causes the same kind of eye clutter we try to avoid when we limit our use of quotation marks.

Parentheses

Though often used in print media for asides and stage whispers, the parentheses have a much more circumscribed and mechanistic task in radio/television copy. Simply stated, they are used to set off stage directions and technical instructions from the words the announcer is supposed to read aloud. In the following classic example, which was actually read on air, the copywriter neglected to use parentheses:

```
It's 8 P.M. Bulova watch time. On Christmas, say Merry
Christmas. On New Year's, say Happy New Year.
```

The correct translation of the copywriter's intent should, of course, have been punctuated this way:

```
It's 8 P.M. Bulova watch time. (On Christmas, say Merry
Christmas. On New Year's, say Happy New Year.)
```

Do not omit parentheses around any private communications between you and the talent who will read your copy. On the other hand, do not persist in the print-oriented approach to parentheses and put anything between them that you *do* wish the listener to hear. In the following piece of broadcast copy, parentheses have been used in a manner common to print media.

```
Even been in a Lumber camp? (If you had, you'd remember
the meals the guys stowed away.) They needed good, hot
food (and plenty of it) for all the muscle work. And no
meal was as important as breakfast. They wanted a hot
breakfast that stayed with them (a hot meal like Mama
Gruber's Corn Mush cereal). No, her Mush isn't modern.
(In fact, Mama Gruber's Corn Mush is kind of
old-fashioned.) But so is hard work.
```

The announcer accustomed to the electronic use of parentheses would quite properly read the commercial this way:

```
Ever been in a lumber camp? They needed good, hot food for
all that muscle work. And no meal was as important as
breakfast. They wanted a hot breakfast that stayed with
them. No, her Mush isn't modern. But so is hard work.
```

Does the spot still make sense? Not only are we left with at least ten seconds of dead air in a 30-second spot, but we have also lost the name of our product and sponsor. Restrict radio/television parentheses to their intended use. If your copy contains words and phrases that, in print, would constitute parenthetical expressions, use dashes or commas in your script to set these expressions off.

Punctuation Postscript

Parentheses and all the other punctuation tools we have discussed are indispensable if we are to communicate properly to our talent intermediaries and, through them, to our target audience. Use punctuation carefully; its abuse can change the entire meaning of your message. In the Depression-ridden 1930s, a little American girl emigrating with her work-seeking father to Canada was reported by a U.S. newspaper to have lamented at the border:

```
Good-bye God, I'm going to Canada.
```

An enterprising copywriter at the Toronto Board of Trade converted this negative implication about his homeland's remoteness into a glowing endorsement by arguing that her statement had merely been mispunctuated. The copywriter's "corrected" version?

```
Good! By God, I'm going to Canada.[4]
```

Even when used correctly and in accordance with widely accepted electronic practices, punctuation of copy meant to be read aloud remains a comparatively tenuous and approximate tool. In his eighteenth-century *A Course of Lectures on Elocution*, English authority Thomas Sheridan focused on the "unprintable components of good speech"; components that words and spaces arranged uniformly on a page were incapable of indicating. The ancients, he pointed out, had no system of punctuation whatever but used written material merely to enable a speaker to learn the words by rote so he could recite them, in his own unique manner, from memory.[5] Because announcers do not often memorize their scripts and because the radio/television industry as a whole has some more or less uniform expectations for how copy is to be read, today's copywriters *need* punctuation, no matter how tentative. A commonly accepted system of punctuation is essential if electronic writers are even to hope for an adequate means of communicating with the announcers and other performers who will bring their copy to life.

Tools to Read/Consult

Punctuation is only one of the copywriter's implements. Reference books comprise another. Though the following list does not attempt to be comprehensive, it does include the types of volumes that are an essential part of the copywriter's library. Basically, these works group themselves into three categories: dictionaries, word-finders, and style/usage aids.

Dictionaries

Any writer must be an ardent dictionary user if for no other reason than its utility as a spelling aid. Because words are our prime stock in trade, misspelling is inexcusable and makes the writer seem as incompetent as the physician unable to read a thermometer. A dictionary is also helpful to print writers in separating the syllables within a word to facilitate proper hyphenating of it at the end of a line. For electronic writers, however, this is a function that should rarely be used. Announcers' eyes do not like to have to jump lines in the middle of a word, and there is no reason the copywriter should require them to do so. If the word does not fit completely on one line, it should be moved in its entirety to the one below. Whole words are more important to copy comprehension than is an unwavering right-hand margin.

For most people, a dictionary is consulted primarily to learn the meaning of words. As a mass communicator, the copywriter should seldom need to use this dictionary capability—at least in selecting words for a radio/television script. If you, a supposed wordsmith, do not already know the meaning of that term, how do you expect members of the mass audience to be able to understand it as the word goes flitting past their ears? Of course, if your spot is aimed at a highly specialized or technically oriented audience (auto engineers or dairy farmers, for example), words unfamiliar to you as well as to the general public may need to be used and their precise meanings sought out in the dictionary.

In most cases, however, a standard abridged dictionary will serve the copywriter better than a massive unabridged volume that is difficult to handle and store and that will include thousands of words, or archaic definitions for words, of which most of your audience will be totally ignorant. Since commercial and continuity copy is intended to be understandable to the audience *as it is* rather than striving to increase their vocabularies, exotic words and meanings are communication hindrances. If the word and the meaning you seek to use are in a good abridged volume, you can proceed with at least a little more confidence in considering its use in your copy.

Besides the standard dictionaries, a number of specialty ones serve the requirements of certain professions. Unless you find yourself consistently writing copy aimed at doctors, computer specialists, or similarly distinct groups, such volumes will not be required. The one type of specialized dictionary that is a helpful addition to any copywriter's library is the rhyming dictionary. Even in straight copy, and especially in campaign slogans or tag lines at the end of spots, a simple rhyme can greatly enhance memorability. The rhyming dictionary can be of significant assistance in this regard as long as we never distort message meaning and clarity in pursuing some forced doggerel.

A few copywriters also find slang dictionaries useful, but such volumes can pose unacceptable dangers. Slang varies widely by era and region, and nothing kills copy credibility more quickly than a slang term your audience misunderstands or feels is outdated. If you don't naturally "speak" the slang yourself, either seek out and listen to people who do, or avoid attempting to write it. Most slang usages are superseded before a book listing them can get into print.

Word-Finders

The most commonly known book in this category is *Roget's Thesaurus*, which is a complete compilation of *synonyms* (words meaning the same) and *antonyms* (words meaning the opposite) active in American and British usage. Any writer develops a preference for, or a pattern in, the selection of certain words. The *Thesaurus* helps break these patterns by giving the writer alternate choices of words that thereby avoid interest-robbing redundancy in the copy. Further, this type of volume allows you to find and select a word possessing a more precise meaning or one with a syllabic construction or phonetic makeup that better promotes sentence rhythm and rhyme. To the radio/television writer, this aural function can be of prime importance given the preeminence of sound in effective oral communication. Consequently, you may discover a word-finder like the *Thesaurus* to be your most often consulted reference work.

Roget's is the classic, but by no means the only, volume in the field. Because to use it, you must first look up a word category and then refer to various subcategories, some writers find the volume to somewhat time-wasting. They prefer books like J. I. Rodale's *The Synonym Finder*, which lists the specific word and its specific alternatives in the same place. Though such works do not generally possess the scope of *Roget's* or provide closely associated categories of words, their ease and speed of use are important advantages in such a volatile and time-bound field as broadcast/cable copywriting.

Style/Usage Aids

In general, style aids tell us the "correct" thing to do and usage guides tell us what is actually being done out there in the world in which real people speak, write, and read. This is not to imply that style aids are worthless for a copywriter. Even though electronic media style and punctuation frequently modify print-oriented practices in striving to reproduce conversational speech, the mechanics of good composition remain more applicable than inapplicable to radio/television writing. As McCann-Erickson's John Bergin insists, "This is not a break-the-rules business. It is a know-the-rules-before-you-break-them business; there's a big difference."[6] A good stylebook such as Strunk and White's venerable *The Elements of Style* provides you with that essential appreciation of those starting-point strictures. Periodic sessions with such a book help ensure that you never become so specialized that, should the time come, you are incapable of branching out into print media, memo composition, corporate report fashioning, or the myriad of other verbal tasks that call for a wordsmith's talents.

Meanwhile, usage guides such as Roy Copperud's *American Usage and Style: The Consensus* and H. W. Fowler's *Dictionary of Modern English Usage* can be counted on to give sensible advice and guidance on the connotations and evolving tendencies of our language.

Tools to Pound on, Write with, Write on

Once we have the germ of a message, know how to spell words it requires, and where to uncover alternative word and stylistic choices, we need some vessel in which to contain all this verbiage while we trim and refine it. Though everyone is aware of the implements serving this function, here are some special considerations that pertain to the copywriter's use of them.

Typewriter

In *Shopping in Oxford*, English poet laureate John Masefield described the typewriter as

> *the black-bright, smooth running,*
>   *clicking clean*
> *brushed, oiled and dainty*
>   *typewriting machine.*[7]

This is as apt and memorable a description as any copywriter could ask for in regard to the "care and feeding" of this traditional appliance on our idea production line.

Even though word processors (see the next section) have muscled their way into what was once the typewriter's exclusive domain, many copywriters still prefer this old instrument for banging out at least the first drafts of their usually brief scripts. Often, a 30-second spot can come to life on a typewriter before we have time to fire up a computer and access its word processing program. Besides, many copywriters feel there is something physiologically and psychologically stimulating about instantaneously crackling out impressions on a piece of paper right above your fingertips.

Word Processor

As most people know, a word processor is a microcomputer primed with the proper writing software (program) and tied to a printer that can eventually produce hard (on-paper) copy. The breakneck technological advancements in the microcomputer industry have put the word processor within economic reach of virtually every copywriter.

There are several advantages to word processor use—particularly in television, with its comparatively complex script format. In conjunction with a software package like New Horizons' *ProWrite*, Comprehensive Video's *Script Master*, or Ixion's *Split/Scripter*, the word processor largely eliminates the tedium involved in setting up a left side/video, right side/audio TV script and maintains the proper spatial and horizontal relationship between modules in the two columns. Many programs also allow you to condense or expand type size to fit a variety of script formats up to and including large characters that can be read by on-camera performers directly off a teleprompter. Some software, like Lake Compuframes' *ShowScape*, further provide your word processor with the capability to create and assemble complete storyboards.

Even basic word processing programs save the copywriter a great deal of time by making additions, deletions, corrections and rearrangements easy to accomplish. Rather than manually retyping the entire script, the writer can simple work with the lines or words that require modification and then reinsert them into the copy, which will be automatically realigned to accommodate the new material. Because you are making your corrections on a cathode ray tube (CRT) rather than on unforgiving paper, correction fluid bottles and sheets of opaquing film become artifacts of the past. Other software can even check for accuracy in your spelling and variety in your sentence lengths.

Nonetheless, the word processor also entails some potential disadvantages that must be considered. First, you must be willing to train yourself to understand this instrument—or, more to the point, to make certain that this instrument understands *you*. Two separate functions must be comprehended. The first, the *editing* function, is the input portion of the operation. This is where you create, modify, and finalize your script. In the second or output function, called *formatting*, the finished draft is delivered in the proper arrangement and spatial style.

Some software packages perform these two functions as a single operation. But in others, they are handled separately and require discrete and systematic instruction from the user (that's *you*) to create a script that looks like a script. In some cases, such as short pieces of radio copy, it might be more efficient just to pound out the copy on a conventional typewriter. Many copywriters, in fact, have both a typewriter and a word processor in their office. They go to the typewriter for brief spots or for quick capture of basic copy ideas and then use the word processor for longer assignments and final script assemblage.

There are still copywriters who believe that writing must be an intensely *physical* activity. They find the word processor keyboard's prim electronic patter totally out of character with this conception and much prefer the feel of a manual typewriter beneath their fingers as it converts their verbal energy into the mechanical assault of keys against paper.

Ultimately, of course, it is not the power of your keyboard that is important, but the power of the ideas that you ask it to share.

Pens and Pencils

Because all copy must be typed (or 'processed') before it can be shown to anyone important, pens and pencils are selected for their utility in a variety of preliminary roles. Pencils are ideal for sketching out material, whether alone or with a colleague copywriter or art director. When capped by a pliable eraser, a pencil allows us to play with words, diagrams, and pictures without having to sit down in front of a keyboard to stare at its roller or monitor. "Leo Burnett used to write with a black pencil on a white pad," recounts Burnett agency executive Chuck Werle. "We're a sophisticated company, but the creative process is still associated with that black pencil."[8] With a highly portable pencil and pad, writers can brainstorm anywhere.

If you're still a typewritter enthusiast, soft pencils (#2) can be used to modify copy while it is still in the typewriter. Higher-numbered (harder) leads should be avoided because they can tear through the paper and mar the roller. Many copywriters also find that a small, inexpensive pencil sharpener, available in any drug or discount store, is handy to keep in their pocket to prevent disruptive trips to a wall-mounted or electric model just as the creative juices are starting to flow.

When it comes to pens, don't be taken in by the "eight for a dollar" specials some emporiums sell. Jotting down fleeting ideas is difficult enough without being harassed by a constantly clogging pen or one whose burred tip scratches across the paper like a cat clawing through the screen door. Shop around for pens that present a pleasing shape and weight in your hand. Note taking and copyediting are both much easier if you can grip the pen firmly without the scrawl that results from having to squeeze it. The pen point should be narrow enough to make a neat, clean, editing incision on a piece of printed copy, though not so pointed that it pierces the paper.

In our desktop publishing era, it is easy to dismiss pens and pencils as quaint irrelevancies. But as *Chicago Tribune* columnist Mike Royko reminds us, "libraries are crammed with great books written with pencils, scratchy pens or even goose quills. Shakespeare didn't worry about how much RAM he had. And Mark Twain didn't feel deprived for the lack of a laser-jet printer."[9]

Paper

Once you go to work for a station, agency, or other institution, your stationery needs will be provided for and should not be of overt concern. You will be issued, or can ask for, pads of lined paper for note taking and doodling, plain typing paper for creating your first draft work, and printed letterhead or other formatting manuscript for preparing subsequent drafts that have to be seen and evaluated by a supervisor or client. If word processors are used in the office, printer paper and letterhead also will be available. Your only responsibilities will be to make certain that you keep your office stocked with a sufficient quantity of each variety and that you follow whatever format is mandated by preprinted letterhead and copy worksheets (format is discussed further in subsequent chapters).

If you are freelancing or otherwise self-supervised, you must provide this paper supply for yourself. You will find that having three distinct varieties of stock (lined pads, plain typing paper, and letterhead) will help you divide your tasks mentally and put you in the proper frame of mind for idea exploration, first-draft experimentation, and final-draft polishing, respectively. When ordering your own stationery on which you will prepare the actual scripts that go to clients and stations, keep these two considerations in mind:

1. Even if you are only a part-time freelancer, professional looking, preprinted letterheads will help establish an initial impression that you know your business. A sleek letterhead won't save a bad piece of writing, but it does help open doors for a good one. Give your copy every chance for a favorable evaluation by clients and a positive treatment by performers. Showcase a solid copy painting within a suitable frame.

2. For durability, paper on which finished scripts are typed should be of at least medium weight and definitely *not* onion-skin or corrasible bond. The thin paper issued forth from some cheap word processing printers also does not pass muster in this regard. Performers need to be able to hold the script without its crackling or rustling. Such extraneous sounds will be picked up by the station or sound studio microphone and, at best, become distractions to the listener. At worst, they resemble the old radio sound effect used to signify fire, and your message might sound like it's coming from hell.

Time—The Tool That's Master of All

Speaking of hell, the inexorable demands of the clock on everything the commercial and continuity writer produces can create our own occupational torment. A 30-second spot was not, is not, and will never be a 35-second spot. No matter what the message and regardless of the writer's talent, all elements of broadcast/cable communication must ultimately conform to the rigorous demands of the station program day, the network feed schedule, the budget our client has to spend, and the amount of available air time on which to spend this money. Unlike a newspaper or magazine, an electronic outlet cannot add "pages" onto its air schedule when advertising volume is high, or contract that schedule when volume is down. On the contrary, the radio or television station or cable network is on the air for a set number of hours each day, and all available program matter, commercial fare, and continuity segments must fill and compete for this time.

The following time standards constitute a general yardstick of spot length as reflected by word count. Copy requiring a relaxed and languid style should contain fewer words than these norms, and material meant to be more rapid and upbeat may contain slightly more. Because the majority of video spots do not have wall-to-wall audio copy, these guidelines can be helpful in television only to provide a rough indication of how much time individual copy segments within the spot will expend.

"Sixties"

Though broadcast television is largely abandoning the costly one-minute message, in radio (and to a lesser degree, cable) sixty seconds remains the dominant spot type. Industry figures show that approximately four out of five commercials recently aired on United States radio stations were one minute in length. A 60-second radio script will usually contain from 135 to 145 words.

As seen later, this number is proportionately less than the word count for two "thirties." Such a determination is based on the presumption that we cannot expect our audience to take in quite as much copy in one continuous minute of listening as they can in two separate messages of thirty seconds each. In short, once initial attention is gained., we can anticipate people's vigilance dwindling the longer the message progresses. If a nonprerecorded radio spot exceeds 150 words, the station may charge the client an additional premium. Because PSAs depend on the station for gratuity airing in the first place, public service announcements that are supposedly "sixties" but contain more than 150 words will probably not be aired at all.

"Thirties"

Since 1971, as a result of both the escalating cost of air time and of research showing that many video messages can be as effective in half-minute as in full-minute form, the 30-second spot has vastly eclipsed the "sixty" as the most commonly used unit of broadcast television time. This phenomenon has had a spin-off effect on both PSAs and in-station continuity, whose lengths had to conform to the type of schedule openings mandated by this buying pattern. Tables 3–1 and 3–2, based on data garnered by the Television Bureau of Advertising, graphically illustrate just how pervasive is the half-minute length in both local (nonnetwork) and network buying patterns. In fact, the trend to "thirties" began as early as the late 1950s in the form of the *piggyback* spot: a one-minute commercial sold to a single advertiser who then broke it in half to promote two separate products.

Half-minute wall-to-wall television soundtrack copy or the same-duration radio spot can each accommodate from 70 to 80 words. Some radio stations, however, will levy a penalty charge for "thirties" of more than 75 words, since such spots, if not pretimed and preproduced, may therefore spill over into the station's own air space. "Thirties" are the second most common radio commercial length; but they tend to be priced in such an inflated way that, given radio's need to establish a picture through more extended sound, the "sixty" is usually the more prudent and economical buy.

"Fifteens"

Though rarely encountered on U.S. radio, where it would be allowed to consume up to 40 words, this newest length has become the most controversial and fastest growing unit on the broadcast television scene. It began through efforts by Alberto-Culver, Beecham, Gillette, and other packaged goods advertisers to sell two separate products with a 30-second spot. This

TABLE 3–1
Local (Nonnetwork) Television Commercial Activity by Length of Commercial

	10s	15s	20s	30s	45s	60s	90s+
1965	16.1%	NA	13.3%	0.8%	–%	64.0%*	
1966	15.6	NA	12.7	0.8	–	61.4	
1967	16.1	NA	12.3	3.0	–	56.7	
1968	14.0	NA	10.6	16.0	–	47.2	
1969	12.3	NA	7.7	32.0	–	36.2	
1970	11.8	NA	4.5	48.1	–	26.5	
1971	12.1	NA	2.4	60.5	–	20.7	
1972	11.6	NA	1.2	67.4	–	17.8	
1973	9.8	NA	0.9	72.7	–	15.2	
1974	8.9	NA	0.6	77.0	–	12.6	
1975	9.1	NA	0.5	79.2	–	10.4	
1976	8.1	NA	0.5	82.2	–	8.3	
1977	8.2	NA	0.4	82.2	–	8.3	
1978	7.8	NA	0.2	83.8	–	7.4	
1979	8.2	NA	0.2	83.9	0.1	7.6	
1980	7.8	NA	0.2	85.1	0.2	3.9%	2.8
1981	7.1	NA	0.1	86.2	0.5	3.4	2.7
1982	6.0	NA	0.1	87.5	0.8	3.3	2.3
1983	6.0	NA	0.1	87.8	1.2	2.9	2.0
1984	5.8	0.4%	0.1	88.2	0.7	2.8	2.0
1985	5.5	1.3	0.1	88.0	0.6	2.7	1.8
1986	5.3	2.6	0.1	86.7	0.3	2.9	2.1
1987	4.8	4.4	0.1	85.3	0.2	3.1	2.1
1988	4.8	5.2	0.1	84.2	0.2	3.5	2.0
1989	4.3	6.4	0.1	83.0	0.2	4.4	1.6
1990	4.0	5.9	0.1	84.4	0.2	3.7	1.7
1991	4.2	6.4	0.3	84.1	0.1	3.5	1.4

Table compiled from material courtesy of Hal Simpson, Television Bureau of Advertising, Inc. (TVB) originating from data supplied by Broadcast Advertisers Reports (BAR) 1965–87, and Arbitron (ARB) Annual Averages, 1988–91.

NA: data not available

*Units of 60 seconds and longer were tabulated together until 1980.

Some year totals do not add up to 100% because columns include neither odd-length spots nor, for 1965–77, piggybacks (a single unit of time split into two spots on behalf of different products from the same advertiser).

created the "split thirty"—actually two 12½-second messages with a brief segue line (such as, "Here's news of another fine product from ___") between. Under intense pressure from these major advertisers, the television networks acceded to experimental acceptance of "split thirties." When station groups (companies owning several local outlets) refused to accept these same-length messages, Alberto-Culver brought a class action antitrust suit against them. In 1984, the group owners backed down and the "split thirty" became a fact of life. Just as important, Alberto-Culver's agreement with the groups did *not*

TABLE 3–2
Network Television Commercial Activity by Length of Commercial

	10s	15s	20s	30s	45s	60s	90s+
1965	–%	NA	NA	–%	–%	76.7%	NA
1966	–	NA	NA	–	–	68.5	NA
1967	–	NA	NA	6.4	–	49.2	NA
1968	–	NA	NA	7.9	–	40.1	NA
1969	–	NA	NA	14.4	–	33.9	NA
1970	–	NA	NA	25.1	–	27.0	NA
1971	–	NA	NA	53.3	–	15.8	NA
1972	–	NA	NA	67.6	–	10.3	NA
1973	–	NA	NA	71.8	–	8.5	NA
1974	–	NA	NA	75.4	–	6.8	NA
1975	–	NA	NA	79.0	–	5.6	NA
1976	–	NA	NA	80.2	–	5.8	NA
1977	–	NA	NA	81.8	0.1	4.5	NA
1978	0.5	NA	NA	82.6	0.7	3.3	NA
1979	0.6	NA	NA	83.3	0.8	2.8	NA
1980	0.7	NA	NA	85.2	0.7	2.1	NA
1981	1.0	NA	NA	86.5	0.2	1.6	NA
1982	1.0	NA	NA	87.2	0.2	1.6	0.1%
1983	1.0	NA	NA	87.3	0.2	1.9	0.5
1984	1.0	5.2%	–	89.2	2.0	2.1	0.5
1985	1.3	10.1	0.8%	83.5	1.7	2.2	0.4
1986	0.5	20.9	1.2	73.6	1.4	1.8	0.6
1987	0.2	30.9	1.0	65.1	0.9	1.5	0.4
1988	0.2	36.6	1.0	59.5	0.8	1.5	0.4
1989	0.3	37.9	1.2	57.4	1.0	1.8	0.4
1990	0.1	35.4	1.4	60.1	1.0	1.7	0.3
1991	0.1	33.6	0.8	62.5	0.9	1.7	0.4

Table compiled from material courtesy of Hal Simpson, Television Bureau of Advertising, Inc. (TVB) originating from data supplied by Broadcast Advertisers Reports (BAR) 1965–87, and Arbitron (ARB) Annual Averages, 1988–91.

NA: data not available

Year totals do not add up to 100% because columns include neither odd-length spots nor, for 1965–84, piggybacks (a single unit of time split into two spots on behalf of different products from the same advertiser).

impose on the advertisers "production requirements such as opening statements identifying the message as advertising 'products from ___' or bridges between the two messages."[10] In short, the way had been paved for the entirely self-standing 15-second spot.

Most industry studies indicate that quarter-minute video spots are cost effective. Backer & Spielvogel Advertising's director of research, George Fabian, found that "the recall, communication, and persuasion ability of a :15 is about 75–85 percent of a :30" for familiar brands or strategies, although these percentages may drop dramatically for new or unfamiliar products or strategies.[11] Not surprisingly, then, in her later study of the fifteens' creative evolution, Professor Roberta Asahina discovered that agency creative directors reported communication of *product key benefit* was the objective for their "fifteens" about 54 percent of the time; publicizing *new product or use* was their intent in only 14 percent of such spots.[12]

At least for advertisers of known commodities, therefore, the quarter-minute can result in real savings because networks price it at little more than half the cost of a "thirty." (Local outlets, seeking to reduce clutter and administrative costs, charge much more; a "fifteen" sometimes is priced as high as 75 to 80 percent of the 30-second rate. This is one reason Tables 3–1 and 3–2 show a much higher percentage of "fifteens" on network than on nonnetwork broadcast television.)

For the message creator, the quarter-minute television spot offers special challenges. As one agency executive put it, "The creative thinking must be more focused. Discipline must be exercised so the concept focuses on one, and only one central point. Visually, the concept must be able to quickly capture the central focal point you want to emphasize and avoid confusing the viewer."[13] From an execution standpoint, ":60s, :30s, or :15s take the same amount of pre-production, production, and post-production,"[14] another creative director adds. The copywriter's search for innovation within quarter-minute time constraints thus is still a high-stakes enterprise. Short does not mean cheap to produce.

One of the most notable of these innovations is the "interrupted thirty" or "bookend" format in which a pair of fifteens open and close a commercial *pod* (the cluster of spots between two segments of program material). In the Figure 3–1 pitch for Banquet's Hot Bites, the $2\frac{1}{2}$ minute pod begins with a "fifteen," in which the talent shoves the product into the microwave. The pod ends in real time two minutes later with the now-cooked treat ready to be enjoyed.

Whether bookending a pod or self-standing, 15-second spots allow the copywriter no margin for error. "They reward discipline and selectivity," observes one creative director, "and punish the greedy and ambivalent."[15]

"Tens"

Especially on radio, where it can include up to twenty-five words, the 10-second spot remains viable as a *shared ID* in which the station's call letter/city of license announcement can be married to a brief commercial pitch for a given sponsor. "Tens" are also effectively exploited to convert bits and pieces of leftover radio and (much less frequently) television airtime into program promos and PSAs. In noncommercial broadcasting, they often serve as the vehicle for the *underwriting billboard*—the sole sponsor identification

Banquet MICROWAVE HOT BITES

"BOOKENDS" A TRULY UNIQUE PRODUCT DEMONSTRATION COMMERCIAL.

FIRST 15: GILBERT: Ooh a commercial break. I'm so hungry, what am I gonna fix. I've got it.

New Microwave Hot Bites Chicken Nuggets

made especially for microwaves.

To taste great. Perfect.

I'll be back in 2 minutes when they're done.

(PAUSE FOR OTHER COMMERICALS)

SECOND 15: GILBERT: Ok I'm back.

Oh great six nuggets with dipping sauce.

It's too good to be true. Well, on with the show.

ANNCR: New Microwave Hot Bites from Banquet.

You could have made some in 2 minutes, too.

This spot for Microwave Hot Bites is the first commercial in history to employ the innovative media technique of being "split" in two parts (with other commercials sandwiched in between) to demonstrate product cooking time.

© 1987 CONAGRA FROZEN FOODS CO.

DMB&B Advertising, St. Louis, Missouri.

Figure 3–1

(Courtesy of Stephen Nollau, D'Arcy, Masius Benton & Bowles, Inc.)

allowed in the noncommercial sector. In addition, though they are seldom logged as such, 10-second spots permeate syndicated programming in the form of PCAs (promotional consideration announcements), which publicize a product or service that has been provided free to the show's producers.

On nonnetwork television, "tens" have served to limit the incursion of "fifteens" because, since 1971, when "thirties" became the prime local unit of sale, stations have been able to price a "ten" at from 50 to 60 percent of a "thirty's" cost. Thus, if the outlets were to accept "fifteens" as the networks do (roughly half the cost of a "thirty"), they would actually have to reduce the asking price for 10-second spots that, up to now, advertisers have been willing to pay.

Like the comparatively expansive "fifteen," the "dime" spot must register its selling idea and brand recognition in an immediate, high-profile vignette, as in the following spot that illuminates the lunacy of paying high prices for the lodging extras offered by Red Roof's competitors.

Video	Audio
OPEN CU OF MARTIN MULL HOLDING SUN REFLECTOR UNDER IIIS CHIN	<u>MULL</u>: Okay, so I paid a little more to stay in this motel.
WIDE SHOT REVEALS MULL IN PARKA, RECLINED ON LOUNGE CHAIR. BEHIND HIM IS BRICK-SIDED, SNOW AND ICE COVERED POOL. A FROZEN DRINK SITS NEXT TO HIM.	But hey, it's got this lovely pool.
STANDARD BUMPER: RED ROOF INN AT DUSK WITH CAR PULLING IN	<u>VO</u>: Next time hit the roof, Red Roof Inns.

(Courtesy of Ed Klein, W.B. Doner and Company.)

"Twenties"

Encompassing up to fifty words of wall-to-wall copy, "twenties" have never been a significant factor in radio and, as Tables 3–1 and 3–2 indicate, are a very minor presence in U.S. television as well. On network air, a few multiproduct advertisers have purchased one minute and subdivided it into three "twenties" to create their own pod. But as long as most nets and stations refuse to sell "twenties" on a stand-alone basis, most time will continue to be sold in half- and quarter-minute units. The only other notable use of this format has been by packaged goods sponsors who split a "thirty" into a 20/10 arrangement in which the first two-thirds of the message is for one product, and the last 10 seconds for another. An "and also from __" bridge usually connects the two, with the newer or more complex product normally preceding the older or more basic one.

"Forty-Fives"

Over a decade ago, some television advertisers used the "forty-five" as a Trojan horse to unlock network/station acceptance of the "fifteen." They purchased a minute of time and then divided it into a 45/15 piggyback. Avon, for example, used the "forty-five" to sell the breadth/image of its line and the "fifteen" to spotlight a particular beauty-care product. A 'full-copy' TV "forty-five" could consume up to 105 words. This computation would also hold true for radio, of course. But few radio stations offer the length, and advertisers have not demanded it in radio or, for that matter, in their recent TV buys.

"Nineties" and "One-Twenties"

The modest growth in one-and-a-half and two-minute message units has occurred chiefly in cable television and on independent (nonnetwork affiliated) stations, which have the scheduling flexibility (and the comparatively lower advertising demand) to handle these extended commercials. Technically, the "one-twenty" is called an *Infomercial* and, as the name implies, provides the advertiser with the time to offer in-depth information about the product/service and its range of benefits. For this reason, the format has special appeal to marketers of such things as magazine subscriptions, book and travel clubs, and special-purpose products aimed at specific occupational and life-style groups.

"Nineties," "one-twenties," and even "one-eighties" (three-minute pieces) are no longer confined to television; they also show up on the screens of movie houses, where they are referred to as *sponsor trailers.* Whatever the environment, the copywriter must make certain that the infomercial (or *short-form program* as it is alternatively labeled) features an interesting storyline to keep consumer attention over this extended time frame.

On radio, a few financial, health care, and political clients have experimented with these lengths—principally in talk-related formats. (On most music stations, long-form spots simply clash too much with the predominant aural element.) When the spots are created, a "ninety" can carry approximately 185 words, and a two-minute spot a maximum of 225 words.

"Time Compression"

We cannot leave the tool of time without mentioning a technique designed to manipulate it. Dubbed a *Lexicon,* after the Waltham, Massachusetts, company that pioneered it in 1979, this time compressor/expander device allows audio material to be played back at a faster or slower speed without degrading it. The television version of this process, using time base correctors (TBCs), is sometimes referred to as "Squeezeplay."

The process must not become a crutch for careless copy, however. Lexicon Inc. boasts that "you can time compress station IDs and promos for extra punch. You can speed up the production of commercials, too, because your announcers will tape them just once—allowing compression or expansion to make them the proper length. And advertisers will never argue with packing an additional 10 seconds of their commercial material into a 30-second spot."[16] While this may be a technical statement of fact, the copywriter should remember that audiences are intolerant of stimulus overload. Electronics wizardry must not be used as a quick tool to deflate bloated copy. Instead, time compression should remain primarily a tool for adding brief temporary or seasonal information to complex commercials that would be prohibitively expensive to reproduce from scratch. Compression is not a fix-it for sloppy writing. It just makes it go by faster.

Tooling Up

Now that we've discussed the tools available to the broadcast/cable copywriter, we can begin to apply them to the situations and problems to be encountered in the chapters and tasks ahead. But in wielding all of these tools, we must not make the mistake of thinking that our audience is breathlessly waiting for us to apply them, like some chair-encased patient alert to the dentist's next probe. For unlike that dental patient, our prospect is neither captive nor in abject need of the message we sell. As copywriters, we have to use our tools to be as relevant, as appealing, and as stylish as possible in coaxing our audience first to *attend to,* and then to *agree with* the proposition our tools have helped us construct. More than two decades ago, Bernard Owett, creative director for J. Walter Thompson/New York, stated the matter well in the following comment, which, though focusing on television, can be applied at least as well to the radio listener:

> One of the great mistakes made by people in this business is to think of the
> viewer—our potential customer—as one who sits in front of a television
> set, eyes alert, mind honed to a keen edge, all interior and exterior anten-

nae eagerly adjusted to receive the message. I think it's far better, far sager and far more realistic to think of the viewer as maybe lightly dozing— maybe semicomatose.

If he's thinking at all, it's probably about his child's orthodontist bill, his wife's scrappiness, his latest problem on the job. . . . So what do we have to do to make this worthy, troubled citizen listen to our pitch? First, we have to get his attention. Then we have to be ingratiating, disarming and, above all, persuasive. And this we have to do through execution, through style.[17]

In gaining attention and being persuasive, copywriters exploit a potent arsenal of emotional and rational attractions. These appeals are examined in the next chapter.

Endnotes

1. "Quips, Quotes, Gripes, Swipes," *Winners* (December 1987), 48.
2. Pico Iyer, "In Praise of the Humble Comma," *Time* (June 13, 1988), 80. Copyright 1988 Time Warner Inc. Reprinted by permission.
3. Ibid.
4. "Immigrants/Emigrants," *Canada Today*, 1 & 2 (1985), 6.
5. Thomas Sheridan, *A Course of Lectures on Elocution* (London: J. Dodsley, 1787).
6. Whit Hobbs, "Same Old John," *ADWEEK* (April 6, 1987), 36.
7. From "Shopping in Oxford" in *Gautama the Enlightened and Other Verse* by John Masefield (Copyright 1941 by John Masefield, renewed 1969 by Judith Masefield). By permission of Macmillan Publishing Company Inc., and the Society of Authors as the literary representative of the Estate of John Masefield.
8. Dylan Landis, "Creatives and Computers: An Uneasy Alliance," *ADWEEK* (April 22, 1985), 22.
9. Mike Royko, "Want to Be a Writer? Buy a Pencil, Not a Computer," (Mt. Pleasant, MI) *Morning Sun* (November 6, 1991), 4A.
10. "Alberto-Culver Wins Split-30 Battle," *Broadcasting* (March 19, 1984), 42.
11. George Fabian, "15-Second Commercials: The Inevitable Evolution," *Journal of Advertising Research* (August/September 1986), RC 3–4.
12. Roberta Asahina, "The Creative Evolution of the 15-Second Television Commercial: Creative Structure and Impact upon the Shorter Message Format" Paper presented to the Association for Education in Journalism and Mass Communication, 1989 convention (Washington, DC), 3.
13. Ibid., 6–7.
14. Ibid., 7.
15. Ibid., 6.
16. "2400 and 2400 TCF Stereo Audio Time Compressor/Expanders," Lexicon Product Brochure, 1991, 3.
17. Bernard Owett, writing in "Monday Memo," *Broadcasting* (October 13, 1975), 11.

Chapter 4

Rational and
Emotional Attractions

Deriving successful broadcast/cable messages involves more than choosing words and phrases that sound appealing. The process also transcends the elements of proper punctuation, tidy typing, and accurate timing. Though all of these aspects play a part in effective continuity writing, they cannot, by themselves, comprise a cohesive and purposeful communication. Such a communication can come about only by combining these ingredients within an overall structure that reflects a thorough understanding of human motivation. Especially in radio/television, where the absence of immediate feedback forces us to make continuous hypotheses about how the members of our audience will react, we must constantly refine our knowledge and questioning of human response patterns.

A host of authorities, both in and outside the field of mass communications, see these response patterns as the result of a volatile mixture of the rational (sometimes call the cognitive) and the emotional (also referred to as the affective). In his *Rhetoric*, Aristotle thousands of years ago isolated the mutually supportive *pathos* (appeal to the emotions) and *logos* (reasoned consideration) ingredients of the persuasive message. Today, psychologists tie similar constructs to cranial geography in discussing the hemispheric right brain/left brain nature of people. As Patricia Einstein delineates it, the left side governs "linear, logical, analytical, critical, rational, judgmental thinking" and the right side controls "creative, intuitive, inspired, playful, symbolic thinking."[1]

Thus, when an advertising message becomes more "intense linguistically" (when the words/concepts used increase the perceiver's emotional involvement), right brain engagement increases, report Stacks and Melson. Because the right brain can process such "qualitative" information faster than the more analytical left hemisphere, this emotionally "intense information is quickly evaluated and transferred to the left with the right's 'interpretation' attached to it."[2] This process thus suggests that use of a strong emotional appeal to grab interpretative right-brain attention will get our message noticed and will also, at least in part, influence the decision making of the logical/rational left.

More simply put, and as Lowe Marshalk's director of strategic planning, Stuart Agres, discovered in his research, commercials with combined rational/emotional benefits scored better from both message recall and persuasion standpoints with consumers than did those using only rational benefits. "It really does take two kinds of benefit promises to persuade a consumer to buy a product," Agres says. "A commercial should address product benefits such as 'Our detergent gets clothes whiter and softer,' [the rational] as well as psychological [emotional] benefits such as 'Our detergent will boost your esteem in the eyes of your mother-in-law.' "[3]

No, you don't have to be a psychologist to write effective copy, but it is important to understand the long-standing circumstances of human perception and human nature. As advertising giant William Bernbach once remarked, human nature "hasn't changed for a billion years; it won't even vary in the next billion years. Only the superficial things have changed. . . . One thing is unchangingly sure, the creative man with an insight into human nature, with the artistry to touch and move people, will succeed."[4]

There are several human-nature-based reasons that would make someone want to buy your client's product, listen to a program your station is promoting, or patronize the civic function described in your PSA. But all of these reasons relate in some way to *solving a problem*—even if the problem is merely deciding how to spend a Saturday night. The difference, however, between appealing to yourself and appealing to your audience is your willingness or unwillingness to put listener/viewer needs *first*. The unproductive salesperson uses an approach that comes across as "I'm trying to sell you something." The effective salesperson's proposition promises "Here's a difficulty I can help you with."

Whatever the problem to be solved, its resolution can be expressed as the satisfying of a fundamental want—a basic rational attraction. As mentioned earlier, it is important to encase this rational pitch in a pleasing, involving emotional package; but the emotion cannot *replace* a functional reason to buy, contribute toward, vote for, or tune in to. Thus, we examine rational appeals first, and then turn our attention to the supporting emotional appeals. Many complicated systems have been devised for defining and categorizing these rational wants. For our purposes, and as a memory aid, however, just think "SIMPLE."

Rational Attractions

"SIMPLE" is a mnemonic (memory-building) device to help you recall the six rational appeals that motivate people to buy, use, or attend to the subject of your message. Each letter of "SIMPLE" is the first letter in the word that denotes one of these six attractions. Specifically, "SIMPLE" stands for:

S afety
I ndulgence
M aintenance
P erformance
L ooks
E conomy

Let's examine each of these rational attractions in more detail. Keep in mind that every persuasive message—and that's virtually every piece of electronic media continuity—must cater to at least one of these appeals in order to trigger an appropriate solution-seeking response by each member of our target audience. As will be seen, a given message can be constructed several different ways to focus on and stress a separate need than that being emphasized by competitors. If, for example, they're all pushing the *economy* of their products, your accentuating of *safety* or *performance* will help your client to stand apart from the pack and stand out more in the minds and memories of your audience. Any product or service can be promoted via any one of the six rational attractions. Sometimes, the least obvious appeal will be the source of the most stirring and powerful sell.

Safety

Though this has always been a buyer's or user's consideration, the rise of the consumer movement in the 1960s gave it much greater prominence in people's hierarchy of values. Listeners and viewers want to know if the product or service being marketed will make them sick, ruin their plumbing, or injure the psyches of their children. With the prodding of many consumer and industry action groups, the question of safety, of absence from probable harm, is being addressed in more and more pieces of copy. The banning entirely of cigarette advertising from the airwaves is an extreme example of this phenomenon; other examples include car ads stressing their air bags, the laxative commercials focusing on the gentleness of their ingredients for people of all ages, and even the program promotion emphasizing a show's suitability for viewing by the entire family.

Given today's threatening and mistrusting environment, the prospect of assured safety is an extremely potent factor in listener/viewer decision making. For the 1990s, asserts market researcher Faith Popcorn, the tendency is "to pull a shell of safety around yourself, so you're not at the mercy of a mean, unpredictable world."[5] Particularly if the concern is central to your product

Figure 4-1

(Courtesy of Kathy Kane and Nancy Thompson, Foote, Cone & Belding/ San Francisco.)

or service category—as is the Supercuts spot in Figure 4–1, you probably heighten credibility by tackling safety head-on. Worry about hairstyling is rampant. But most salon ads ignore this fear by showing only model-perfect hair. Supercuts stands out because it dares to recognize customers' anxiety about trusting their hair to someone else's shears.

Indulgence

We all like to be comfortable, to be self-indulgent. And we frequently are willing to sacrifice one of the other rational appeals in order to obtain this quality, which is so integral to the good life. Water beds and bean-bag chairs may be ugly—but they feel so good. Frozen dinners may not be as tasty as home-cooked—but just look at the time and dirty dishes they save. Conversely, subcompact cars are cheaper to purchase and operate—but they can jar your bones and cramp your style. Because, in the words of a famous beer campaign, we "only go around once in life," the indulgence attraction, and its comfort and convenience corollaries, are oft-used devices in a consumer-oriented society such as ours. The rosier financial conditions are, the more susceptible most of us become to the siren song of self-indulgence.

In the Figure 4–2 Standard Federal storyboard, the comforts of a worry-free retirement are shown as the positive outgrowth of using the bank's services. The 'board does not stress economy for economy's sake, but saving as a means toward attaining indulgence results.

Maintenance

If a product maintains its usefulness for a long time, or if a service has long-term benefits, we are in a much better position to justify a comparatively high cost or to overlook drawbacks in comfort/convenience. Automotive accounts such as Mercedes-Benz and Volkswagen, the lonely Maytag appliance repairman, and the entire stainless steel industry have had significant success by accenting maintenance factors over any of the other rational attractions. In what many people complain is a plastic society, the possibility that something will actually survive into downright longevity is an enticing prospect indeed. If a meaningful durability claim can be made and substantiated, it weaves aspects of performance, economy, and indulgence into a very compelling and logical strand. To function in the future, a maintenance-efficient product must certainly work now (performance). Because its life expectancy is long, it saves on replacement costs (economy) while eliminating the bother and inconvenience of having to do without while the thing is being fixed (indulgence).

Sometimes the durability attraction can be extended to encompass not just a single product, but an entire company. In the following television treatment, the longevity of Canadian Tire as a retailer that generations have counted on to maintain their dreams is nostalgically documented. "A Bike Story" strongly suggests that the store chain has lasted a long time because its services can be counted on to prolong happy memories.

WIFE: I'd say we've gone 4,200
      miles so far.

There's no schedule. It's
wonderful.

ANNCR: That's when good planning
       with long and short term
       savings accounts from
       Standard Federal Bank can
       really pay off.

WIFE: Let's see, what else?
HUSBAND: Yesterday she ate three
         hot dogs at the
         amusement park.
WIFE: Well, you don't have to
         tell them that.

Figure 4-2

(Courtesy of Andrew Schmittdiel, DDB Needham Worldwide.)

I mean, it's not like we have to
be back to work Monday morning.

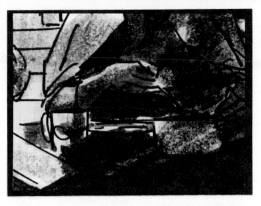

ANNCR: Retirement is the time to
really enjoy life. To do
what you want.

ANNCR: Standard Federal Bank. For
all of life's financial
needs.

Video	Audio
BOY RUNS TO MEET 1940s MAIL TRUCK. BOY RECEIVES MAIL FROM DRIVER.	<u>V/O (MAN IN SIXTIES REMINISCING:</u> I'm sure a lot of folks can tell you
BOY FLIPS THROUGH CANADIAN TIRE CATALOGUE TO PICTURE OF BIKE.	the same story.
BOY RUNS HOME, PASSING FARMER FATHER.	You just don't forget a thing like that.
BOY SITS ON BED AND CUTS OUT PICTURE OF BIKE.	I can still tell you the page number in that Canadian Tire catalogue.
BOY TAKES PICTURE TO SCHOOL.	That bike went everywhere with me.
FATHER NOTICES MISSING SECTION AND GLANCES AT SON.	But I knew Dad had more important things to worry about.
BOY IN BED STARES AT PICTURE.	I slept, ate, lived and breathed that bike.
BOY WATCHES FATHER WORKING IN FIELD.	But I just couldn't ask him for it.
BOY ENTERS YARD AS FATHER WASHES UP.	<u>DAD:</u> Hey boy. I got a couple new tires you can help me unload.
BOY FOLLOWS TO BACK OF PICKUP TRUCK.	
FATHER PULLS BIKE FROM TRUCK.	

Continued

Video	Audio
CU OF BOY'S FACE	V/O: Boy, what I'd give to have seen my face that day.
SUPER: LOGO AND THEMELINE: Some things from Canadian Tire are priceless.	

(Courtesy of Lynda Snage, W.B. Doner & Company Advertising.)

Performance

Even though this rational attraction often overlaps with several of the others, its essence is workability. Will the product function for me? Will my donation help solve the community problem? Will staying up late to watch TV-8's movie really "round out my weekend on a happy note"? With performance, we are not primarily concerned with what it looks like, how much it costs, how long we can maintain it, even with how safe it might be. Instead, we simply want to be convinced that the product, or service, or charity drive will meet the need at hand. *"But does it work?"* is a central question copywriters seldom are able to duck.

A straightforward problem/solution progression is often the most efficient technique for performance appeal validation. The following 30-second radio commercial bears this out. Though the copy is sparse, the effectiveness of the soda nonetheless is convincingly depicted.

MAN: (Whistling <u>Bridge on the River Kwai.</u> After a few bars his whistle starts to go dry, and he is unable to whistle any longer.)

        (SFX: CAN OPENS---GLUB, GLUB, GLUB, GLUB)

MAN: (Starts to whistle again.)

ANNCR: For that intense thirst, don't just wet your whistle, crush it. Crush. Available in orange, grape, lime and cream soda.

MAN: (Whistling winds up to time.)

(Courtesy of Cordelia Chhangte, Saatchi & Saatchi Compton Hayhurst Ltd.)

Looks

Often the least rational of our rational attractions, the looks element evaluates a subject based on how pleasing it is to the eye or, as in the case of the 20-second British spot that follows, how pleasing 'it' might be if the product was applied.

Video	Audio
OPEN IN LADIES' POWDER ROOM AT A DANCE CLUB. WE VIEW THE SCENE AS IF SITTING BEHIND A TWO-WAY MIRROR.	(MUSIC: MUFFLED DANCE MUSIC UNDER AS IF HEARD THROUGH A WALL)
A TRENDILY DRESSED TEENAGE GIRL IS IN FRONT OF THE MIRROR APPLYING HER MAKE-UP.	
A SECOND GIRL COMES INTO THE POWDER ROOM AND STANDS NEXT TO THE FIRST GIRL. THE SECOND GIRL HAS A BUCKET OVER HER HEAD.	
FIRST GIRL IS A BIT STARTLED BY THE BUCKET.	GIRL 1: Did yer perm go wrong? GIRL 2: (Muffled by the bucket) No, spots.
GIRL 1 RUMMAGES THROUGH HER HANDBAG AND PULLS OUT A PACK OF OXY 10, WHICH SHE HANDS TO GIRL 2.	GIRL 1: Well, this stuff really works. Oxy 10. You gotta ask the chemist for it. Here.
GIRL 2 TAKES IT.	GIRL 2: Ooh, ta!
TIME WIPE VIA SUPER TITLE: "One Week Later"	
BACK IN LADIES POWDER ROOM, VIEWED FROM THE SAME POSITION.	

Continued

Video	Audio
BOTH GIRLS ARE AT MIRROR APPLYING MAKE-UP. THE 'BUCKET GIRL' NO LONGER HAS HER BUCKET; WE SEE SHE IS ATTRACTIVE WITH SMOOTH, SPOT-FREE COMPLEXION.	
THIRD GIRL WALKS IN WEARING BUCKET OVER HER HEAD.	
'EX-BUCKET GIRL' NOTICES HER OUT OF CORNER OF HER EYE AND NUDGES HER FRIEND.	GIRL 2: You gonna tell her or shall I?
CUT TO PACKAGE SHOT. SUPER TITLE: "Blitz Those Zits. Clinically Tested from Beecham.	VO: Blitz those zits with Oxy.

(Courtesy of Helen Willsher, Grey Ltd.)

Radio as well as television can use the physical likeness of an object to promote it or the product's impact on it. In fact, the looks appeal is often even more potent on radio because the sound medium actively involves listeners in constructing their *own* mind pictures out of their own experiences. In the following spot for Mr. B's, a well-crafted looks attraction not only conjures up an image for the eye but also engages the senses of smell and taste.

ANNCR: Look deep into your imagination. Picture full, red, ripened tomatoes. Tender, young onions. Oregano. Basil. Parsley. Ladled lavishly onto our own fresh, enriched, wheat flour dough. Crown it with mozzarella. Grated parmesan cheese. Fresh mushrooms. Pepperoni. Italian sausage. And garden fresh peppers. Slide it into the oven. The aged cheeses begin to bubble. Sizzle. And bake themselves into the completed creation. Now comes the time for the ultimate test. Your first bite. Then and only then, you'll know why people call it Best. Mr. B's Best pizza. We bring out only the best. It's what you deserve. Mr. B's.

(Courtesy of Stewart Saacklow, Wolkcas Advertising, Inc.)

Economy

Few of us, and few members of our various target audiences, can totally ignore the *cost* of the goods and services used to make our lives safer and more self-indulgent. Even the decision to devote our time to watching that program or listening to this station must often be weighed against the other more productive responsibilities to which we might better attend. Life is a constant cost/benefit comparison, and the disbursement of our time and of the money that is a product of that time is a more or less continuous concern. Nothing comes free, and the farther from free it is, the higher will be consumer resistance to obtaining it. "Your have to stress worth," points out Ammirati & Puris research director Alan Causey. "Consumers have to know that they'll be getting what they pay for. If something is expensive, it's because it's worth it."[6] It is probably easier for most of us to decide on a brand of cereal than on what new car to buy; simpler to determine that we'll watch a thirty-minute show than a six-hour miniseries, which expends three nights' viewing. Depending on the product category, asking *how much* it costs is at least as important to consumers as asking *how safe* it is or *how long* it will last.

Sometimes, the most effective economy appeal is one that presents a comparison between doing it the way our copy suggests and the alternative. In the following radio commercial, this alternative is ludicrously misunderstood by a stubborn noncustomer who thereby makes the economy point in an even more graphic manner.

```
CONSUMER:    You know that SEMTA bus commercial of yours?

SEMTA REP:   Uh, the one where we say you can save eight
             dollars a day by riding the---

CONS:        Hold it right there, that's the one.

REP:         What about it?

CONS:        Well, your figures, they just don't add up.

REP:         First of all, do you live in Birmingham?

CONS:        Right.

REP:         Do you ride the bus to and from work?

CONS:        Every day.

REP:         Well, by not having to pay gas and oil and
             parking, we conservatively figure eight dollars
             a day is what you'll save.
```

CONS: Save! Ha! It cost me $112 a day!

REP: Impossible!

CONS: Okay, you just check my math, buddy.

REP: Go ahead.

CONS: First, there's $72,000 for a used bus---

REP: You bought a bus?

CONS: Interest, gas and parking is $12,0000---

REP: He bought a bus.

CONS: And there's $6,000 to raise the roof on my garage---

REP: He bought a bus.

CONS: Finally, I spent six bucks for snow chains.

REP: Hold it! You save eight dollars a day if you ride our bus.

CONS: Your bus?

REP: SEMTA.

CONS: SEMTA?

REP: Yes.

CONS: Oh, I see.

REP: See?

CONS: You already probably got them tall garages and everything, huh?

REP: Exactly.

CONS: Okay. How'd you like to buy a good used bus real cheap?

REP: (Yelling to someone off-stage) He bought a bus!

(Courtesy of John J. Saunders, Southeastern Michigan Transportation Authority.)

Whatever rational attraction package you end up constructing, check to make certain it does not attempt too much. In spots of sixty seconds or less, it is usually unwise to try to cover more than one, or at most, two closely associated rational appeals. Some vacillating copywriters employ multiple rational pitches in the same message and think they thereby are playing it safe. "But what they end up with is not an advertisement," warns audience researcher Kevin Clancy, "but a laundry list with so many messages that none are memorable."[7]

Emotional Attractions

The rational appeals are the underlying justifications for why anyone chooses to buy, listen to, or watch something. But for any of these attractions to make their impact on audiences' decision-making processes, the attention of those jaded consumers must be engaged. The emotional attractions provide the copywriter's most potent instruments for grabbing this attention. Like Mary Poppins's 'spoonful of sugar helping the medicine go down,' the emotional appeals offer an immediate reward for stopping to listen and watch. "The best advertising has always touched people somewhere where they feel," points out Ken Robbins, chief executive officer of Lintas International. "If they can find those universal [emotional] touchstones, that advertising can run anywhere."[8] Further, as Professor Esther Thorson observes, "In a society like ours where there are a great many goods, there are so many parity products that they basically have to be sold on emotional value. . . . An emotional backdrop for a brand is really important."[9]

Thorson and her colleague, Jacqueline Hitchon, discovered in their research that "an execution that clearly creates a positive emotion in the viewer can be used with greater frequency without danger of damaging attitude to the commercials, brand attitude or motivation to purchase."[10] In other words, emotional attraction is not only important in the single reception of an ad;[11] it also is a key factor in making multiple exposures to the same message palatable. In both single and repeated encounters with our spot, the emotional triggers in our copy provide the incentive for audience members to stick around long enough to absorb that rational attraction designed to promote memory, belief, and action.

As we made it "SIMPLE" to remember those rational appeals, we can make it a "PLEASURE" to keep the emotional attractions in mind. "PLEASURE" is decoded this way:

P eople interest
L aughter
E nlightenment
A llurement
S ensation
U niqueness
R ivalry
E steem

Even though there are many ways to categorize and subdivide the various factors that solicit an emotional response, this "PLEASURE" approach is an uncomplicated yet reasonably comprehensive one as regards the appeals put into play in electronic copywriting. In its simplicity, "PLEASURE" may not satisfy many psychologists or motivational research experts, but it does possess real utility for the preoccupied copywriter (and it is the nature of the business for all of us to be preoccupied). "PLEASURE" serves constantly to remind us that human beings are emotional as well as rational creatures. As Bonneville Media's marketing director Jeff Hilton puts it, "People remember what they feel a lot longer than what they heard."[12]

Let's now examine, in order, each of these powerful feeling-good PLEASURE vehicles.

People Interest

This attraction might be less charitably called "nosiness." We tend to have a well-developed and, occasionally, even perverse fixation on what other people are doing and how they are doing it. The testimonial spot seeks to exploit this characteristic by showing what the stars are drinking, wearing, or shaving with. But, as seen in later chapters, we have equal interest in the doings and preferences of "real people," people we ourselves can identify with and relate to.

In a more uplifting way, a concern with the lives and problems of others is a very warm and charitable phenomenon that motivates folks to give of their time and treasure. Many PSAs seek to tap this aspect of the audience's humanity. Whichever cause it aids, the people interest appeal works only if the characters it features and the way they are presented can compel the audience's curiosity.

The following spot heightens our attention by letting us eavesdrop on the malicious revelation of someone's adolescent past. The commercial's people interest works to support the rational attraction of performance.

```
(SFX:           DOORBELL; DOOR OPENING)

AL:             Yeah?

MARTY:          Uh, Al Linkus? It's me, Martin Flink.

AL:             Marty, I haven't seen you since the seventh
                grade. How you---

MARTY:          Let me cut right to the chase here.

AL:             Okay.

MARTY:          August 12, '61, Saturday Matinee, The Rialto,
                Laddie, the Farm Dog. Ring a bell?

AL:             No.

MARTY:          You cried like a baby, said if I never told the
                guys, someday you'd give me anything I want.

AL:             (Laughing) Oh, year, right!

MARTY:          Well, I want your Jeep Cherokee.

AL:             (Laughing again) Are you serious?

MARTY:          Hey, I always wanted a Jeep Cherokee. It's a
                legend. You have one---I want it.

AL:             Marty, that was thirty years ago!

MARTY:          And I've been monitoring your life. Up until
                now you haven't had anything I wanted.

AL:             This is stupid!

MARTY:          Your Jeep Cherokee has the available four-wheel
                and anti-lock braking system.

AL:             Yeah, but I---

MARTY:          I'm gonna love my new Jeep Cherokee!

AL:             It's not yours!

MARTY:          It has the most powerful available engine in
                its class.
```

```
AL:            Look, I'm not giving you my new Jeep Cherokee
               as hush money. I was twelve years old. I don't
               care who knows I cried at Laddie the Farm Dog.

MARTY:         You don't?

AL:            No.

MARTY:         Would your wife care that I have pictures of
               you and Gail Hellman at your thirteenth
               birthday party playing Post Office?

               (SFX: DOOR SLAMS)

MARTY:         (Shouting) They're in color!

ANNOUNCER:     See your California Jeep and Eagle dealer now.
               For the Jeep vehicle you've always wanted.
```

(Courtesy of Dick Orkin, Dick Orkin's Radio Ranch.)

Because of its primacy in the human psyche, people interest has been exploited from advertising's very beginnings. Note, for example, the following copy penned in 1840 by telegraph inventor Samuel Morse to promote his earlier business:[13]

```
How cold must be the heart that does not love. How fickle
the heart that wishes not to keep the memory of the loved
ones for after-times. Such cold and fickle hearts we do not
address. But all others are advised to procure miniatures
at Professor Morse's Daguerreotype Establishment.
```

Laughter

Human beings need to laugh, need to have the capacity to stand back and make light of the problems and conditions around them. Individuals who trudge through life taking themselves and everything else completely seriously are asking for a mental breakdown or a peptic ulcer. Laughter is a vital release mechanism for all of us—copywriters especially. That is why we seek it in our entertainment fare and try to use it to our advantage every chance we get. Comedy is disarming. It can effectively break down a reluctance to listen and at the same time build good will. Though not every product, service, or program can be approached in a humorous vein, laughter tends to be the most coveted emotional attraction in a family-oriented, home entertainment medium. If it's appropriate, comedy can even scale attention barriers that, for some functionally disagreeable subjects, are all but insurmountable via any other emotional approach.

Lactose intolerance—in people or dogs—is not a pleasant concept. But this Joy Golden commercial deftly uses laughter to define both it and the product that caters to its canine variation.

> <u>Production Note:</u> Fifi's voice that of a canine Julia Child.

DOGS: (RANDOM BARKING)

FIFI: Welcome to Fifi Beagle's nutrition class. Today, I have some wonderful news for you ice cream lovers.

DOGS: (RAPID PANTS)

FIFI: As you know, we dogs shouldn't eat ice cream because of our (whispers) little <u>lactose intolerance</u>. Milk products upset our tum tums.

DOGS: (DISAPPOINTED OOOOHH!)

FIFI: And so, I'd like to announce that a leading animal nutritionist has just developed new Frosty Paws Frozen Treat for dogs. With the same creamy texture as ice cream, but with almost no lactose. Isn't that a whizzer?

DOGS: (EXCITED BARKING)

FIFI: And Frosty Paws is nutritious and yummy too. Should we try some, class?

DOGS: (MORE EXCITED BARKING)

FIFI: Please wait your turn. Mr. Chihuahua---get off my back. I <u>have</u> talked to you about that before.

ANNCR: Introducing Frosty Paws, the world's first frozen treat for dogs. It's not ice cream, but your dog will think it is.

FIFI: Oh no! Mr. Dachshund's just run off with the Frosty Paws. There he is at the hydrant. Get him, class!!

DOGS: (ANGRY SNARLING)

FIFI: Grab him by the other leg!

ANNCR: New Frosty Paws Frozen Treat for dogs. Now in your
         ice cream section.

DOGS: (HAPPY, EXCITED BARKING)

(Courtesy of Joy Golden, Joy Radio.)

The Frosty Treat spot is also noteworthy because it successfully utilizes a technique known as *anthropomorphizing*—endowing nonhuman subject with human attributes (see Figure 4–3). Anthropomorphizing can be an effec-

"ANTHROPOMORPHISM — THAT'S OUR
TICKET OUT OF HERE."

Figure 4-3
An Insider's View of Anthropomorphism

(© 1992 by Sidney Harris—The Chronicle of Higher Education.)

tive copywriting tool if you remember to (1) keep the spokesthing(s) in character throughout the spot, and (2) periodically re-identify those characters for late tuners-in so they are not confused as to who (or actually, *what*) is speaking.

Enlightenment

Though we often do not recognize it as such, the need for enlightenment, the need to know, is itself an emotional function. Human beings can feel more in control of themselves and their environment if they are aware of what is going on around them. If you've read *Man without a Country*, been in solitary confinement, even survived a week in the wilderness minus radio and newspapers, you are aware of the real emotional ramifications that flow from a lack of information about the places, people, and institutions with which you are familiar. Our increasing reliance on near-instantaneous electronic news has deepened our information dependency. The promise that we will receive useful data on a subject or event is often enough to initiate attention that can be sustained as long as valuable and relevant data seem to keep coming.

The Figure 4–4 commercial for the Arizona Office of Tourism takes Florida's greater knowledge base among the target Chicago audience as its starting point. But it then converts this familiarity into a boring drawback by enlightening viewers about Arizona's comparative and as yet unexperienced advantages.

Allurement

Few red-blooded copywriters require a detailed explanation of this emotional attraction, which, in a more exploitative sense, is called "sex." Actually, allurement is something of a hybrid as it contains elements of people interest, sensation, and sometimes rivalry or esteem all rolled into one. Because the use of allurement is so widespread in several product categories, however, we tend to treat it as a distinct classification. But one definite caution must be raised in regard to this appeal, a caution that has nothing to do with taste or moral standards. Because allurement has such utility, it has been exploited in irrelevant contexts in which it was totally unrelated to the copy approach and rational appeal of the message as a whole. In such a case, sex becomes an unjustified attention-getter that makes promises the subsequent copy never fulfills. This technique has caused listeners and viewers to develop a real suspicion, if not deep distrust, of any message using the allurement appeal, even those where its solicitation is pertinent.

Figure 4-4

Video	Audio
MIDDLE-AGE COUPLE IN LIVING ROOM, SURROUNDED BY FLORIDA MEMORABILIA, LOOKING AT CAMERA. SUPER: <u>FLORIDA, AGAIN</u>?	<u>MAN</u>: So, we going to Florida again? <u>WOMAN</u>: Where else?
SPEEDBOAT ON LAKE	<u>JINGLE</u>: <u>If you</u>
GRAND PRIX RACE DANCERS AT SAN XAVIER	<u>knew Arizona</u>--- (MUSIC, FIREWORKS SFX)
SAME AS SCENE ONE	<u>MAN</u>: How many years we been going to Florida?

Continued

Video	Audio
	WOMAN: It's in the Guinness Book.
COUPLE CAMPING BY RV IN FLAGSTAFF	JINGLE: If you
FAMILY BICYCLING IN SEDONA	knew
COUPLE SHOPPING	Arizona---
FOURSOME GOLFING	(GOLF SFX)
CLOSE-UP, MAN PUTS ON "SAGUARO" SUNGLASSES.	MAN: I got a crazy idea---
WOMAN RESPONDS, SURPRISED.	WOMAN: Animal!
RESORT SWIMMING POOL	JINGLE: If you knew
WESTERN TOWN COWBOY WITH HORSE IN HIGH COUNTRY SHOOT-OUT	If you
TENNIS MATCH	knew
WESTERN TOWN SHOOT-OUT SUPER: FREE VACATION KIT 1-800-247-4000	Arizona---
INDIAN GUIDE AND TOURIST COUPLE	
COUPLE HIKING IN GRAND CANYON SUPER: SIG AND SLOGAN. ARIZONA OFFICE OF TOURISM.	ANNCR (VO): Arizona, If you knew it, you'd do it.

(Courtesy of Shirley S. McCalley, Taylor Advertising.)

Allurement can be an effective emotional attraction. It also can be appropriately adapted to a wide variety of adult-oriented products and services with which it is not now paired. The copywriter must, however, make certain that the use of sex is both relevant and helpful to the assignments at hand and is an effective vehicle for the rational appeal or appeals that are stressed. "People have been hit over the head so often with sex," complains *Victoria* editor

Nancy Lindemeyer, "they don't feel the hammer anymore. We have to reach them through their sensibilities, not just their hormones."[14]

A lighthearted, almost satiric projection of allurement is accomplished in the following radio spot for Broduer Collision. The commercial illustrates the attention-heightening value of this appeal when it is used in a product category with which it is not normally associated. The trick for the writer is to find words and phrases to pull the allurement motif all the way through the copy. Otherwise, if sexiness is used only at the outset, it becomes an extraneous, cheap, and resented gimmick.

> <u>Production</u> <u>Note:</u> Male voice is helpfully businesslike, female voice is warmly sexy, and on filter mic.

(SFX: PHONE RING, PICKED UP. BACKGROUND NOISE OF BUSY BODY SHOP)

MAN: Broduer Collision, may I help you?

WOMAN: Is this the---body shop?

MAN: Yes, but Broduer offers a lot more than your average body shop.

WOMAN: That's why I called.

MAN: Y'know, our 20-thousand-square-foot facility here is very high-tech.

WOMAN: Imaginative toys are so important.

MAN: (Confused) Uh, and Broduer isn't greasy and grimy like other body shops.

WOMAN: Nothing 'dirty' going on there, right?

MAN: Even our waiting room is plush and comfortable---

WOMAN: Mirrors on the ceiling, of course.

MAN: Ye---uh, no. I mean---

WOMAN: I'm sure we can do business, but first, tell me about your 'special' body work.

MAN: (Gulps) Well (Voice cracking), it's unitized repair, and we explain <u>everything</u> before we do <u>anything</u>.

WOMAN: Ooooh. Talk to me.

MAN: Broduer offers 24-hour towing, with rentals and loaners available.

WOMAN: I'm always looking for a loaner.

MAN: Then there's our European down-draft bake-spray painting that---

WOMAN: Body paints! Mmmmmmmm

MAN: And all work done with our state-of-the-art equipment comes with a year's full warranty.

WOMAN: Ooooh. This 'Art' must have <u>some</u> equipment---

MAN: (Quite unnerved at this point) Uh---Excuse me??!!?

WOMAN: I'll be right over. (PHONE CLICKS)

MAN: M-mmaam???

ANNCR: Broduer Collision, Groesbeck, north of 14 Mile Road. Call 296-51-hundred. 296-51-ooh-ooh.

         (SFX: DOOR OPENS. BODY SHOP NOISE HEARD)

WOMAN: (NO FILTER MIC) Hello. I'm here to see Art.

MAN: (Gulping) Oh boy---

(Courtesy of Christopher Conn. WHYT–FM.)

Sensation

The sensation attraction requires no literacy, no social insight or ambition on the part of the audience. Instead, it uses the basic senses of sight, sound, taste, smell, and touch to achieve its emotional impact. Even a very small child can respond to the taste-whetting stimulus of that rich chocolate cake or the depicted softness of that Downy-washed blanket. In fact, research conducted by marketing professor James McNeal shows that 64 percent of children's ads express the sensation appeal, making this attraction the number one appeal in kid-aimed messages.[15] For their part, adults bring more depth to their appreciation of the beads of condensation running down that bottle of beer, but the same fundamental emotional attraction is in operation.

Sensation requires less social or scholastic experience of its audiences than do any of its colleague appeals. That is why it is recruited so often to market the low-cost, mass-consumed products and services sold to such broad sections of the listening and viewing public. When properly selected and employed, the sensation appeal enables the audience to participate most rapidly in the message-building process by plugging in their own experiences almost as soon as the copywriter-stimulated image reaches them.

Because it brings us the actual visual, television's use of the sensation appeal usually demands even less verbal acuity of the audience than does radio. Nevertheless, television sensation can be heightened still further by orchestrating the counterpoint of compelling copy, as is accomplished in this Canadian Dairy Foods Service Bureau script:

Video	Audio
MASTER SHOT: ECU OF A CHEESE KNIFE AS IT STARTS TO SLICE THE FRONT OF A WEDGE OF CHEDDAR IN SLOW MOTION.	MUSIC UNDER ANNCR VO: This could make you very hungry for the taste of Canadian Cheddar.
CUT TO ECU OF A CHEDDAR SANDWICH.	VOICE: Cheddar in a sandwich.
CUT TO ECU OF CHEDDAR ON PIE.	Cheddar with some pie.
CUT BACK TO MASTER SHOT AS KNIFE CONTINUES TO SLICE.	ANNCR VO: Think of the clean, honest taste of Cheddar. Think about Cheddar and something crisp and tangy with it.
CUT TO ECU OF CHEDDAR ON CRACKER.	VOICE: Cheddar on a cracker.
CUT TO ECU OF CHEDDAR AND PEAR.	Cheddar and a pear.
CUT BACK TO MASTER SHOT.	ANNCR VO: Or maybe melted, golden Cheddar.
CUT TO CHEDDAR ON OPEN 'BURGER.	VOICE: Cheddar on a 'burger.
CUT TO ECU BROCCOLI DIPPED IN CHEDDAR FONDUE.	Cheddar in a pot.

Continued

Video	Audio
CUT BACK TO MASTER SHOT AS KNIFE BREAKS OFF PIECE AND LIFTS IT TOWARDS CAMERA.	ANNCR VO: Go on. Your Cheddar's waiting.
	MUSIC UP: SHOW YOUR CHEDDAR MORE WARMTH.
PIECE OF CHEDDAR DISAPPEARS.	ANNCR VO: That's the way!
CU OF CHEDDAR GOING INTO SHOPPING BASKET. SUPER: C.D.F.S.B. LOGO.	MUSIC: TAKE IT HOME FROM THE STORE MORE OFTEN!

(Courtesy of Mary Jane Palmer, Vickers & Benson Ltd.)

Uniqueness

Alternately referred to as "newness" or "novelty," this emotional attraction is exploited unmercifully in the marketplace as just-developed products and services try to make their mark and old established items attempt to demonstrate how up-to-date they've become. Being "where it's at" is an important concern to many consumers—especially younger ones with higher discretionary incomes. As these are the people most advertisers like to reach, not only commercials but also whole programs and the continuity that promotes them will often invoke this novelty aspect.

Because the Federal Trade Commission allows the term *new* to be applied to a product characteristic, in general, for only the first six months of national advertising, the novelty approach as attributed to the product has a severely circumscribed lifespan. But fortunately for clients and copywriters, the uniqueness appeal can also be exploited in how we write and design the message itself. Even vintage products, services, and programs can appear fresh and modern within the proper contemporary framework.

What follows is a unique way to present the benefits of radio, a way that, by implication, makes the old sound medium itself seem more novel. Clearly, the rational attractions of performance and economy are also major considerations that this spot brings forth.

CUSTOMER: Your ad agency is highly recommended.

AD REP: Oh, thanks. What do you sell?

CUST: Fruits and vegetables. Here, I brought some
          along.

REP: Great. We'll do some TV spots.

CUST: Oh, I'd rather use radio.

REP: Why?

CUST: TV is too expensive.

REP: Well, look---

CUST: Anyway, people don't have to see my fruits and
          vegetables as long as they can hear them.

REP: What?

CUST: When we play music on them.

REP: Are you kidding?

CUST: No. See, I put an all-produce band together just
          for our radio commercial.

REP: Oh, come on now.

CUST: Hand me that squash there.

              (MUSIC: LONG SAXOPHONE RIFF)

REP: How did you do that?

CUST: Practice. I'm also proficient on three leafy
          vegetables and two tropical fruits.

REP: Really?

CUST: It's economical to advertise on radio, and I can
          target the people who like to listen to fresh
          fruits and vegetables.

REP: This, uh, band you---

CUST: Seven rutabagas, five cucumbers, and a bass broccoli.

REP: Uh-huh.

CUST: So, we'll play our theme song, 'Yes, we have no bananas,' and then we'll eat our instruments. Okay?

REP: (Laughs) Okay!

CUST: You'll buy radio for us then?

REP: Sure. Listen, could you teach me?

CUST: Sure. Here, start with the celery.

        (SFX: BLOWING SOUND)

        You don't blow on celery. You strum it.

REP: Oh, sorry.

        (MUSIC: HARP STRUM)

CUST: Beginners!

ANNCR: Radio. Red hot because it works. For all the facts, call this station or the Radio Advertising Bureau.

(Courtesy of Dick Orkin, Dick Orkin's Radio Ranch)

One caution about uniqueness must be observed. In exploiting the appeal, you must make certain that the novel aspect is one you have established as clearly significant to our customer's needs. Then take it from there. For, as star copywriter Tom McElligott reminds us, "communicating a meaningful product point of difference—assuming you're lucky enough to have one—is only half the battle. Doing it with wit, charm, intelligence and imagination is the other half."[16]

Rivalry

Dramatists and literary experts tell us that no good story can be without this element. The rivalry or conflict between two opposing entities or points of view provides the motive force for a story and constitutes a constant pull on our attention. As ministories, many pieces of commercial and continuity writing must use similar conflict mechanisms but within a very reduced time frame. On several classic occasions ("Will Shell with Platformate Out-Perform Other Gasolines?"; "Can the Timex Take This Licking and Keep on Ticking?"), the conflict itself has become the message's prime emotional attraction, with the attainment of the advocated rational appeal constituting the specific rivalry resolution. Yes, our Timex has the maintenance reliability and can take that licking. Yes, our client's vinyl covering does have the looks, the appearance, and feel of real leather. Yes, our cracker is more economical than the national brand but still tastes just as crispy. These and dozens of other little contests are constantly played out before listeners and viewers.

If the rivalry is too contrived, if its results and main copy point are telegraphed from the beginning, the impact and, consequently, the emotional attraction will be seriously impaired. In order to succeed as the primary emotional appeal, the conflict must build and heighten as the message progresses. Such is the case in the following Arby's commercial where crisis 'reports' gradually escalate the tension. Also notable in this spot is its innovative point of view. We see 'the revolution' not from the expected client's perspective, but from that of its unnamed competitors.

Video	Audio
LS MODERNISTIC OFFICE WITH SUNSET PANORAMA BACKDROP. OLDER EXECUTIVE (ED) FACES CAMERA AS YOUNGER EXEC (BILL) STRIDES IN	BILL: Well, Ed. Burgers are BOOMING.
MCU ED'S WORRIED FACE	ED: Have you seen this?
CU ARBY'S SANDWICH	BILL (VO): Arby's beef and cheddar.
OVER-SHOULDER SHOT BILL'S FACE	BILL: Nothing to worry about.
M2S BILL AND ED	ED: These reports say it otherwise.
CU ED'S WORRIED FACE	ED: People stepping out of our
CU ARBY'S SANDWICH	ED (VO): burger lines to go to Arby's

Continued

Video	Audio
M2S TWO EXECS	BILL: Because Arby's roast beef with cheddar sauce is different.
CU ED	ED: Thing is---they're not coming back to burgers.
REACTION SHOT BILL	ED (VO): They have a slogan: Beef & Cheddar's better.
ED WALKS OUT OF FRAME TO FAVOR CU BILL	BILL: Come on, Ed. It's still a burger world out there.
MS. BOTH MEN TURN BACK TO CAMERA	ED: That may be. But it's a changing one.
LS OF ABOVE WITH SANDWICH NOW CU IN FOREGROUND	ANNCR (VO): The revolution continues. Taste the Arby's difference.

(Courtesy of David R. Sackey, W.B. Doner and Company.)

Rivalry is also the motivating force in the people-versus-the-elements sagas in which the product is shown to tip the balance in our favor. In the Hefty spot reproduced as Figure 4–5, the universal struggle of taking out the trash is overlaid with the rivalry between Hefty and wimpy trash containers.

Esteem

This final emotional attraction may be more readily recognized as self-realization, keeping up with the Joneses, becoming a beautiful person, and even blatant snob appeal. Goods that are among the most expensive in their product category often use this approach in an attempt to turn an unfavorable economic rationale into a positive looks or indulgence statement. Seventy years ago, when Cadillac Motors stopped emphasizing the technical aspects of its automobiles and began instead to position them within regal and ultrastylish tableaus, the effectiveness of the esteem appeal became continuously entrenched in modern advertising.

When combined with ego-building copy that compliments the audience member's taste, professional life-style, or value to the community, the esteem appeal becomes a potent generator of charity pitches in PSAs as well as an effective means to cultivate consideration of commercial products. Even in

Hefty® MAINSTREAM BAG

"HEFTY/WIMPY"

CLIENT: MOBIL CHEMICAL CO.
PRODUCT: HFFTY
COMM'L CODE: MBHB0419
LENGTH: 30 SECONDS

VO: (Enthusiastic) What would you rather rely on. . . Something Wimpy. . .? (Music throughout) . . . or something Hefty!?

SINGERS: Hefty . . . Hefty! Hefty!

Wimpy. . . Wimpy . . . Wimpy!

Hefty!

Wimpy!

VO: Wimpy bags are fine for wimpy jobs

But don't send one . . . To do a Hefty job! When the pressure's on . . . Hefty stretches . . . Where wimpy bags break!

SINGERS: Wimpy . . . Wimpy . . . Wimpy!

Hefty . . . Hefty . . . Hefty!

VO: Want a bag you can rely on? Then don't send a wimpy bag

to do a Hefty job!

SINGERS: Hef . . . Hef . . . Hef . . . Hef . . . Hefty!

Figure 4-5

(Courtesy of Belinda Perez, Wells, Rich, Greene, Inc.)

program promos and station IDs, the esteem attraction can be used to get audience members to watch the program or listen to the station that "astute people like you are talking about." Esteem is why you display your client's toilet tissue on a golden baroque holder instead of dangling it from a bent coat-hanger.

In the radio spot that follows, esteem is intertwined with its frequent rational partners, performance and looks. Notice how the ego-building prospect of success helps bolster the reason to buy. The copy also strengthens the case for PIP Printing by comparing its esteem gratification with a more obvious, but less effective, esteem alternative. PIP, in short, is your passage to business eminence thereby accomplishing what BBDO agency head Phil Dusenberry refers to as "turning the customer into a hero and the product into a catalyst."[17] This commercial also illustrates the frequent practice of *local tagging*. It is deliberately written "short" so that customized identity lines for individual locations can be added.

```
(SFX: AUDITORIUM AMBIENCE)

ROYCE:   So, there I am, strolling in to that critical sales
         meeting

ANNCR:   You're listening to Sixty Seconds to Success, a
         motivational seminar for ambitious listeners, funded
         by PIP Printing.

ROYCE:   Now, I know going into that meeting that I'm going
         to be successful because I look successful. Perhaps
         you've noticed this massive gold watch on my wrist.
         I know you're thinking, 'Royce, who cares what time
         it is. I could gaze at that watch for hours.'
         Expensive? You bet. And absolutely worthless (SFX:
         WATCH SLAMS DOWN) in that big sales meeting. When I
         leave the room, it leaves the room. My sales
         brochure stays behind. You say, 'Royce you destroyed
         your watch.' I say, 'Friend, I made my point.' It's
         your business printing that needs to look
         successful. Now you say 'Royce, good point but where
         do I go?' I say, 'PIP Printing.' Because at PIP
         Printing, they print success stories. And when you go
         to PIP printing, don't say: I want to be a
         millionaire. They'll think you're an underachiever!

(:05 Local Tag)
```

(Courtesy of Maria Chaiyarachta, BBDO/Los Angeles.)

An Appeals Addendum

This chapter demonstrates that, though our messages are brief, they still are required to engage both those right (affective) and left (cognitive) brain functions. The real skill comes in keeping these two spheres in balance. Communication researcher Dolf Zillman agrees that this can best be accomplished by leading with emotional arousal to set up the rational appeal. However, he adds, "Don't make the arousal so intense that the receiver has difficulty focusing on the tandem rational product message. . . . You don't want to over-arouse or the receiver will become pre-occupied with the emotional element. . . . What is needed is *moderate* emotional arousal; get attention without diverting subsequent orientation from the rational point of your message." [18]

Putting the matter in a societal context, agency head Andy Berlin asserts that "great advertising, really great advertising doesn't persuade just by saying, 'Here are the features, here are the benefits, here is the rational analysis.' It also works because it becomes a little ink blot on the communal id of America."[19]

But perhaps the most concise and graphic prescription for emotional/rational blending in our copy comes from Foote, Cone & Belding's Eric Weber, who supports both Zillman's and Berlin's observation when he submits that

> the advertising I love best has a rational benefit for the consumer running down the middle of it and imagery that would be attractive to the consumer wrapped around it. [20]

Try to keep that blueprint in mind as you fashion your own scripts.

Endnotes

1. Barbara Lippert, "The Right Brain Gains Share of Mind at Agencies," *ADWEEK* (June 10, 1985), 29.
2. Don Stacks and William Melson, "Toward a Hierarchical Processing Model of Audio Advertising Messages." Paper presented at the Association for Education in Journalism and Mass Communications 1987 Convention (San Antonio), 8.
3. Kim Foltz, "Psychological Appeal in TV Ads Found Effective, *ADWEEK* (August 31, 1987), 38.
4. "The Quotable Bill Bernbach," *ADWEEK* (October 11, 1982), 26.
5. Faith Popcorn, "All Wrapped Up in a Cocoon Boom," *ADWEEK* (August 26, 1991), 24.
6. Jon Berry, "Agencies Respond to Uncertain U.S. Economy," *ADWEEK* (July 30, 1990), 23.
7. Debra Goldman, "Marketing's Biggest Myths," *ADWEEK* (January 27, 1992), 29.

8. Mary Huhn, "Learning Advertising Esperanto," *ADWEEK* (June 6, 1988), G. 14.

9. Cathy Madison, "Researchers Work Advertising into an Emotional State," *AD-WEEK* (November 5, 1990), 30.

10. Esther Thorson and Jacqueline Hitchon, "Effects of Emotion and Product Involvement on Responses to Repeated Commercials." Paper presented at the Association for Education in Journalism and Mass Communication 1990 Convention (Minneapolis), 14.

11. Single exposure studies cited by Thorson and Hitchon that demonstrate "consistent superiority in performance of emotional over non-emotional commercials" include the following: Aaker, David, Stayman, Douglas and Hagerty, Michael (1986). "Warmth in Advertising: Measurement, Impact and Sequence Effects." *Journal of Consumer Research,* 12(4), 365–381; Choi, Young, and Thorson, Esther (1983). "Memory for Factual, Emotional and Balanced Ads under Two Instructional Sets." In A. D. Fletcher (ed.), *Proceedings of the American Academy of Advertising* (Knoxville: University of Tennessee); and Thorson, Esther, and Page, Thomas (1989). "Effects of Product Involvement and Emotional Commercials on Consumer's Recall Attitudes." In David Stewart and Sid Hecker (eds.), *Nonverbal Communication in Advertising* (New York: Academic Press); Thorson, Esther, and Friestad, Marian (1989). "The Effects of Emotion on Episodic Memory for TV Commercials." In Pat Cafferata and Alice Tybout (eds.), *Advertising and Consumer Psychology* (Lexington, MA: Lexington Press).

12. Jon Berry, "Bonneville Puts Emotion on the Screen," *ADWEEK* (February 6, 1989), 34.

13. Richard Rudisell, *Mirror Image: The Influence of the Daguerreotype on American Culture* (Albuquerque: University of New Mexico Press, 1971), 215.

14. "Romantics," *ADWEEK* (November 3, 1989), H.M. 18.

15. Jon Berry, "Spotlight: Kids," *ADWEEK* (April 15, 1991), 32, 34.

16. Tom McElligott, "Great Advertising Breaks the Rules," *ADWEEK* (May 6, 1985), 46.

17. Michael Kaplan, "The Last Temptation of Phil Dusenberry," *Winners* (October, 1988), 8.

18. Dolf Zillman, remarks to the Broadcast Education Association Convention (Las Vegas), April 28, 1989.

19. Betsy Sharkey, "The Scribble That Won an $80-Million Account," *ADWEEK* (November 25, 1991), 31.

20. "Eric Weber," *ADWEEK* (March 30, 1992), 26.

■ *Chapter 5*

Making Sense of Our Audience

Having explored "SIMPLE PLEASURE" in the previous chapter, we now turn to the audiences at which these coupled emotional and rational attractions are directed. We begin with a look at the general attitudinal sets that audiences adopt. Then, we examine the life-style or *psychographic* delineations into which today's consumers are more and more narrowly segmented. Finally, we present a copy structure that is calculated to resonate with most peoples' behavioral patterns because it mirrors how human beings typically encounter and react to life.

Audiences and Attitudes

As our "SIMPLE PLEASURE" discussion recognizes, any electronic media audience presents the copywriter with a two-pronged communication challenge. Listeners and viewers must be approached with a balanced blend of both emotional and rational cues because, although they constitute a mass audience, it is an audience that is geographically divided into very small units.

Psychologically, our audience members share certain characteristics common to both large and small groupings. Because it is a mass, the radio/television audience needs an emotional stimulus to cut through the impersonality of the one-to-many communication setting. Like Marc Antony's "Friends, Romans, Countrymen" speech in Shakespeare's *Julius Caesar*, our copy must quickly strike emotional chords that each member of the audience can easily personalize, even though that audience is not actually being addressed as distinct individuals.

But because members of the broadcast/cable audience are also largely separated from one another, pure emotion alone won't compel and convince them. As solitary units of one and two, they are not prey to the sort of mob psychology that can magnify the response and dull the inhibition of individuals who find themselves part of the crowd at a rock concert, religious revival, or hockey game. When we are addressed alone, or as part of a very small group, we expect our intellect to be solicited; we are less susceptible to purely emotional pitches.

Aiming at a quantitative mass that is physically isolated into very small, even single-person units, the broadcast/cable copywriter must not only resort to a balance of the rational and the emotional, but must also be aware of the fundamental *attitudinal set* of the consumers being targeted. Lacking immediate audience feedback, and with a minute or less in which to communicate, we must call on as much market data and raw intuition as are available. Then it becomes a matter of selecting from among the "SIMPLE PLEASURE" appeals those most likely to dovetail instantaneously with what we believe to be our target audience's predominant disposition.

There are four main attitudinal orientations that an audience may reflect. Each orientation must be dealt with somewhat differently in order to achieve maximum copy effectiveness. These four varieties can be identified respectively as (1) Affirmative (2) Dissident (3) Skeptical and (4) Apathetic.

1. Affirmative Audience

Unfortunately, this audience is a rare commodity in the copywriter's world. It is the assemblage already favorably impressed with the fundamental thrust of your message; it is an audience that simply needs to be coaxed into tangible action or, at least, into extending their positive posture.

As graphically as possible, such a group must be shown why/how they should *energize* their belief. It's fine that they agree that making videos of the kids is a swell idea. But unless they are activated into buying the 'machine,' you haven't sold many Camcorders. It's great that they think our candidate is tops. But unless we motivate them to go to the ballot box, she's not going to win no matter how far ahead the polls put her. It's gratifying to know how highly they think of our news program. But it doesn't mean much unless they develop the habit of tuning in.

With the Affirmative Audience, we don't have to sell them on the basic premise. In the following KUTV public service announcement, for example, we can assume that an expectant parent wants the delivery of a healthy rather than an unhealthy baby. The task is to activate the viewer to take the prenatal precautions that will help achieve that highly desirable goal.

Video	Audio
OPEN ON CU OF HUSBAND BY WIFE IN DELIVERY ROOM. (SERIOUS TONE TO BIRTH W/DOCTORS & NURSES BUSY.)	HUSBAND: It's ok---everything's ok---

Continued

Video	Audio
	VO: Despite what you may think, a lot of things can go wrong during pregnancy.
DISSOLVE TO HAZY FLASHBACK OF COUPLE IN LIVING ROOM HUGGING AND LAUGHING.	HUSBAND: So, when do you see the doctor?
	WIFE: Aaah I'll wait till---I show!
CUT TO REAL TIME IN DELIVERY ROOM AGAIN. PAN SERIOUS LOOK OF DOCTOR TO NURSE.	VO: But many serious problems can occur at the beginning of pregnancy.
DISSOLVE TO FLASHBACK OF WIFE OPENING MEDICINE CABINET (FROM INSIDE CABINET). SHE LOOKS THROUGH PILLS.	WIFE: We both have a headache.
CUT TO DELIVERY ROOM, DR. SENDS NURSE TO CALL FOR ASSISTANCE.	VO: And what you may think is helpful---may actually be very harmful for you and your baby.
CUT TO CU OF WIFE WITH CIGARETTE IN HAND.	WIFE: It's my last one, promise.
CUT TO DELIVERY ROOM, DR. SENDS NURSE TO CALL FOR ASSISTANCE, AS NURSE WALKS BY HUSBAND, HE STOPS HER.	VO: If you're pregnant,
	HUSBAND: What's going on?
	VO: Don't wait to see your healthcare provider.
CUT TO BLACK	Baby Your Baby, now.
SUPER SLOGAN AND LOGO.	

(Courtesy of Deborah Hamberlin, KUTV, Inc.)

2. Dissident Audience

These folks have a real bone to pick either with your client's category in general or, worse, with your client in particular. There is no way you are going to sell them on anything until you first alleviate their antipathy. One way to accomplish this is to approach them with total frankness. Bring the element they don't like right up front and then show why it isn't so bad after all or why there are other factors that outweigh this disadvantage. Historically, Volkswagen pretty well neutralized the negative esteem appeal its "Beetle" had with upper-income types through a campaign called "Live Below Your Means." A & P Supermarkets put "Price and Pride" together to repair the damage done in a previous approach that had stressed economy at the expense of the company's long-time reputation for quality and integrity (performance). The copy admitted A & P had strayed and most people forgave them. Listerine turned the "Taste People Hate Twice a Day" from an anti-indulgence debit into a positive performance credit. In the Figure 5–1 ten-second spot, Brown & Haley's agency concedes, even accentuates, the "ugliness" of their client's product while revealing that the taste more than compensates for its visual unattractiveness.

If frankness is too difficult for the client to swallow, your copy can take a more indirect approach that starts by establishing some common ground, some principles with which both the copy and the Dissident Audience can agree. That gives you some place figuratively to hang your hat before tackling the point of controversy. Nobody, for example, likes to endure the cost and potential discomfort of trips to the dentist. But if we can show people the ravages of untreated gum disease, they'll be more likely to make regular appointments. Your liquid deodorant may take longer to dry than a spray, but if we can first appeal to an audience interest in saving money, the inconvenience may be shown to be worth it. As in the following radio spot, the positive aspect must be both well presented and unequivocally held now by the Dissidents. If they don't subscribe to even your alleged common ground principle, you'll be selling two concepts and they'll buy neither.

```
ANNCR:  We all like peace and quiet. It's nice to hear
        yourself think. So the noise in downtown Carrington
        must be driving you up the walls. Jackhammers;
        riveting; truck engines. When will it stop? It'll
        stop by the end of next year. It'll stop when our
        new mall is ready for your enjoyment. It'll stop
        when we all have a downtown mall that we can
        comfortably shop in; winter or summer. Your
        Carrington Chamber of Commerce asks that you let us
        continue to make some noise about the new downtown
```

HORROR MUSIC BUILDS
WOMAN: AHHHHHHHHHHH! ! !

WOMAN: AHHHHHHHHHHH! ! !

WOMAN: AHHHHHHHHHHHH! ! !

MUSIC STOPS

VO: They're only ugly until you
taste them.

VO: Brown & Haley Mountain Bars.

Figure 5-1

(Courtesy of Pam Batra, McCann-Erickson/Seattle.)

mall. Things will be peaceful again when it's done.
Much more peaceful, much more relaxing than they
were before we started. The new Carrington Mall.
Better shopping, better business, a better city. The
Carrington Mall. It'll be the quietest ever then;
because we're raising the roof now.

3. Skeptical Audience

A target universe with this attitudinal set is certainly not hostile to your
product or cause—but neither are they preconvinced. If anything, the Skeptical Audience would like to buy what you have to sell but has a nagging doubt
or two that requires resolution. For them, the copywriter must present evidence and validation that the claim is true; that more people *do* watch your
news team than the crew down the street; that (even) "for a dollar forty-nine,
it's a pretty good lighter." All the common ground in the world won't satisfy
the Skeptics if we don't come to grips with their objection. Ignoring weaknesses in your subject may convert them into diehard Dissidents. The Skeptical Audience, unlike the other three types, is passing through a temporary
stage rather than displaying a stable condition. If you ignore them, they may
lapse into indifference. If you try to mislead them, they'll be interested
enough to exhibit a very active Dissident attitude. But if you can convince
them with appropriate and sensible documentation, they'll be Affirmatives
for a long time to come.

Red Roof Inns, for example, are known to have substantially lower prices
than most other motel chains, *but*—doesn't that mean you get many more
amenities at the other motels? In the following message, comedian Martin
Mull quantitatively proves to the Skeptic that the "more" at the other places
is not worth the premium you pay for not staying at Red Roof.

Video	Audio
OPEN MS MULL SEATED AT MOTEL ROOM TABLE NEXT TO WINDOW. ON TABLE ARE CALCULATOR AND OTHER ITEMS HE'LL MENTION.	MULL: What do 60-dollars-a-night
CAMERA SLOWLY TRUCKS RIGHT	motel chains offer you that you can't get at Red Roof Inns? Let's add them up and see.

Continued

Video	Audio
HE HOLDS CAPS UP	This handy shower cap, 59 cents;
CU MULL; HOLD UP TINY PLASTIC BOTTLE, THEN FLOSS PACKET	shampoette, two dollars. Ah, dental floss; always a plus.
PUTS FLOSS IN SHIRT POCKET, STARTS PUNCHING CALCULATOR	Ooh,
ECU HIS FINGER PUNCHING CALCULATOR BUTTONS	we're still spending 27 dollars a night more than at Red Roof Inns.
ECU MULL'S FACE; HOLDS UP ROUND, FOIL-PACKAGED MINT	Huh, wait a minute, I forgot the mint.
LS STANDARD SHOT OF INN EXTERIOR AT DUSK WITH CAR PULLING IN	ANNCR: (VO) Don't pay too much, hit the roof, Red Roof Inns. Call 1-800-THE-ROOF.
CU MULL; TAKES BITE OUT OF MINT	MULL: It's a good mint. It's not worth 27 dollars, but it's good.

(Courtesy of Ed Klein, W.B. Doner & Company Advertising.)

4. Apathetic Audience

This is by far the most numerous attitudinal set that the electronic media copywriter will encounter. Most mass consumable products and services do not create a strong enough impression on people to generate love, hate, or even the interest needed to be active Skeptics. Such a vast number of commercials, PSAs, and other continuity fill the airwaves that audiences can muster little more than profound indifference to most of them. Most copywriters' lives are a constant battle against this malaise, a continuous struggle to break through to Apathetics long enough to make an impression and stick in their memory. A wordsmith's fundamental job, then, is to crack this disinterest with a compelling image that flows smoothly into a relevant problem/solution vignette.

We would be hard pressed to find a less top-of-mind or more boring subject than a light bulb, for instance. But Figure 5–2's commercial shatters this apathy with a deliciously demented illustration of just how important reliable Philips bulbs can be.

(SFX: VACUUM)

(SFX: BULB BLOWS OUT)

(SFX: CAT HOWLS, VACUUM SUCKING NOISE)

ANNCR (VO): It's time to change your light bulb.

Philips Longer Life square bulbs last 33% longer than ordinary round bulbs.

Figure 5-2

(Courtesy of Arthur Dijur, DFS Dorland.)

Psychographics

Of course, the contemporary marketing world often subdivides audiences into more precise and sophisticated segments than merely our four broad attitudinal types. As Burson Marsteller's Al Schreiber observes, "If you talk about how people are selling their products and services today, you would see this whole evolution toward what we call life-style approach. And that is: 'I don't want to keep hitting you with just plain old ads; I want to surround you with my message.' "[1] *Psychographics* is the broad term that encompasses this lifestyle approach, or what industry analyst Ron Gale describes as "a way of getting beyond pure demographics to get under people's skin and discover what makes them tick."[2]

The Evolution of Psychographics

Well over a decade ago, public relations executive Henry J. Kaufman amplified the difference between demographics and psychographics in these terms:

> Years ago, everything was demographics. Age. Sex. Wealth. Education. Now there's a thing called psychographics that deals with lifestyles. Like cancer or the common cold, psychographics are not based on your social status or your wealth. You can have a taste for great books and be as poor as a churchmouse, and be willing to spend your last sou on them. Or you can be poor as a churchmouse and own a Leica camera, if your interest is photography.[3]

Thus, people in the same demographic category may, through their preferences, self-concepts, and world views, be distributed among several separate psychographic categories. In like manner, folks from different demographic groups may cluster together in the same psychographic category. The impoverished Leica camera owner to whom Kaufman referred may be in the same psychographic circle as people with twice the education and ten times the income. This would depend on how salient the values associated with the practice of advanced photography are to the individuals in question.

These life-style dynamics were set in motion, argues James Ogilvy, in the burgeoning affluence of the 1960s, when large numbers of middle-class young for the first time joined upper-class youth in the quandary of having all their physical needs comfortably met. "Once the basic needs had been satisfied," says Ogilvy, "then the common denominators of material wealth no longer served as an adequate way of keeping score in the great game of life. . . . Instead of satisfying universal needs with the same universally available products of mass marketing, more and more mainstream consumers began to define themselves not as having more or less of what everybody wanted, but as having precisely what only they wanted. More of the mainstream moved from a commonly understood standard of living to an individually defined life-style."[4]

By the mid-1970s, a number of advertising agencies were conducting their own psychographic research, and psychologist Daniel Yankelovich had firmly established his *Yankelovich Monitor*, which was first introduced in 1970. The Monitor tracked more than four dozen trends in consumer attitudes about such things as family, money, and social institutions. These are trends that marketers attempt to consider when planning new campaigns and rolling out new products.

While increasingly prominent on the media scene, this evolving *life-style segmentation* orientation is neither universally accepted nor uniformly focused. Different companies and different researchers have developed distinct methodologies for trying to segment that mysterious audience pie—and different terminologies to describe that pie's individual pieces. In cooperation with the Times Mirror group, The Gallup Organization, for instance, regularly surveys the U.S. electorate, dividing it into ten groups ranging from *"Enterprisers* (Republicans, well-educated, pro-business, anti-government and concerned about the deficit)" to *"The Partisan Poor* (very concerned with social justice issues and believe strongly that the Democratic Party can bring about the social changes they want)."[5]

VALS

A much more widely applicable and widely used psychographic schema is VALS—the Values and Life-styles research tool developed principally by Arnold Mitchell of SRI International. As in other psychographic models, "the underlying thesis of VALS is that people and their buying habits are driven by their values and lifestyles, as well as their needs. It looks to the motivation behind the act . . . Using values enables them [companies and agencies] to give consumers shape and texture—a face and a psychology as well as a demography."[6] In its standard form, VALS is divided into four categories and nine segments, as outlined below:

Need-Driven
  1. Survivors
  2. Sustainers
Outer Directed
  3. Belongers
  4. Emulators
  5. Achievers

Inner-Directed
6. I-Am-Me's
7. Experientials
8. Societally Conscious
Integrated
9. Integrateds

Need-Driven people are the poor whose financial concerns are so pressing that any other options beyond basic subsistence are largely irrelevant. The Survivors tend to be rooted in poverty, and the Sustainers' fortunes drastically ebb and flow with the state of the economy. As a result, some advertisers, particularly those offering costly or upscale items, avoid this category entirely, whereas "necessity" product producers (such as grocery chains and staple foods manufacturers) must put their advertising focus on price and guarantees.

Outer-Directed individuals want, above all, to fit in. Often referred to as Middle America and comprising up to two-thirds of the U.S. population, they perceive of products as status symbols. Belongers are the largest (and least wealthy) segment in this category and the ones for whom being accepted is of overwhelming importance. They are seldom likely to try something new, preferring instead what are often labeled "heritage" brands—even if these brands are not price competitive. Emulators want not just to be accepted but also to be noticed (even envied) for how well-accepted they are. In rational appeals terms, Emulators usually sacrifice indulgence and performance for looks. They are seeking to pattern themselves after the Achievers, who may be the most driven segment in the VALS typology. Achievers already possess the success for which the Emulators are striving but continue to push themselves for more socially prized material goods. Unlike the less secure Emulators, Achievers know they have made it but don't want to be patronized by advertising that tells them that.

Representing approximately 20 percent of the U.S. (and assumedly, other developed Western countries') population, the *Inner-Directeds* are most concerned with self-expression. They believe more in social responsibility and meeting personal goals than in conforming to an external standard. The I-Am-Me segment is a group in transition from *Outer-* to *Inner-Directed* values. Thus, they tend to be impulsive, rather self-consciously independent, and highly unpredictable. Because of the small size of this segment and its volatility, it is extremely difficult (perhaps even counterproductive) to attempt to aim a campaign at them.

Experientials, conversely, are secure in their inner-directedness and wholeheartedly pursue a rich personal life regardless of how other people may perceive their possessions and activities. Because they do not necessarily subscribe to status quo values, they are most likely to try a new product or brand if it can be shown to meet their intensely personal needs. For the

Societally Conscious segment, meanwhile, personal needs are defined by what they believe to be *society's* needs. They seek not status but to act in harmony with what is best for the world as they see it—even if that course of action is not viewed as socially popular. Generally highly educated, they look for real value and environmental harmony in their product purchases. Thus, safety and maintenance appeals would be especially useful in reaching the Societally Conscious.

Integrateds are the smallest category and segment in the VALS universe. Making up no more than 2 percent of the population, they are so mature and self-assured that they can deftly combine both *Inner-* and *Outer-Directed* values in their preferences without self-contradiction. Because of the small number of Integrateds and their variegated behavior, few marketers make them a prime target.

To illustrate how VALS principles translate into copywritten communication, here are five separate television scripts prepared by Ketchum Advertising/Philadelphia for Provident National Bank. Each spot is aimed at a different VALS segment: Belongers, Emulators, Achievers, Experientials, and Societally Conscious. Each script features the financial product most likely to appeal to the needs of the VALS segment being addressed. Notice how the copywriter has zeroed in on the product and its associated need. Notice, too, that VALS is so central to the creative concept that it becomes a key part of each script's visual description. Finally, review our earlier VALS descriptions to determine why Provident National did not target in this campaign the other four VALS segments (Survivors, Sustainers, I-Am-Me's, and Integrateds).

Spot 1: Outer-Directed Belonger

Video	Audio
1. OPEN ON PROTOTYPE OF BELONGER TENDING HER PLANTS. THIS MIDDLE-AGED WOMAN WHO LIVES IN CHELTENHAM WAS WIDOWED EARLY IN LIFE (5 YEARS AGO) AND IS IN CHARGE OF HER OWN FINANCES.	1. <u>SFX:</u> NATURAL SOUNDS <u>PERSON:</u> I thought I should have a money market account. I mean, everyone else was talking about high interest---why shouldn't I get it? So I went down to my bank---The Provident. And they took the time to explain things to me. Helped me turn my savings account into a Gold Edge Money Market Account.

Continued

Imagine. For my money, The
Provider was the right place
to start. and a pretty good
place to stay, too.

2. FADE TO BLACK
   SUPER: THE PROVIDENT
      PROVIDENT NATIONAL BANK
      MEMBER FDIC WE'RE
      PREPARED TO HELP.
	2. SFX: NATURAL SOUNDS

Spot 2: Outer-Directed Emulator

Video	Audio
1. OPEN ON PROTOTYPE OF EMULATOR HAVING LUNCH. HE'S BLACK, LATE 20'S TO EARLY 30'S. HAS A CLERICAL JOB, BUT STILL WEARS A 3-PIECE SUIT. HE'S MARRIED WITH ONE OR TWO YOUNG CHILDREN.	1. SFX: NATURAL SOUNDS PERSON: The money wasn't the problem. In fact, I had to do something before I filed my tax return. And I'd seen all the ads, but I still didn't really understand Individual Retirement Accounts. Well, The Provident is my bank---so I decided to start there. You know what? I didn't have to worry. By the time I left The Provident, I knew all I needed to know about IRAs. (Humorously) Tax deductions. Investment options. Ask me anything!

2. FADE TO BLACK
   SUPER: THE PROVIDENT
      PROVIDENT NATIONAL BANK
      MEMBER FDIC WE'RE
      PREPARED TO HELP.
LEGAL SUPER: SUBSTANTIAL
   PENALTIES FOR EARLY
   WITHDRAWAL.
	2. SFX: NATURAL SOUNDS

Continued

Spot 3: Outer-Directed Achiever

Video	Audio
1. OPEN ON PROTOTYPE ACHIEVER IN THE LOCKER ROOM OF HIS COUNTRY CLUB. HE'S A BRIGHT ENGINEER WHO'S MADE A GO OF HIS OWN COMPANY. AND EVEN THOUGH HE STILL WORKS EVERYDAY HE HAS MADE A GOOD DEAL OF MONEY.	1. <u>SFX</u> NATURAL SOUNDS <u>ACHIEVER:</u> We were just college kids with a good idea. Ever since, it's been good business. But while I was getting ahead professionally, I was getting nowhere managing my own money. Professional investment management? Protect my family with a Trust? Well, I called The Provident; my company bank. They're known for their trust department. Now I understand personal financial management. I'm doing this, because they're helping me do that.
2. FADE TO BLACK <u>SUPER:</u> THE PROVIDENT PROVIDENT NATIONAL BANK MEMBER FDIC WE'RE PREPARED TO HELP.	2. <u>SFX:</u> NATURAL SOUNDS

Spot 4: Inner-Directed Experiential

Video	Audio
1. OPEN ON PROTOTYPE OF EXPERIENTIAL WORKING OUT IN A GYM. THIS YOUNG LAWYER LIVES IN CENTER CITY OR THE MAIN LINE WITH HIS GIRLFRIEND. BECAUSE HE IS A SPECIALIST HE IS ALREADY MAKING A DECENT INCOME.	1. <u>SFX:</u> NATURAL SOUNDS <u>PERSON:</u> I have always made my own decisions. And after all, I have been following the stock market since law school. So it made sense to switch to a discount broker. Which one? Well, I called my bank, The Provident. After I explained

Continued

my needs, they explained
Tradesaver---Provident's
brokerage alternative, that
exccutes and clears through
BHC Securities. Now I have
access to my brokerage account
where I have my bank account;
at The Provident.

Video	Audio

2. FADE TO BLACK
    SUPER: THE PROVIDENT
      PROVIDENT NATIONAL BANK
      MEMBER FDIC WE'RE
      PREPARED TO HELP.
LEGAL SUPER: TRADESAVER IS AN
    INITIATED BROKERAGE SERVICE
    ACCOUNT CARRIED BY BHC
    SECURITIES, INC., A
    REGISTERED/BROKER DEALER.
	2. SFX: NATURAL SOUNDS

Spot 5: Inner-Directed Societally Conscious

Video	Audio
1. OPEN ON PROTOTYPE OF SOCIETALLY CONSCIOUS PERSON SITTING IN HER DEN, WORKING WITH A HOME COMPUTER. SHE'S A MIDDLE MANAGEMENT TECHNICIAN OR PROFESSIONAL WHO'S BEEN OUT OF COLLEGE FOR A WHILE.	1. SFX: NATURAL SOUNDS PERSON: Like everyone else I started an Individual Retirement Account when they first came out. Opened one at my bank---The Provident. But I decided I could do more with the money in it---like put it into a mutual fund or money market investment. So I went down to The Provident. Explained what I wanted to do. And guess what! They explained to me I could do everything I wanted with my IRA right there at The Provident. That's my bank.

Continued

```
2. FADE TO BLACK                    2. SFX: NATURAL SOUNDS
     SUPER: THE PROVIDENT
         PROVIDENT NATIONAL
         BANK MEMBER FDIC
         WE'RE PREPARED TO
         HELP.
LEGAL SUPER: SUBSTANTIAL
     PENALTIES FOR EARLY
     WITHDRAWAL
```

(Courtesy of Lynda M. Lee, Ketchum Advertising, Philadelphia.)

Other Psychographic Tools

As we've stated, VALS constitutes a major but by no means the only example of psychographic research and its impact on the copywriter's work. Newer derivations strive to extend the process by attempting to link audience values to current and projected social conditions thereby *anticipating* the kinds of appeals that will be most attractive to target prospects.

For instance, the Yankelovich Environmental Scanning Program, a further evolution of the Monitor, focuses on thirty-five social values that are considered to be the building blocks of social change. Applying its findings, Yankelovich researchers have isolated eight key attributes they believe are important to today's cautious consumers as these prospects evaluate products and brands:

1. Is it owned or used by winners?
2. Does it minimize short-term risk or reduce long-term risk?
3. Does it enhance the feeling of connectedness to another person or group?
4. Is there real or implied delivery of service?
5. Is the level of technology appropriate?
6. Does it reduce stress, either by saving time or by allowing more control over one's life?
7. Does it enhance daily experience without costing too much?
8. Is it a "smart" purchase?[7]

If the psychographic profile of your target audience includes cautiousness as a prime characteristic, the more of these questions your copy addresses, the better your chances of resonating with that audience. Consider the following radio spot, for example:

```
MAN:   Some drivers brake for animals. Some brake for
       railroad crossings. I, on the other hand, brake for
       no apparent reason whatsoever. Someday you'll be
```

cruising down the road and the three cracked tail
lights that still work on my chartreuse Galaxy 500
will suddenly light up like a trio of giant red hots
as I realize I missed my turn. As you try to stop in
time, and the sight of my wrinkled, grease-covered
license plate just above my titanium-reinforced
bumper looms larger, you'll wonder if you're
properly insured. Of course, if you had American
Spirit insurance you'd know. You see, they make
certain you're not over or underinsured. And since
they don't cover people like me, you get good rates.
A feature that becomes even more attractive as you
pull around to see me frantically cleaning up the
Big Gulp I spilled on the crossword puzzle I'd been
working.

ANNCR: American Spirit. Smart insurance for smart drivers.

(Copyright 1992, Great American Insurance. Produced by The Richards Group, Dallas. Copywriter: Mike Renfro.)

This copy gives the cautious consumer multiple reassurances. As referenced to the Yankelovich eight questions, it is "smart insurance for smart drivers" (1). The whole point of insurance is risk-reduction, of course, and American Spirit protects you from problems caused by people like this guy in the chartreuse Galaxy (2). If you consider yourself a "smart driver," American Spirit coverage "connects" you with other people sharing this same laudable quality (3). With American Spirit, you won't "wonder if you're properly insured" (4), because the company's implied expertise with client analysis will "make certain you're not over or underinsured" (5). The overall stress reduction of knowing you're protected in case of encounters with vehicular idiots (6) is amplified by the "good rates" that accrue from American Spirit's refusal to cover these bad drivers (7). Ultimately, this *is* "smart insurance" (8) for a person like you.

Our copy can still appeal successfully to cautious consumers without covering all eight questions, of course. But with this or any other values-cluster group, the more of our audience's psychographic hot buttons we can push (without fragmenting our message), the better our chance of stimulating client-advantageous responses.

Another trend-reflecting psychographic matrix has been developed by Faith Popcorn and her consulting firm, Brain Reserve. In brief, Popcorn has isolated ten often contradictory values factors that can either separate or link people who are drawn from discrete population cells. By analyzing which factors are likely to be present in the prime target audiences for our specific product or service, we can get a better idea of the appropriate themes our copy might stress.

1. *Cocooning*—protecting oneself from the increasingly harsh and unpredictable world by gravitating toward the home and its family-friendly environment.
2. *Fantasy/Adventure*—the flipside of cocooning; the search for the exotic, the unusual, "safe thrills."
3. *Small Indulgences*—economically-stressed consumers want to splurge on *affordable* luxuries like gourmet treats or minivacations.
4. *Customization*—we crave individuality to offset the sterile computer era; seek ways for self-expression in order to stand apart.
5. *Vigilante Consumerism*—manipulate the market through pressure, boycotts; demand for corporate accuracy, accountability, and environmental responsiveness.
6. *Staying Alive*—prolong your existence by looking better, feeling better, and improving the overall quality of a healthy life.
7. *99 Lives*—search for things that expand time, reduce chores, and offer flexibility, often through quickness and convenience.
8. *Cashing Out*—working men and women now questioning career satisfaction; sacrifice power and dollars for more personal freedom and sense of control.
9. *Growing Young*—think young and age slowly; mature consumers' return to old symbols and products associated with *their* (not current) youth.
10. *S.O.S. (Save Our Society)*—support and promote ethics, education, and the environment (the 3 E;s).[8]

Examine the Figure 5–3 photoboard for the Beaver Canoe clothing store chain. Which of Faith Popcorn's psychographic trend factors does this 15-second spot seem to reflect? Do you believe these factors are most relevant to the concerns of the likely target audience for this product? Are there other trend factors that should be addressed in this or other Beaver Canoe commercials?

Progressive Motivation

Putting together a blend of rational and emotional attractions that serve a psychographically defined audience is a formidable task. But it is not the entire copy task. As copywriters, we must also concern ourselves with how these appeals are unveiled in our messages; in other words, with the overall order and progression of the spot. To persuade consumers—particularly those

Beaver Canoe

Base Brown
& Partners Limited

SFX: Early morning sounds of birds, wind and rustling leaves.

SFX: Creaking Sound of chair rocking after shirt has been lifted from it.

SFX: Rustling of shirt being pulled over teen's head.

SFX: Birds, wind and rustling of leaves as teen walks to open door.
VO: When you wear beaver canoe...

SFX: Sound of waterdrop hitting water.

VO: ...you wear the wilderness.

Ripples dissolve into Beaver Canoe logo

Figure 5-3

(Courtesy of Barry R. Base, Base Brown & Partners Ltd.)

attitudinally-most-numerous Apathetics—it is important that the message draws them in *before* making a lunge for their wallets. What we refer to here as Progressive Motivation is a proven persuasive structure, one calculated to maximize listener/viewer involvement in what we have to say, show, and sell.

Though the study of multistep persuasion has a long history, it was most lucidly configured some fifty years ago by speech professor Alan H. Monroe. He coined the term *Motivated Sequence* to refer to a persuasive process that he divided into five steps: attention, need, satisfaction, visualization, and action.[9] According to Monroe, a communicator must first attract the indifferent listener (attention), then identify the problem (need), provide the solution (satisfaction), project that solution into the future (visualization), and, finally, get that solution manifestly adopted (action).

Grounded as it is in interpersonal communication, Monroe's formula must be somewhat modified to conform to the needs of the electronic media. Because people are not socialized to give the same initial attention to a radio or television set that they give to other people, broadcast/cable copywriters must devote some of their already scarce time to an *attention-enlarging* step. We must strive to ensure that our unseen audience is still with us before plunging ahead into problem-solution unveiling. Therefore, what we call *Progressive Motivation* deletes Monroe's visualization step in order to have time earlier to lock in attention. A summary comparison between Monroe's speech-oriented Motivated Sequence and our electronic-media-favoring Progressive Motivation is given below:

Motivated Sequence	*Progressive Motivation*
1. Attention	1. Entice
2. Need	2. Engage
3. Satisfaction	3. Disclose
4. Visualization	4. Demonstrate
5. Action	5. Activate

In other words, we must first *entice* audience notice (1), which is usually the job of one of the "PLEASURE" elements. Then we must *engage* that notice (2) by providing stimuli that involve audience members' past experiences in a way that gets them to help us construct our selling scene. Next, we apply this involvement toward the *disclosure* of a consequent need (a rational appeal) the listener or viewer has for our product or service (3). We then *demonstrate* how our product or service can fulfill this need (4), and, finally, we encourage the audience to make some overt, *activated* response (5)—even if only to remember the name of our product or the call letters of our station.

The Henry Ford Hospital spot in Figure 5–4 is a prime example of Progressive Motivation. In fact, the purpose of many health care commercials is to break through the audience's fearful avoidance of "illness" subjects so that their focus can be directed to the offered remediation. The Roman numerals added to the Henry Ford commercial indicate where each of our five steps begins.

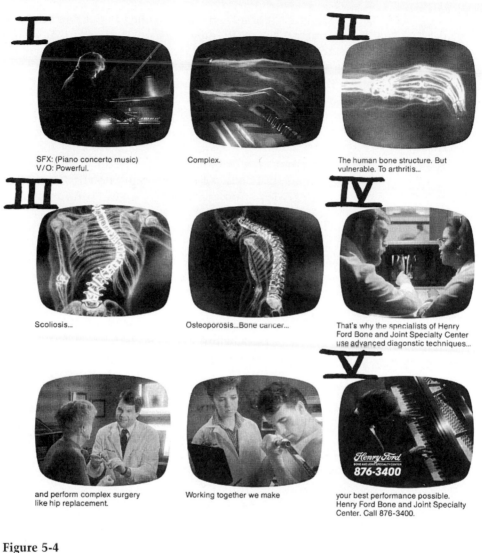

I
SFX: (Piano concerto music)
V/O: Powerful.

Complex.

The human bone structure. But
vulnerable. To arthritis...

III
Scoliosis...

Osteoporosis...Bone cancer...

IV
That's why the specialists of Henry
Ford Bone and Joint Specialty Center
use advanced diagonstic techniques...

and perform complex surgery
like hip replacement.

Working together we make

your best performance possible.
Henry Ford Bone and Joint Specialty
Center. Call 876-3400.

Figure 5-4

(Courtesy of Brogan & Partners Advertising/Public Relations.)

Progressive Motivation can fight audience apathy on radio, too. Here is a spot that exploits laughter, people interest, and just a hint of allurement to carry rational economy/performance attractions. Roman numerals again have been added to highlight the commercial's structural flow.

111

CATHY: Our kids are three and four and [I] they're picking
         up on everything we say. So we decided if we were
         ever to mention 'making love' we needed some sort of
         code. [II] We came up with---'The Furnace kicked
         on.' Kinda cute. But I forgot. (Fading off) And
         yesterday---

STEVE: Honey, the furnace just kicked on.

CATHY: Well, I'm not surprised. That thing kicks on every
         20 minutes. [III] I told you we should change from
         oil to gas. It's so much more efficient.

STEVE: Fine. But the furnace kicked <u>on</u>.

CATHY: I know. It's giving me a headache. I also know that
         [IV] Washington Natural Gas will lease us a
         conversion burner for $4.20 a month.

STEVE: Fine. We'll convert to a new one, but right now, the
         <u>old</u> furnace has kicked on.

CATHY: Exactly my point. But if we switch from oil to gas---

STEVE: Honey! This old furnace thing is not working.

CATHY: Well, it's never worked like it's supposed to.

STEVE: I'm gonna go take a shower.

CATHY: It'll probably be cold.

STEVE: (Off mic) That's what I'm thinking.

ANNCR: [V] Think about this. Washington Natural Gas will
         install a gas furnace or conversion burner and, if
         for any reason you're not satisfied after one year,
         they'll re-install a new electric or oil furnace at
         no cost. Think about it. Gas makes sense.

KID: Mommy, why is Dad kicking the furnace?

(Courtesy of Holly J. Roberts, Chuck Blore & Don Richman Inc.)

Listed below are several of the spots presented in Chapter 4 and others featured earlier in this chapter. Turn back to them now and put your own numbers on each message to indicate where each of the five Progressive Motivation steps begins:

Supercuts example of a "safety" appeal (Fig. 4–1)
Crush example of a "performance" appeal
Oxy 10 example of a "looks" appeal
Frosty Paws example of a "laughter" appeal
PIP Printing example of an "esteem" appeal
Philips example of an Apathetic Audience approach (Fig. 5–2)
American Spirit example of a "cautious consumer" pitch

After examining these spots, you should have discovered that the proportional length of each Progressive Motivation stage may vary and that some of the early steps may even occur simultaneously. Nonetheless, the basic order of step introduction remains the same as the spots all strive to penetrate the barrier of audience apathy. You should also recognize that, once product name is mentioned, the copy is unequivocally at Step IV—is already "demonstrating" the solution. And if solution occurs before problem exposition, the spot will contradict the dilemma/resolution rhythm of real life. In real life, people encounter problems first and then seek solutions; not the other way around!

An Audience Sense Summation

Radio/television writing is more than word assemblage. As a copywriter, you must ascertain the type of audience you are striving to reach, both in terms of its demographic makeup and its predominant attitudinal and value sets. Then develop copy goals and strategy based on these sets and execute this strategy through calculated evoking of compatible rational and emotional attractions presented in a properly persuasive order.

Building on the experiences and needs of our audience requires effective electronic communication that is neither involving imagery nor stark product data—but a painstakingly tailored blend of both. Copywriters don't write for themselves. We write for the values-laden consumers we are paid to stimulate. Or as German advertising executive Wolfgang Ullrich reminds us:

"Die Werbung muss dem Fisch schmecken, nicht dem Angler."
(The fish, not the fisherman, must like the advertising.)[10]

Endnotes

1. "Event Marketing Adds to Radio's Coffers," *Broadcasting* (June 17, 1991), 35.
2. Ron Gales, "Mind Games," *ADWEEK* (October 30, 1989), M.O. 62.
3. "At Large: Henry Julian Kaufman," *Broadcasting* (June 25, 1979), 72.
4. James Ogilvy, "From Universal Needs to Particular Wants: A Vertigo of Possibilities," *Marketing Communications* (November 1986), 15–16.
5. David Hill, "What's Behind Political Labels," *ADWEEK* (July 18, 1988), 26.
6. Betsy Sharkey, "The Father of VALS Looks Ahead," *ADWEEK* (December 1984), F.6.
7. Cathy Madison, "The Flip Side of Bush Bonhomie: Study Sees 'Society Under Stress,' " *ADWEEK* (January 16, 1989), 10.
8. Carolyn Wall. Presentation to the International Radio & Television Society Faculty/Industry Seminar, February 8, 1991 (New York).
9. Alan Monroe, *Principles and Types of Speech*, 3rd ed. (Chicago: Scott, Foresman and Company, 1949), 310.
10. Greg Farrell, "Marketing Is a New Game in the Old East Germany," *ADWEEK* (October 29, 1990), 24.

 *Chapter 6*

CDVP Factors

Before proceeding in subsequent chapters to discuss the separate specifics of radio writing and television writing, we need to lay down some additional groundrules that apply equally to copy developed for both media. We must ascertain what we as copywriters are striving for, how to describe and evaluate the results of this striving, and the nature of the organizational and regulatory boundaries within which the whole game must be played.

All of this is encompassed by what we refer to in this chapter as copywriting's CDVP FACTORS: **C**reation, **D**efinition, **V**alidation, and **P**rohibition.

Creation

Creativity is probably the most often used and often abused word in our business. Although the term didn't even appear in dictionaries until the 1970s,[1] it is used to describe what we intend to do, how we intend to do it, and what we'll have when we're through. 'Creativity' is invoked to excuse our faults and failings ("I just can't turn on creativity at will") and is cited as justification for the ignoring of client instructions ("How do *they* know what creativity is? They only make the product"). In derivative form, *creative* is also a noun that comprises the material our profession constructs. The plural *creatives,* meanwhile, refers to the copywriters and art directors who are supposed to accomplish this constructing. Most functionally, creativity is what we're paid to exercise (when feasible) and why we're paid more than somebody else to exercise it. Still, none of this addresses the question of what constitutes creativity's essence.

That question is the focal point for volumes on aesthetics. But since we cannot take time right now to read and discuss them, let us borrow the definition from legendary copywriter and agency founder Leo Burnett. He maintained that creativity is

THE ART OF ESTABLISHING NEW AND MEANINGFUL RELATION-SHIPS BETWEEN PREVIOUSLY UNRELATED THINGS IN A MANNER THAT IS RELEVANT AND IN GOOD TASTE.[2]

Burnett's is a real-world orientation that well serves the copywriter who deals in real-world products and services. Unlike some of art's more mystic extremities, the copywriter's creative product must be openly logical, must make sense, and the *same* sense, to a very large number of people on the other side of those radio and television sets. This is the kind of creativity that everyone has the chance to bring to his or her life's work and, therefore, that everybody can appreciate.

Robert Fulton (hardly an avant-garde weirdo) brought this kind of creativity to bear when he put together a tea kettle's steam and a boat's ability to traverse water. The consequent steamboat was dubbed Fulton's Folly—until it worked, until the meaningful nature of the relationship was established. The World's Fair concessionaire who ran out of ice cream containers exercised this same sense of creativity when he bought funnel-shaped cookies from the booth next door and gave birth to—the ice cream cone. Even the first Western mass communicator, Johannes Gutenberg, was an undistinguished goldsmith until he fed some paper through his partner's coin punch to multiply written messages. And the copywriter who put a Bic pen on a flamenco dancer's boot got a no less creative (if less global) result in the process of proving the pen point's durability.

Here are some additional classic examples of radio/television copy creativity. The "previously unrelated things" are identified, as in the central copy point—the "new and meaningful relationship"—which ties them together in a relevant way:

The Polaroid print in the goldfish bowl   equals/proves
   the camera's self-processed photos are water resistant.

The six-foot 'sub' sandwich in the Pacer auto   equals/proves
   a small car need not be uncomfortably cramped.

The Jergens Lotion on the dry autumn leaf   equals/proves
   the softening attributes of this skin creme.

The monk scribe using the Xerox machine   equals/proves
   original-like copies are 'miraculously' easy with
   this photocopier.

The Milk Bone Dog Biscuit and the toothbrush the biscuit's dental hygiene properties.	equals/proves
The diver in the wet-suit and the Wendy's hamburger the sandwich's exceptional juiciness.	equals/proves
The Mercury Monarch and the diamond cutter the luxurious smoothness of the car's ride.	equals/proves
The gorilla hurling the American Tourister suitcase the luggage's durability.	equals/proves

To fully succeed, the copywriter's "meaningful relationship" (equals/proves statement) will be (1) the central copy point (2) the entire fabric from which the message is woven and (3) an important *consumer* benefit for our target audience.

In the Figure 6–1 spot, the two "previously unrelated things" are (a) the Baltimore Symphony and (b) professional baseball. The central copy point flowing from the continuous sports motif showcases the consumer benefit that Baltimore Symphony Concerts (equal) vigorous, competitive, *major league* entertainment.

A packaged goods commercial that also demonstrates our brand of creativity in action appears in Figure 6–2. What are the "previously unrelated things" and the "new and meaningful relationship" presented here? You can note from this spot that we sometimes use more than two 'things' to establish our creative synergy.

To make and hold an impression on the audience, radio also seeks to capitalize on the sort of creativity we've defined. That radio's creative linkage must be engendered entirely through sound increases both the challenge and the need for a clean, clear relationship that stands out and draws its conclusion in a visualizable way. The following radio spot juxtaposes a border-straddling house with Black Label beer to establish that buying this brand is the trouble-free way to obtain "great Canadian taste at a great American [domestic] price."

```
ANNCR:  We're talking to a man who lives on the
        Canadian-American border.

MAN:    If you're in my kitchen you're on the Canadian side.
        If you're in my living room you're on the American
        side.

ANNCR:  What made you build a house right on the border?
```

Continued on page 122

117

MAN #1: I think they're one of the best teams playing today.

WOMAN: I just love their uniforms.

VIOLINIST #1: He's got the best stuff---

V/O: ---of any righthander I've ever seen.

COP: The crowds are getting bigger every year.

MAN #3: I remember Beethoven, top of the ninth. It was beautiful.

Figure 6-1

(Courtesy of David R. Sackey, W.B. Doner and Company.)

118

SPORTSCASTER: Here's a team that can do it all; adagio, allegro, molto vivace.

MAN #2: Great stadium, no rain delays.

FRANK ROBINSON: We could never play like that.

VIOLINIST #2: (Heavy accent) We're feeling good, we're looking good, we're playing good.

MAN #4: Man, can they play that Tchaikovsky!

KID #1: I'll trade you a Mishi Virizlay for a David Zinman.
KID #2: No way, I've already got three cellists.

119

FLUTIST: We're psyched.

CHANTING CROWD: David! . . .
David!

MUSIC: (OPENING BARS OF
BEETHOVEN'S 'FIFTH SYMPHONY')

ANNCR VO: The Baltimore Symphony
Orchestra. Baltimore's other
major league team. For tickets,
call 783-8000.

Figure 6-1 *(Continued)*

MAN #1: They don't chew tobacco,
they don't spit, and they're
very polite.

"CAR WASH"
:15 Television Commercial

Anncr: The joys of traditional cooking.

(MUSIC & SFX)

Anncr: Why get steamed?

(MUSIC & SFX)

Anncr: Do away with baked-on mess...

...And heavy duty clean-up with...

...Reynolds® Oven Cooking Bags.
Real cooking! Why make it tough?

TITLE: "CAR WASH"
COMM. NO.: RMCB 9075

Figure 6-2

(Courtesy of John Lowrie, Reynolds Metals Company.)

MAN: Beer.

ANNCR: So you didn't mean to.

MAN: I sure did. See, I love Canadian beer. But living on
          the American side I'd have to pay high imported
          prices.

ANNCR: So?

MAN: So now I buy my Canadian beer in Canada, walk
          through my Canadian kitchen---

ANNCR: Yes?

MAN: Then sneak into my American living room and drink it.

ANNCR: Why don't you just buy Black Label beer, sir?

MAN: Black Label?

ANNCR: It's the beer born in Canada but brewed in America.
          Black Label's got that great Canadian taste at a
          great American price and it costs less than imported
          Canadian beers.

MAN: If I woulda known about Black Label it sure woulda
          saved me some grief.

ANNCR: You wouldn't have built your house on the border?

MAN: And I wouldn't have to go through customs every time
          I have to use the bathroom. Excuse me.

ANNCR: Black Label Beer. G. Heileman Brewman Company,
          LaCrosse, Wisconsin and other cities.

(Courtesy of David R. Sackey, W.B. Doner and Company.)

To find other examples of treatments that exhibit our creativity characteristics, turn back to Chapters 4 and 5 and examine the spots listed below.
Once again, sharpen your ability to appreciate genuine copy creativity by
isolating the "previously unrelated things" and the "new and meaningful
relationship" that has been forged by combining them:

Crush example of a "performance" appeal
Oxy 10 example of a "looks" appeal
Radio Advertising Bureau example of a "uniqueness" appeal
Brown & Haley Mountain Bars example of a Dissident Audience pitch
    (Fig. 5–1)
Philips example of an Apathetic Audience pitch (Fig. 5–2)
Henry Ford Hospital example of Progressive Motivation (Fig. 5–4)

Is creativity achieved in most commercials and continuity segments being aired? Spend some time in front of a radio or television set with a pencil and paper. Try to detect the previously unattached subjects and the new, logical linkage between them in each spot, PSA, and extended piece of continuity to which you are exposed. You will undoubtedly find a great many identical relationships to those being emphasized by same-category competitors. Alternately, you may also find copy that strives to construct a new relationship but ends up with a linkage that is either illogical or unrelated to the message's central copy point.

Deriving a great creative concept is a hard and extended process. Award-winning copywriter David Johnson of Young & Rubicam maintains that this process can actually be broken down into three stages. "In the first stage, you come up with every cliché. In the second stage, you run dry and you realize you're hacks. In the third stage, you do the work you're meant to do. It would be easy to stop at the first stage—a lot of clients and a lot of agencies wouldn't know the difference. But we do good work because we demand it of ourselves."[3] Purposeful creativity is especially difficult to achieve within the electronic media's unyielding time limits. If it weren't, the manufacturers and humanitarians would be tempted to turn out their own commercials and PSAs. No one would feel they needed the special talent and expertise of the copywriter. And that could make us very hungry!

In many assignments, a competent, straightforward description of the subject and what it will do for the prospect is all that is mandated—and difficult enough for even expert copywriters to supply. Forced, irrelevant creativity can be counterproductive and get in the way of the task to be done. Still, *creativity,* as we have defined the term, is something often to be reached for if seldom attained. Robert Browning's observation that "a man's reach should exceed his grasp, or what's a heaven for?" is an apt encouragement for the copywriter in this regard.

Creativity is not something "out there" but something that derives from within us. As creative director Curvin O'Rielly observes, "Creative thinking, after all, is no more than an echo of your personal perceptions."[4] In our profession, at least a portion of creativity, confesses star radio copywriter Joy Golden, "comes from fear, desperation, panic—from terror that if I don't write something funny, I'll be living in a box in front of Tiffany's."[5]

Despite the fear, keep searching, whenever the assignment permits, for that new and meaningful relationship between previously unrelated things. Keep in mind that this relationship should be both your central copy point and an important consumer benefit. And whatever you do, don't get too scientific or aesthetic about the process. "The only purpose of advertising, is to sell products," advertising executive Malcolm MacDougall reminds us. "The only true measure of our creativity is the number of customers our advertising creates. Only those who are willing to work and be judged on that basis will survive."[6]

But most important to your own mental health, learn to take pleasure in the fact that, as ad agency chairman Joey Reiman puts it, "Creativity is intelligence having *fun*."[7]

Definition

In the mass communication setting, creativity means very little if even a detectable minority of your target audience fails to decipher the sense of the terms you've used to achieve it. A meaningful and consumer-beneficial relationship can appear insignificant when couched in language that is vague or subject to misinterpretation. Thus, copywriters must clearly define the terms and images inherent in their subject matter. At the same time, we must also beware of introducing additional elements that are more in need of definition than those with which we started.

Definitional Hazards

There are five categories of terms that, when used in your copy, possess the potential to cloud comprehension. These hazards consist of (1) abstractions (2) analogies (3) generalities (4) technicalities and (5) multiplicates.

Abstractions.   These are words that fail to activate the "mind's eye" because they lack tangibility. The undefined abstraction is therefore especially dangerous on radio, where successful communication requires active picture-building by the listener. General Electric must always provide a concrete example of the "good things" they "bring to life." Banks may prattle on about customer *service,* but to little effect without graphic descriptions of the forms that service take. The *love* stressed in some PSAs exists in a vacuum unless illustrated with concrete referents of love in action.

Analogies.   These are terms that attempt to illuminate the resemblance of two things to each other. Copywriters often encounter analogies in client/brand names. Sometimes these symbolic or figurative terms may be wonderfully appropriate, as in the computer repair shop that calls itself *Slipped Disc Inc.* or the *Grandma Had One Like That* antique store. For other clients, however, such as the Chinese-made *Fang-Fang* lipstick, the analogy can be ludicrously counterproductive. Either way, since we normally can't change the brand name, copywriters must make certain that the relevance of the analogy is understood by the audience, and understood in a way that puts the product in the most favorable light possible. *The Little Zephyr* may be a potent brand name for a fan—but only if the audience is made aware that a "zephyr" is a cooling west wind. *Barracuda* may be a fine name for a predatory fish, but when applied to a Chrysler compact car, it dredged up a gobbling image that hinted of gas pump gluttony. *Kurl Up and Dye* may be cute as beauty shop signage, but raises threatening prospects when voiced in a radio spot.

In addition to client names, analogies may exist as copywriter-originated devices to make product operation or benefit come alive. One radio wordsmith, for example, successfully conjured up the image of a baby's bath as an analogy for how gentle his client's car wash would treat the listener's automobile. Because most such analogies tend to be manifestations of creativity, however, they share our core creativity requirements of establishing an *obvious* meaningful and benefit-centered relationship. If you have to define your own analogy, your tool misguidedly has become your task.

Generalities. The third definitional hazard, generalities, are terms with such broad meaning that, unless we can stake out the particular aspect of the meaning we're invoking, our audience members will be led in several irrelevant directions. To some pharmaceutical companies, it is essential that consumers be aware of the characteristics of a *capsule* that differentiate it from the broader classification of *pills*. Likewise, some beauty cleanser manufacturers are especially concerned that you not lump their product under the general category called *soap*. In any case, generalities are seldom as graphic as clear radio/television copy requires and may blur the key distinction your product depends on to stand apart from the competition. Worse, if generalities in your copy are allowed to multiply, they may give the impression of deliberate vagueness, with a consequent rise in consumer mistrust.

Technicalities. These are specialized terms such as those used by certain occupational groups. Unless the message is aimed at a narrow and exclusive universe (farmers, doctors, auto mechanics), these jargonlike references can be counted on to repel the audience by either making them feel inferior (because they aren't 'smart enough' to speak that language), or by irritating them because you haven't cared enough to select the plain talk they can understand. If milk is people's only referent for the term *homogenized*, telling them your peanut butter is homogenized will not, by itself, have a positive/meaningful impact. A skin creme designed to penetrate the *epidermis* had better be described in a message that shows and tells just what the epidermis is.

Sometimes, a technical word or phrase is deliberately enlisted early in the copy as a means of heightening the seeming importance of the subject being discussed. This is most often done in spots promoting products for your body, your dental work, or your car. *Eczema, iron deficiency anemia, plaque, halitosis, hydroplaning,* and *rotary power plant* are all used to document the seriousness of the communication to follow and thereby to increase consumer attention. But unless you then clearly articulate what type of malady eczema is, plaque's character and location, and the fact that the rotary power plant in "the Mazda goes hhmmmmmmmmmmmmmmmm," the technicality alone won't hold attention long enough to accomplish your purpose.

Multiplicates. Our final definitional hazard, multiplicates are terms having more than one use or application. If audience members think the Malaga *Pipe* Company turns out products for plumbers when it in fact makes the kind you smoke, your message won't sell many meerschaums. ('Meerschaums,' however, is a technicality we could productively exploit to attract our real target universe.) With the capability to visually specify from the very first frame, television can clarify a multiplicate much more quickly than radio, of course. But on either medium, the longer you allow your audience to play mentally with their own favorite referent for *pipe, plane,* or other multiplicates (like *conductor, organ,* and *range*), the greater the probability that they will be irretrievably off on their own mental tangents. If your spot inadvertently stimulates the consumer to muse about a keyboard instrument (one type of *organ*), he or she will seldom be prepared to worry about a bodily 'organ's' excess acidity.

The Five Definitional Tools

Now that we are aware of the kinds of terms requiring definition, we can focus on the available mechanisms for accomplishing this definition. Generally speaking, a word or phrase can be clarified via any of five methods: (1) negation (2) context (3) correlation (4) derivation and (5) exemplification.

Negation. This is an old rhetorical technique that sets a thing apart by showing what it is NOT or by demonstrating the conditions to which it does NOT apply. Definition by negation can be a very effective copywriter device because it often lends itself to a highly developed copy rhythm in which both the sound and the sense push the message forward:

Not a roll-on, not a cream, new Mennon with Pers-stop . . .

This is NOT---your father's Oldsmobile.

Provided we don't attempt to milk it too long, negation is also an effective suspense-builder that encourages the listener or viewer to stay tuned to discover just what the thing *is:*

If you think it's butter, but it's not; it's---Chiffon.

Guinness. The beer that isn't for snobs or the ignorant masses.

Definition by negation can also be more subtle. It can be used to encourage the audience to reevaluate a product or procedure in order to see it in its proper light; to appreciate that its attainment is easier than the audience has been led to believe. This is the brand of negation used in the PSA below to explain that eliminating litter does *not* entail immense self-sacrifice.

ANNCR: Presenting great discoveries during Stamp Out Litter Week. Three years ago, little Tommy Ferguson discovered that his arm would not fall off if he held onto his candy wrapper until he reached a wastebasket. Two years ago, Miss Edwina Perkins discovered it would not take forever to walk twenty extra feet and trashcan the newspaper she'd finished reading. Just last week, Alvin 'Big Al' Bustamonte discovered that bagging his empties, instead of stomping them into the pavement, did not destroy his great macho image. This Stamp Out Litter Week, you too can discover how easy it is NOT to litter. You'll also discover how safe, suave and desirable it is not to have litter around.

In employing negation on radio, however, remember that the listener can't picture a 'not.' So, negations must be wrapped in imagery that keeps audience mind's eyes filled with concrete, positive images. Notice how the following student-composed copy lines blur the benefit that the writer is attempting to erect in the listener's imagination:

Our disinfectant's aroma is not displeasing.

(But how *does* it smell?)

```
The Kitchenaide Cheese Slicer prevents slices where you
don't want them.
```

   (What/where *does* it slice?)

```
You won't get diluted drinks or messy melting when you put
Fairmont Ice Wedges in your beverage.
```

   (What *will* I get?)

The same principle applies to station-positioning promos. As Miami program director Bill Stedman points out, "Stations that use a combination of 'not too hard, not too soft,' 'no silly DJ chatter' and ' no contests that you could never win' may reflect listeners' attitudes, but they don't establish a positive image. . . . The solution is for a station to tell a listener exactly what it *is* and then live up to that promise."[8]

Context.   This is the most straightforward and least time-consuming of our Definitional Tools. With context, the meaning of the term is made clear simply by the environment in which the term is placed—by the words and phrases that immediately precede and/or follow it:

```
We pasteurize to purify.
```

```
Tercel---Toyota's answer to the small car question.
```

```
The Serta Perfect-Sleeper mattress.
```

   In the following radio spot, for example, the copywriter makes certain to continuously position the word 'cheese' immediately after the unusual 'Alpine Lace' brand name. The listener thereby is given no opportunity to wander off in musings about mountain climbing or tapestries; musings that the unqualified term might otherwise engender.

```
BERNIE: And how can Bernie's Better Deli help you?

LADY:   My husband's cholesterol is up, his weight is
        up, and he's having an affair. What do you
        recommend?

BERNIE: Alpine Lace Cheese.

LADY:   Is that the cheese that's lower in cholesterol,
        sodium and fat?
```

BERNIE: Right. Bring home an Alpine Lace American Cheese sandwich, and everything works out. His cholesterol, his pressure, his weight, even his tootsie.

LADY: You really think Alpine Lace Cheese will change Phil into the man he used to be?

BERNIE: Absolutely! He's only running around because she makes him feel healthy. If he had a good piece of cheese, he'd dump her like a bad habit.

LADY: And that's Alpine Lace Cheese, right?

BERNIE: Right.

LADY: You're so sensitive.

BERNIE: That's because we're an official Alpine Lace Cheese healthier cheese deli---we care about you.

LADY: So what's my plan?

BERNIE: Just walk in the door with the Alpine Lace Cheese sandwich, and say, Phil---

LADY: I can him Pookins---

BERNIE: Okay, say Pookins, I'm gonna give you the greatest thing you've ever had in your life.

LADY: I'll do it!

BERNIE: How's Pookins like it?

LADY: On white, no crust, and a toothpick with a colored frill.

BERNIE: The man is an animal!

LADY: Yeah, a rabbit.

ANNCR: Ask your deli for a sandwich with Alpine Lace, the healthier cheese. If they don't carry it, they don't care.

(Courtesy of Joy Golden, Joy Radio.)

Correlation. Our third Definitional Tool, correlation involves comparing the term to be defined with more familiar terms that can be shown to have a somewhat similar meaning. Through this device, we attempt to connect the less known or less vibrant term systematically and colorfully with a term possessing clearer audience image potential. Thus, unique definitions by correlation also constitute examples of *creativity:*

```
Like a thousand busy fingers, Lustre Creme works to smooth
wrinkles.

Wash 'N Dry is like soap and water to go.

Peak Anti-Freeze is like chicken soup for your car.
```

In the Figure 6–3 Allnet photoboard, the negative business impression made by low fidelity long-distance lines is graphically correlated (defined) with the impact made by sloppily typed correspondence.

Derivation. This method defines a term by expressing its semantic or geographic heritage. The original meaning of the whole term can be illuminated, or we can break it down into its constituent parts and show the specific significance of each:

```
In Europe, where our beer originated, Fassbeer meant draft
beer.

Mata Hari: an intriguing fragrance inspired by the
seductive spy.

Named for the inventor who made rubber tough: Goodyear
Tires.
```

Even though a dictionary quotation can sometimes be used to present the derivation, many audiences will be turned off by such a boring and stilted approach. It is true that for a professional/technical market already interested in the field from which the term comes, the dictionary blurb may be the quickest available way to sketch the word's history. For more general consumer groups, however, a less bookish approach is needed to retain attention. In the commercial on page 132, for instance, copywriter Joy Golden constructs an entertaining marital dialogue to define not only the product's origin for New York audiences, but also the cooking process through which it and part of its name are derived.

ALLNET
Long Distance

"Business Letter"   :30 television commercial

©1986 Allnet Communications

Figure 6-3

(Courtesy of Marjorie Nugent, Fallon McElligott Advertising.)

WIFE: Fred, do you remember when I said let's go to
          Hawaii?

FRED: (Disinterested) Yeah.

WIFE: And you said no.

FRED: Yeah.

WIFE: And I said why?

FRED: Yeah.

WIFE: And you said because all they've got is pineapples
          and coconuts.

FRED: Yeah.

WIFE: Well, do you want to hear something?

FRED: No.

WIFE: I bought new Eagle Snacks Hawaiian Kettle Potato
          Chips today, and guess where they came from?

FRED: Potatoes?

WIFE: No, I mean the recipe.

FRED: Columbus Avenue.

WIFE: No, Fred---from Hawaii. Eagle Snacks slow cooks them
          in a great big kettle and a man stands there and
          gently rakes them back and forth until they're so
          crunchy you wouldn't believe it.

FRED: I wouldn't?

WIFE: Think of it, Fred. In this day and age, in a big
          American factory they actually do what they do in
          Hawaii.

FRED: The hula?

```
WIFE:   No, Fred. Slow kettle cooking. Here. Taste this
        Eagle Snack Hawaiian Chip.

FRED:   (After biting down on it with large crunch) You're
        right. They're terrific. What a crunch.

WIFE:   See, Fred? Hawaii isn't all pineapples and coconuts.
        I know it's not Rockaway, but let's go sometime.

FRED:   Why? We've got Eagle Snacks Hawaiian Kettle Potato
        Chips right here.

WIFE:   But what about the glamour? The weather? the lei you
        get when you land?

FRED:   (Suddenly interested) The what?

ANNCR:  New Hawaiian Kettle Potato Chips. Nothing tastes
        like an Eagle Snack.
```

(Courtesy of Joy Golden, Joy Radio.)

Exemplification. Our final Definitional Tool, exemplification accomplishes its task either by (1) citing examples of situations to which the term best can be applied, or (2) enumerating the essential components of what the term represents.

With the first method, for instance, we help define the term/brand *Excedrin* by stating:

```
Excedrin is great for relief of mild headache pain. If pain
persists, see your doctor.
```

Thus, the commercial has been both truthful with the audience and respectful of the Federal Trade Commission and Food and Drug Administration in citing, in *exemplifying*, situations for which the product is and is not intended. Similarly, in the following promo for TV-24's Sunday evening movie, we learn that the 'product' is especially applicable when you desire a flick Sunday night—but have to get up Monday morning.

```
(SFX: TV SET UNDER. KNOCK-KNOCK; DOOR OPENS.)

WILSON:      Yes?

MR. SANDMAN: Mr. Wilson-comma-Edgar?
```

WILSON: Yes?

MR. SANDMAN: It's time, Mr. Wilson.

WILSON: Hey Edith, did you order a pizza?

MR. SANDMAN: I'm Mr. Sandman, Mr. Wilson.

WILSON: Oh lord.

MR. SANDMAN: You know the rules. No more TV. Tomorrow's a work day. It's beddy-time.

              (SFX: TV SET CLICKS OFF)

WILSON: Hey, I was right in the middle of that movie!

MR. SANDMAN: You should have been watching the Over By Midnight Sunday Night Movie on TV-24, Mr. Wilson. TV-24's movie starts at 10:30 and is over before 12.

WILSON: Can't I stay up just a little longer?

MR. SANDMAN: Aren't you the same Wilson-comma-Edgar who always complains about being tired and/or cranky come Monday morning?

WILSON: (Angrily) I don't get cranky!

MR. SANDMAN: SSH!

WILSON: Well, I <u>don't</u>.

MR. SANDMAN: Next time remember: TV-24's Over By Midnight Sunday Night Movie.

WILSON: You sure you're not the tooth fairy?

MR. SANDMAN: Do I <u>sound</u> like a fairy, Mr. Wilson?!

WILSON: No, well it's the peach-colored pajamas that made me think---

```
MR. SANDMAN:   It's the uniform, buddy. At least mine don't
               have feet in them.

WILSON:        They were a gift.
```

(Courtesy of Steve Eichenbaum, Curro/Eichenbaum, Inc.)

Our second exemplification method, enumerating the term's essential components, is more of a dissection process. We can, for instance, define the performance of the Little Zephyr Fan through exposition of its namesake's effect and behavior as a gentle, cooling breeze. We identify the original zephyr's key characteristics and thereby simultaneously identify how the product itself is promised to perform. Correspondingly, as in the television spot in Figure 6–4, the viewer is shown a number of facilities and qualities that collectively exemplify the consistent excellence of Inter-Continental Hotels.

A copywriter may choose whichever Definitional Tool or Tools best fit(s) the problem at hand. There is nothing wrong in using more than one of these devices in the same spot as long as message coherence is maintained. In the following Dick Orkin radio commercial, for instance, definition by *context* is applied via use of the complete brand name: Wilcox *Family Farm Dairy* Products. The vague notion of product quality is made much more tangible by *correlating* it with being 'particular,' 'picky,' or even 'obsessed.' All Wilcox foods are *derived* from an enterprise that has been in operation "just down the road" for "about 80 years" (right here in the state of) "Washington." And Wilcox products are *exemplified* by those pampered cows and chickens working to produce "the cottage cheese . . . yogurt . . . the sour cream . . . butter . . . the eggs." The copywriter even uses a bit of anti-*negation* by starting to define the Wilcox establishment as "not too picky"—and then retreating from this premise to further bolster the correlated quality claim.

```
WOMAN:    Oh, we've lived just down the road from the
          Wilcox family our whole life.

MAN:      About 80 years they've been there.

WOMAN:    Nice folks.

MAN:      Very nice folks.

WOMAN:    They make all those delicious Wilcox Family Farm
          Dairy Products, you know.

MAN:      It's just, well, you know---
```

Announcer V.O.:
All over the world

3 out of 4 of our guests

return to
Inter-Continental,
again and again.

London—
for a jolly good business hotel...

Inter-Continental London GM:
Inter-Continental,
again and again.

Paris—
for true French flair...

Inter-Continental Paris GM:
Inter-Continental,
encore et encore.

Vienna—
for hearty hospitality...

Inter-Continental Wien GM:
Inter-Continental,
wieder und wieder.

Washington—
for the residence
of presidents...

Willard Inter-Continental GM:
Inter-Continental,
again and again.

100 hotels
around the world!
Inter-Continental,
again and again.

Figure 6-4

(Courtesy of George Lois, Lois/USA Advertising.)

WOMAN: Oh, go ahead, say it.

MAN: They're just so darn particular.

WOMAN: That's it. Particular.

MAN: I might even say obsessed.

WOMAN: Obsessed.

MAN: I mean, you've never seen anything like it.
                Constantly fretting over those dairy cows, those
                egg-producing chickens---

WOMAN: I hear that they treat those cows practically
                like members of the family.

MAN: Oh, yeah. They take such pride in the Wilcox
                Family Farm milk, the cottage cheese---

WOMAN: Yogurt---

MAN: The sour cream---

WOMAN: Butter---

MAN: The eggs.

WOMAN: Ahhhh.

MAN: They're so darn particular.

WOMAN: Very particular.

MAN: Some might even say obsessed.

WOMAN: Obsessed.

MAN: Or picky.

WOMAN/MAN: Picky, picky, picky.

ANNOUNCER: At Wilcox Family Farms, we <u>are</u> picky about
                our quality dairy products, all made with
                pride, in Washington. Some might say too
                picky.

WOMAN: Well, I wouldn't say they're too
                picky.

137

```
MAN:         Oh, no, they're not too, uh, they are fussy,
             though.

WOMAN/MAN: Fussy, fussy, fussy.

ANNOUNCER: Wilcox Family Farms, we're obsessed with quality.
```
(Courtesy of Dick Orkin, Dick Orkin's Radio Ranch.)

One thing more before leaving the subject of definition. As the number of radio examples we've used in this section attest, *any* radio assignment presents the copywriter with unavoidable definitional challenges. In television, as long as we have enough sense to point the camera at the product-in-use, the fundamental definitional task is automatically (if not necessarily persuasively) accomplished. On radio, however, there is no product-in-use, there is no product or benefit picture, until we capture these elements with carefully chosen definitional words and supporting sounds.

Validation

Let's suppose you've achieved our meaningful relationship between previously unrelated things. Let's even assume that the relationship in unbreakable. And let's further assume you've isolated the terms in need of defining and employed the appropriate Definitional Tools. You are now ready, not to relax, but to take a step back from your copy and attempt to evaluate it as a whole; to predict its overall effect on those listeners and viewers who are definitely *not* waiting breathlessly for your next message to reach them.

This stepping back, this organized speculation about how your communication will be received, can be dubbed *Validation.* It's a process best delineated via the *Ten Guidelines for Professional Copy* developed by Stone & Adler's copy supervisor, Paul Connors.[9] When all ten of Connors's questions are brought to bear, they help ensure that copy technique has not been permitted to overshadow the ultimate marketing objective.

1. Does the Writer Know the Product? If you are not fully cognizant of the benefits of what you're selling, you are in no position to choose the advantage that has the greatest appeal to the audience you're striving to reach. And if you're unaware of your subject's drawbacks, you may end up constructing a spot that only serves to publicize a client weakness. You don't have to personally use something to promote it. But you do need to be fully conversant with its attributes before attempting to explain some of them to somebody else.

2. Does the Writer Know the Market?   As we stressed in Chapter 5, mass communication does not mean trying to talk to everyone, but rather, entails targeting ever more segmented groups, each of which coalesces around distinct needs and attitudes. "In 1970," MTV sales executive Douglas Greenlaw reminds us, "there were 9,000 items available in a traditional supermarket; in 1990 . . . in excess of 26,000. The ability to send a rifle shot directly to a specific consumer is not a luxury, but a necessity."[10]

Once you have done the market research, the best way to make certain your copy reflects the results of that research is to visualize one person to epitomize your prime prospects. Picture that fifteen-year-old sophomore boy, or that thirty-eight-year-old female secretary, or the retired factory worker who sat next to you on the bus. Next, forget that you're a copywriter; forget that you've written the spot; forget everything about the assignment and just go blank. (If going blank is too easy for you, consult another book.)

Now, thinking as that sophomore, secretary, or bus-rider (or some other person who represents your client's prime target)—does this piece of copy make sense? Is it believable? Does it come across through terms and images with which you can identify? Or does the message make you want to skip out, take a coffee break, or move to another seat? And whatever your audience, as we stressed at the end of Chapter 2, never talk down to them. "We'll only be in trouble," cautions agency founder Jerry Della Femina, "if we . . . give in to the cynics who say that the consumer is a boob and we should treat him like he really believes he has ring around the collar and a head filled with arrows in his nasal passages."[11]

3. Is the Writer Talking To the Prospect?   Beyond identifying and attracting our market via concepts most likely to push these folks' 'hot buttons,' Validation also required wrapping the concept in a friendly, conversational package. Arthur Godfrey, radio's first great salesman, achieved his success after a lengthy convalescence in which he had nothing to do but listen to the radio. Godfrey tried to discern why some commercials were so much more effective in convincing him than others. The explanation he formulated was that too many spots simply blabbed at "you folks out there in radio land." Even given these messages' targeting to a particular demographic group, there was little or no *personalization*, little or no attempt at simulating and stimulating a sense of one-to-one communication before dragging the product in by the foot. Successful commercials, conversely, took the time and trouble to establish a feeling of trust and good will before waving the product in front of the listener's ear.

Good copy, in other words, must sell itself before it can sell the product. Like any successful door-to-door salesperson, it radiates enough warmth and interest to keep the door to the listener's or viewer's attention open long enough to get the product out of the sample case. Copywriters "tend to forget that they are door-to-door salespeople, invading people's privacy for less than altruistic purposes," chides advertising executive Malcolm MacDougall.

139

"They seem to ignore the fact that people are just as wary of advertising that knocks on their door—and just as quick to slam the door. People slam the door on almost 80 percent of the advertising we send them. When you look at some of the commercials on the air today, it's easy to see why."[12] Imagine yourself standing on an endless street of stoops mouthing the essence of your commercial. If that conjures up doors being slammed in your face, it is time to re-examine how you are really addressing that prospect.

4. Does the Writer Make a Promise and Back It Up with Evidence? Our promise, as stated in Chapter 4, is the rational attraction our copy expresses. But this attraction/promise will not be credible if we fail to support it with proof. Consumers are constantly asking "Why?" or "How?" in response to copy claims. If the message merely moves on to another unsupported assertion, as in these two lines from a student-written spot, believability evaporates.

```
Simon's Watermelon Candy captures the nostalgia of an era
gone by (How?). And this candy is better for the kids than
a chocolate bar (Why?). Treat yourself and your family to
Simon's today.
```

Conversely, the following commercial provides extensive evidence to validate Dollar General Stores' (economy appeal) promise of low prices—and even introduces this evidence *in advance of* the full articulation of the "always make it worth the trip" claim. Thus, by the time the promise arrives, the listener has been pre-assured.

```
ANNCR:  'Well now,' you're saying to yourself, ' where in
        the world is one of those Dollar General Stores I've
        been hearing about?' Well, ask somebody. Or look us
        up in your phone book. It'll be the best 30 seconds
        you ever spent. If you don't know where a Dollar
        General Store is, you've been hanging around those
        big expensive malls too much. You won't find us
        there. The rent's too high. Nope, we're right on
        down the road. Somewhere in a smaller, older center
        where you might even be able to find a parking
        place. Or sometimes we're in a building that
        somebody else deserted in order to get up there with
        the big boys in the new mall. Don't kid yourself,
        They aren't losing money when they move up. You are.
        And we won't let that happen to you at Dollar
        General Stores. You may have to look for us a little
        bit, but we always make it worth the trip, every
        time.
```

(Courtesy of Miller Leonard, Madden & Goodrum & Associates, Inc.)

5. Does the Writer Get to the Point at Once? Even in the comparative expansiveness of sixty seconds, electronic media copywriters do not have the time to wander leisurely into their subject. We must know where we are going from the very beginning. In addition, radio/television audiences tend to give us only three to four seconds before they make the decision to tune in or tune out. One technique for dealing with this condition is to imagine your target consumers with empty cartoon bubbles above their heads. Then try to fill those bubbles with a relevant and interesting image within the very first 'panel' of your message. Don't draw a blank for your audience or they will quickly 'go blank' to your spot.

6. Does the Writer Make Every Word Count—Is Copy Concise? Not only must we get right to the point, but we must also direct every word we use toward that point. Unlike print writers, we can't afford a throwaway paragraph here or there because our *entire spot* is usually the equivalent of a single paragraph. So radio/television copywriting is a continuous *streamlining* process. Anything that doesn't directly relate to your selling picture must be eliminated. Everything that does relate must be re-examined to see if it can be expressed even more succinctly. As a training technique, some agency creative directors pay a token "bounty" on unessential words that their copy trainees locate in each other's scripts.

7. Is Copy Logical—Does It Flow? Our discussion of Progressive Motivation in Chapter 5 deals directly with this requirement, of course. But whether you use Progressive Motivation or some other selling structure, it is essential that

a. every phrase should drive the message forward;
b. one sentence must lead directly to the next;
c. no part of the message should be susceptible to cutting without breaking the idea flow.

Aristotle, who created some pretty fair copy in his own idiom, called this process *organic unity.* As he discussed in his *Poetics,* organic unity culminates in the whole being greater than the sum of its parts. Each part leads so inevitably to the next part that the conclusion (the central copy point) is itself inevitable.

Beethoven's music reflects this quality of inevitability, and so does a well-crafted legal brief or debate case. Beginning with an original concept that is compelling to the audience, we then couple together a string of little agreements that ultimately lead to audience satisfaction with the message in its entirety. Because the parts of the pitch are so fused, the listener/viewer cannot carve it up and attack these parts piecemeal. Instead, the discourse must be either accepted or rejected in its entirety. When organic unity is employed, "Somehow, in the blend of image, words and format, there is a larger meaning that emanates from them like a bloom," advises the advertising/public relations firm of Arnell/Bickford Associates. "Each element serves the larger purpose of the advertisement: There seems to be a 'natural order' to a successful creation."[13]

The following 60-second commercial is an example of well-executed organic unit. Beginning with its "Did I hear that right?" opening premise, it elicits both listener involvement and step-by-step acceptance of the advocated action.

ANNCR: This year, billions of bugs will lose their lives on the nation's highways. Chances are, a lot of them will end up on the front of your car. And if you don't get them off, they'll come back to haunt you.

(EERIE MUSIC: FEATURE AND UNDER)

You see, as bugs decompose, they give off a strong acid that actually eats away at your car's chrome and paint---making it dull. The hotter the weather, the faster the acid is made. But there is a brighter side to all of this. Come to Hot Springs Auto Wash. We've developed a way to completely remove bugs before they kill your car's finish. In fact, Hot Springs is the only car wash to make this guarantee: if you find as much as one single little mosquito on your car after we've washed it, we'll give you your money back.

(MUSIC: OUT)

Next time, we'll talk to you about the problem with birds.

(SFX: BIRDS CHIRPING)

(Courtesy of Diana Monroe, Siddall, Matus & Coughter, Inc.)

8. *Is Copy Enthusiastic—Does the Writer Believe in What's Being Sold?* This is sometimes a difficult stipulation to meet. As we establish earlier in this chapter, you don't have to personally use a product to promote it. But you must believe that it will do what you are claiming. Agencies have resigned accounts when they could no longer subscribe to the claims a client wanted articulated. This, of course, is a wrenching business decision that may have severe financial fallout. An individual copywriter may face the same credibility-based decision. If you're in a large enough shop, you may be able to get

transferred off that account. If you're stuck where you are, the most feasible strategy is to try to fashion copy that at least puts the claim in accurate perspective—while keeping your eyes open for more reputable pastures.

Functionally, most clients come to realize that you can't squeeze effective, enthusiastic copy from people who don't believe in what they are selling. That is why "the match of agency and client culture" is such an important, if illusive, quality when a company seeks out a firm to handle its advertising. As Dan Wieden, co-founder of Wieden & Kennedy Advertising maintains, "We do what we are. If you're having fun, it shows up in your work. If you're bright and focused, that shows up. If you're trying to con somebody, that shows up."[14] "The best writing," adds Professor Howard Good, "is done not under outside pressure, but from some inner compulsion. Only then is it possible to write something that really matters, first to you, and later to others."[15]

9. Is Copy Complete—Are All Questions Answered? Copywriters most often run into trouble with this Validation when they try to cover more than one main point in their message. Raising multiple issues/claims in a spot also means you must answer all their associated questions and doubts—an impossibility given the limitations imposed by fifteen, thirty, or even sixty seconds of time. If you follow the advice given with Validation Questions #5, 6, and 7, the danger of incomplete copy is greatly reduced.

Sometimes, it is necessary to break the concept up into two or more subthemes and pen separate ads for each. In the Hot Springs Auto Wash commercial above, for instance, the copywriter left "the problem with birds" for another spot rather than attempting to cover both bird and bug impact in a single message.

10. Is Copy Designed to Sell? The ultimate function of any commercial, PSA, or promo is to convince an audience to take the course of action that your client wants them to take: to buy the product, donate to the cause, or tune in to the program. If either the technique you've employed or its execution gets in the way of the 'sell'—change it. Unlike a poem, no piece of copy can exist solely for itself. As copywriting legend David Ogilvy (who began his career selling cooking utensils door-to-door) proclaimed, "I'm a salesman. I don't care if my work wins awards in Cannes or at any other of these ridiculous festivals. I want to sell products."[16]

Prohibition (Regulatory)

Besides all of our other concerns as copywriters, we must avoid certain techniques no matter how much they might seem to enhance our creation, definition, and validation efforts. Several of these prohibitions are mandated by laws and regulations associated with the Federal Trade Commission (FTC), the Food and Drug Administration (FDA), the Federal Communications Commission (FCC), or a host of other national, state, and even local agencies. Other prohibitions are present in network and local outlet "standards and practices" policies, or in similar self-regulatory activities associated with the Council of Better Business Bureaus. "It used to be advertisers just had to worry about the FTC," recalls Wally Snyder, the American Advertising Federation's governmental relations executive. "Now we're fighting battles on 50 different fronts."[17] Because this is not a legal casebook, we cannot delve into all of these battles here. Instead, we can sketch the major war zones that are of most concern to copywriters.

The Federal Sector

The Federal Trade Commission historically has been the prime investigator of deception in advertising. In exercising its overall oversight duties, points out business analyst Craig Stoltz, "the FTC chooses cases not just to prosecute specific offenders but to establish precedents that guide all marketers."[18] In an action brought against Listerine, for example (which was upheld by the Supreme Court in 1978), the FTC established its right to require a client to engage in *corrective advertising* to make up for past misstatements. Listerine's manufacturer, Warner-Lambert, was forced to include the following 'corrective' comment in its next $10 million of advertising (an amount equal to Listerine's average annual advertising budget for 1962–72):

```
Listerine will not help prevent colds or sore throats or
lessen their severity.[19]
```

In 1984, the FTC also reaffirmed and refined its commitment to its *advertising substantiation* program whereby advertisers and agencies must be certain they have concrete evidence in hand before disseminating product performance claims. And, in a 1992 case involving advertising for Klondike Lite dessert bars, the Commission made it clear that it is prepared not only to carefully scrutinize assertions about fat content and 'lite-ness,' but also to move beyond the stated facts in the copy to examine its *implications and inferences.* The FTC cited Klondike for making a "low in cholesterol" claim that, while factually accurate, implied (in the FTC's eyes) that the product was also low in fat.[20]

Actual food labeling, as well as monitoring of advertising and promotion by pharmaceutical manufacturers, is the province of the Food and Drug Administration. Claims and labels permitted by the FDA will also pass FTC muster. Therefore, copywriters on food and drug accounts are wise to follow FDA decisions closely. Like the FTC, the FDA's authority allows it "in effect, to legislate by precedent," says Craig Stoltz. "Marketers making claims similar to those subjected to FDA actions must make changes or face investigations, too."[21]

Additional federal oversight has come about as a result of the Trademark Law Revision Act of 1988. Under prior law, advertisers' main concern was to avoid misrepresenting their *own* products. But the new act has enlarged this concern by holding companies liable for misrepresenting the qualities or characteristics of *competing* products as well. "Competitors are watching one another more closely than the FTC ever did, or could," asserts attorney Stephen Bergerson. The 1988 act "gives them the ability to move more quickly and effectively. . . . Marketers today use litigation as a competitive weapon."[22]

The State Sector

Not only must advertisers worry about what legal action the federal government and their competitors might precipitate, but they also have to be sensitive to more aggressive state regulation. In the 1980s, when Reagan administration deregulatory and budget-pairing tendencies substantially reduced FTC activities, state law enforcers took notice. "When the FTC wasn't doing anything, we saw dynamic growth of the National Association of Attorneys General because the state ag's saw themselves filling a void in regulation," advertising law attorney Felix Kent points out. "NAAG has grown in power and influence and, even though the FTC is back in business, NAAG isn't necessarily resigning."[23]

Although it has no statutory legal standing in its own right, NAAG's membership is using its collective resources to approach advertisers with a united voice and, implicitly, with the threat of law suits if its recommendations are ignored by the advertising community. Beginning with actions against airline ticket and rental car price advertising, NAAG members have moved on to additional battlegrounds. In 1990, pressure from the Minnesota Attorney General forced General Mills to pull an ad that showed psyllium (an ingredient in Benefit cereal) as a PacMan-like cholesterol-eater. The company also agreed to pay $7,000 to each state in which the ad ran in order to cover legal costs incurred by those states in bringing the action.

The following year, acting on a tip, the Texas attorney general's office discovered that a Volvo commercial shot in Texas featured client cars in which roof supports had been reinforced with steel girders and lumber to prevent collapse when a monster truck rolled over them. Once the ads ran, the AG went after Volvo and extracted a $316,250 fine plus corrective advertising. (Volvo later fired its long-standing advertising agency in retribution for the deception.) Still later, the same state attorney general threatened suit against Pfizer *as well as its advertising agency* for alleged deception in regard to the plaque-reducing qualities of Plax mouthwash. Clearly, copywriters as well as their clients face state legal hassles if their claims appear deceptive or unsubstantiated. (At the national level, the FTC also has served notice that it will hold agencies co-responsible for problem ads.)

The Self-Policing Sector

For their own legal protection, broadcast/cable networks and outlet owners have devised a number of guidelines governing what they will and will not permit in their commercials and other pieces of continuity. The copywriter must be aware of these policies *before* the script creation stage. If a network, system, or station "standards and practices" executive refuses your copy, it can play havoc with your campaign's air schedule, bring you and your client into disrepute, and create public relations problems that nobody needs and few can solve.

Every year, for example, the major broadcast television networks receive about 50,000 storyboards and scripts for preliminary review. According to CBS vice-president Beth Bressan, of the 15,000 ads her office reviews per year, one-third require substantiation. Because postproduction changes are very expensive, most agencies bring in their spot at the storyboard stage in which modifications are relatively easy to accomplish.[24] "Once the networks give approval to an advertisement, odds are it will be able to air outside of the networks without going under the microscope again," reveals industry reporter Joe Flint. "Some cable networks have their own standards and practices departments but most seem to operate on the theory that 'if it's good enough for the [broadcast] networks, it's good enough for us.' "[25]

Another self-regulatory apparatus is maintained by the National Advertising Division (NAD) of the Council of Better Business Bureau. NAD's staff monitors national advertising, responds to consumer and competitor complaints, and arbitrates unresolved cases that originate with local Better Business Bureaus. In 1990, for instance, 79 advertising claims were called to NAD's official attention. Of these, "19 were substantiated; 58 were modified or discontinued; and 2 cases were referred to the National Advertising Review Board (NARB), which is called to arbitrate cases when the NAD cannot resolve its decision with an advertiser."[26] At the local level, some 32 Local Advertising Review Programs (LARPs) operate in major cities throughout the country as joint ventures of the Better Business Bureau and each city's chapter of the American Advertising Federation (AAF).

While such self-regulatory activities are certainly preferable (and considerably less punitive) than the actions of the governmental overseers, having to defend your copy in even these forums is stressful, time-consuming, and client-irritating. The most efficient self-regulation is accomplished by the copywriter at the moment of the spot's conception. Making certain the copy is clear and accurate before it leaves your office is the best way to prevent later catastrophes. "The few exceptions to otherwise truthful advertising that do occur sadly reinforce the negatives and give a distorted image of our industry," asserts AAF chairman David Bell. "It's not that we have an enormous problem; it's just that any problem that comes up—at a time when the microscope is on us and what we do—goes ballistic almost instantly."[27]

In addition to carefully weighing the words you use, Attorney Richard Kurnit suggests four cautions designed to keep you and your spot out of potential legal quagmires:

1. Early in the creative process, get written permission from the appropriate people if an ad carries the potential to violate copyright and/or privacy laws.
2. During production, make sure no one hires someone to sound like, look like, or otherwise represent a celebrity.
3. Before the [television] shoot, get producers' affidavits signed to substantiate that demonstrations are not mockups.
4. Have regular seminars with a lawyer to update staff on how to specifically stay within the limits of advertising law.[28]

Prohibition (Stylistic)

Even though they are largely outside the scope of governmental and industry regulation, four audience-offending stylistic crimes do so much damage to the client that they merit special attention here. With a little self-policing, you should be able to respect these stylistic prohibitions against (1) fraudulent attention-getters (2) disparagement (3) repulsiveness and (4) superlatives.

Fraudulent Attention-Getters

Some people will do anything to attract attention to themselves—or to their copy. As we've seen previously, a good attention-getter is vital if your message is to grab the audience's eyes and ears. But an attention-getter that has nothing to do with the copy's main point, or a main point that has nothing to do with the offered product or service, is both a lie and a theft. It promises prospects something your message is never prepared to give and robs them of the time each expended in taking the whole message in. Loud noises, screams, and other "now that I've got your attention" ripoffs resurrect the specter of the huckster copywriter. Spots like this may show imagination, but such imagination is both unprincipled and undisciplined:

```
(SFX: WAILING SIREN UP AND UNDER)

ANNCR:  (In a panic) Fire! Fire! What a tragedy! What a
        disaster! All those poor people and what it does to
        them. Makes you sick right down to your stomach.
        Yes, the tragedy of heartburn, of excess acidity
        that comes from eating all that 'fast food,' is a
        national calamity. But all the flaming agony can be
        prevented. Stop burning yourself out at those
        plastic food palaces and start enjoying how 'cool' a
        good meal can be at Barney's Beefsteak Bistro.
        Barney's Beefsteak Bistro, corner of Fulton and
        Business Route 9, takes the time and care to prepare
        a meal that stays with you; but stays with you the
        right way. A lunch or dinner at Barney's leaves you
        cool and collected; not hot and bothered. Plan now
        for a relaxing noon or evening at Barney's Beefsteak
        Bistro, Fulton and business Route 9. Barney fires up
        his trusty charcoal; not your tender stomach.

(SFX: WAILING SIREN UP AND OUT TO TIME)
```

Barney's itself deserves to burn, most listeners would conclude. And so does the copywriter who wrote such fraudulent trash.

Disparagement

People do not enjoy having their egos bruised—especially by some jerk on the television or radio. Thus, copy that tries to bludgeon the audience into accepting your point of view through sarcasm and ridicule is bound to go down in flames, just like Barney's steaks. Few writers deliberately attempt to disparage their audience, but ill-considered lines like the following do no less harm just because they are oversights.

```
Even you can operate a Sharkfin outboard on the very first
try.
```

```
Well, Mom, are you about to bake another batch of those
drab, dull, everyday cookies?
```

```
It's time the Hades Oil and Gas Company taught you a few
things about home heating.
```

```
Banking is simpler than ever at Fidelity. That's why we
know you'll enjoy it.
```

Disparagement is also a problem when directed at the competition. Until 1971, both CBS and ABC refused to accept advertising that "named names," and their stance helped keep both fair and unscrupulous product comparisons off most of the airwaves. If two of the networks wouldn't accept the copy, it was just too difficult to get proper penetration for it. Then the Federal Trade Commission ruled that euphemisms such as "Brand X" and "our larger competitor" were confusing the public and depriving them of meaningful consumer information. The two networks got the message and joined NBC in permitting the specification of which "Brand X" copy was talking about. This resulted in a significant upswing in what are officially known as "comparative" commercials and in the consequent rise in advertiser-versus-advertiser litigation.

It must be clarified that comparison, by itself, is neither evil nor disparaging. As long as the focus of the message is on the positive aspect of your product (comparison) and not on the alleged negative attributes of the competition (disparagement), the practice can play a beneficial role for both the advertiser and the cause of public enlightenment. According to Janet Nciman, "35 percent to 40 percent of all advertising is comparative, and 25 percent to 30 percent identifies the competition."[29] But comparative ads become *negative* ads, states agency chairman Allen Rosenshine, "when there's stridency in the tone of voice—when it puts down a competitor."[30] And if the allegations underlying this put down cannot be substantiated, warns attorney James Astrachan, "courts will not tolerate deceptive claims and are willing to impose large damages when the circumstances warrant."[31]

Therefore, in constructing a comparative spot, the American Association of Advertising Agencies advises that you respect the following ten guidelines:

1. The intent and connotation of the ad should be to inform and never discredit or unfairly attack competitors, competing products or services.
2. When a competitive product is named, it should be one that exists in the marketplace as significant competition.
3. The competition should be fairly and properly identified but never in a manner or tone of voice that degrades the competitive product or service.
4. The advertising should compare related or similar properties or ingredients of the product, dimension to dimension, feature to feature.
5. The identification should be for honest comparison purposes and not simply to upgrade by association.
6. If a competitive test is conducted, it should be done by an objective testing service, preferably an independent one, so there will be no doubt about the veracity of the test.

7. In all cases the test should be supportive of all claims made in the advertising that's based on the test.
8. The advertising should never use partial results or stress insignificant differences to cause the consumer to draw an improper conclusion.
9. The property being compared should be significant in terms of value or usefulness of the product to the consumer.
10. Comparisons delivered through the use of testimonials should not imply that the testimonial is more than one individual's thought unless that individual represents a sample of the majority viewpoint.[32]

In short, any honest, comparative message should concentrate on placing your client in the best verifiable light—not on placing the competitor under some unsubstantiated cloud (a cloud that could all too likely rain on your own parade).

The following radio commercial illustrates a *positive* comparison. The competing Ajax candles aren't disparaged—in fact, they're conceded to look the same and be less expensive. But the Re-lites advantage is described in such a manner that a key superiority shines through—a superiority that comes from concentrating on an honest Re-lites *attribute* rather than a competitor *flaw*.

```
ANNCR:  If you're searching for something to brighten up
        your next birthday party, then you're searching for
        Re-lites. Re-lites look just like ordinary Ajax
        birthday candles. And Ajax candles are a lot
        cheaper. But unlike ordinary Ajax candles, when you
        blow Re-lites out, they re-light. By themselves.
        Magically. And they'll keep on relighting as long as
        you have the breath to keep blowing them out. Don't
        miss out on the laughs that Re-lites can bring to
        your next birthday party. Re-lites. The more you
        blow, the more they glow.
```

Repulsiveness

This third stylistic prohibition addresses the issue of offensive or unpleasant words and pictures. Particularly with an entertainment medium such as radio or television, people will be patently unwilling to expose themselves voluntarily to extended periods of agony. Gone is that poor suffering mortal with the hammers pounding and the lightning flashing through his skull. Gone, too, are the people bent over with the torment of constipation and unrelentingly assailed by the torture of skin itch. Spots that dwell on such images can appeal only to masochists—and there aren't enough of them to bolster many sales curves. If you must depict a discomforting image in your commercial, don't wait too long before introducing relief. And in order to avoid violating our first stylistic prohibition, that relief had better be a *relevant* result of using our product. As *Modern Maturity* magazine's advertising standards appropriately suggest, "Instead of a message that says, 'I feel terrible, give me product X,' we welcome ads that say, 'I feel great with product X.' "[33]

Public service announcements may be tempted to ignore this prohibition more than do their commercial counterparts. How many PSAs expend virtually their entire time in showing us starving orphans or ravaged wildlife? Certainly these are vital concerns. But the message that illuminates nothing but the grotesque effects of this or that calamity will cause listener/viewer tune-out before folks learn how they can help. It does the starving orphans or endangered species little good if the people who could have mitigated their plight were driven away prematurely.

Don't remain repulsive. If you must use a disagreeable image, get through it as soon as possible to make way for the relief. And make certain such relief is a tangible and logical outgrowth of the product or service for which you have drawn the assignment. The Figure 6–5 television PSA adheres fully to this principle. Even though the target problem is vividly illustrated in Frame #3, the spot gets into and out this negative depiction quickly. In this way, the viewer is turned off to cigarettes—not to the message itself.

Superlatives

Inexperienced copywriters tend to try too hard; they tend to oversell the product or service to such a degree that the listener or viewer may conclude it is just too good to be true. If the product, service, or program sounds so unbelievably divine that we expect the Three Wise Men to come over the hill, the copy needs total rethinking. Superlatives (words of overpraise) will not be credible to an audience that is bombarded daily by hundreds of spots and promotion pieces. Our jaded receiver is well aware that heaven is not "just around the corner from where you live" or "yours by mail for only six ninety-eight." Copy that attempts to say different is begging to be scorned. Imagine how you would react to the following pitch:

```
ANNCR:  Spectacular! Stupendous! Those are just some of
        the words used to describe Gramma Hubbard's Hominy
        Bread. Gramma Hubbard's Hominy is the best thing
        ever to come out of an American oven. Its texture
        is unsurpassed. Its taste is incredibly delicious.
        And Gramma Hubbard's Hominy Bread makes the most
        tremendous toast your taste buds have ever
        experienced. Try a loaf of this fantastic bread
```

V/O: You can do your hair.

You can do your eyes.

But when you smoke, you can't do a thing with your mouth.

Smoking stinks.

Figure 6-5

(Courtesy of Marcie Brogan, Brogan & Partners.)

```
breakthrough. Witness the marvel of real milled
hominy. Gramma Hubbard's Hominy Bread.
```

In fact, even if your product is as good as you claim, describing that goodness too enthusiastically may still be counterproductive. Several years ago, a spot for Dupont's Xerex antifreeze showed a hole being punched into a can of the stuff and the product package then resealing itself. The claim seemed so incredible that many viewers thought it was phoney. So did the Federal Trade Commission. They required Dupont to substantiate the claim that Xerex would work in a similar way to seal small holes in a car's cooling system. Dupont did substantiate it and the FTC backed off. But some viewers still could not believe a coolant could perform so amazingly well. As one advertising executive on an aspirin account observes, "When you have a superior product claim, it's difficult creatively because we're all used to parity in this business. Everybody is already out there trying to position their product as a superior one, and it's an even more difficult assignment to do that right when the claim is true. . . . And every time you have a real superiority, you face the risk of unbelievability."[34] Moral: sometimes even a truly spectacular product needs more humility than it deserves.

Don't canonize your product or service. Don't make a saint out of every account to which you're assigned. Superlatives cause mistrust to mushroom and may prevent the audience from accepting suggestions that would otherwise have been truly beneficial for them. And whatever you do, don't get carried away and use the words *guarantee* or *offer* unless your client really intends to extend a guarantee or an offer. "Such wording," Professor George Stevens points out, "has been used to support findings for plaintiffs"[35] that an oral contract thereby had been made.

A CDVP Reassurance

If it seems as though everyone—government, industry, client, and consumer—is looking over your shoulder, you have acquired a healthfully paranoic view of copywriting today. By its very nature, radio/television's power and potency attract the close scrutiny of a wide variety of groups with both legitimate and self-serving axes to grind. It is not easy to balance the conflicting pressure and cross-purposes of the various forces at work in and on the electronic media. But try to keep it all in perspective or you'll drive yourself looney.

Try to see the humor in even a pressure-cooker situation. For along with the four "CDVP Factors," a sense of humor must also accompany the copywriter as part of the baggage he or she brings to each new assignment. Recognizing the incongruity if not the downright ludicrousness of some work situations will do a lot to keep your blood pressure down and your enthusiasm up. The resilient ability to find humor in all things—even in occasional failure—is what preserves a copywriter's vitality. It is exactly in this spirit that creative director John Lyons counsels, "Don't worry about rejection. There isn't a profession anywhere that pays you more for revising your own stupidity."[36]

Granted, the "establishing of new and meaningful relationships" that make sense to regulators as well as to target audiences may not be an easy task—and often is simply not feasible. But even if it doesn't meet our criteria for true

CREATIVITY, copy that is properly DEFINED and VALIDATED and respects the PROHIBITIONS we've just outlined is well positioned for success.

Radio commentator Earl Nightingale put the whole struggle in reassuring perspective when he reminded us that

> most products advertised and sold in this country are good products. A lot of hard work, research and brains have gone into them, and there's a market for them. So all we have to do is tell the truth about them, in a straightforward, interesting and even creative way. There's an interesting story lurking in every product or service. It is the job of the advertising people, and especially the copywriter to ferret it out and present it in an interesting and believable way to the consumer.[37]

In undertaking the "ferreting" of which Nightingale spoke, the copywriter's main governor is not some external regulator but a sense of professional *responsibility*. As described by advertising veteran Whit Hobbs, this means that

> When I sit down to write, I feel a strong sense of responsibility to a lot of people—to my client, to my associates, to my customer/reader/viewer. This is what creative people in advertising are *supposed* to feel, and I wish all of them did. . . . I keep seeing advertising that seems to be designed by creative people in agencies primarily to impress *other* creative people in other agencies—inside jokes that leave the customers out there relatively unmoved. It is very nice to win praise from one's peers, but it's far more important to win *customers*.[38]

The *responsible* winning of customers is the ultimate COPYWRITING DIMENSION, the central and candid goal that motivates everything we write. Let's now turn our attention to how this goal can be achieved on radio.

Endnotes

1. Richard Morgan, "A How-To on Managing Creatives Has More Clues Than Answers," *ADWEEK* (May 18, 1990), 2.
2. Leo Burnett, *Confessions of an Advertising Man* (Chicago: private printing, 1961), 20–21.
3. "David Harner and David Johnson," *ADWEEK* (March 30, 1992), 24.
4. Curvin O'Reilly, "Why Some People Have More Ideas," *ADWEEK* (February 15, 1988), 57.
5. "Who's Your Muse?," *ADWEEK* (February 1, 1988), C.R. 17.
6. Malcolm MacDougall, "The Night They Stole the Statues," *ADWEEK* (June 24, 1991), 6.
7. "Quips, Quotes, Gripes, Swipes," *Winners* (December 1987), 48.

8. "Format Gold Rush: Staking a Claim in Oldies," *Broadcasting* (June 17, 1991), 36.

9. Paul Connors, "Copywriting and the Importance of the Offer." Presentation to the Direct Marketing Educational Foundation Faculty Institute, June 4, 1986 (Chicago).

10. Douglas Greenlaw, writing in "Monday Memo," *Broadcasting* (May 13, 1991), 14.

11. "Quips, Quotes, Gripes, Swipes," *Winners* (January 1988), 48.

12. Malcolm MacDougall, "Getting the Foot in the Door," *ADWEEK* (March 12, 1984), 32.

13. "Creative Theft: A Primer in Advertising's Grand Tradition," *ADWEEK* (May 2, 1988), 30.

14. Cathy Taylor, "Wieden & Kennedy," *ADWEEK* (March 23, 1992), R.C. 9.

15. Howard Good, "Teaching Writing as a Beautiful and Bleak Passion," *Chronicle of Higher Education* (July 17, 1991), B.3.

16. Kenneth Jacobsen, "David Ogilvy," *ADWEEK* (January 28, 1991), 16.

17. Craig Stoltz, "Hammer Time!" *ADWEEK* (September 16, 1991), 20.

18. Craig Stoltz, "Weighing In," *ADWEEK* (June 1, 1992), 22.

19. "FTC Power on Corrective Ads Left Untouched by Supreme Court," *Broadcasting* (April 10, 1978), 80.

20. Stoltz, "Weighing In," 22.

21. Craig Stoltz, "The Enemies List," *ADWEEK* (October 28, 1991), 28.

22. Cathy Madison, "Come Nov. 16, What Your Ads Don't Say Can Land You in Court," *ADWEEK* (October 30, 1989), 10.

23. Barbara Holsomback, "Ad Agencies Feel Piercing Glare of Watchdogs," *ADWEEK* (December 3, 1990), 18.

24. Interview with Beth Bressan (New York), February 8, 1991.

25. Joe Flint, "Network Handling of Comparative Ads Causing Concern," *Broadcasting* (October 29, 1990), 55.

26. "National Ad Review," *American Advertising* (Summer 1991), 9.

27. Stephen Battaglio, "Ad Industry Braces for New Rules," *ADWEEK* (March 18, 1991), 9.

28. Holsomback, 18.

29. Janet Neiman, "The Trouble with Comparative Ads," *ADWEEK* (January 12, 1987), B.R. 4.

30. Ibid., B.R. 5.

31. James Astrachan, "When to Name a Competitor," *ADWEEK* (May 23, 1988), 24.

32. Ibid.

33. Robert Wood, "Attacking Ageism," *Media & Values* (Winter 1989), 8.

34. Noreen O'Leary, "What if 10 Out of 10 Doctors Agree?" *ADWEEK* (February 1, 1988), 4.

35. George Stevens, "Contractual Offers in Advertising," *Journalism Quarterly* (Spring 1990), 34.

36. Sarah Stiansen, "Subtitle This Book 'The Joy of Advertising,'" *ADWEEK* (October 12, 1987), 46.

37. Reprinted with permission of Nightingale-Conant Corporation, Chicago, 1979 copyright, producers of the Earl Nightingale radio program "Our Changing World."

38. White Hobbs, "Biting the Brands That Feed You," *ADWEEK* (October 4, 1982), 20.

■ *Chapter 7*

Key Elements of Radio Writing

For years, many people thought radio to be a second-class medium, a kind of "television with the picture tube burned out," as master radio humorist Stan Freberg once protested. Broadcast copywriters saw the building of their "TV reel" as the way to fame and glory and looked on radio assignments as hardship duty. So they (along with a number of sponsors) abandoned the medium in droves, leaving it to the tender mercies of cookie-cutter hacks. As N. W. Ayer chairman Jerry Siano recalls, "When television came along people started watching that. Radio didn't change. But our perception of it did. We forgot a quarter of a century of people watching their radio sets. And this might be what led to the development of the 'secret' to bad radio advertising. . . . Just stuffing the commercial full of twaddle, wall-to-wall words, endlines and some cheap music is the sure-fire formula for ineffective radio advertising."[1]

Slowly, things have begun to change; partly, it is true, as a result of broadcast television rate-card increases that have priced many advertisers out of that medium. But the rehabilitation of radio is also due, argued then-president of the Radio Advertising Bureau, Bill Stakelin, to the renewed realization that "Radio *is* visual. It is one of the most visual if not the most visual medium in existence today. Where else can you see 5,000 albino rhinos stampeding down Pennsylvania Avenue? Only on the radio. Radio is visual, and as you plan for it, as you create for it, as you write for it, think of it visually."[2]

This visual imagery through solo sound is not, however, easy for a writer to capture. Everything you want to say must be wholly transportable via words, sound effects, and music. There is no camera lens to convey automatically what the product looks like and how it works; the radio copywriter must explain these things through audio-only sensations. Because of this challenge, the creation of radio messages "offers something unique in this day and age," points out advertising executive Ed McCabe; "the opportunity to stand up and be counted, which is why radio can be a scary medium for creative people who aren't so sure of themselves. . . . Radio separates the doers from the talkers."[3]

If *you* want to be a doer, the next three chapters are designed to assist you. Along the way, you will discover the audio medium to manifest a respect for language like that print accords—but a respect that must be rationed into segments of a minute or less. Also unlike print, the radio message cannot be "re-read" by our audience. Nor can they slow down the speed with which they consume it. A radio spot exists in real time, at one predetermined velocity, and then disappears until the next occasion it airs. If the listener doesn't comprehend it the first time, there may not be another chance.

Yet, despite all these drawbacks, the radio communication can become more integral to our consumer's life than messages on any other medium. This is because the appropriate sound cues from us force the perceivers to recall specifics from their own past experiences in order to complete the picture. "Unlike TV, which is at the mercy of the size of the screen," points out Stan Freberg, "the monitor of our head is limitless."[4] The visually compelling radio spot thus becomes a part of the listener, and the listener becomes a part of the spot. Award-winning copywriter Sarah Cotton deftly manipulates this unique radio attribute in the following commercial that promotes the medium itself.[5]

```
WOMAN.   (In conversational style) Every Tuesday she'd wear
         the same pale pink nylon blouse. And she always wore
         scuffed black flat-heeled shoes. All run down in the
         back. Underneath that pale pink nylon blouse you
         could seen the faintest outline of a very functional
         slip. No lace. Ever. Not Mrs. Pennybaker. Not my
         second grade teacher. Her hair looked like a tight
         fuzzy brown cap. I think she went to the beauty
         parlor on Saturdays and then wrapped her head in
         toilet tissue when she slept. Sometimes there'd be
         little pieces of it stuck to the back of her neck.
         She had dangly skin on the bottom of her upper arms.
         When she wrote on the blackboard it would swing back
         and forth like a turkey's wattle. We'd snicker. I
         know she heard us. She always smelled like orange
         blossoms and chalk. And she had five perfect
         vertical lines running from under her nose to the
         top of her upper lip. And they were yellow. From
         eating Cheeze-its, maybe. Or smoking. We weren't
         sure.

ANNCR:   Pennybaker has just come to life before your very
         ears. Radio can take your customers anywhere. Back
         to the second grade—or directly on to your product
         on the second aisle on the left. You'll reach more
```

```
people more often with affordable radio advertising.
To put radio to work for you, call this station
or the Radio Advertising Bureau. As for Mrs.
Pennybaker? Well, now you can say, 'I met her---
on the radio.'
```

The copywriter who feels abused because she or he has been dealt a radio rather than a television assignment would do well to recall master communicator Garrison Keillor's observation that "the spoken word, not pictures, is the doorway to memory. . . . If I tell stories on radio, I will run into people months and years later who can repeat back to me what I said, word for word. This never ceases to amaze."[6] In short, the impact of your writing may be felt much longer via the sound medium than through the picture tube.

Standard Radio Format

In order to properly prepare that listener-involving radio concept for airing, we must construct a clear script blueprint. As we mention in Chapter 2, even the most innovative message must first be set down in standard script format.

The body of the copy, the script's working section, is our concern here. It is in the body that we must indicate our precise structuring and manipulation of any or all of the parts of radio's sound element triumvirate: words, music, and sound effects. The commercial in Table 7–1 has been constructed not as a "hall of fame" spot but to demonstrate a useful and cogent pattern for script organization. It features all of the key ingredients that might need to be scripted. Reference numbers have been added to facilitate dissection. (As with all of our scripts in this book, what is single-spaced here would be double-spaced on actual copysheets, and what is double-spaced here would be triple-spaced.)

As [1] shows, an indented production note may precede the actual copy and is used to give a general casting or stage direction that will pertain throughout the script. This keeps clutter within the copy to a minimum and segregates continuing elements from those relevant only to limited sections.

Specific talent movement and stage directions, such as the one marked by [2], exist in parentheses, with the first letter capitalized. These directions are placed in the copy at exactly the point when they're to become operative.

Sound effects are likewise in parentheses and, unlike stage directions, are entirely in CAPS. They may or may not be preceded by the designator SFX. When they occur between character speeches but within the same scene, sound effect directions are indented at least three spaces more than are lines of dialogue. The [3] marks such a situation. When sound effects occur within a speech they, like stage directions, are placed at the actual point of occurrence, as [4] demonstrates. Sound effects' FULL CAPS format is the prime means by which actors can distinguish these technician-activated devices from the lower-case stage directions for which these actors themselves are responsible. Finally, when sound effects comprise the bridge between scenes or are the prime means of initial scene establishment, their cue begins at the far left margin, as [5] points out.

Music cues are also in parentheses and are also in CAPS. They are further distinguished from sound effects by being fully <u>underlined</u> but may or may not begin with the term MUSIC. As reference numbers [6], [7], and [8] illustrate, the location of music cues within speeches, between speeches, and as scene-bridging devices respectively, follows the same rules as do sound effects serving similar functions. When separate music and sound effect cues assist each other to shift the scene, both directions are normally placed at the left margin with a separate line for each, as [8] and [9] designate.

The spacing of each subsequent line of copy is also important in providing both talent and sound engineers with the clearest possible blueprint of what the copywriter has in mind. Typical professional practice is to DOUBLE SPACE WITHIN SPEECHES and TRIPLE SPACE BETWEEN THEM.

This includes triple-spacing between a speech and a sound effect or music cue that completely separates that speech from another character's line to follow (see [3] and [7]). It also applies to the triple-spacing that precedes and follows music and/or sound-effect bridges between separate scenes (such as [5] and [8-9]).

A commercial announcement or piece of continuity will seldom be extensive enough to require the use of even half the specialized cues called for in Table 7–1's Elixir script. In fact, such a cluttered productional orgy would be a technical and cognitive nightmare. The Owen's Elixir presentation does, however, demonstrate a standardized plan for message typography, a plan that promotes consistent script layout and ungarbled communication with the skilled voices and technicians who must mold your copy into sound-propelled images.

Productional Terminology

The copywriter's adaptability to the technical requirements of radio is more than a matter of proper format. It also encompasses an understanding of those basic radio terms that, for the writer, translate into sound capabilities. For our purposes, we divide terminology into three categories: (1) talent instructions, (2) control booth instructions, and (3) other writer-used technical terms. It is not our intent here to cover all of audio production's specialized vocabulary. Instead, we call attention only to words you are most likely to need in preparing the actual script.

Table 7-1
Radio Copy Format Guide

[1]Production Note: All talent should convey lines like actors in an early 1930s movie.

ANNCR: Motion sickness; that queasy feeling. And it's hard to imagine a better place for it than this choppy cruise. Doesn't seem to bother that guy out on deck though. [2](Fading off) Let's try to find out why---

[3](FADE IN: CREAKING TIMBERS, SPLASHING WAVES)

BILL: (Fading on) What? No, I'm no sailor. I'm Bill the Bookie from Davenport. [4](TIMBERS/WAVES OUT) Motion sick? Not me. Not since that day (Fading off) back at George's Drug Store---

[5](STORE SOUNDS UP QUICKLY AND GRADUALLY OUT)

GEORGE: Hey, Bill. [6](MUSIC: OFF-KEY WHISTLING OF 'CAMPTOWN RACES' FIRST FOUR BARS) Know this tune?

BILL: Give it some hay, George. Oh, that bumpy flight from Vegas. Like riding a swayback steer.

[7](TWO MORE WHISTLED BARS OF 'CAMPTOWN RACES')

GEORGE: Then saddle up to this. It's Owen's Elixir.

BILL: Owen's what?

GEORGE: Owen's Elixir. Makes you feel like it's post time.

[8](TRADITIONAL 'AT THE POST' TRUMPET CALL)

[9](CROSSFADE TO SHIP SOUNDS UP AND UNDER)

BILL: From then on, it was Owen's for me. You can bet your calm stomach on it. It's Owen's Elixir to win, every time.

Talent Instructions

This category can be thought of as traffic- or stage-directing devices, several of which are included in the above Owen's Elixir commercial. In essence, they tell talent where they should be in relationship to the microphone and whether they should stay there. Because talent are expected to be *on mike* unless told otherwise, this instruction requires writing out only when needed to indicate the desired completion point of a long move toward the microphone. Walking toward the microphone is called *fading on,* as Bill's portrayer does in his first Elixir spot speech. The reverse effect is called, not surprisingly, *fading off.* The Elixir announcer does this to give the impression that he is walking away from the listener and out on deck to Bill. Bill does the same thing at the end of his first speech to suggest the feeling of a gradual flashback in time. If we instead want the talent to stay "in the distance" for any significant portion of their dialogue, we use the term *off mike* at the beginning of the first line to be delivered in that mode.

Moving talent in and out creates a much more realistic sound picture than the mere adjusting of volume in the control room. When someone walks away from us in real life, for example, our ears do not suddenly pick up less sound from our total environment. Instead, quieter but closer sounds grow more prominent as the receding person's voice grows less distinct in the distance. The total sense of presence is what radio seeks, and we therefore move people accordingly. As a slightly more sophisticated application of this principle, we sometimes use the terms *behind barrier* or *thru soundscreen* when we want the effect of someone talking through a wall, behind a closed door, or locked in a trunk, to name just a few possibilities. A special acoustical panel is placed between the talent and the microphone to suggest this condition. When the fictional door is opened or the trunk is unlocked, the talent can simply move quickly around the barrier to be instantaneously *on mike.* Alternatively, if our aural scene depicts a long partition or pictures a door that is supposed to be some distance from the listener's central vantage point, the talent can be instructed to *fade on* (either *quickly* or *slowly*) *from behind barrier.*

Control Booth Instructions

As mentioned above, volume is the most obvious productional function to be manipulated by the control booth engineer. Sound effects and music are commanded to *FADE IN* or *FADE OUT* when respectively introduced and removed from the scene. Sound effects and music that are *already present* in the scene may be requested to FADE UP or FADE DOWN in order to enlarge or diminish their part in that total sound picture. We can also use refinements to these general directions, such as ESTABLISH, SNEAK IN/SNEAK OUT, FEATURE/FEATURE BRIEFLY, or construct hybrids, such as FADE UP AND OUT, FADE DOWN AND UNDER, FADE UP AND UNDER, and FADE DOWN AND OUT. As the conclusion to the Elixir spot in Table 7–1 demonstrates, we can, in addition, CROSSFADE one music or sound effect cue to another by overlapping the receding element with the sound source just taking the stage. Especially when both elements are musical in nature, the CROSSFADE is also known as a SEGUE.

You may occasionally need certain more rarefied control booth instructions, too. The FILTER MIKE effect may be accomplished by having the talent talk into a tin can but is often accommodated through a more sophisticated microphone or control room modification of the input line that carries the talent's voice. A FILTER MIKE mechanism is used to give the effect of a voice coming over a telephone, through a public address system, or to denote unspoken thoughts and musings in a character's mind. As these musings get more and more unreal or frenzied, we may also want to bring REVERB—electromechanical echo—to the sound source. Varying amounts of REVERB are also effective in denoting such specialized locations as an empty warehouse, the bottom of a well, the Grand Canyon floor, or the inside of your refrigerator. (In a precise engineering sense, "echo" is *delayed* sound whereas "reverb" is *deflected* sound that is then "bounced back" to the listener's ear.)

In distinguishing control booth instructions from talent instructions, remember that people fade *on* and *off* whereas control-booth-originated sounds fade *IN* and *OUT*, and *UP* and *DOWN*. In addition, as the Elixir commercial shows, stage ("people") directions are not in full caps. Control-booth directions and music and sound effects cues, on the other hand, are entirely set IN CAPS even in those rare instances when sound is created "live" in the studio rather than in the control booth.

Other Writer-Used Technical Terms

The following miscellany is comprised of additional productional designations commonly understood in the radio industry. These terms might find their way into, or border, the actual body of our copy.

ACTUALITY: *production that seems to be originating live from some scene external to the studio*

AD LIB: *impromptu dialogue not written out in the script. We might, for example, ask background "crowd" to ad-lib reactions to what is being said or portrayed by the characters on mike.*

AMBIENT SOUNDS: *sounds that are a normal and expected part of the scene/environment being presented (train station, jungle, cocktail lounge, etc.).*

ANNCR: *the standard abbreviation for "announcer."*

ATTENUATE: *reducing the level of an electrical signal via volume or loudness controls or by using acoustically absorbing materials.*

BB: *abbreviation for "billboard" (see below).*

BG: *abbreviation for "background"; normally referring to sound that will not be at full volume.*

BILLBOARD: *a brief announcement that identifies the sponsor at beginning and/or end of program.*

BRIDGE: *aural transition (normally via music or sound effects) between two separate scenes or vignettes.*

CHAIN BREAK: *station or network identification occurring between programs.*

CONTINUITY BOOK: *loose-leaf collection of spots and promos in the order they are to be read or played over the air; also called* copy book.

COWCATCHER: *a portion of time that immediately precedes the actual start of a program and thus allows space for brief unrelated spots or continuity.*

CUT: *a particular band on a disc recording from which a specific music bed or sound effect is retrieved.*

DEAD AIR: *period of time when no discernible sound is being transmitted.*

DISTANT MIKING: *placing microphones several feet from performers to accomplish a listener feeling of physical distance from the subject.*

DRY: *a recording made without the introduction of any echo or reverberation.*

ET: *an electrical transcription; a recording. This abbreviation can be used to indicate that a scripted music or sound effect is already available in a prerecorded form.*

FLIGHT: *a series of announcements for the same product or service that are usually done in the same style and format as part of a single campaign.*

GAIN: *the radio sound term for "volume."*

HITCHHIKER: *a portion of time that immediately follows a program and can accommodate brief, unrelated spots or continuity.*

JINGLE: *customized musical creation used throughout a spot or as the articulation of a key copy point or brand identification.*

KILL DATE: *last day on which a particular piece of copy is authorized to be aired.*

LIVE TAG: *a line at the end of a recorded message that is added by a local announcer to help adapt the copy to local/seasonal programming, personalities, and conditions.*

LOGO: *the visual or auditory/musical corporate symbol used by a station or client to identify itself.*

MASTER: *the "original" recording of a disc or taped message from which duplicates can be dubbed.*

MIX: *two or more separate signals brought into a desired collective balance.*

OUT CUE: *last word of a message and the signal for the next message/program to begin.*

OUT TAKE: *recorded segment not used in creating the final production.*

PAD: *material added at the end of a message to bring it to the exact time specified; also referred to as* fill.

ROS: *abbreviation for "run of schedule"; the announcement may be rotated anywhere in the program day rather than remaining at a particular time or near a particular show.*

SC or SP: *abbreviations for "station continuity" or "station promotion"; designates local copy meant to further the station's image or activities.*

SFX: *the standard abbreviation for "sound effects."*

SIGN OFF: *the piece of continuity used to end the program day.*

SIGN ON: *the piece of continuity used to begin the program day.*

SITTING MIKE: *a microphone placed on a table rather than mounted on a floor-length stand* (stand mike) *or from an overhead boom* (boom mike).

SOTTO VOCE: *stage whisper; often used to comment on an off-mike event without disturbing it.*

SOUNDER: *short musical/copy identification of a particular programmatic element.*

STAB: *musical or sound exclamation used at the beginning of or within a spot.*

STING: *a stab used at the end of a spot.*

SYNTHESIZER: *audio signal processor that can produce conventional sounds (including music) or create entirely new sounds.*

TF: *abbreviation for " 'til forbid"; announcement may be run until originating source instructs otherwise. May also be designated* TFN—" 'til further notice"—*or* TN—" 'til notified."

TIMBRE: *the tonal makeup and quality of any sound that is the sum of its frequencies and overtones.*

UNIVERSE: *the particular demographic group, the particular part of the total available audience, at which the message is directed.*

VOICE OVER (VO): *an announcer reading over a music segment.*

WET: *a recording to which reverberation or echo has been added.*

Using Sound Effects

Today, few effects need be "custom made" during the production of the radio message. Readily available sound effects libraries like those provided by the Thomas Valentino, FirstCom, or Sound Ideas companies contain virtually every effect piece a copywriter might need to specify. But whether a SFX is "canned" or specially produced, the vital thing to keep in mind is that it should be used to further the message rather than as an end in itself. The spot or PSA that becomes "that pitch with the locomotive" instead of "that pitch *for*" whoever the client might be, is a waste of everybody's effort (unless you're really selling locomotives).

Whether used to set locale, heighten a product-use situation, or give substance to something that is silent in real life, a sound effect must (1) advance message progression, (2) enhance the main copy point, (3) integrate well with the copy's style and form, and (4) accomplish its task without creating aural clutter. Sound effects should not be used in a misguided attempt to duplicate reality. The only result will be a muddled jumble of noise. Instead, the writer should select, as the human ear selects, the most prominent or more relevant sounds in a given situation, use these with discretion, and forget about the rest.

In addition, Foote, Cone & Belding's group copy head Larry Rood long ago cautioned that, "If you are going to use sound effects, make sure they register. The sound of a car skidding and crashing is easily recognizable. A boulder rolling down a mountainside may not be. It helps to describe the action at the same time you use the sound effect."[7] The "slamming door" PSA featured below is a good illustration of immediately discernible SFX and also demonstrates how even a single, stark sound effect can characterize a complex condition.

(SFX: SLAMMING DOORS, RAPID FIRE, REVERBERATING)

ANNCR: Behind millions of doors in America, people are
        trapped alone---(SLAMMING DOOR) suffering from a
        contagious disease; which has reached epidemic
        proportions. (SLAM) The disease can be passed from
        parents to children and from those children to the
        children of the next generation. (SLAM) Every year,
        that disease hurts an estimated one million
        children. Countless others are emotionally crippled
        for life. An estimated eighty percent of America's
        prison inmates have suffered from the disease. That
        disease (SLAM) is child abuse. (SLAM) Child abuse
        hurts everybody. But it doesn't have to happen. With
        enough people who care, we could help form crisis
        centers and self-help programs. Together, we could
        help prevent child abuse. For more information on
        child abuse and what you can do, write: Prevent
        Child Abuse, Box 2866, Chicago, Illinois 60690. What
        will you do today that's more important?

(Courtesy of The Advertising Council, Inc.)

Alternatively, as in the following message for the National Council on the Aging, specific copy identification of the sound effect can be deliberately withheld for a few moments to build listener interest. This approach should be risked, however, only when (1) you have but a single sound effect, (2) it well represents your central copy point, and (3) you don't try to string the listener on too long before providing unequivocal verification of just what that sound *is*.

```
(SFX: CREAKING OF ROCKING CHAIR---FEATURE)

MAN:     Do you know you're slowly becoming part of the
         fastest growing minority in the country?

WOMAN:   What?

MAN:     Would you mind standing up for a moment?

WOMAN:   Huh---(SFX: CREAKING STOPS) Hey, where are you going
         with my rocker?

MAN:     Are you willing to take old age sitting down?

WOMAN:   Sitting---?

MAN:     You are going to be old some day.

WOMAN:   All right, all right; but you didn't have to take my
         rocker to prove your point, did you?

MAN:     You have to get off your rocker to stand up. Stand
         up, or be prepared to just sit back and rock your
         life away.

WOMAN:   I see what you mean.

MAN:     This message has been brought to you by this
         station, The Advertising Council, and the National
         Council on the Aging.

WOMAN:   Thank you.
```

(Courtesy of The Advertising Council, Inc.)

Sometimes, sound effects are most effective when contrasted with a much quieter or nearly silent condition. In a classic commercial, Farrell Lines, a large shipping firm, once used this principle to undercut some executives' stereotypes about Australia by dramatizing the vitality of its business climate.

Against a cacophony of bustling, industrial SFX, the voice-over copy pointed out that

```
Australia is so booming that you can't hear the sheep being
sheared. You can't hear tennis balls pinging off rackets.
You can't hear koala bears eating leaves off eucalyptus
trees. Listen to the sounds of booming Australia.⁸
```

One caution: sound effects should never be expected to accomplish identifications beyond their intrinsically recognizable aural capabilities. Examples like the following are impossible to portray adequately without the assistance of spoken copy.

```
(SFX: WATER BEING POURED INTO CAR RADIATOR)
```

How does listener know the receptacle is a *radiator*? How does the listener know it's *water* and not some other liquid?

```
(SFX: HORSE CHOMPING ON APPLE)
```

How does listener know it's a *horse*, not a slovenly human? How does listener know it's an *apple*?

```
(SFX: 10-YEAR-OLD GIRL GOING UP STAIRS)
```

How does listener know she's *10*? How does listener know she's a "she"? How does listener know she's going *up* and not *down* stairs — or on stairs at all?

Using Music

Like sound effects, music is readily available to the commercial and continuity writer in conveniently prepackaged form from a wide variety of sources, such as Associated Production Music, Network Production Music, DeWolfe Music Library, and Capitol Production Music. This availability is especially helpful to the in-station writer. If the station has purchased the library or service from any of these or several other firms, all relevant copyright fees have already been paid, and the often formidable task of obtaining copyright clearances is thereby avoided. While this is not a casebook on copyright law, it must be emphasized that music virtually never comes "free." Mechanical, synchronization, performance, and grand dramatic rights may all be involved in your using even a brief musical cut and may often be held by several different firms or individuals. The fact that your station has ASCAP, BMI, and

SESAC performance rights licenses does *not* give you the automatic prerogative to take popular compositions licensed by them as background music for your continuity. In fact, such unauthorized appropriation usually constitutes overt copyright infringement.

Especially if you're a freelancer, or an in-station writer directly involved in the production of your message, make certain the music you've selected has been properly cleared—and for more than just performance rights. Advertising agencies and other larger organizations will normally have specific employees who assist with these clearance concerns.

Wherever the music comes from, take special care that it is of professional quality in styling and sound reproduction. As more and more sources of production music come on the scene, there is a natural tendency on the part of some companies to underprice the competition by offering an underproduced product. If the music bed sounds like it emanated from the group shown in Figure 7–1, don't use it to accompany your copy. Bargain basement music is a cellar, not a stellar commodity. If it is cheap, it will sound cheap—and so will your client.

As the third of radio's trio of potential sound elements, music has unsurpassed utility in quickly and comprehensively constructing an environment for the message it complements. William Stakelin, former president of the Radio Advertising Bureau, observes that "music is the most natural way to stimulate thought and action. . . . Music sets up our expectations—brings a pastoral scene into focus, swells up feelings of love or affection, hints at troubles to come, establishes movement and, using a basic sound motif, heralds an important idea or event. Music plays to the moods and desires of customers. The right music, in the right format, on the right stations establishes an instant unspoken bond with your target audience."[9] The necessity for this appropriateness cannot be overstated. The copy style, the product or service category, the situation being conveyed in the spot, and the station(s) on which the spot will be run must all be considered in music specification. Because, for the radio copywriter,

```
M   U   S   I   C
e   s   e   n   o
a   i   n       n
n   n   t       t
s   g   i       e
        m       x
        e       t
        n
        t
        s
```

Intrinsically, music *does* mean using sentiments in context. Even a very short musical passage can simulate and stimulate a wide variety of feelings. Your job as a copywriter is to make certain that the passage and context you have

Figure 7-1
Have you ever wondered where some production music is recorded?

(Courtesy of Michael Anderson, Network Production Music, Inc.)

built will call up sentiments appropriate to your selling message. Notice how, in the spot below, brief snippets of the song *I Get Around* are perfect enhancers of the product's functional and esteem-building properties while keeping the mood light rather than institutional. Together, the music and the copy affirm that a Southwestern Bell cellular phone is not just for buttoned-down corporate types, but for 'regular' folks as well.

> Production Note: MUSIC is a jaunty version of I GET
> AROUND. 'Guy' has a low, deadpan delivery.

(MUSIC: QUICK FEATURE AND OUT)

GUY: I get around. I put a Southwestern Bell cellular
         phone antenna on my head and walked into a crowded
         restaurant. Forty-two attorneys tried to dial out on
         me.

169

```
        (MUSIC UP, THEN OUT)
```

GUY: When I talk on a Southwestern Bell cellular phone,
        my voice is crystal clear. That's amazing,
        considering it's not really that clear in person.

```
        (MUSIC UP, THEN OUT)
```

GUY: Southwestern Bell cellular service is so clear, that
        when I talk to my girlfriend on my car phone, it's
        like she's right next to me. I can actually hear her
        withdrawing.

```
        (MUSIC UP, THEN OUT)
```

GUY: Southwestern Bell Mobile has cellular service that's
        trouble-free. Then again, trouble is always free.

```
        (MUSIC UP, THEN OUT)
```

ANNCR: More people---go more places---with Southwestern
        Bell Mobile Systems.

GUY: Someday Southwestern Bell will be able to break us
        down molecularly and send our bodies through
        cellular phones. This might be a long way off. But
        just in case, I'm getting a haircut.

```
        (MUSIC CLOSE AND OUT)
```

(©1992 Paul & Walt Worldwide. Writer: Walt Jaschek. Producer: Paul Fey.)

If, on the other hand, your music implies one thing and your copy says something else, it will probably be the music's point of view that predominates in both the listener's short- and long-term recollection. Never start off with a musical "bed" just because you like it and then try to construct a message around it. You may end up with a nice commercial for the tune but only at crippling expense to your central copy point.

In radio, the introduction of music will be much more attention-getting than it is on television, where audience focus is already heavily oriented toward the visual. But if the music's style or character at all clashes with the flow and approach of the copy, the melody will invariably become a disrupting rather than an enabling element. Don't be afraid *not* to use music in your copy. In fact, if surrounding messages tend to make heavy use of music, a solid piece of straight copy will stand out very well by comparison. This is especially true when your client's main competitors have all tripped down Melody Lane and you want your campaign to be distinct. We have more to say about music's use in Chapter 8.

The Radio Copywriter as Poet

While it may not be immediately apparent, radio copywriters have as strong a bond with the art of poetry as they do with the art of music. After all, *Webster's New Collegiate Dictionary* describes a poet as "one endowed with great imaginative, emotional, or intuitive power and capable of expressing his conceptions, passions or intuitions in appropriate language." The radio copywriter's job, in fact, is to find words and other sound elements that are so *appropriate* to our message that the listener will not only comprehend but also remember them as the means of recalling the workings of our product and service. Thus, through the years we recall what will "double our pleasure, double our fun," where to go for a "sandwich that's a manwich," whom to call "when it absolutely, positively has to be there overnight," and maybe even how to feel "the heartbeat of America."

These electronic slogans are simply the latest manifestations of an age-old tradition. Before the age of print and, consequently, before the age of significant literacy, fables, sagas, and folklore in general were passed down orally. From the ancient Greek rhapsodes and Biblical psalmists to the medieval minstrels and beyond, poets seeking to communicate with significant numbers of preliterate "common folk" did so by casting their messages into concise yet colorful verses that could be understood easily by all and remembered, at least in part, by many.

Like these earlier poets, the radio copywriter performs in a totally oral and fundamentally nonliterary environment. Our listeners, like those of our historic predecessors, have no concrete, permanent record of the subject being communicated. Everything the radio audience carries away with them must not only be visualized but also implanted in the mind through an unusually harmonious juxtaposition of sounds and ideas. In a process with which any past or present minstrel can identify, the radio writer continually struggles to attain the perfect marriage between *sound* and *sense,* a marriage that will enable the message to spring to life and stay alive in the listeners' memories during the days and weeks to follow.

As eighteenth century poet Alexander Pope once wrote:

True ease in writing comes from art, not chance,
As those move easiest who have learned to dance.
'Tis not enough no harshness gives offense,
The sound must seem an echo to the sense.

Much more recently, semanticist S. I. Hayakawa observed that the "copy-writer, like the poet, must invest the product with significance so that it becomes something beyond itself. . . . The task of the copywriter is the poeti-cizing of consumer goods."[10] Yet, in many ways the radio copywriter's task is even more difficult than that faced by most other poets. Conventional poets can usually choose their own subject, the attitude they will take toward that subject, the form to be employed, and the length to which that form will extend. Radio copywriters conversely, virtually always have the subject as-signed to them together with a compulsory subject attitude, which is nearly always positive (unless it is something like an *anti*-litter PSA). The specified form is certain to be budget- and time-bound. If there is no time or money for a dialogue spot to be produced, for example, the copywriter must proceed with a univoice approach regardless of personal or professional preference. And the dictated length is precisely the length decreed by the campaign managers and the media selection plan they have adopted; no longer and no shorter.

The nonradio poet can decide to write in praise of a solitary stalk of corn. The copywriter is told to pen a corn flakes spot. The conventional poet may decide this particular cornstalk represents man's constant search for inde-pendence. The radio poet is instructed to demonstrate how the one brand of corn flakes meets the whole family's breakfast requirements. The traditional poet decides to discuss the corn stalk in Italian sonnet form: fourteen lines in iambic pentameter grouped into two subsections of eight and six lines. The broadcast writer has thirty seconds of air-time to be devoted to a univoice homemaker testimonial. The remarkable aspect of all this is that, despite the comparatively cramped boundaries within which they have to maneuver, radio copywriters must still construct a message that is just as meaningful and memorable to the mass audience as the traditional poet's message is to his or her far fewer and initially more attentive constituents.

Just for a moment, let's see how a conventional poet and a "copywriter poet" might approach and describe the identical subject. In this case, the topic is the same small-town cafe. Certainly, the nonradio writer's imagery is more descriptive and extended. But does the the poet make Bannerman's *benefit* as 'significant' and discernible as the copywriter's 30-second spot?

DINER

A new day's procrastination
Lets night's veil still opaque the sun.
The silky mist floats on the highway
And the dew embosoms the grass,
While sleepy truckers and travelers,
Draped in coats, soon discarded,
Gather in bleary-eyed company,
Sipping the heavy-mugged coffee.

The morn's high tide arrives.
Rays of sunshine put neon to shame;
The grey road crawls toward tomorrow
And the ground is a mottled pastel.
A carpet which grade school children
Imprint with rubber-ribbed gym shoes
In their jumbled, vibrant rush
To the charm-filled gum machine.

Exhausted, a spent afternoon
Plods by in thankful surrender,
Leaving a dusked thoroughfare
Flanked by the darkening earth
Where the bachelors and creased businessmen
Stretch out their day-piled stiffness
While stepping from autos and vans
In pursuit of the house specialty.

A suit with a moon for lapel pin
The ebony mystery of midnight
Makes the highway a concrete river,
Gives each blade of grass a new boldness
To the starry-eyed couples,
As linked pairs of feet
Drift through the door
For the evening's last talk.

ANNCR: A place to start the day off right; a place to stop
         before saying good-night. Tempting food, relaxing
         atmosphere, and an always-here-to-please-you
         attitude. That's what you'll find every day,
         twenty-four hours a day, at Bannerman's Diner. From
         that first up-and-at-em cup of coffee, to a
         late-night home-cooked snack, Bannerman's Diner
         serves you the food you like---when you like it.
         Bannerman's Diner on Route 23. Your any-time,
         every-time restaurant.

Poetic Packaging

In comparison with the above poem, the copywriter's radio-tailored effort may seem somewhat humdrum. But our words must be instantaneously accessible to an audience that is paying only partial attention. The commercial must sell

Bannerman's. The poem need only promote itself. This distinction aside, both poets and copywriters are required to energize and activate audience member's visual and other senses via media that are not, in and of themselves, pictorial. This is not a mutual drawback but a shared advantage. For, as award-winning copywriter Robert Pritikin once noted, "When you write a radio commercial for the eye, instead of for the ear, you can expect to achieve enormous recall value. The most elementary memory course will teach you that to remember something, you must visualize it."[11] Pritikin himself created one of modern radio's most poetic illustrations of this principle in a series of spots that illuminated a paint's very visual essence via the supposedly "blind" radio medium:

ANNCR: The Fuller Paint Company invites you to stare with
        your ears at---yellow. Yellow is more than just a
        color. Yellow is a way of life. Ask any taxi driver
        about yellow. Or a banana salesman. Or a coward.
        They'll tell you about yellow. (PHONE RINGS) Oh,
        excuse me. Yello!! Yes, I'll take your order.
        Dandelions, a dozen; a pound of melted butter;
        lemondrops and a drop of lemon; and one canary that
        sings a yellow song. Anything else? Yello? Yello?
        Yello? Oh, disconnected. Well, she'll call back. If
        you want yellow that's yellow-yellow, remember to
        remember the Fuller Paint Company, a century of
        leadership in the chemistry of color. For the Fuller
        color center nearest you, check your phone
        directory. The yellow pages, of course.[12]

This Fuller Paint spot is a perfect example of radio's using its own unique advantages to capitalize on television's disadvantages. Every member of the audience was enticed into poetically painting, in his or her own mind, what was most appealing about yellow. There was no forced dependence on the film processor's yellow, videotape's yellow, the kind of yellow that the television station engineer admired, or even the brand of yellow the home receiver was adjusted to reproduce. Instead, it was everyone's perfect yellow displayed in everyone's most perfect showcase—the individual mind.

Like any successful radio copywriter, Pritikin engaged in a little *Poetic Packaging*—he isolated the element of the subject on which he wanted to focus and then derived some picture-potent symbols to bring that element to mind's-eye life. Broken down, the development of the above commercial, like the development of any image-filled piece of *Poetically Packaged* radio, results from a unified process that springs from three successive questions:

1. What is my subject? (Yellow Fuller Paint)
2. What is its key element or quality that I want the listener to appreciate? (the vibrancy of its yellow color)
3. How can I *poetically package* this quality? (relate it to other prominent examples of the color yellow; taxis, bananas, dandelions, melted butter, lemon drops, a canary, even the yellow pages and cowards)

Many aspiring writers realize they must use imagery to make their message come alive, but they neglect the vital second step. They mistakenly try to describe, to *Package Poetically*, the product or service as a *whole* rather than first selecting its key attribute and the central copy idea that must be fashioned to display that key attribute. Since no short piece of copy can ever be expected to make more than one memorable point, the adopted *Poetic Package* must likewise work in undistracted service to that point instead of attempting to characterize the product's totality.

For practice, take the following items and try to pull out what the key element or quality of each might be:

a ball-point pen
a pizza pie
a life insurance policy
a watchband
an automobile shock absorber
an underarm deodorant

Do you and, given your subject's specific advantages, *should* you focus on the pen's shape, the pizza pie's convenience, the policy's low monthly cost, the watchband's strength, the shock absorber's gentleness, and the deodorant's aroma? Or do you stress the pizza pie's shape, the deodorant's convenience, and the policy's strength? Whatever you decide, you must then as a radio writer encase that central concept in the most vivid and meaningful wrapping you can derive. Does the pen fit your hand like an extra finger? Does the watchband's strength come from "tank-track" weave? Does the deodorant go on "gentle as a goldfish's kiss"? And what about that pizza with its shape or convenience? Keep digging until you find your subject's most appropriate element and a convincing *Poetic Package* to match. It's not easy, and a lot of seemingly unproductive "think time" may be expended before you ever start setting your copy to paper. But hang in there. Once you have successfully dealt with all three of *Poetic Packaging's* questions as they apply to the assignment at hand, you'll have a message that is truly effective because it's intrinsically *radio*.

Isolate how *Poetic Packaging's* trio of queries might have been answered in the formulation of this commercial:

(MUSIC: FEATURE SINGLE SOPRANO OPERATIC VOICE)

ANNCR: In today's competitive business atmosphere, it isn't easy for a small business to be heard.

(ORCHESTRA SWELLS TO DROWN OUT VOICE)

(FADE DOWN ORCHESTRA TO FEATURE BASS VOICE)

ANNCR: Truth is, even if you're a big business, there's no guarantee that you'll be heard.

(ORCHESTRA SWELLS TO DROWN OUT BASS VOICE, THEN UNDER)

ANNCR: But when it comes to property and casualty needs, the CIGNA Companies listen to businesses of every size. From the neighborhood corner store to the multi-national corporation. And though their needs may be worlds apart, they are both given the same attention to detail. Whether its implementing a global insurance program or helping to put together a tailor-made business package policy. The CIGNA Companies have been providing property and casualty insurance for nearly 200 years. And in today's ever-changing business climate, doesn't it pay to listen to the voice of experience?

(A TENOR VOICE RISES ABOVE THE ORCHESTRA TO TIME)

(Courtesy of the CIGNA Companies.)

Other Techniques for the Radio Poet

In addition to the umbrella concept of *Poetic Packaging,* there are seven precise writing techniques for improving your message's sound and sense potency. Specifically, skilled "radio poets": (1) vary length (2) deploy pause (3) erect fulcrum phrases (4) exercise evocative phonetics (5) lighten up on alliteration (6) explore onomatopoeia and (7) paint a backdrop.

1. Vary Length

Compelling copy projects a sense of flow. And flow is enhanced best by a progression of related thought units that vary in length. If all of its sentences expend about the same number of metric beats, a spoken message will develop a lock-step character that is enjoyable as a music lyric, but monotony incarnate as unaccompanied copy. In a jingle like the Spangles' spot below, for example, the pulsating, *uniform* stanzas propel the flow in an ear-pleasing, foot-tapping progression totally appropriate for musically depicting a lively nightspot.

```
Spangles is where the fun begins.
Party times that never end.
Great food, great prices, great service too.
It's all waiting here for you.

Call all your friends in the neighborhood.
You don't have to settle just for good.
For a sit-down dinner, or a quick bite,
Make it Spangles; Spangles tonight.

When you feel like relaxin',
You know that we're gonna treat you just right.
When you feel like some action---
Make it Spangles, make it Spangles,
Make it Spangles; Spangles tonight.

Spangles is where the fun begins.
Party times that never end.
Great food, great prices, great service too.
It's all waiting here for you.

Make it Spangles; Spangles tonight.
Make it Spangles; Spangles tonight.
Make it Spangles; Spangles tonight.
Make it Spangles; Spangles tonight.
```

(Courtesy of Fran Sax, FirstCom.)

In the case of straight copy, conversely, there is no music to embellish the pulse. So the attainment of flow variety is totally dependent on the words and sentences themselves, which should proceed in contrasting short and medium units. After all, flow is best appreciated when balanced by ebb. The shorter units help hold the thought up momentarily before the medium ones propel it ahead again.

The copywriter should be enough of an artist that the listener will not notice the means by which flow is regulated but will only experience its pleasing effect. The tedium of unaccompanied same-length sentences, on the other hand, is a dulling distraction for audience attentiveness. Often, listeners may not b able to identify consciously what caused their attention to wander. But the lack of contrast inherent in uniform-length thought units takes its toll no matter how glowing the word choices that made up those units. The sample Talbot Reinforcement spot below demonstrates the sluggish sameness undiversified length begets. Each succeeding thought unit has the same five beats, which pound relentlessly on without regard to copy meaning or aural flow. The beats are marked to identify further the lack of variety in sentence duration:

```
1          2               3         4       5
Paper's cheap but your time and effort aren't. Ripped

  1      2           4     5         1       2        3
 binder holes mean lost homework. Now's the time to stop

    4    5              1        2        3       4
this problem. Surround those holes with Talbot Gummed

       5             1        2         3         4
Reinforcements. A round Talbot circle will keep the hole

         5           1        2        3         4
from tearing. So keep that valuable work right there in

         5             1       2       3           4
your notebook. Don't waste the time and effort you put in

         5           1           2         3           4
that essay. Get Talbot round Gummed Reinforcements before

            5
it's too late.
```

Length, then, is measured in *beats,* which combine to create copy *rhythm.* It is not the number of words but the number and arrangement of beats that comprise the framework for copy flow. Take the measure of some of your own material in the way we've just measured the Talbot spot. That should help you detect metrical monotony in the making in time to prevent it.

Contrast the mechanical effect of the Talbot commercial with the non-repetitive progression in this Pawprint dog food spot. Compute the beats in each thought unit. Here, the sentence lengths are varied enough to retain rhythmic interest without eclipsing copy comprehension.

```
ANNCR:  Life. It's a beautiful thing to behold. From a
        newborn baby to a newborn puppy. Remember that old
        cardboard box and all those puppies clinging to
        their mother? Remember smiling? When you finally
        decided which puppy was going to be yours? That was
        a big decision. You took on responsibility for
        another's life. And you handled that responsibility
        by making sure your puppy got the best. Pawprint dog
        food. Pawprint nurtured your pet from a clumsy pup,
        to a mature adult. And Pawprint's rich beef flavor
        gave your dog all he needed to live a long, healthy
        life. That beautiful dog's still part of your life.
        And so is Pawprint dog food. Because when
        something's this genuine, you want to keep it.
```

2. Deploy Pause

Too many copywriters think they are paid to gather words rather than create communication. These scribes pack their copy with as much linguistic baggage as possible and then wonder why listeners stop listening. The poetic copywriter, on the other hand, just like the consummate composer, knows that silence can be as powerful as sound. So this wordsmith orchestrates meaningful pauses within the message. As audio producer Eric Larson tells his clients, "If you make a good point, sometimes . . . the best thing to do is just give a break to the copy right there, so that strikingly convincing sales point can be absorbed."[13]

If you can learn to follow Larson's suggestion, you will get a lot closer to becoming a "real writer." This is the central quality that art director Don Easdon ascribes to his counterpart, Bill Heater, when Easdon acclaims:

> He's a real writer, and a real writer is a student of the way people talk, what they say, phrases they use. And more importantly, what they *don't* say. The little pause in between the sentences. He's the first [copywriter] who ever talked to me about that. He said we really don't have to fill up the 30 or 60 seconds with copy. It's what he doesn't say that makes the work so powerful.[14]

Pauses can be created by punctuation, by the natural separation in time of one thought unit from the next, and even, if necessary, by the stage direction: (Pause). However you indicate it, the pause allows you to isolate what comes on either side of it for easier contemplation by the listener. Read the following Australian commercial aloud. Observe how its unignorable bits of silence help achieve brand name recognition.

Production Note: Les is a right-wing Australian with
a wife and two grown-up children who believes things
aren't what they used to be.

LES: There it was staring me in the face. 4 Play! Then my
        youngest, Sharlene, said that's what she wanted. 4
        Play? Now admittedly this Philips 4 Play is a pretty
        good hi fi. Turntable, tuner, double cassette and a
        vertical compact disc. And all from just $899. But
        to call it a Philips---4 Play. I mean, what's a man
        supposed to do?

(Courtesy of Troy Sullivan, Ogilvy & Mather Pty. Ltd.)

3. Erect Fulcrum Phrases

A *fulcrum* can be described as the brace-point of a seesaw. When positioned
exactly halfway between the board's two ends, it can hold the board perfectly
horizontal once the weights on the ends are in balance. Linguistically, the
fulcrum phrase possesses this same capability. It is a thought unit constructed
in such a way that its midpoint is obvious because there is an equal metrically
balanced load on each end. Such a line is intrinsically pleasing to the ear and,
therefore, like any pleasing rhythm, makes it easier to remember the message
being carried. True, listeners may not be able to define just what a fulcrum
phrase *is*, but, to paraphrase Justice Stewart's comment on obscenity, they'll
"know it [and appreciate it] when they hear it."
    A landmark series of spots for the Fuller Paint Company employed an
excellent example of the fulcrum phrase. Not coincidentally, that phrase was
also the company's identity line:

a century of leadership in the chemistry of color

Where is the fulcrum? Between the words *leadership* and *in*. This balance
point, as shown in Figure 7–2, is literally *composed* into the line to give it the
appealing sense of proportion, of stability, so important in aiding and stimulating recall.

Figure 7-2
The Fulcrum Phrase Visualized

Other classic commercial fulcrum phrases that have served to enhance brand identify include:

```
Our L'Eggs ∧ fit your legs.

K-Mart is ∧ your savings place.

You can't do better ∧ than all AAAs.

GE. We bring ∧ good things to life.

The proud bird ∧ with the golden tail. (Continental
Airlines)

Best of all ∧ it's a Cadillac.

McDonald's ∧ and you.

You're in the Pepsi ∧ generation.

Take the Nestea plunge.

We sell no wine ∧ before its time. (Paul Masson)

With a name like Smucker's ∧ it has to be good.

Bandini is the word ∧ for potting soil.

Chock Full 'O Nuts ∧ is that heavenly coffee.

Like a good neighbor ∧ State Farm is there.
```

Like the refrain of a recited poem, a well-crafted fulcrum phrase endows the radio writer's central idea with a propelling clarity that is especially important in aural-only communication.

If the fulcrum phrase is a valuable asset to a spot, it can be downright vital to the comparatively abbreviated program promo that often has a *total* of only one or two lines in which to accomplish its objective. There, the fulcrum phrase may be a necessity to add interest to a line that exists in virtual isolation. Notice how even these one-liner promos seem confident and complete in themselves because they are conscientiously balanced:

```
The tunes roll on with Mel St.John ∧ and they never stop
'til ten.

Let Dialing for Dollars ∧ give your purse a silver lining.
```

181

Here are four more fulcrum program promos. Plot the balance point in each for yourself.

```
Take the pressure out of rush hour with The Jim Mead
Show.
```

```
Lou Day has better weather 'cause he helps you understand
it.
```

```
Cool, mellow sounds for a warm Akron night as Kay Lenox
grooves jazz just for you.
```

```
Play-by-play baseball with Bobby Mack sticks the bat and
ball in your ear.
```

4. Exercise Evocative Phonetics

As a true soundsmith, a radio-television copywriter will choose words not only for the precision of their meanings and the feel of their rhythm and balance, but also for the appropriateness of their phonetic makeups.

Audiences as a whole tend to respond in different ways to different sounds. They are conditioned by certain quirks of the language to perceive some words as much for their aural composition as for their denotative meaning.

The *i* sound as in the word little, for example, very often occurs in words that depict something little: *bit, kid, mitten, chick, tiff, whiff, pill, kilt, thin, pin, inch, lint, snip, wisp,* even *witticism.* Similarly, a crisp, decisive effect is auditorially suggested by words that end emphatically, such as *pep, jet, swept, attack, act, clap, clout,* and *catapult.* Or, a rapid, lightninglike impression can often be conveyed more fully by words that begin with the *fl* sound, such as *flash, flurry, fling, flay, flag, flaunt, flail, flare, flee, flame,* and *flourescent.*

Want your phonetics to suggest humor? Then, Ira Schloss advocates choosing words that start with or contain *k* and *p* sounds—words like *chicken, pickles, cucumber,* and *porcupine.*[15] Conversely, words featuring the syllable *-ain* can help to paint a generally listless or unpleasant image, as evidenced in *pain, bane, rain, drain, stain, strain, wane, abstain, complain, inane, mundane,* and *profane.* Thus, a sensitivity to evocative phonetics would cause you to take care that the *-ain* sound is enlisted to describe the condition your product or service is designed to alleviate and not the product or service itself.

Examine the following program promo. How are evocative phonetics used to further its pitch and portray program character?

If talk is a pain and country's a drag, flip your dial to
rockin' 98 and <u>The Andy Acne Show.</u> Join the jump to
Denver's fast track.

Contrast that characterization of Andy's show with the way evocative phonetics help to depict this one:

The mystery of moonlight on Lake Erie shorelines. Midnight
in Buffalo with the mellow melodies of Larry Languid's
<u>Sonatas 'til Sunrise.</u>

Lyrics, of course, are especially deft evocative tools when instrumental
and copy sounds combine to further the same overall mood. The dulcet music
that bedded the following "Here with You Tonight" song was complemented
by euphonious long vowel sounds as in radi<u>o,</u> l<u>ow,</u> kn<u>ow,</u> g<u>o,</u> and y<u>ou.</u> This
last word possesses special utility because, other than his or her own name,
you is the most pleasing sound in the world to any listener.

Sitting here with you
The lights and the radio way down low
We listen to a song or two
And I know it's gonna be awhile before I go

Here with you tonight

Everything is just exactly right
Here with you tonight
Chicago 101 is our special friend
WKQK playing our song again
Here with you tonight
WKQK Chicago 101
We hear it with you tonight
Here with you tonight

(Courtesy of Jim West, FairWest.)

Whether radio promo, PSA, or commercial, read your copy aloud to see if
its phonetics are appropriate to the ultimate meaning you want to convey.
Your choice of sounds begins without boundaries. As Gary Provost tells us,
"In writing, there are no intrinsically good or bad sounds, just as there are no
good or bad notes in music. Just as giggling is a 'good' sound during recess and
a 'bad' sound during a geography test, the sound of your words must be
considered in the context of what you have written."[16] Analyze the following
commercial by copywriter Wally Wawro. Observe how he manipulates the
phonetic makeup of succeeding thought units to give his copy just the right
pace, mood, and character.

ANNCR: For your pleasure---a daydream from Southwest Marine
        Sales. The sails are full. The vessel glides quietly
        and gracefully through the water. White, foaming
        waves, cascade over the deck. The refreshing spray a
        coolant from the mid-day sun's warming rays.
        Seagulls soar overhead---specs of white against a
        backdrop of blue. Gentle gusts of a salt-scented
        breeze and you. The strain of muscles conquering
        wind and wave. The thrill of motion. <u>This</u> is
        sailing. Man and the elements. Willful. Strong.
        Exciting. This passage a thought from Southwest
        Marine Sales---Texas' largest sailboat dealer. See
        Texas' finest sailing vessels at Southwest Marine
        Sales, today, on Highway 146 at Seabrook Shipyard.
        Once sailing's in your blood, you may never be a
        land-lubber again. Southwest Marine. Number One at
        making daydreams reality.

(Courtesy of Wally Wawro, WFAA-TV)

In radio copywriting as in poetry, we employ evocative phonetics to achieve *descriptive* rather than merely *declarative* writing. In penning a spot for Gold Dragees (small, beadlike confections used to decorate cakes) one student wordsmith, for example, wrote that they provided a "great decorating touch." This is declarative writing only. It asserts product benefit but paints no picture to visualize it. Another student more deftly praised the "glistening crunchy sparkle" that the product brought to the cake. This is descriptive writing. The words evaluate the product by conveying a specific and positive *image* of that product in use. And the very sound of those words suggests their flashy appearance and tactile firmness.

In pursuit of evocative phonetics, "It is the word alive the writer wishes to capture," points out Judson Jerome. "Its vowels pure and unfaded, its consonants brittle, unchipped, its sinews tough. The syllables of the word should articulate for you with all the give and spring of a rattlesnake's jointed spine. Sniff the word for its sweat-and-leather smell. Does it ring on the counter like silver or clang like brass or chink as dully as lead? When you squeeze it, does it squirt?"[17]

5. Lighten Up on Alliteration

Unlike poetry, radio copy tends more to avoid alliteration (the repetition of the same initial sound in succeeding words) than to embrace it. The listener may marvel at the announcer's ability to enunciate the "pervasive Peruvian poverty that the penniless peasants personify in patient passivity" but, in the process, will undoubtedly miss the appeal's main point. Thus, the peasants persist in their penury.

Our job is not to trip up the voicers of our copy. Nor is it to distract the listener by favoring sound *over* sense. Articulating your own writing out loud will immediately flush out unintended tongue-twisters. If it trips you up—change it. There is no broadcast poetry in a sprung tongue.

6. Explore Onomatopoeia

Onomatopoeia is the ultimate extension of evocative phonetics. It results from using words that sound the same as the subject/action to which they refer. A copywriter spelled his beer client's name BUSSSSSCH rather than BUSCH as a means of portraying its can's sound when opened. The Mazda rotary engine went 'hmmmmmmmm' in a sung spot to convey how smoothly the motor purred without pistons. And the Weed *Whacker* actually spits out that sound while it works.

These and many other such phonetically imitative devices help us reach through the radio to the listener's other senses. If there's no word to describe the sound of your subject, don't be afraid to invent one:

```
ANNCR:  Listen to your car. Properly inflated tires should
        purrrr down the road. But under-inflated tires
        foo-wapp, foo-wapp, foo-wapp. So check your tires
        for proper air pressure with the Accu-Test tire
        gauge. Just a quick pssssst with the Accu-Test lets
        you know if your tires need more air. Prevent
        tire-wearing foo-wapps with a tire-saving pssssst.
        Use the instant tire checker from Accu-Test. The
        quick pssssst that keeps the purrrr in your driving.
```

If nothing else, onomatopoeia (and evocative phonetics in general) should serve as constant reminders of the importance of *sound* in successful radio communication. Certainly, our copy must make linguistic sense. But it must move beyond this sense into the realm of auditory sensation. This latter requirement sometimes takes real labor to satisfy. "A lot of times, I'll do something again and again, and it still won't be right," admits Massachusetts copywriter Paul Silverman. "You feel sour notes. It isn't right inside your ear; it bumps and thumps all over the place. It's gotta go bdlmp, bdlmp, and if it breaks that speed, it's no good."[18]

7. Paint a Backdrop

Finally, the radio poet must recognize that audio presentations should reflect a locale, should seem to arise from some specific setting. Television, with the camera's opening shot, can easily show the viewer the context of the message to follow. Radio has no such automatic establishing device. Unless special care is taken, the listener can immediately become disoriented. Therefore, like a curtain that rises on a carefully dressed stage, the opening seconds of your radio presentation should frame and spatially locate the action to follow. Granted, you don't want the listener to "walk out whistling the scenery." But you do want to construct a mind's-eye habitat that heightens *visual* memorability while dramatizing your central copy point. In the following spot, for instance, the locale and its tension are both swiftly established in the first three lines of dialogue.

MAN: Susan, this is Mr. Rudolpho. You're my star model, now <u>please</u> come out of there.

WOMAN: I'm not leaving this dressing room!

MAN: But the fashion show's about to begin!

WOMAN: Not until you take me to Kempner's Clothing Store.

MAN: What have they got that my designs don't have?

WOMAN: Wonderful fit, low prices, great selection---

MAN: Just put this dress on.

WOMAN: How can I! There's only room for one leg!

MAN: It's so avant garde! It's part of my 'Hop Into Spring' collection.

WOMAN: And this sweater top---it's ugly! And there's no opening for my head to go through!

MAN: It's my sweater they want to see, not your head.

WOMAN: When I go to Kempner's Clothing Store I know I'll find something that's---just right for me, that fits---and at the right price.

MAN: If I take you there, will you take one quick hop down the runway here?

WOMAN: On one condition. First, you go to Kempner's too.
        They have great men's clothing.

MAN: What's wrong with my clothes?

WOMAN: Paisley tights and a Nehru jacket?

MAN: Okay, I'll go there. What else?

WOMAN: Let me take off this stupid belt.

MAN: But it's a fashion statement.

WOMAN: It's a live boa constrictor!

MAN: Shhh! He thinks he's a belt. Easy Binky, you're a
        belt, you're a belt---

WOMAN: I don't believe this---get this thing off me.

ANNCR: Good fit. Good selection. Great prices. If Kempner's
        Clothing Store has something you haven't had lately,
        perhaps you'd better drop by---before your next
        public appearance! Kempner's Clothing Store, 370
        15th Street, at Yale Boulevard.

(Courtesy of Fran Sax, FirstCom.)

Despite its brevity, even station continuity can create a sense of locale. That may, in fact, be its prime mission in encouraging listener identification with the program or station being plugged. The following two snippets illustrate how time and place can be quickly communicated and capitalized on in your continuity:

Don't you just love coming back to work on Monday? Well, I
do. This is The Bill Robinson Show and I'm ready to go with
Big Lake Country music on KJCK.

It's springtime where the hills meet the plains. What a
great place to be, in 1420 country and The Bill Robinson
Show.

(Courtesy of Jon R. Potter, The Musicworks, Inc.)

Whether its a commercial or brief piece of continuity, if you give your listeners a vague or blurry scene, they'll tune out. Notice how your mind's eye draws a blank with this copy opening:

```
Service is something we'd all like to expect from those we
do business with.
```

Far better to give the listener's imagination something tangible to *play with* as an incentive to *stay with* our developing story:

```
The old corner gas station. Where they'd wash your
windshield and check under the hood without you having to
ask.
```

Likewise, if you try to begin your scene with a question that can be answered negatively,

```
Can you see yourself on a Caribbean cruise?
```

those listeners who do answer "no" will decide the rest of the spot must not pertain to them and summarily depart. As any good salesperson knows, its much more productive to elicit initial agreement from which to build a persuasive pitch:

```
Wouldn't it be great to get out of the snow for awhile?
```

This is a line that promises localized pertinence to the listener's life (assuming they live in the frost belt). So they're tempted to listen a little longer.

As star radio copywriter Joy Golden concludes, "In television, a commercial writer works with the art director to create the picture. In radio, the listener is the art director, because you're giving him the material from which he has to create his own visual image. The reason a lot of radio commercials don't work, is that they give the listener bad pictures."[19]

Radio's Essence

Poetic Packaging and the radio poet's other techniques, as well as proper format, terminology, sound effects,and music use are the essential elements to be relied on in styling radio messages that truly engage the "theater of the mind." Whether it's a short piece of continuity, a public service announcement, or a commercial for a client's new room freshener, radio can be any copywriter's greatest challenge. "After all," urges associated creative director Ed Butler, "radio is all yours. You create it. You select the talent. You may even get the chance to direct your brainchild. And, more often that not, radio is 60 seconds. Epic proportions in a world that seems to be measured in 10- and 30-second segments. It's my opinion that if you can write good radio, you can write great television."[20] Besides, radio doesn't have the hobbling blinders of TV's picture tube casing or print's column inch. Radio, when professionally written, is as expansive and unbounded a medium as you can induce yourself and your listener to make it.

Endnotes

1. "The Marriage of Radio Advertising and New Product Lines," *Broadcasting* (June 22, 1987), 43.
2. "Stakelin Accentuates the Positive of Radio," *Broadcasting* (May 20, 1985), 85.
3. "Testifying to Radio's Powers," *Broadcasting* (June 24, 1985).
4. Claudia Puig, "A Special Holiday Roast with Satirist Stan Freberg," *Los Angeles Times* (November 28, 1991), F13.
5. Andrew Jaffe, "Why Sarah Cotton Can't Conform," *Winners* (March 1988), 13.
6. Reed Bunzel, "Garrison Keillor: An American Radio Romance," *Broadcasting* (January 6, 1992), 86.
7. Larry Rood, writing in "Monday Memo," *Broadcasting* (November 11, 1974), 14.
8. Emery Dobbins, writing in "Monday Memo," *Broadcasting* (May 18, 1970), 14.
9. William Stakelin, writing in "Monday Memo," *Broadcasting* (December 10, 1984), 26.
10. S. I. Hayakawa, *Language in Thought and Action* (New York: Harcourt Brace and World, 1964), 262.
11. Robert Pritikin, writing in "Monday Memo," *Broadcasting* (March 18, 1974), 22.
12. Ibid.
13. "Orchestrating the Commercial," *ASAP* (January/February 1988), 17.
14. Curtis Feldman, "Bill Heater's Reality," *Winners* (July 1988), 6.
15. Ira Schloss, "Chicken and Pickles," *Journal of Advertising Research* (December 1981), 47–49.
16. Gary Provost, "Sound Advice," *Writer's Digest* (December 1985), 34.
17. Judson Jerome, "How Words Work," *Writer's Digest* (June 1986), 34.
18. Susan Korones, "Something's Burning," *Winners* (October 1987), 17.
19. "Ad Agency Creativity: Radio's Needed Dimension," *Broadcasting* (June 25, 1990), 46.
20. Ed Butler, "Why Creatives Avoid Radio," *ADWEEK* (October 1983), R.R. 38.

 ## Chapter 8

Radio Commercials

Having survived the previous chapter, you should now be able and perhaps even *willing* to hone in on the subject of radio commercials. Writing effective audio advertising can be a gratifying and potentially lucrative enterprise. It can deepen your insight into the beauty of language and heighten your sensitivity to the power of sound. It can acquaint you with music and sharpen your diction. Besides all of this, as compared to composing print ads, devising radio commercials is more ecologically responsible. Why? Well, as F. Joan Roger of Berkshire Broadcasting points out,

> Radio advertising is clean. Radio messages are crisp and to the point. radio advertising doesn't require growing trees, manufacturing paper, printing and distributing, carrying it home, shifting and sorting through it and then carrying it out to the trash. There's no depletion of national and natural resources with radio advertising.[1]

Whether or not you accept Roger's argument, you should concede that radio allows us to convey richly colored mind pictures at frugal black-and-white prices.

Commercial Noncopy Data Block

As with most commercial/continuity scripts, a radio spot begins, not with copy, but with a heading known as the *noncopy data block.* This block serves as a standardized memorandum that helps writers, media outlets, and clients keep track of the scripted message and its scheduling. The skeleton of the data block is set forth as pre-printed stationery. The specifics pertaining to the particular commercial are then typed in on the appropriate lines. A typical example of a radio commercial block appears as Table 8-1.

The series of dates in the upper left portion of the copy head pertain, respectively, to when the commercial was originally submitted for review to a supervising officer, when the resulting revision was prepared, the date on which that revision was approved, and, for a message released in recorded rather than script-only form, the date of sound studio production. The complete chronology of the spot is thus available at a glance and any unusual time lag between stages can be noted. If this same lag begins to appear in the development of other commercials, management can conduct an appropriate investigation to ascertain if there is an organizational bottleneck that needs attention.

Moving to the block's right column, and below your agency's centered name, the client line contains the contracting firm's official corporate designation. On the next line, the specific product being advertised is identified. For very small, one-product companies, these client/product lines may carry identical entries.

Next, the spot title is the colloquialism that illuminates the copy's central concept and provides a quick means of identification for those who will be cooperating in its creating and production. Forcing the writer to set down a spot title is also a good quality control device. If the writer has difficulty evolving a title, or if the title does not relate well to the script as a whole, perhaps the central concept is either faulty or missing altogether. In the

Table 8-1
Radio Commercial Data Block

```
                    AIMED-WRITE ADVERTISING
                    (radio-TV division)


2/21/94              client:    B & E Chemicals
3/9/94 rev.
3/13/94 rev. apprvd. product:   Dynamite Drain Opener
4/2/94 prod.         title:     Plunger Parade
                     length:    60 seconds
                     script
                     no.:       BE-167-94R (as recorded)


. . . . . . . . . . . . . . . . . . . . . . . . . . . . . . . . . . . . . . .

        Production Note: ANNCR is middle-aged female.

ANNCR:  I've got five sinks in my house. All different
        sizes. With different size drains. But they had one
        thing in common. They all clogged. So I owned five
        different size plungers. Which all
        worked---sometimes. Then I found out about . . .
```

following pre-adolescent perfume spot, the "good 'ol Karen" designation chosen as a title encapsulates the message's pivotal character as well as its pivotal
problem—a problem our product is adroitly positioned to solve.

```
ANNCR:   Good 'ol Karen. She had more male friends than she
         could handle. But she wasn't satisfied. Problem was,
         they treated her like one of the guys. Good 'ol
         Karen. She just couldn't put up with it anymore. She
         wanted boys to treat her like they did the other
         girls. With romance, candle-light and flowers,
         rather than candy bars, pencil-borrowing and study
         trips to the library. Then good 'ol Karen discovered
         Ben Hur perfume. Its sweet, gentle fragrance stayed
         with her. And more importantly, it made the boys
         take notice. That's because Ben Hur perfume touches
         that special sense in guys. And Ben Hur is only 99
         cents for a three-quarter-ounce bottle. Now good 'ol
         Karen is asked to parties and dances and her
         boyfriends treat her just the way she wants. Ben Hur
         perfume. Let it bring out the new Karen in you.
```

The title of this spot captured the very essence of its selling storyline.
That's a good indication of a commercial that serves a single, focused, and
specific purpose.

A script number, such as BE–167–94R in our Dynamite Drain Opener
format sample, is a more objective and necessarily bureaucratic means for
designating a given spot. It is used in intra-agency correspondence as well as
in correspondence with the outlets whose facilities have been contracted to
air the commercial. With a numerical designation, the outlet does not have to
take the time to audition the entire spot in order to ascertain whether it is
actually the "Plunger Parade" treatment for which time has been purchased.
The number makes such a chancy subjective judgment unnecessary. Further,
a numerical designator serves to identify the commercial as it wends its way
through the various continuity acceptance offices at networks and stations.
Everyone concerned will therefore have an accurate record of which spots
have been previewed by the outlet and cleared for airing. (Review the 'prohibition' section in Chapter 6 for a discussion of industry clearance processes.)

Script numbers may be constructed in several different ways but usually
with an eye toward identifying any or several of the following:

a. the originating agency
b. the client or company for whom the spot is written
c. the spot's location in the total sequence of advertisements produced by the
   agency for that client

d. the year in which the spot is produced or in which it is intended for first airing
e. the medium for which the spot is intended
f. the spot length

Our sample "BE-167-94R" indicates that the client is B & E Chemicals (BE), that the spot is the one-hundred-sixty-seventh treatment for that client that this particular agency created, and that it is a 1994 *commercial for use on Radio*. Alternatively, we might use a number like AW–5–167–60r in referring to this same spot. In this case, the script number first reflects the agency name (AW for Aimed-Write), and then uses a client number (5) rather than a letter abbreviation. Everything Aimed-Write creates for B & E Chemicals would thus be identified via symbols beginning AW–5. The specific spot sequence number then follows (167), as does the designation that this is a 60-second radio spot.

Generic Classification of Radio Commercials

The radio spots that these data blocks serve to identify can be divided into four main categories based on the general technique each spot employs: (1) univoice (2) multivoice (3) dialogue and (4) musical.

1. Univoice Commercial

In this category, which is alternatively known as the "straight" commercial, a single voice delivers the selling message without support from any of radio's other sound elements. Most spots sent to stations in script form for live on-air reading by an announcer or disc jockey are therefore, by necessity, univoice treatments. Because it cannot depend on music, sound effects, or the vivifying interaction of different voices, this spot type requires an especially clear and cogent use of the language. On the plus side, a straight commercial is also very inexpensive to produce since only the script need be sent to the stations. It also means that revised versions of the spot can be created very rapidly in order to take advantage of a local condition or seasonal event. An April snowstorm can sell a lot of leftover sleds if appropriate copy can be quickly marshalled.

Of course, the univoice commercial also lends itself to prerecorded rendering by a corporate spokesperson who may be a prominent personality. The copywriter must be careful, however that the words themselves do the selling job and don't become dependent on the personality for the announcement's impact. The spot below, for example, could be voiced by a nationally famous or anonymous local announcer without compromising its concept-centered pitch:

```
ANNCR:   Right now, Perkins Family Restaurants are featuring
         a dinner special that could very well lead to world
         peace. For example, say you want to know Boris
         Yeltsin a little better, but not enough to be stuck
         with a big dinner tab. With Perkins Restaurants 2nd
         Dinner Deal, you can order any dinner and buy a
         second dinner of equal or lesser value for $1.99.
         You can order Crispy Fried Chicken, Boris could have
         Liver and Onions. Who knows, you might become
         buddies. At a buck 99, it's worth the risk. Perkins
         2nd Dinner Deal also applies to steaks, fish, and
         Fidel Castro. But to get the $1.99 dinner you
         must---repeat must---tell your waitress: '2nd Dinner
         Deal please.' Otherwise, the second dinner will be
         at its regular price. And we wouldn't want that to
         happen as international tensions are high enough
         already.

TAG:     (LOCATION OF LOCAL PERKINS OUTLET GIVEN HERE)
```

(Courtesy of Gary A. White, Weinstock Marketing.)

Because of their sparseness and audio-only delivery, univoice radio spots present the copywriter's greatest challenge. If you can create a high-impact 'uni,' you will probably have little trouble with spot techniques that allow you more tools than the stark presentation of spoken words alone.

2. Multivoice Commercial

This is a derivative of the univoice commercial since, in both types, the voices talk directly to the listener. In the multivoice, *two or more* characters who are *not* in conversation with each other are used to deliver the selling message. The employment of more than one talent is a means of bringing vocal variety to the spot and/or helps suggest universality. Especially in a commercial that is required to impart a significant amount of specific information, the multivoiced approach can keep jogging the listener's attention more than would a straight spot. Still, don't make the multivoiced method a crutch on which to hang weak writing. Like any radio technique, it cannot do the selling job without well-directed copy that is appropriately styled to the task at hand. In the following multivoiced application, three mutually supportive testimonials all speak directly to the listener in a persuasively interlocked fashion:

FRAT LEADER: The fraternity of 'Alpha Pizza PI' welcomes
                 this year's pledges to our noble brotherhood
                 of pizza pie lovers. The pledges have
                 successfully completed the most difficult of
                 initiations. It was tough---eating all those
                 inferior pizzas that---

PLEDGE #1:   Yeah, it wasn't too funny when the guys made
                 me scarf those soggy things from Pizza Pit.

PLEDGE #2:   And me? I hadta choke down all those greasy
                 pizzas from Mr. Joey's. I missed a whole day
                 of classes trying to recover.

FRAT LEADER: Sure. They've all been there. They know what
                 it's like. But it was worth it. Because now
                 the guys can really respect the excellence of
                 Uncle Mario's Pizza. Now they're ready to
                 discover what real pizza is. I'm going to
                 open this box and---

PLEDGE #1:   Look at all the cheese!

PLEDGE #2:   And Uncle Mario's wholewheat crust. Really
                 something to sink your teeth into.

FRAT LEADER: If you're a pizza freak, like the brothers of
                 'Alpha Pizza PI,'---

PLEDGE #1:   You skip our initiation.

PLEDGE #2:   And initiate <u>yourself</u> to real decp-dish pizza
                 from Uncle Mario's.

FRAT LEADER: That's Uncle Mario's on South Jefferson. Or
                 check the white pages for Uncle Mario's free
                 delivery phone number.

ALL: All right, Mario!

As the Uncle Mario's treatment shows, universality is implied when
we have several voices all saying similar things about the product, service, or condition. Sometimes, these lines accrue from phone or on-the-

street interviews, which are taped and later edited into an audio montage. In such semiscript cases, the copywriter sets down the interviewer's questions and the desired direction in which the responses should be led by that off-mike interrogator. Provided a large number of answers can be taped from which to choose, the results are often more effective than if writers try to script out all the lines themselves. When copywriter Mike Sullivan created a series of ads in which an announcer calls people named Goodrich in search of the real "BF" Goodrich, for example, his team phoned more than 200 Goodrichs to get enough usable tape.[2] When you fully script out a multivoiced message, it should project similar credibility. If your draft spot seems contrived, it is much better to return to a simpler (but still conversational) univoice approach.

3. Dialogue Commercial

With this technique, rather than talking to the audience, the multiple voices used *are* in conversation, in *continuous* conversation, with each other. Usually, one voice is a salesperson surrogate and the other voice or voices represent the prospect by asking the kinds of questions and expressing the kinds of doubts we believe our listeners would vocalize. Though radio lacks the immediate feedback of the point-of-purchase setting, the dialogue spot allows us to simulate that environment. Thus, in convincing our substitute buyer in the commercial, we are striving to persuade that real listener at the other end of the radio waves.

To be effective, the dialogue must seem natural, feature distinctive characters, and possess dramatic tension. "When characters have words put in their mouths, the conversation sounds phoney," radio creative director Christine Coyle points out. "But when the writer steps back and allows the characters to interact as they wish, what results is far more dramatic and real."[3] Inept dialogue conversely, sounds as though the characters are either delivering soliloquies to no one in particular or are attempting to pitch directly to the audience like a uni- or multivoice message. Remember, if it's believably juicy dialogue, the listener will want to eavesdrop on it—and no eavesdropper wants suddenly to be addressed directly by the parties he's spying on. This is why you cannot intermix both multivoice and dialogue methods in a single spot. The disoriented audience will not know whether they are intended to be in the conversation or simply to overhear it.

Therefore, if you want your listener to be approached directly, stick to a straight or multivoice technique. Similarly, when a direct-sell line is mandatory at the end of overheard dialogue, don't compromise your characters by making one of them deliver it. After all, observes agency creative chief Virgil Shutze, "God created announcers to say the poison stuff."[4]

Natural dialogue also requires that product exposition be delivered in brief snippets rather than in one big chunk of information. You will sometimes hear a dialogue spot that begins interestingly enough, with short, alternating exchanges between the characters. But then, right in the middle of the commercial (and usually about the time the product first appears), the "seller" voice mouths twenty to twenty-five seconds worth of uninterrupted details that drone on like a blurb from a mail-order catalog:

LOU: I hate my grass.

MAC: What's wrong with it?

LOU: It keeps growing and growing. My old lawnmower just
      can't keep up with it.

MAC: I knew the feeling.

LOU: How do you keep your grass under control?

MAC: With my new Pasture Master, The Pasture Master is
      that great riding mower from Beasley Products. It
      features a tilt steering wheel, adjustable cutting
      heights in 10, accurate-to-the-millimeter settings,
      and accelerates from zero to 15 miles-per-hour in
      just 45 seconds. And the XKE Pasture Master even
      comes with roll bars, racing stripes, and a 30-db
      horn. Right now, you can put yourself behind the
      wheel of a brand-new Beasley Pasture Master for no
      more than the price of a small luxury sedan.

LOU: Sorry I asked.

Don't abandon your sense of dialogue halfway through the spot. Instead, permit your characters to volley back and forth briskly rather than laboriously pushing bowling balls at each other.

Dialogue characters should also be thoroughly distinguishable, one from the other. If taking a line from Character A and giving it to Character B makes no difference, that line should not have been included. One good way to foster distinctiveness is to maintain that buyer/seller demarcation mentioned earlier. One voice can be knowledgeable about the product while the other voice (along with the listener) has the problem or question that the product can deal with. The seller need not be cast in the role of an actual salesperson. He or she could, for example, be a co-worker with an over-the-water-cooler testimonial to product/service advantages that the seller has personally experienced.

Be careful never to let seller and buyer switch roles, however. If the *buyer* suddenly starts spouting torrents of product information, for example, then the situation's believability is crippled. A further means of character separation is to create contrasting types: a man and a woman; an oldster and a youngster; a straight voice and a colloquial one.

Whatever delineation method you choose, it should help promote *tension* between the two conversants. Author Gary Provost describes this tension as "that quality of 'something else going on' during the dialogue."[5] It doesn't have to be two people slugging it out, just an issue or quandary in which they, and our listener, can become immersed. This quandary, of course, should be solvable by our product or service in a way that drives home the central copy point. Then make certain that each line in the spot advances our march from problem introduction to solution exposition. However, don't complete the sell (get buyer concurrence) too soon. If you do, the tension will evaporate before the end of the commercial and your listener will be irritated by the anticlimax.

The Canadian dialogue spot below introduces natural and distinct characters for whom a tension-fueled problem is quickly identified and a solution gradually unfurled. Note that all the speeches are short and mutually responsive. Each one moves the selling situation forward without bringing the scene to a premature climax. We don't get the feeling that the lines are predetermined but instead are led to believe that each little comment is a natural— and spontaneous—reaction to the line that preceded it. Finally, we bring in an announcer for the product tag rather than forcing one of our characters suddenly to pitch to the audience.

(<u>MUSIC</u>: JAPANESE FLOURISH)

FATHER: Ah, my son, you have troubled countenance.

SON: I know, pappa-san.

FATHER: Today pussy willow in bloom. Sky without cloud. Yet you drag butt. Wassamatta?

SON: Ah, I save and save money to buy colour television, but more I save, more infraction drive colour TV price out of reach.

FATHER: Oh, infraction is a fract of life.

SON: But I find out Japanese colour TV go to Canada. There, Granada TV <u>rent</u> colour set for small monthly payment in <u>Canadian dollar.</u>

FATHER: Holy mackerel. In Tokyo you can't even blow <u>nose</u>
          with Canadian dollar.

SON: Granada include all parts, all service, even color
          loaner if shop service is needed---no extra charge.

FATHER: No kidding!

SON: So I call Granada long distance, say send me one,
          and you know what?

FATHER: What?

SON: Granada colour TV available only in Canada.

FATHER: Only in Canada you say? Pi-pi-pir-pirr-Tough ruck!

ANNCR: Granada TV rental. Worry free colour TV. Forever.

(Courtesy of Barry Base, Base Brown Partners Ltd.)

An engaging dialogue spot, asserts radio master Dick Orkin, can overcome radio's comparative disadvantage with television. "With TV you just plop yourself down on the couch and just look at it," Orkin says. "In radio we have to attract the attention of listeners who are actively involved in other things at the time. In order to grab their attention you have to do something at the top . . . so the listener gets the idea that he's eavesdropping on a personal, private conversation. It's this eavesdropping quality that makes radio work so well."[6]

4. Musical Commercial

As suggested in Chapter 7, music can establish itself more rapidly and more powerfully than can any other sound element. Provided the music matches the product category and blends well with your product's personality and your campaign style, it can bring an unparalleled dimension to your selling message. But before we examine the four main types of musical commercials, we should briefly discuss how best to specify musical effects in our copy.

Much of the music a copywriter might choose will be of the straight instrumental variety and so will have no lyric cues to be used as script referents. In such instances, there are several possible methods for indicating how you wish music to be handled:

A. In the case of many music services and libraries, you can identify the music you want via the catalogue number and/or the musical segment title that the packaging firm has assigned to it. Thus, your music cue might look like this:

(MUSIC: FADE IN 'COUNTRY TWANG,' EZQ 634-R2

B. Similarly a particular passage within a larger work that exists independently of a sound library can be specified as follows:

(MUSIC; ESTABLISH SECOND THEME FROM BEETHOVEN'S 'EGMONT OVERTURE')

(MUSIC: SNEAK IN FLUTE SOLO FROM RIFKIN'S 'THREE JAZZ NIGHT'—SOLO IS 2:40 INTO THE PIECE)

C. Alternatively, for the copywriter who does not have direct access to a music library, it is sufficient to construct a phrase that specifically describes the musical effect sought. The tempo, the style, and, if possible, the instrumentation of the desired passage should be indicated. If the particular musical effect is important and precise enough to enhance your copy, you as a writer should have little trouble finding the proper adjectives to describe it:

(MUSIC; FADE UP LANGUID OBOE DAYDREAM)

Or, for an entirely different effect:

(MUSIC: FEATURE FRANTIC PERCUSSION EXPLOSION)

In this Spam commercial, copywriter Steve Kahn set down the essential requirements for the music but without locking in to any one song or recording that might be unclearable or prohibitively priced. This is generally the most feasible practice. Identify the musical specifications you desire but try not to make them so inflexible that the whole spot must be junked if a single tune or cut is unobtainable.

(MUSIC: IMPRESSIVE DRUM ROLL)

ANNCR: In 1985, an old American soft drink changed its formula.

    (MUSIC: BRASSY FANFARE STARTS; WINDS DOWN TO A PITIFUL STOP)

ANNCR: You were not amused

        (MUSIC: DRUM ROLL AGAIN)

ANNCR: Now, another American favorite has changed its
        formula.

        (MUSIC: REINVIGORATED FANFARE; THEN FEATURE DRUM
        ROLL AND UNDER)

ANNCR: Introducing Less Salt Spam, with twenty-five percent
        less salt, twenty-five percent less sodium. Taste
        tests prove that Less Salt Spam Luncheon Meat tastes
        great. But just in case you're not amused---

        (MUSIC: FEATURE ABRUPT STOP OF DRUM ROLL)

ANNCR: ---we still have classic Spam.

        (MUSIC: RAUCOUS PARTY HORN BLEAT)[7]

You may be constructing music-related script cues for any of the four distinct forms that the musical commercial can assume:

1. The pseudo-sound-effect
2. The slogan/sales point enhancer
3. The backdrop
4. The end-to-end lyric vehicle

Music as *pseudo-sound-effect* is epitomized in the above Spam spot. In such an approach, we are not using music for its emotive, melodious qualities but rather for its ability to punctuate our copy statements quickly in a humorous or attention-riveting way. As long as it is relevant to our context, music can focus the product-in-use scene more quickly and sharply than any sound effect. This is so because music, unlike SFX, also reflects an attitude. Reread the Spam spot to see just how unequivocally those musical 'opinions' come through.

In our second category, music as *slogan/sales point enhancer*, a musical tag line is linked to what is otherwise a completely nonmusical production. Lyric tags such as "From the Valley of the Jolly—ho ho ho—Green Giant," "Ace is the Place with the Helpful Hardware Man," "You're Looking Smarter Than Ever—J.C. Penney," "And Like a Good Neighbor, State Farm Is There," all epitomize this brief but nonetheless incisive enlisting of music's recall power. In the following eatery commercial, singers are used to punch out the product-in-use slogan as a bumper between brief dialogue vignettes:

MAN: Every once in a awhile, I---get lonesome. So I just---go there.

DOCTOR: To Munchie's Delicatessen?

MAN: Yeah, I know I should feel guilty, but just one little order, that's all. One for my baby and---maybe---one more for the road, but that's all. I can take it or leave it alone really.

DOCTOR: Can you <u>really</u> leave Munchie's alone?

MAN: Well, except when I see all of that great food. Then I think---one quickie can't hurt. I mean, one teensey-weensey bite? It---(CROSSFADE TO SINGERS)---oh---ohhhh---

SINGERS: <u>Oh, Oh, open your mouth; and put Munchie's great food in.</u>

WOMAN: Well, for a woman to function properly, she needs emotional escape.

DOCTOR: And Munchie's Delicatessen offers these escapes?

WOMAN: It's awesome. Of course, it's a very personal thing. Just one little bite. (CROSSFADE TO SINGERS) Oh---ohhhh---

SINGERS: <u>Oh, Oh, open your mouth; and put Munchie's great food in.</u>

ANNCR: Others make promises. Munchie's delivers.

(Courtesy of Fran Sax, FirstCom.)

Sometimes, the musically heightened slogan has been extracted from a complete spot-length lyric and used as a tie-in to other spots that are primarily straight copy. Such a practice helps keep an entire campaign integrated while, at the same time, avoiding the cost and copy limitations of having every commercial fully scored.

The third musical commercial form, music as the *backdrop*, is exemplified by the Chanel spot below. There is no lyric in whole or part in such an approach. Instead, instrumental music provides the complete mood/motif proscenium within which the product and situation can more graphically be set. As in all good commercials of this type, the copy here is not *dependent on* the music in achieving its objective but rather *works with* the music to acquire an extended and more vibrant dimension. To enhance the copy/music integration, note that the script is set down as a series of lyric-like phrases rather than a single paragraph "block." In this way, the copywriter conveys a sense of the length of the melodic subelements that the selected music bed should contain.

We have omitted the specific music description here. What precise musical backdrop would *you* select in order to complement this product and copy texture?

(MUSIC: UNDER)

MAN: Why do you give a woman Chanel Number Nineteen?
Because she called one evening, and asked if you'd
like to go out and grab a hamburger.
You said sure, why not?
She said she'd be by in an hour.
And she was. In a hired limousine, complete with a
uniformed chauffeur and a bar stocked with chilled
French champagne.
Hamburgers to go were never like this.
You drove slowly around the city, looking at the
lights.
And at her.
Finally, she closed the window between the front and
back seats so the chauffeur couldn't hear the
conversation.
She smiled slightly, and gave you a conversation
you'll never forget.

WOMAN: There's a single fragrance to give that woman---
Chanel Number Nineteen. Witty. Confident.
Devastatingly feminine. Inspire her today,
and pick up some Chanel Number Nineteen
to go.

(MUSIC: QUICK FEATURE TO TIME)

(Courtesy of Melissa Wohltman, DDB/Needham Advertising.)

In selecting appropriate backdrop music, there are two key provisos to keep in mind. First, you must be sure that the musical bed will sound appealing as low-volume scenery. If it has to be placed at 'full gain' (engineer talk for high volume) in order to register, the music will control center stage. Your talent—as well as your copy—will have to shout from the wings. "Possibly the most stupid thing advertisers do," complains Robert Snodell, "is allow their agency to have background music, usually loud, rock-type music, played while the person is trying to explain the features of the product. Frequently the music is louder than the voice, so the commercial goes down the drain."[8] Even if the volume is kept under control, backdrop music does not work well with an announcer who sounds down-in-the-mud—whose vocalized pitch range is so low that, explains soundtrack creator Steve Carmine, "you can't get solid music under him. Ed McMahon is in such demand because he's good. He always gets his voice up and out front."[9]

Second, in most cases it is prudent to stay away from melodies that have had a previous life of their own. At best, the listeners' prior associations with the piece may totally divert them from your copy point. At worst, warns John Motavilli, "People who truly love a given artist's music are the most likely to be irritated by its commercial exploitation."[10] Creative director Lee Garfinkel adds, "What you often have in commercials are songs being used *instead* of an idea. Conceptually, you're not left with much of a message, except that they've used an old song."[11]

Music as a carrier of copy that is entirely cast in lyric form, our fourth and final category, goes back even to the earliest days of commercial radio. Usually called jingles, these end-to-end lyrics have evolved a great deal from the banal rhymes and melodies of the thirties and forties. Today's jingles or musical images are carefully sculpted and orchestrated to bring together a particular target universe and a particular product.

Contemporary musical treatments are often selected for lyric spots because most clients want to appear in tune with the times and because a modern sound blends well with the formats of the greater number of radio stations. But because few advertisers seek to associate their products with the uncertainty of the *newest* musical trends, the style of the lyric commercial tends to mirror the "Top 40" sound from two or three years previous. Normally, as shown in the Figure 8–1 Jersey Fresh *lead sheet* (a tune's basic blueprint), the musical/verbal syntax is kept uncomplicated for easy listener ingestion and inadvertent recall.

The copywriter usually creates the lyric before the tune is composed. It thus is especially important that the rhythm and sound of your words (those Radio Poet Techniques) accurately convey the personality of your product. If your copy is rotund and relaxed, permeated with long vowel sounds, there's not much a composer can do to give the message more pep. Conversely, if your words and phrases are short and percussively consonant-filled, the music bed

Figure 8-1

(1987 Copyright Sarley/Cashman Creative Services.)

must be briskly up-tempo as well—as in this spot promoting attendance at major league baseball parks:

```
SINGERS:      IT'S A BAT, IT'S A BALL
              IT'S A MIT, IT'S A CALL

              IT'S A SACRIFICE BUNT DOWN THE LINE

              IT'S A CATCH AT FIRST BASE

              IT'S THE SUN IN YOUR FACE

              IT'S A FLAME THROWER SHAKING A SIGN

              IT'S A TIME WITH YOUR FRIENDS
              HOPING IT NEVER ENDS.

              'CAUSE IT'S STILL TIED AFTER NINE---

              GET UP AND GO FOR ALL THE ACTION

              GET UP AND GO FOR ALL THE FUN

              IT'S MAJOR LEAGUE SATISFACTION

              GET UP AND GO.
```

ANNOUNCER: A message from Major League Baseball.

(Courtesy of Laurie Rhame, Bonneville Media Communications.)

One further musical device, though not a category unto itself, most be mentioned. Termed the *doughnut* technique, it is a means of customizing a preproduced national or regional spot to meet local needs and situations. The doughnut normally uses a lyric and an instrumental accompaniment. At a point clearly specified in the accompanying cue-sheet, the lyric stops while the accompaniment continues. This allows the local announcer a "hole" over which can be read information relating to the locations or specials being offered by the client's outlets in that area. In the "closed" doughnut, the preproduced lyric is featured again after the locally filled hole and before the end of the spot. In the "open" doughnut, the hole runs from the point of its introduction to the very end of the message without the lyric ever being reintroduced. Because timing is especially crucial in achieving a smooth "closed" doughnut effect, a safety valve is sometimes added in the form of a brief hummed or "la-la" phrase by the singers. If the local announcer runs over the actual hole, the "la-la" lets him or her know that fact and provides a bit more time to wrap up the live copy without stepping on the lyric.

Even if the specific copy in the hole does not *demand* content localization, its reading by each station's own air personality helps blend the message much more effectively with the program on which it appears. The following closed donut for a franchise food establishment, for instance, sets up a hole that can be used to promote a currently featured "fresh and fast" item and/or stress the location of the Whistle Stop Deli in this particular town.

```
SINGERS:    THERE'S SOMETHING ABOUT THAT SPECIAL PLACE
            THAT BRINGS YOU BACK, YEAH BRINGS YOU BACK
            THE FOOD'S SO GOOD IT BRINGS YOU BACK
            THERE'S NOTHING QUITE LIKE THAT DELI TASTE
            IT BRINGS YOU BACK, YEAH BRINGS YOU BACK
            THE WHISTLE STOP IS THE KIND OF PLACE
            YOU SIMPLY CAN'T IGNORE
            SO FRESH AND FAST, IT BRINGS YOU BACK
            THE WHISTLE STOP DELI
            BRINGS YOU BACK!

ANNCR:      (:23 hole copy)

SINGER:     SO FRESH AND FAST, IT BRINGS YOU BACK
            THE WHISTLE STOP DELI
            BRINGS YOU BACK
```

(Courtesy of FirstCom Broadcast Services)

When you write a doughnut, don't think of the lyric as something separate and discrete from the spoken copy. This is, after all, a single commercial. So try to make the *sense* of the message flow smoothly from lyric copy to spoken copy and back again. In other words, if the entire spot was sung, or if the entire spot was spoken, would the progression of ideas still be cohesive? If not, you have some rewriting to do.

Stephen Ford, of Chicago's Godfrey & Ford, has developed a checklist to help ensure that *clarity* is indeed the cornerstone of any musical message, in both its lyric and instrumental aspects:

First, hone in on style. Think of a musical piece which most nearly approximates what you want. A tune on the radio, a popular artist, a classical piece, anything akin to the mood you want to create. We're all pretty much exposed to or bombarded by the same music and four bars truly are worth a thousands words. . . .

When dealing with orchestration, communicate in terms of mood. A nice method, particularly for art directors, is to use visual color descriptives. Red could be a trumpet or a screaming electric guitar. Woodwinds are earth tones, clarinets yellow, oboes orange, bass clarinets dark brown, French horns a deep blue, and flutes a light green. This technique works especially well when creating sounds electronically on a synthesizer. . . .

Who is the announcer? Male? Female? The tonal range and attitude of a voice will determine the selection of instruments in orchestrating an underscore. . . .

If you don't have an idea of what sort of musical treatment would be suitable, that's what music houses are for—to offer creative input that could enhance your concept. Maybe put an Addy on your wall.

However, be wary of those producers who talk above you and hide behind a technical bush with words like "echo tweaks," "digital delay" or "square waves." They're probably technicians, not musicians.[12]

In short, when it comes to music, don't be afraid to trust your own instincts and don't be mesmerized by technicalities. Advertising music and its production are a mass communicative tool, not a secret cult.

Putting 'PUNCH' in the Radio Spot

Whatever its generic form, *any* radio spot of a half-minute or more can and should accomplish five product-related tasks. While, at first glance, this seems a huge assignment to complete in thirty or sixty seconds, the spot that in some way encompasses all five will possess real marketplace PUNCH. Specifically, this PUNCH consists of

P   roduct specification(s)
U   ser experience(s)
N   otable competitive advantage(s)
C   ost/value ratio
H   eightened listener benefit

What follows is a one-minute univoice commercial for Motel 6. Let's see if it possesses PUNCH:

```
TOM:  Hi. Tom Bodett for Motel 6 with some relief for the
      business traveler, or anyone on the road tryin' like
      the dickens to make a buck. Well money doesn't grow
      on trees and I'm probably not the first person who's
      told you that, but maybe I can help anyway. Why not
```

stay at Motel 6 and save some of that money. 'Cause
for around 27 bucks, the lowest prices of any
national chain, you'll get a clean comfortable room,
free TV, movies and local calls. And long distance
ones without a Motel service charge. No, we don't
have a swingin' disco or a mood lounge with maroon
leather chairs and an aquarium where you can
entertain clients, but that's OK. I got a better
idea. Take the money you save and meet that client in
town. Besides they probably know all the best places
to go anyway. So let them tell you what they know
best and you do what's best for business. Call
505-891-6161 for reservations at Motel 6. I'm Tom
Bodett for Motel 6 and we'll leave the light on for
you.

(Courtesy of John Beitter, The Richards Group.)

Product Specifications

Even from this single commercial, listeners learn a great deal about Motel 6. They know that it's a national chain, offering clean rooms as well as free TV, movies and local calls plus long distance calls without a service charge tacked on.

User Experience

The spot shows that the spokesperson (and, by extension, the management of Motel 6) is aware of the needs of the average business traveler and how best to meet those needs. When you're "on the road tryin' like the dickens to make a buck," it is clear Motel 6 can and has helped—not with extraneous luxuries, but with services and suggestions to conserve those hard-earned dollars. Motel 6, in short, helps you "do what's best for business."

Notable Competitive Advantages

The central and overriding advantage is, of course, the low price—in fact, "the lowest prices of any national chain." Still, Motel 6 doesn't neglect any of the things you require to be comfortable, including the homey promise to "leave the light on for you."

Cost/Value Ratio

In this spot, as is often the case when the rational appeal of economy is used, Cost/Value Ratio and Notable Competitive Advantage become the same thing—as long as the *cost* doesn't come at the expense of customarily perceived *value*. Therefore, this Motel 6 commercial indicates that the low price does *not* result from cutting corners in value-significant areas. Credibility is then enhanced by specifying exactly what *has* been trimmed to keep the price low—and then demonstrating why the absence of these items ("swingin' disco or a mood lounge with maroon leather chairs and an aquarium") is probably all for the best. You can "take the money you save and meet the client in town" because "they probably know all the best places to go anyway."

Heightened Listener Benefit

If you're a business traveler, and you want to obtain comfortable lodging without inflated prices, Motel 6 is your place. If it's an economical motel you need rather than a pricey nightspot, Motel 6 has "got a better idea." As in most effective commercials, Heightened Listener Benefit thus constitutes the cumulative and persuasive sum of all the other PUNCH factors.

Here is a commercial with a generically different approach and for a different product category. Let's examine its PUNCH factors:

Production Note: Woman should convey lines like innocent girl-next-door. Man emotes with lusty impatience.

SALLY: Tom, dear, I've got a treat for you when we reach the honeymoon cabin.

TOM: (Devilish) Heh-heh-heh-heh. I know, Sally. I've been counting the minutes.

SALLY: (Hurt by spoiled surprise) Who told you?

TOM: Told me? Someone had to tell me?

SALLY: How else would you know I made your favorite cookies?

TOM: Cookies?

SALLY: Sure, the ones made with Blaine & D'Arcy's new cherry-flavored bakers' chips. You said you loved them 'cause they taste like fresh-picked cherries.

TOM: (Bewildered) Blaine & D'Arcy's cherry chips <u>do</u> taste tartly sweet. But I had something else in mind for the first night of our honeymoon.

SALLY: (Revelation) Of course! I'm sorry, Tom. I'm such a silly. We'll stop at the store and get some cherry chips for munching. I can get a whole bag of Blaine & D'Arcy's for only 59 cents.

TOM: (Defeated) Good grief.

ANNCR: Blaine & D'Arcy's cherry-flavored chips. Their newest flavor. Blaine & D'Arcy's. Candy chips for your baking that taste like fresh-picked fruit. Good <u>any</u>time.

TOM: Or <u>almost</u> anytime.

Product Specifications

The eavesdropper on this little vignette knows that Blaine & D'Arcy's cherry-flavored chips are a recent addition to their product line (thus evoking the emotional attraction of uniqueness/newness). More important, it is clear that they taste "tartly sweet" just like their fresh-picked namesake and are easily obtainable in bags at the grocery.

User Experience

Even though the honeymoon may be off to a rocky start, the spot gives ample evidence of past positive associations the couple has had with the product. She has baked cookies for the trip after success with a previous batch that he enjoyed. They apparently also like eating the chips right out of the bag since she berates herself for not buying the means to replicate that experience.

Notable Competitive Advantages

Unlike Motel 6, this product has no direct competitors other than fresh cherries themselves, which are obviously more expensive and more difficult to obtain and store. Secondary competition consists of conventional chocolate and, perhaps, butterscotch and peanut butter chips. Thus, it is important to focus on the novel alternative Blaine & D'Arcy's *cherry* chips now provide.

Cost/Value Ratio

Blaine & D'arcy's cherry-flavored chips are only 59¢ a bag and seem well worth it since they can do double-duty as a candylike snack in addition to their testified-to success as a baking ingredient.

Heightened Listener Benefit

Though cherry-flavored chips are not as thrilling as a honeymoon, they seem capable of bring more pleasure even to that experience. They are inexpensive, highly portable, easy to obtain and, apparently, offer baking success even for the driftily naïve. They are furthermore *different* both in product characteristics and in the way these characteristics are introduced to the listener.

In attempting to achieve PUNCH in your copy, two considerations are especially important. First, make certain that a product specification *is always converted into a listener benefit.* The product attribute alone will be meaningless to the consumer unless it is shown to make a difference in that consumer's life. Inept copywriters restrict themselves to mere characteristic listing and then wonder why prospects aren't motivated:

```
Clean Gene detergent's filled with sparkling blue granules.
And because of their unique molecular structure, these
granules are more tightly compacted than any powdered
competitor.
```

So What? Who Cares? What difference do "sparkling blue granules" and "unique molecular structure" make in the listener's washing machine? Far better to write it this way:

```
Clean Gene. The detergent with the sparkling blue granules
that are easy to see in your measuring cup. And Clean
Gene's granule form packs more cleaning power into each
ounce. That means a box of Clean Gene is kind to your
budget because it goes farther than other laundry powders.
```

Here the product specifications make sense because the writer has empowered them with the customer benefits of "easy to see in your measuring cup" and "kind to your budget because it goes farther."

Second, do not require your product to share the benefit acclaim with other props or its desirability will be overshadowed. For example:

```
The elegant china, the vintage wine, and your new hairstyle
from Cut 'N Run. Everything you need to make your dinner a
triumph.
```

Is the triumph due to the client's beauticians? The china? The wine? Or all three? Will my Cut 'N Run coiffeur bring me success even in the absence of these other commodities? Change the line so the benefit spotlight shines on your product *exclusively:*

```
You've worked hard on your dinner. And the table looks
beautiful. But what makes you most confident about the
evening is your new hairstyle from Cut 'N Run.
```

Through this revision, those other props still help dress the scene, but your client is clearly the star.

The Ten Radio Commandments

In addition to putting PUNCH in their spots, successful radio copywriters follow these ten tenets to keep their commercials on the right selling track:

1. Stay conversational.
2. Voice and time the copy.
3. Remain present and active.
4. Beware uncertain pronouns.
5. Avoid TV soundtracks.
6. Keep humor in bounds.
7. Stress sponsor identification.
8. Concentrate the attack.
9. Conclude with energy.
10. Ask for the order.

1. Stay Conversational

Radio copy must be conversational, not only because that quality helps simulate an essential feeling of one-to-one communication but also because conversation is the style in which we are most conditioned to pick up aural meaning and to pick it up the first, and often the only, time the message is delivered. The sentence just completed is a good example of print communication. It is an extended thought unit that pulls several related elements together into one package whose meaning can be garnered by rereading or simply reading more slowly the first time. For radio communication, on the other hand, we have to sacrifice the unity of one extended "lead" idea for shorter thought units that will cumulatively give us the same information in a more "aurally digestible" serving. Rewriting this paragraph's lead sentence to meet radio's requirements might give us something like this:

```
Radio copy has to be conversational. A conversational
quality helps simulate the needed feelings of one-to-one
communication. Besides, we're used to picking up aural
meaning when it's delivered in a conversational style. And
we realize conversation won't often be repeated. So we work
harder to understand conversation; the first time.
```

Sometimes, as this example shows, radio must use just as many if not more words than print to cover the same ground. That's why on radio, where real-time communication is so brief, we can seldom afford to deal with more than one main point in any commercial or piece of continuity.

Yet, too many writers still try to send out the same piece of copy to both newspapers and radio stations. This practice results either in print copy that does not offer enough information to hold a reader's focus or, more often, in radio copy that is just too congested for most listeners to decipher. Here is a piece of newspaper copy that was sent to radio without rewriting. Is it styled conversationally? Does it make one main point? Does that point come through clearly?

```
Honest Abe is the wood burner for big jobs. For $269 you
can heat your entire home with this amazing wood-burning
stove and save one half or more in fuel costs. Clean and
safe burning, it's free of smoke and fireplace odor.
Minimum maintenance with easily emptied ash drawer. Roomy
24 by 20 firebox allows one fire to burn for hours. And
Honest Abe is easy to install. Call Harry's Heating at
320-8865.
```

Though the copy conforms to the word limit inherent in a 30-second spot, there is little else about it that shows adaptation to the radio medium. In reaching the *listener* as opposed to the *reader*, some of the technical data would have to be omitted so that the main copy point can be allowed to surface:

```
It's been a cold winter, with more to come. And those high
heating bills have probably given your budget a real chill,
too. Harry's Heating offers the solution; the Honest Abe
woodburner which can cut those fuel costs in half. The
easily installed, Honest Abe wood-burner is the clean,
safe, economical way to bring cheery warmth to you and your
```

```
budget. Call Harry's Heating at 320-8865. Get Honest Abe
warming for you. Call 320-8865.
```

Radio copy obviously cannot depend on typeface alterations, layout patterns, and the other graphic implements through which print can present and arrange a comparatively vast quantity of information. And unless they are composed into the very essence of the copy, paragraphing and headlining are also undiscernible to the radio listener, who receives the message only one word at a time in the order in which the announcer's voice is unveiling it. On the other hand, radio can paint pictures in the mind—pictures that can be much more involving and multidimensional than the pen-and-ink starkness on which print must so often depend. If our radio copy can escape "printese," it can attain what Richard Mercer long ago recognized as the "freedom from print's static vulnerability. Radio doesn't just stand there like a four-color proof begging to be nit-picked into appalling mediocrity."[13]

Contractions are especially helpful in promoting conversationality while avoiding printese. Contractions shorten time-wasting helping verbs while mirroring the way most people talk in real life. To illustrate the importance of contractions, we have removed all of them from the following spot and substituted complete helping verbs (underlined for easy recognition). Read the commercial aloud and note how stilted and unnatural the absence of contractions makes it.

```
DICK:      What is wrong with the way I sell cars?

BOSS:      Go ahead. Sell me a car.

DICK:      You say you would like a good deal on a car. Tell
           you what I am gonna---

BOSS:      Hold it. That is enough. At J. K. Chevrolet we are
           very low key. There is no pressure, no hype.

DICK:      Who is hypin'?

BOSS:      No shouting.

DICK:      Who is shoutin'?

BOSS:      We are all very relaxed.

DICK:      That is why I wear this pink coat and white shoes.
           It relaxes me.
```

BOSS: <u>It is</u> very nice.

DICK: <u>You would</u> like to buy it? Tell you what <u>I am</u>
gonna---

BOSS: No. No. At J. K. Chevrolet we believe in selection,
value, service.

DICK: All right. I get it. <u>I am</u> just a fast talkin',
slicky car salesman.

BOSS: Why <u>do you not</u> try our competition?

DICK: They fired me.

BOSS: How come?

DICK: They <u>did not</u> think I was aggressive enough.

BOSS: <u>I will</u> see you around.

(SFX: DOOR SLAM)

ANNCR: J. K. Chevrolet. 3901 North Broadway at the bypass.
(Courtesy of Fran Sax, FirstCom.)

Unless you really want to portray a character as pompous or verbose, let that character communicate in the conversational contractions of oral speech.

2. Voice and Time the Copy

As we've just seen, words and sentences that look fine on paper can sound stilted, awkward, or even incomprehensible when launched onto the air-waves. Great writing is not necessarily great *radio* writing. Actually voicing the copy is the only way to test your words in a manner comparable to the way your listeners will encounter them. Here is a piece of great writing from William Faulkner's *Light in August*. Can it also be used as great *radio* writing? Try reading it aloud to find out:

> All the men in the village worked in the mill or for it. It was cutting pine.
> It had been there seven years and in seven years more it would destroy all
> the timber within its reach. Then some of the machinery and most of the
> men who ran it and existed because and for it would be loaded onto freight
> cars and moved away. But some of the machinery would be left, since new
> pieces could always be bought on the installment plan—gaunt, staring, mo-

tionless wheels rising from mounds of brick rubble and ragged weeds with a quality profoundly astonishing, and gutted boilers lifting their rusting and unsmoking stacks with an air stubborn, baffled and bemused upon a stumppocked scene of profound and peaceful desolation, unplowed, untilled, gutting slowly into red and choked ravines beneath the long quiet rains of autumn and the galloping fury of vernal equinoxes.[14]

Vocalize everything you write for radio as you write it. Your copy may not approximate classic literature but, as we've just demonstrated, classic literature will often not succeed as digestible aural copy. Perform the message you've created exactly the way you would want an announcer to read it. If something trips you up, change it. That same imperfection is likely to cause similar problems later for both talent and listeners.

If you neglect to voice your copy, you're likely to be deaf to its true tonality. This deafness is especially likely on copy you've revised several times. As writing authority Gary Provost points out, "Often when you write and rewrite and constantly rearrange information, your ear for the sound of the writing becomes corrupted. Reading out loud will return to you the true sound of your story. You will hear the sour note of the word that's 'just not right,' and the drastic changes in tone will cry out to you for editing. You'll notice that you are breathless at the end of one long sentence and you know that you must break it up into two or three. Read out loud. Listen for the music, the variety, the emphasis."[15]

While reading aloud, you should also obtain the actual running time of the copy. Word count, as noted in Chapter 3, is only a general indication of the number of seconds a given piece of material will expend. The only exact method is to put a stopwatch to the copy as you are voicing it. And make sure you do *really* voice it. Some copywriters invariably come up with material that is over-time because they whisper the message to themselves. Since it takes longer actually to vocalize a word than it does simply to form it with the mouth, lip-read copy will always time out shorter than when fully articulated by an announcer. The result (assuming that stations accept the material at all) is a forced accelerating at the end of the copy as the talent strives to fit it into the allotted time. Nothing can be more detrimental to listener attention than this involuntary speeding up. Avoid it by careful timing of several fully articulated run-throughs performed at the tempo at which you wish the announcer to read. In this way, your message will be as succinct in form as it should be in content.

3. Remain Present and Active

With its extreme availability and portability, radio is a "right-now" medium. Thus, good radio copy is normally expected to convey a sense of immediate, present-tense vibrancy. It is easier for any of us to become involved mentally in something happening *now* than to meditate on the past or speculate on the future. Radio copywriters, therefore, usually keep verbs in the present tense. This not only makes it easier for listeners to visualize the action our copy depicts, it also cuts down on the drab, time-wasting helping verbs that can destroy copy conciseness. In case you slept through junior high English, here is a list of these always dull and often extraneous helping or linking verbs. They are divided into five sets to facilitate heightened familiarity if not downright memorization:

1. be, am, is, are, was, were, been
2. have, has, had
3. do, does, did
4. may, might, must
5. can, could, will, would, shall, should

Thus, it's:

We play it for you on 93 KHJ.

Not:

We WILL play it for you . . .

The first set of helping verbs (all forms of the verb *to be*) should be avoided for another reason as well. Because they all convey only state of being rather than action, they put your ideas into the dreaded *passive* voice, which destroys the sense of dynamism so important to vibrant copy. Sometimes the passive voice is grammatically unavoidable. But the less we use it, the less the danger that we are projecting static stills to our listener's mind's eye rather than compelling motion pictures.

For a comparison, here are two versions of the same spot. The first version (the commercial that actually aired) stays in the present tense and active voice by holding helping verbs to a minimum:

ANNCR: Say, teen, let's celebrate Premiere style. Get your Easter vacation off to a really great start. Grab a partner or a group of friends and come on down to Premiere Center for a night of fun you won't want to miss. This Saturday, April the second, dance on the area's largest dance floor to today's hot tunes. Played by the area's most talked-about deejay. The fun happens from 6:30 p.m. until 11:30 p.m. That's

```
      this Saturday, April second. Dress up in
      your favorite fashions and come on down to
      where it's happening. The Premiere Center.
      Three-three-970 Van Dyke Avenue in Sterling
      Heights.
```

(Courtesy of Christopher Conn, WHYT-FM.)

Though most of the words are the same, the second version illustrates how energy drains from a spot when helping verbs and the passive voice are allowed to predominate:

```
ANNCR:  Say teen, you can be celebrating Premiere style.
        You'll soon be on Easter vacation so you will want
        to have that vacation start off great. All your
        friends should be coming on down to Premiere Center
        for a night of fun you will not want to miss. This
        Saturday, April the second, you could be dancing on
        the area's largest dance floor as today's hottest
        tunes will be featured. They'll be played by the
        area deejay who is the most talked-about. The fun
        will happen from 6:30 p.m. until 11:30 p.m. That
        will be this Saturday, April second. So you should
        be dressed up in your favorite fashions and come on
        down to where it will happen. The Premiere Center.
        It's located at three-three-970 Van Dyke Avenue in
        Sterling Heights.
```

The second set of helping verbs (*Have/has/had*) also deserves disdain. Too many writers allow them to solo as a thought's only verb. Because these words are so colorless both in their own phonetic makeup and in what they contribute to their subjects, *have/has/had* should not be permitted to stand alone. Compare this copy line,

```
The Vistacruiser has a European-style grille.
```

with these possibilities:

```
The Vistacruiser sports a European-style grille.
The Vistacruiser displays a European-style grille.
The Vistacruiser flaunts a European-style grille.
The Vistacruiser boasts a European-style grille.
The Vistacruiser brandishes a European-style grille.
```

4. Beware Uncertain Pronouns

We have previously established that, unlike newspaper or magazine readers, radio listeners cannot go back to pick up ideas missed the first time. By the same token, these listeners cannot regress to find the referent for pronouns like *he, she, it, they, them,* or *that.* Because pronouns have such a high potential for listener confusion and diversion, they should be used with great care in radio copy. Particularly to be avoided is the use of the relative pronouns *this* and *that* to refer to a complex idea. Listeners will certainly tire of mentally retracing their auditory steps and may overlook the entire point of the spot in the process.

This trainee-written commercial for Sanford's Mucilage illustrates how pronoun proliferation can clog continuous auditory revelation. Even if they bother to remain tuned in, listeners become so preoccupied with determining which nouns the pronouns replace, that they have little time to focus on the product use situation.

```
ANNCR:  Many of you may not know what Sanford's
        Mint-Flavored Mucilage is. Some may say it's a new
        kind of dessert, or maybe it's an after-dinner
        drink. Well, it's not. It's an adhesive that's used
        like licking a stamp. Just apply it to what you want
        bonded. Then lick it and hold its two surfaces
        together. It bonds in seconds. And with Christmas
        getting close, children can use it to make more tree
        decorations. Yes, it can make it even more fun for
        them because it's mint flavored. Its rubber top
        regulates the mucilage flow so they get out only
        what is needed. The bottle is unbreakable too so you
        won't have to worry about their mess. Try Sanford's
        Mint-Flavored Mucilage. It's great fun for them
        because it tastes like mint.
```

Count the number of pronouns that have been inflicted on this poor, harmless product and on the poor, harmless listener at whom this spot is aimed. Not only must time be taken to locate the referent for all of these pronouns, but at several points the identity of this referent also may be in considerable doubt. *What* "bonds in seconds?" *Who* will "it" be even more fun for and what is the "it?" *What* has a rubber top and *who* makes that mess? Little wonder if listeners get bored with the guessing game and turn their minds to other things.

Keep pronouns to a minimum in your copy. If a pronoun has been used to avoid the redundant use of the same term, either find an appropriate synonym or try rearranging the sentences so that term does not appear at the same place in succeeding thought units. On radio, most pronouns are confusing stumbling blocks to listener comprehension.

The main exception to this rule is the pronoun *you,* which represents each individual listener's name in simulating a sense of one-to-one communion. Notice, for example, how the following commercial propels the listener into The Fifth Season Lounge through the copywriter's discrete exploitation of *you:*

```
ANNCR:   Where do you go for live music? Free hors d'oeuvres?
         All right in the middle of one of the most plush
         night spots in the state. You go no further than
         Greensboro to The Fifth Season Lounge in the Holiday
         Inn Four Seasons. The music? The best top-40 and
         beach. Free hors d'oeuvres Monday through Friday
         from 5 to 7. The company you find is the
         cream-of-the-crop in the triad. And the dancing is
         outrageous. Dance to your heart's delight---and meet
         the people you want to meet. At The Fifth Season
         Lounge. In the Holiday Inn, Greensboro. Your kind of
         fun.
```

(Courtesy of Bernard Mann, Mann Media.)

5. Avoid TV Soundtracks

Having been continuously exposed to so many television spots from the virtual moment of birth, it is easy for today's writers to create radio copy that's really *television.* Specifically, this means scripting *up* to the point at which the product is to be used—and then jumping ahead to discuss the glowing *results* of the use. What's missing? The vital revelation of *product-in-use.* Why does the novice writer miss it? Because in the familiar world of television, the visual can actually unveil the product doing its thing, thereby leaving the audio free to anticipate and amplify the consequences. But radio is NOT television; radio cannot illustrate product-in-use *unless* that use is translated into the aural pictorialization of words, music, and sound effects. Note how the following commercial introduces Baker's Guild Gold Dragees and then leapfrogs directly to use aftermath. Unfortunately, since the actual manipulation of the product was omitted, listeners are unsure of how the "All-Occasion Cake" was achieved, uncertain as to whether they can duplicate this positive result. This makes the commercial much less involving and puts the decision to buy much more in doubt.

> ANNCR: I'm the All-Occasion Cake. Being in the cake family
> hasn't always been easy for me. Especially with a
> popular big brother like the Birthday Cake. But now
> I'm special too---thanks to Baker's Guild Gold
> Dragees. Gold Dragees are cake decorations that look
> like tiny gold beads. Before trying them, I was a
> plain, ordinary cake. But now, I'm a beautiful
> All-Occasion Cake. For creative cake decorating, use
> Baker's Guild Gold Dragees from your Wise Frog
> grocery store. Baker's Guild: for the sparkling
> All-Occasion Cake.

You don't necessarily need a lot of time or a battery of sound effects to demonstrate product-in-use aurally. Even thirty seconds of straight copy can do the job if the words are well chosen and well arranged, as in this univoice demonstration of the Lintaway. How (with what words) is product-in-use articulation accomplished in this commercial?

> ANNCR: Going out? Got everything you need? Chances are you
> have more than you need. Chances are you're carrying
> lint. There---on your favorite sweater. On your new
> suit. On that special jacket. But now, you can roll
> lint off with Lintaway. Lintaway's specially
> designed adhesive roller actually peels lint off in
> smooth, easy strokes. Glide the 6-inch Lintaway
> roller up that sleeve and watch as the lint, hair
> and other unsightly particles vanish. Next time,
> leave lint at home with the Lintaway adhesive
> roller.

6. Keep Humor in Bounds

Particularly on radio, the trend has been toward more and more humor as a means of promoting an ever-widening range of products and services. The proponents of comedic commercials observe that you can't reason with people if you don't have their attention. And radio research by Duncan and Nelson suggests that "humor appears to increase attention paid to the commercial, improve liking of the commercial, reduce irritation experienced from the commercial, and increase liking of the product."[16] These findings are in line with legendary radio humorist Stan Freberg's belief that, "At the end of any commercial that I've every created, you have the feeling, whether you can articulate it or not, subliminally even, you have the idea 'This must be a pretty good company because they don't take themselves too seriously.' "[17]

On the other hand, as Duncan and Nelson also discovered, "Humor does not appear to reduce mental arguing of the advertised message, improve product-related beliefs, increase intention to buy, produce distraction, or increase recall of the commercial's selling points."[18] In other words, even though a comedic approach will help attract your listener's ear and set up a presumption of agreeableness for your message, humor cannot consummate the sale nor compensate for the absence of a clearly articulated consumer benefit.

It must be recognized that you can be use comedy to promote everything. As a general rule, the more expensive an advertised product or service is, the less appropriate a humorous appeal becomes. When is the last time you chuckled at a Lincoln or Cadillac spot? Guffawed at an ad for a $60-an-ounce perfume? Giggled at a brokerage firm's commercial? Things seem to become less humorous the more money they will siphon from our wallets or bank accounts. If for this or any other more rarefied reason, humor does not seem appropriate to your client and/or your client's product category, don't use it.

You must also beware of the extraneous humor that ad man Robert J. Wanamaker long ago labeled *parasite advertising* because it feeds off, chews away at whatever positive image the product or service heretofore possessed. If listeners remember the joke but not the product that joke was supposed to promote, the quip has sustained itself entirely at the expense of the client with no beneficial return in either brand recall or product knowledge.

Because humor is so prevalent on radio, and because when radio humor fails, it fails so abjectly, copywriters for the aural medium must be especially suspicious and wary of giving birth to anything that might translate itself into parasite advertising. To keep your humor in bounds, and to ferret out parasite advertising before it feeds off *you*, stand your proposed comedic treatment up against the these "don't's and do's" fashioned by agency president Anthony Chevins:

1. Don't tell a joke. Jokes wear out fast.
2. Never make fun of the product. Have fun with the product, but not at the expense of it.
3. Don't have a surprise ending. Surprise endings are only a surprise one time.
4. Don't make it difficult for the listener/viewer to figure out whether you're laughing at him or with him.
5. Don't ever let the humor get out of hand and get in the way of selling your product. Don't pull the chair from under the listener/viewer.
6. Don't use humor because you can't figure out anything else to do.

Now the do's:

1. Way out front and number one by far is make the humor relevant—relevant to the product—relevant to its benefits—relevant—relevant—relevant.
2. Involve the listener/viewer in the humor in the first 10 seconds of the commercial.
3. Use humor to point out the product's strong selling points.
4. Be charming rather than funny. It is better to get a smile than a belly laugh.
5. Make your humor simple and clear. Make it basic and broad (Give it a chance to appeal to everybody.)
6. Make sure that the humor is so tightly integrated with the product and its sales message that there would be no way that one could survive without the other. A humorous approach that could be used to sell any number of products by simply picking out one and putting in another is usually worthless—as with all borrowed interest.[19]

The spot below is a typical piece of parasite advertising in which the attempted humor tramples all over the client. Pay particular attention to how the most potent imagery focuses not on the product but on the allegedly funny condition that product is supposed to alleviate:

WIFE: (Syrupy) Good morning, dear. How's my little pigeon?

HUBBY: Awful. My mouth feels like the bottom of a bird cage.

WIFE: That's terrible. Here. Stick your little beak into this.

HUBBY: What is it?

WIFE: It's Apri-Grape. A juice to wake-up crowing about!

HUBBY: Apri-Grape? With a bunch of starlings molting in my mouth?

WIFE: Just try it, ducky. This apricot and grapefruit blend will really get you flying.

HUBBY: (Tasting) Hey! This stuff sure plucks up my spirits!

WIFE: (Sexily) Anything for my little rooster.

In contrast, here is a comedically appropriate commercial. Rather than feeding off the product, this spot meets every one of Chevins's criteria for effective selling humor—while expending only 30 seconds.

```
(SFX: KNOCK ON DOOR AND DOOR OPENING)

CURT:     (Instantly terrified) Rocco!!

ROCCO:    (Calm, yet firm and ominous) Yeah, Rocco the
          Decorator. You strayed from our arrangement.

CURT:     I-I---

ROCCO:    I hate to be crossed.

CURT:     (Groveling)---well, it's this La-Z-Boy
          Motion-Modular Furniture, Rocco. It can be a corner
          unit, a long sofa---I can't stop rearranging.
          (Pleading) You gotta understand!!

ROCCO:    Put it back the way I like it---

CURT:     Sure, Rocco, sure.

ROCCO:    ---or next time I'll rearrange more than your
          furniture.

LOCAL     La-Z-Boy Motion Modulars. So many great combinations
TAG:      and all on sale. See them at Conroy's Furniture, 862
          North Cherry.
```

(Courtesy of Ross Roy Inc. and La-Z-Boy Chair Company.)

In summing up humor's justification and deployment, British actor/writer John Cleese reminds us that "As the old Chinese proverb has it, 'Tell me and I'll forget, show me and I may remember, involve me and I'll understand.' The point of comedy is that it involves the audience."[20] And Fallon McElligott's Bob Barrie concludes, "People like to be charmed by advertising, and it has a better effect on them if you can deliver a message with some humor. We like to do things that attract attention, but our ads are always based on strategy—an understanding of marketing, the media, how the tone of the ad represents the client."[21]

7. Stress Sponsor Identification

The world's most colorful and comedic piece of radio writing won't justify itself if the listener fails to discern the brand name being promoted. It used to be that clients and/or agencies would translate this commandment into a mathematical formula that decreed how many mentions of the brand name must be included in given length spots. Today, it is recognized that you do not necessarily have to mention the product a dozen times or in every other sentence. The particular *placement* of the mentions within the spot and how the spot as a whole hooks the listener are much more important considerations. This Stiller and Meara commercial promotes exceptional brand recognition through their skillful manipulation of a character's name.

ANNCR: United Van Lines presents Stiller and Meara.

ANNE: Welcome to 'Simpatico Singles.' I'm Rowena Pirhana, and you're---

JERRY: Van. Van Linze.

ANNE: (Laughing) Oh, like the moving company.

JERRY: Yeah.

ANNE: Not married are you, Mr. Linze---or should I say, United?

JERRY: Er, no.

ANNE: (Hysterical laughter) United! Get It? If you were married, you and your wife would be the 'United Van Linze!' (Shrieking with laughter)

JERRY: Actually, I work for United Van Lines.

ANNE: How cute!

JERRY: Van's just a nickname.

ANNE: Is it true what they say about United, Van? Can you move practically anything?

JERRY: Anything from computers to trampolines.

ANNE: I thought United only moved household goods.

JERRY: Not any more. Now United's the total transportation company.

ANNE: You totally transport me, Van.

JERRY: United moves new products and equipment direct from manufacturer to distributor.

ANNE: Anywhere?

JERRY: Sure. And United gives the same special handling to
         industrial machinery as they do to your delicate
         Chippendale.

ANNE: Sounds protective.

JERRY: We are. That's why individuals and companies trust
         United to move them.

ANNE: I find you very moving, Van. Get it?

JERRY: Got it and I am.

ANNE: What?

JERRY: Moving. Right out the door.

ANNE: Wait, Van.

JERRY: United Van Lines, Ms. Pirhana. Call 'em.

ANNCR: For the name of your United Van Lines agent, see the
         Yellow Pages.

*(Created by Stiller & Meara and Bob Kelly, President of Kelly, Zahrndt &
Kelly; and Shirley Browne, Director of Public Information. United Van Lines.)*

Especially on radio, a prime component of this audience hook is often the *identity line,* the short but swingy slogan that enhances rapid recognition of the brand or corporate name. It often helps if this identify line has a categorical thrust—if it showcases the brand name *and* the product category of which that brand is a member. Brand names in isolation do not exist in the listener's mind for long. So if the identity line also designates the product category (and thereby the product use), the line will enjoy a longer and much more functional life. Here are some past and present identity lines that establish both the brand name and its category/application:

When you're out of Schlitz, you're out of beer.

The great American road belongs to Buick.

Diet Delight. If it wasn't in cans you'd swear it was fresh
fruit.

Fly the friendly skies of United.

```
You've got an uncle in the furniture business---Joshua
Doore.

When it comes to pizza, who knows? Jenos.

Red Lobster for the seafood lover in you.

We put eight great tomatoes in that little bitty
can---Contadina.

Shasta Root Beer---the foam that you feel.

Post Toasties---the best thing that's happened to corn
since the Indians discovered it.

Piccadilly Circles. The English muffin with the meal on top.

Heinz. The slowest ketchup in the West.
```

Whether or not their spots make use of an identity line, some copywriters like to substitute the pronoun *we* in contexts that would otherwise call for the brand name. This is generally an unwise practice for two reasons. First, each use of *we* is one less use of the client's name in a place in which it would be just as easy to be specific. Second, unless the client has one voice under contract on an exclusive basis, the listener is fully aware that this announcer is not, really, the *we* down at Joe's Service Station any more than he was the *we* at the Ajax Appliance Mart whose message he delivered earlier. Phony *we's* cut down on message credibility and do nothing to facilitate sponsor identification.

Ensuring this identification, says consultant Philip LeNoble, is merely a matter of keeping one design principle in mind: "Make the commercial an event and the business a destination."[22]

8. Concentrate Your Attack

Given all the potential perils of the real-time message that reaches its audience solely via the aural mode, one commercial cannot cover everything there is to say about the product or service. A radio spot is *not* a full-page print ad with its variety of typefaces, graphics, and layout patterns. So radio—even 60-second radio—maximizes its chance for success when it selects a single product appeal/benefit and paints that attribute clearly. "Many radio spots miss the mark because they forget what they want the listener to know," says

Dick Orkin. "They get so deeply involved in the entertainment aspect that they get lost."[23] Bank commercials are notorious for trying to sell too many things to too many different people in a single spot. But in this Dick Orkin message, the pitch is restricted to one universe (business customers) and a single, well-focused benefit/point (deposit pickup service). Nevertheless, the commercial still manages to be entertaining and involving.

JERRY: Listen, Shirley, the boss asked me to
                              take our daily deposit to the bank.
                              Can you cover sales?

SHIRLEY: Oh, alright.

                                  (SFX: INTERCOM BUZZES)

SHIRLEY: Norma? I'm covering sales while Jerry
                              takes the daily deposit to the bank.
                              Could you cover me and finish typing
                              the memos?

NORMA: (FILTER MIC)   O.K.

ANNOUNCER: Sending employees to the bank with
                              daily cash deposits can rock a company
                              boat. That's why San Joaquin Bank
                              offers a deposit pickup service.
                              A San Joaquin messenger shows up
                              everyday to pick up deposits,
                              instead of---

NORMA: (NO FILTER)   Eddie?

EDDIE: Yeah?

NORMA: I'm covering Shirley's typing,
                              Shirley's covering Jerry's sales desk,
                              and Jerry's taking the daily deposit
                              to the bank. Could you cover my
                              inventory numbering?

EDDIE: Again?

ANNOUNCER: The San Joaquin Bank pickup service is
                              even free for most customers.

EDDIE:	Sir, could you cover for me and empty the wastebaskets:
COMPANY PRESIDENT:	Why would I, the president of this company, empty wastebaskets?
EDDIE:	Because I'm covering Norma's inventory, Norma's covering Shirley's typing, Shirley's covering Jerry's sales desk, because some idiot sent Jerry with the daily deposit to the bank.
COMPANY PRESIDENT:	That idiot would be me.
EDDIE:	Uh, huh. So, can you do it?
ANNOUNCER:	Call San Joaquin Bank at 395-1610. That's 359-1610 for more information. San Joaquin Bank, the business bank.

(Courtesy of Dick Orkin, Dick Orkin's Ranch.)

If you *must* make more than one major point, resort to separate spots, similarly styled, that together can constitute a cohesive *flight* of commercials. In this way, the listener will become acquainted not only with each aspect but also with the fact that all of them relate to the same brand or company.

Varying the product appeal in different spots or flights is often the best mechanism for telling a complete story about the product while avoiding individual message fragmentation. With proper spot rotation (a big concern of agency media planners) and consistent copy styling, listeners will get an in-depth picture of your client's wares over the days and weeks of the campaign without sacrificing the individual commercial's integrity and precision.

Whether you use the same appeal in different situations, or vary the appeal from spot to spot or flight to flight, make certain that any and every appeal selected is calculated to aim your copy directly at your target audience. Your entire approach, the appeals used as well as the words that convey them, should show the listeners in your universe that you (and, by implication, your client) know something about them and their needs. A teen-oriented message that tries to use slang, for example, may only imply that the client knows little about young folks. "Teen slang," writes Julie Schwartzman, "is a precise code that obscures meaning and prevents an unwelcome outsider from comprehending an insider's meaning, such as Cockney slang does. A commercial that misuses slang and renders an adolescent way of talking inane and vacuous is more likely to alienate teenagers than impress them."[24]

A similar problem occurs when ethnic audiences are clumsily targeted in copy styling. As Caroline Jones of Mingo-Jones Advertising warns, "slanguage has never worked, and probably never will. Especially if it comes from general advertisers. We still call that 'patronizing' advertising, not ethnic."[25] Ethnic markets should be addressed via the same process as any demographic/psychographic cluster—through careful research into their wants and life-styles rather than by superficial parroting of alleged ethnic verbal patterns.

9. Conclude with Energy

Whatever your target universe and main copy point, your message won't make a solid impact unless each thought unit within that message ends in a crisp, forward-leaning finish. To bring a sense of impending climax to a commercial, announcers need something to *read up to.* They can experience the copy's natural impact and, through their voices, their listeners experience it also. Both announcer and listener need to feel that each succeeding sentence was worth their time and trouble. This helps ensure and heighten further attention as the spot progresses.

Conversely, the anticlimactic sentence or message ending that lets the audience down rather than conferring a reward for listening is like Aunt Eleanor's bright-tinseled Christmas packages—with the perennial underwear inside. The result never lives up to how it was wrapped or the time expended in opening it.

Don't be an "Aunt Eleanor Copywriter." Make sure your messages for radio reveal engaging discoveries as the sentence-by-sentence unwrapping proceeds:

> Production Note: Man with a country preacher's delivery.

MAN: My life used to be empty. Then a miracle took place. A man with a halo came unto me. He spoke of a perfect garden which had been destroyed. And his message rejoiced in the fruits of this life. Soon I quit my job to spread his good news. Yea-ah! And before long I converted millions of people around the world to his teachings. Then one day I bought a pair of glasses from Opti-World. Suddenly I saw the errors of my way. That wasn't god I had seen, it was Emmit Bailey who works at the Farmer's Market. His blond afro must have looked like a halo. Most people like Opti-World because of their service and selection. But I like Opti-Word because they stopped me from worshipping the head of the produce department. Thank you Opti-World.

(Courtesy of Jim Paddock, producer, Fitzgerald & Company. Copywriter: Jerry Williams.)

10. Ask for the Order

Some copywriters get so preoccupied with appeals selection, benefit description, and entertaining imagery that they forget to write a call for action. They fail to close the sale. KMEO general sales manager J. D. Freeman reminds us that "It's not enough to say, 'Oh, by the way, here we are.' It's important for your commercial to ask somebody to do something. 'Come into our business today.' "[26] In this stereo shop pitch, for instance, Santa asks for the order on three separate occasions when he urges his petitioners to "go to Dixie Sound Gallery."

SANTA: Hi. This is Santa Claus with a special message for you car stereo enthusiasts: Get off my back! And that goes for you nimrods who write asking me for cellular phones and car alarms and stuff like that too. What 'd'ya think—we got oil wells at the North Pole? I'm Santa Claus, for cryin' out loud. I do choo-choos and dollies and wagons. I don't do five band graphic equalizers. If you want car stereo equipment for Christmas, go to Dixie Sound Gallery or Sound Gallery 59. They specialize in auto sound, alarms, cellular phones by the top names like Pioneer, Sansui, Jensen and more. And at Dixie Sound Gallery and Sound Gallery 59 they do professional installation. And they're the area's only authorized Alpine dealers. I don't do installation, and as far as I'm concerned, Alpine is Mr. and Mrs. Pine's little boy. Get the idea? I am not the guy to ask for car stereo. Go to Dixie Sound Gallery on Dixie Highway in Drayton Plains or Sound Gallery 59 on M-59 in Pontiac. You want a candy cane, I can take care of ya. Car stereo? Go to Dixie Sound Gallery or Sound Gallery 59. I'm Santa Claus. I'm old. Give me a break---

(Courtesy of Rick Wiggins, WDFX.)

With some clients, "asking for the order" may be enhanced by using a 'radio coupon.' As broadcast researcher Gerry Hartshorn suggests, "Why not design your commercial copy to instruct the listener to ask for a special deal or limited offer at the sponsoring merchant? If the offer is only available through your radio coupon, it gives the retailer a direct means of assessing the effectiveness of advertising on your station."[27]

Commercial Conclusions

Whether it's a lean univoice treatment or a fully dramatized dialogue spot, well-executed radio remains the medium in which writers and their words can conjure up the most vivid and most audience-participatory scenes. With wise selection of generic vehicle, the injection of PUNCH, and a commitment to the ten Radio Commandments, radio *will* sell. It will sell because it most directly and most intensely thrusts the audience into the picture-determination process. Guided by your well-wrought words, radio listeners can fantasize product benefits in use—and in use within the immediate intimacy of their own lives.

Above all, maintains Motel 6 spokesperson Tom Bodett, a radio spot is successful when "we're talking to somebody or having fun with them, and not making fun of them. They're not a target as much as a preferred customer."[28]

Endnotes

1. F. Joan Roger, "The Ecology of Radio," *NAB RadioWeek* (October 3, 1988), 8.
2. "*Adweek* Midwest Creative All-Star Team," *ADWEEK* (June 5, 1992), 54.
3. "Eureka!" *Radio Ranch Wrangler* (Fall 1991).
4. Jeffrey Schoot, "Virgil Shutze and His American Dream Machine," *Winners* (July 1988), 39.
5. Gary Provost, "The Secrets of Writing Powerful Dialogue," *Writer's Digest* (August 1987), 30.
6. "Ad Agency Creativity: Radio's Needed Dimension," *Broadcasting* (June 25, 1990), 46.
7. "The Funniest Spots," *ADWEEK* (June 22, 1987), 42.
8. Robert Snodell, "Why TV Spots Fail," *Advertising Age* (July 2, 1984), 18.
9. Steve Carmine, "You Can't Whistle the Announcer." Speech presented at the Detroit Radio Advertising Group 1986 Creative Seminar, November 11, 1986, at Troy, Michigan.
10. John Motavalli, "Turning Old Hits into New Jingles," *ADWEEK* (January 11, 1988), B.R. 35.

11. Ibid., B.R. 36.
12. Stephen Ford, "You, Too, Can Be a 'Music Man,' " *ADWEEK* (April 16, 1984), 18.
13. Richard Mercer, writing in "Monday Memo," *Broadcasting* (May 23, 1966), 24.
14 From *Light in August* by William Faulkner. Copyright 1932 and renewed 1960 by William Faulkner. Reprinted by permission of Random House, Inc., and Curtis Brown, Ltd., London.
15. Gary Provost, "Sound Advice," *Writer's Digest* (December 1985), 34.
16. Calvin Duncan and James Nelson, "Effects of Humor in a Radio Advertising Experiment," *Journal of Advertising*, XIV/2 (1985), 38.
17. Claudia Puig, "A Special Holiday Roast with Satirist Stan Freberg," *Los Angeles Times* (November 28, 1991), F.13.
18. Duncan and Nelson, 38–39.
19. Anthony Chevins, writing in "Monday Memo," *Broadcasting* (May 18, 1981), 22.
20. "Some Serious Talk about Laughs and Learning," *ASAP* (November/December 1989), 31.
21. Barrie Gillies, "Funny Business," *Winners* (October 1987), 22.
22. Philip LeNoble, "Show Advertisers How Radio Spots Deliver," *NAB RadioWeek* (June 11, 1990), 4.
23. "Ad Agency Creativity," 47.
24. Julie Schwartzman, "The Touchy Task of Talking to Teens," *ADWEEK* (April 6, 1987), H.M. 13.
25. Caroline Jones, letter to the editor, *ADWEEK* (January 31, 1983), 22.
26. Kenneth Chaffin, "Voices from The Broadcast Tower," *ASAP* (January/February 1988), 25.
27. Gerry Hartshorn, "Marketing without Formal Research," *NAB RadioWeek* (March 4, 1991), 5.
28. "Bodett Sheds Light on Motel 6 Success," *Broadcasting* (February 4, 1991), 29.

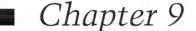

Chapter 9

Additional Radio Endeavors

The previous chapter covers the basics of radio commercial construction. In this chapter, we explore a variety of station-based writing challenges and also examine the special copy challenges posed by retail, co-op, and direct response radio advertising. As with Chapter 8, we begin by setting forth the appropriate noncopy data block that, in this case, services many in-house script assignments.

In-House Noncopy Data Block

When you are creating material that your outlet itself commissions, produces, and airs, the data block need be less formal than the standard commercial version. This is because your script is a piece of internal communication (like a memo) rather than something that must be sent to outside organizations. Nevertheless, for all but the smallest operations, the block should be detailed enough to facilitate production and tracking of the message by staffers other than those who wrote or requested it. Table 9–1 presents an arrangement that accommodates a significant amount of helpful information within a compact space.

    In this particular example, a maintenance promo is one intended to sustain the current audience for the show by reminding listeners of the benefits of staying with us. The completed items in this data block indicate that the promo has been ordered by Sid, the program director, and written by Thelma, the in-station copywriter. The blank items signify that it has not yet been produced (recorded) or finally approved by management. These dates, and the Accepted By line, will be inked-in later to monitor and document announcement completion.

    This data block format should *not* be used if the assignment is a commercial for an outside client. Even though such an advertisement may be produced and written in-house, it is still being generated for an external entity.

Table 9-1
Radio In-House Data Block

```
           WAAD CONTINUITY PRODUCTION ORDER

Subject: Bruce/Lucy Fall Maintenance    Order #: 1383
Date Ordered: 8/20/94                   Length: :30
Format: Univoice                        Start Date: 9/15/94
Ordered By: Sid Sharepoint              End Date: 10/13/94
Written By: Thelma Thesaurus            Scripted: 8/26/94
                                        Produced:
Accepted By:                            Approved:


.................................................

ANNCR: Days are getting shorter and those mornings getting
       darker. But you can keep your pre-dawn bright with
       WAAD's very own early-A.M. toast-burners, Bruce and
       Lucy . . .
```

Thus, the conventional commercial data block presented in Chapter 8 should be used, with the station name/call letters occupying the heading that would otherwise identify an advertising agency.

IDs and Transitions

Turning to actual copy construction, a station identification may just give the information required hourly by FCC regulations—the call letters immediately followed by the community to which the station is licensed. (The only material that can be inserted between these two items is the station frequency.) Often, however, this legal ID is followed by a brief promo or client billboard (*shared ID*) in order to fill a standard ten seconds of time.

An example of the shared ID, with two seconds for the government and eight seconds for the station's sales department, would typically be fashioned like this:

```
This is KTRE, Cedarton. Enrich your day with Nestor's Ice
Cream in fifteen dairy-delicious flavors. Nestor's Ice
Cream makes any meal a party.
```

For variety, the two parts of the ID can also be reversed:

```
Keep your smile, keep your teeth. Cranston's Sugarfree Gum
satisfies without danger of cavities. Chew Cranston's for
enjoyment and safety. This is KTRE, Cedarton.
```

A legal ID that is pressed into service for station promotion can be set up this way:

```
This is KTRE, Cedarton. The week's best music, today's news
and tomorrow's weather. All for you on the Big 102.
KTRE---your hits-happy radio station.
```

Or, it too can be juxtaposed and a mini-PSA thrown in as a public relations gesture:

```
Your hits-happy radio station doesn't want trees to be only
a thing of the past. Be careful with campfires. This is
hits-happy radio, KTRE---Cedarton.
```

Beyond the legal IDs mandated to air as close to the top of the hour as possible and at sign-on and sign-off, stations are free to signify themselves as often, and in any manner, that they see fit. In fact, most outlets schedule many more IDs than required by law as a means of reasserting their identity for the listener. Because these additional (*optional ID*) announcements are not compulsory, they need not even contain the name of the station's home city. Instead, optional IDs can be devoted exclusively to outlet image-building. They may therefore be shorter, or a good deal longer, than the traditional 10-second identification. Most often, optional IDs consist of straight copy that ties into a particular format, show, or personality while always making certain that the station is clearly positioned in the speaker's mind:

```
The Zoo Crew from the Nut Hut. All yours from Z-100.
```

```
Rich Hawkins with the hits on 'CAU-FM.
```

```
The music you remember from the station that never forgot.
68 WCBM.
```

(Above courtesy of Julie Sizemore, Affiliate Relations Director, JAM Creative Productions, Inc.)

```
Join Mary Price from midnight to five on Kickin'
Country 98.
```

We're 101---Gourmet FM---a full course of the music you
want to hear.

(Above courtesy of Rita Lilly, Unistar Radio)

This is Bruce Williams. Glad that we can share the night
together on WJNO Newsradio. AM 1230.

(Courtesy of Richard Greenhut, NBC Radio).

ANNCR: WLOL. (HEAVY LASER SFX) Now playin' more music.

JOAN
 RIVERS: Can we talk?

ANNCR: No! (LASER TRAILS OUT)

(Courtesy of Tom Gowan, Emmis Broadcasting's WLOL.)

The words of a loved one. Tender moments. A joyful reunion.
The 'Music of Your Life' brings it all back crystal clear
on WMAS, Springfield.

(Courtesy of Al Ham, Research Center, Huntington, Ct.)

Optional IDs, like those above are also known as *separators* or *liners* and should be regularly rewritten, updated, personalized, and localized for maximum listener impact. The station strives to rotate these separators throughout various parts of the day and on a week-to-week basis in order to have well-established identity without listener-boring redundancy. Thus, many such separators are usually required from the copywriter.

Some program directors will have you prepare distinct stylings for more precise segue tasks:

1. *Backsell* liners are for use at the end of a 'music set' (back-to-back records) and just before a 'stop set' (series of commercials and other announcements). Ideally, they should be perceived as a natural extension of the music:

That's another classic on WAAD. Your station for soft music
and more of it. Be sure to listen all day at work. Even
your boss will like the music on WAAD.

2. *Return* or *re-entry* liners segue from the end of the stop set back into the next music set. They should reiterate the station's promise/benefit to reinforce overall image:

Now, more of what you came back for: back-to-back
favorites; all in a row. WAAD.

3. *Sweep/transition* liners are quick reidentifiers in the middle of a music
   set (also known as a 'sweep'):

You're spending your evening with WAAD.

(Above liners courtesy of T.J. Lambert, Drake-Chenault.)

4. *Recaps* are backsell liners in which the copy restates the titles of the
   tunes just played. For maximum station recognition, recaps should begin
   with the call sign or dial position:

WQLR, Clear 106, just played---'I Just Called to Say I Love
You,' by Caravelli; Barbara Streisand and 'Somewhere,' and
'Memory' by Frank Pourcel.

(Courtesy of Jeffrey Mathieu, Kalamusic.)

5. Especially important for automated stations, *location* liners "personalize
   your station and involve listeners outside of your immediate city of
   license," instructs programming executive Dennis Soapes. "Location liners can also be used to target listeners in key neighborhoods:

Here's one for our friends in (neighborhood/city) on FM 102
WXXX."[1]

A tightly formatted station will even commission sets of liners geared to
time of day, day of the week, and season of the year:

Starting your day in the very best way, WAAD.

Middleburg's afternoons move to the sound of WAAD.

Another night of favorites, just for you on WAAD.

(Above courtesy of Bill Wolkey, Broadcast Programming.)

We keep you going on a Monday, at WAAD.

Clutter-free on a Thursday. This is WAAD.

You bring your radio and WAAD will bring the best music
this weekend.

```
Let us help you wrap packages with music from WAAD.
```
(Above courtesy of Renee Fleming, Century 21 Programming, Inc.)

```
Celebrating the birthday of our great nation, we're WAAD.

The joy of Thanksgiving to you and yours, WAAD, Middleburg.

Have a happy and safe New Year from WAAD.

A whisper of sweet somethings on Valentine's Day from WAAD.

WAAD; putting on our Sunday's best. Have a pleasant Easter.

Trick or treat! Happy Halloween from WAAD.
```
(Above courtesy of Billy Wolkey, Broadcast Programming.)

Optional ID material can also be cast in lyric form, usually by a writer at a specialty ("jingle") production house. In most cases today, these lyrics are very short *signatures* that tie station recognition to a clear listener life-style benefit. Here are four examples:

```
I'm getting up with Lite
It's another Houston dawn
Start the morning with a song on 93.7 FM---K-Lite.

Bumper to bumper, miles to go
I don't mind
I've got Lite Rock playin' on the radio
93.7 FM---K-Lite.

Meetings, reports, a million things to do
Everyday you play the songs that help me make it through
93.7---K-Lite.

I could never leave you
I listen all day long
You understand my feelings
You play my favorite songs
93.7 FM---K-Lite.
```

(Courtesy of Century 21 Programming, Inc. copyright 1990, Century 21 Programming.)

When expressed as lyrics, optional IDs will usually expend fewer words in the time allotted than would straight copy. You can't pack a music bed full of words and still expect that bed to play a balanced role in the total impact of the message. It should be clear, too, that the style of the music and the swing of the copy must mesh, not only with each other, but also with the overall image sound the station is striving to exemplify.

IDs constitute a station's most available and most important continuing public relations device. It is therefore vital that, whether lyric or straight copy, they be well written, well produced, and carefully oriented in consultation with station programming executives. More than any other type of material a copywriter creates, the ID reflects on the character and identity of the station for which it is constructed. Consequently, it is essential that copy and program personnel be operating on exactly the same wavelength when it comes to aural definition of what the station is, and of what it is striving to say about itself. In today's radio, *format* is everything. It imbues everything the station airs and everything the station sells or fails to sell. Continuity/programming clash makes for a disjointed, schizophrenic station personality that disrupts format and design integrity. The format will *never* be changed to fit the style of your continuity, so your continuity had better be a mirror image of that format from its inception. This rule applies to all continuity but especially to the ID material, which is supposed to promote and epitomize the format's essence.

Even the shortest ID should reflect the heart of your station image line—the one overriding statement that must adhere like glue to the listener's entertainment-seeking consciousness. This may be expressed in straight copy, a musical statement, or a combination of the two. But whatever its form, the line must embody the station and be almost infinitely expandable from both length and seasonal standpoints.

It is generally an efficient practice to ascertain the length of the longest ID requested by the programming department. Then, write this lyric or straight copy first so it can be the fountainhead out of which the shorter IDs flow. These comparatively brief, derivative announcements are thus known as *lift-outs*. Such a procedure not only saves on production costs but also ensures a tight consistency of station image throughout all dayparts and ID applications.

In articulating that image, "don't assume listeners know what your slogan means; tell them what it means," concludes radio consultant Rob Balon. "Simply put, the most eloquent station positioning liners are those that educate and translate for the listener . . . Communicate with the listeners in *their* words, not in yours . . . Save the broadcaster jargon for your next guest piece in the trades, and *concentrate on finding out how your listeners describe the things that your radio station does.*"[2] Thus, it's

```
Five 60's tunes in a row. Neon 92's morning guarantee to you.
```

rather than

```
Tune to Neon 92 for the longest classic rock sweeps in
morning drive.
```

As indicated earlier in this chapter, backsell and re-entry ID liners often do double duty as transitional devices between major programmatic elements. But these are not the only transitions that the radio copywriter may be called on to create. Sports coverage in particular frequently requires an extensive inventory of linking material. The aim here is not literary elegance but cogent, hard-working traffic-directing that 'takes care of business' while propelling the program forward as in the following hockey continuity:

The Herb Boxer Pre-Game Show---brought to you by your friends at Copper Country Ford-Lincoln-Mercury. Your volume price dealer with reliable service; located next to the Mall in Houghton.

. . . .

The first period is brought to you by Superior National Bank and Trust, with offices in Hancock, Hubbell, Baraga, and the Copper Country Mall. And by Aurora Cable Communication---providing Houghton-Hancock with a better picture. The switch is on---to Aurora.

. . . .

The second period comes courtesy of Maki Oil of Ripley, offering you 24-hour emergency fuel oil delivery and furnace repair. And by Thomas Ford-Mercury of L'Anse---where you can drive a little and save a lot.

. . . .

Coming up---the third period---through the courtesy of D & N Savings Bank with offices in Hancock and Calumet and the new Bank-Mart now open in K-Mart at the Copper Country Mall.

. . . .

Stay tuned for The State Farm Three-Star Show brought your way by your local State Farm agents: Ted Gast in Houghton, Gary Sands in Ontonagon and L'Anse, Art Vasold in Calumet, and Mike Lahti in Hancock. Like a good neighbor, State Farm is there.

(Courtesy of Jeffrey Olsen, WMPL and WZRK-FM.)

Sports and other live, out-of-studio events are not, of course, entirely predictable. So, sometimes, a copywriter must prepare *contingency continuity*, which announcers can use in a variety of possible situations. Here is a set of such lines designed to help the sportscasters get into the sponsor's commercials with as little disruption as possible. Like all professional transition copy, it does not call attention to itself but instead, helps conserve and direct that attention to the important event to follow:

(POSSIBLE USE: AT THE START OF THE GAME OR DURING THE PRE-GAME SHOW)

Hey, what a nice crowd out there today! Looks like about (ESTIMATE NUMBER) fans came out to watch the stars shine. To all of them and to all you fans listening to the game---this Bud's for you!

. . . .

(POSSIBLE USE: AFTER AN INJURY OR WHEN A DOUBTFUL PLAYER ENTERS THE LINE-UP.)

Do you believe that? It takes a lot of courage to be playing in such pain. But you've gotta hand it to the trainers, right? Yeah, for all you guys who help keep the players playing---this Bud's for you!

. . . .

POSSIBLE USE: WHEN A PLAYER MAKES A KEY PLAY ROUTINELY---LIKE KICKING A FIELD GOAL OR SINKING FREE THROW.)

What a play! Just like in practice! Now that's what makes these guys so good. They perform under pressure just like it was routine. So for everyone who looks as good during the game as they did in practice---this Bud's for you!

. . . .

(POSSIBLE USE: IN A TIGHT GAME SITUATION.)

Talk about tense situations! Boy, I'd hate to be in the coaches' shoes right now. But win or lose, they know how to handle the pressure---just like Budweiser knows how to

243

```
handle thirst. So for all you coaches pacing the
sidelines---this Bud's for you!
```

```
. . . . . . . . . . . . . . . . . . . . . . . . . . . . . . . . . . . . . . . . . . . . . . . . . . . . .
```

```
(POSSIBLE USE: LATE IN THE GAME WHEN THE TEAM IS HOPELESSLY
LOSING.)
```

```
This Bud's for all the fans who are still here and to all
of you still listening. Yes, to everyone who supports the
(TEAM NICKNAME) win, lose or draw. For all you do---this
Bud's for you!
```

(Courtesy of Annette Abercombie, Mutual Broadcasting.)

Program Promos

Many of the ID construction principles we've just discussed pertain to promotional continuity for individual programs, station personalities, or program series. Like IDs, program promos must mirror the station's overall sound. They also frequently serve transitional purposes:

```
Gary Havens playing the country hits in KIOV Country. And
by the way, there's more great country music with your
favorite starts on Live from the Lone Star Cafe every
Sunday night at 10:05 here on KIOV.
```

```
Big Lake Country Radio and Bill Robinson here on KJCK.
Listen to Swap Shop Monday through Saturday from 9:30 to
10:00 in the morning. If you have anything to buy, sell, or
trade, call us during Swap Shop at 238-0151.
```

(Above courtesy of Jon Potter, The Musicworks, Inc.)

Wherever possible, program promos should also exploit seasonal subjects in order to tie the feature more closely to what is in the listener's mind (and environment) at the time:

```
Look outside. It's finally Spring in New England. the
daffodils, the tulips, the azaleas, the dogwoods. The black
flies! It's finally time to get outside. Work the
flowerbeds, put in the vegetable garden. Your lawn needs
mowing already! And time to check in with WOKQ twice every
```

hour for the radar weather. Jim Witt and his staff
don't get to go outside---they're glued to their
radar screens watching the weather for you. On 97.5
WOKQ.

(Courtesy of Ramsey Elliot, Fuller-Jeffrey Broadcasting Companies, Inc.)

A special challenge arises when the program being promoted by the local outlet originates at a network. In such case, the best solution lies in copy prepared by the station's writer that is then voiced by the network's talent. Following is a promo that makes the most of such a situation by having the network personality plug not only his show, but also the local outlet's baseball coverage that frequently precedes it:

BRUCE: Hi, this is Bruce Williams of Talknet. Stick around
         after tonight's game, because after those ball
         players finish circling the bases, we'll cover all
         the bases concerning your financial matters. On
         Talknet. Right here on KIRO, Seattle.

(Courtesy of Richard Greenhut, NBC Radio.)

If the program in question is prerecorded, the show may help you write its own promo. By taking sound 'bites' from the feature and combining them with announcer commentary, you can create a multivoice promo with the impact of a movie preview:

(MUSIC: MELLOW SAX FEATURE AND UNDER)

PAUL: It's the same as when anyone dies, really.

ANNCR: Paul McCartney.

PAUL: You wish you told him all the stuff you really want
        to tell him. But you don't.

ANNCR: One half of one of songwriting's most influential
        duos.

PAUL: The last phone call I had with John was just very
        warm. We talked all about his kids. And about his
        cats. And about this and that.

ANNCR: On WLOL. To talk about it. And he does.

PAUL: I really don't want to come out as any kind of
        preacher for pot.

ANNCR: Tonight on Phil Houston's <u>Countdown Show</u>. Hear a living legend talk about his music, his new movie, his old friend. An exclusive in-person WLOL interview with Paul McCartney. Beginning at four this afternoon.

(<u>MUSIC: FEATURE TO TIME</u>)

(Courtesy of Tom Gowan, Emmis Broadcasting's WLOL.)

The same technique applies if it's a radio plug for a TV event. In that case, your script's 'bites' are simply pulled from the film or video soundtrack:

(<u>MUSIC: UNDER THROUGHOUT</u>)

ANNCR: The longest war ever fought in America wasn't between two armies---it was fought between two men!

TAPE: You will go to jail and this is the face that's gonna put you there.

(<u>MUSIC: FADE FURTHER</u>)

ANNCR: Tonight at 8, TV-50 presents a very special Detroit television movie premiere.

TAPE: I gotta protect the Teamsters, that's my job. (SFX: CROWD CHANTING 'HOFFA')

ANNCR: The untold story of a ten-year battle that would change America forever---'Blood Feud: Kennedy vs. Hoffa.'

TAPE: You're a spoiled runt. You couldn't get a job as a law clerk if you didn't have a millionaire for a father.

ANNCR: Starring Robert Blake as Jimmy Hoffa.

TAPE: Kid, I make it my business to know everybody who can help and anybody who can hurt me!

ANNCR: And Cotter Smith as Bobby Kennedy.

TAPE: Don't warn me, Jimmy, I don't like warnings.

```
ANNCR:  Watch the Detroit television premiere of 'Blood
        Feud: Kennedy vs. Hoffa.'

TAPE:   If Hoffa goes down, Bobby Kennedy goes down, too.

ANNCR:  Starting tomorrow night at 8 on WKBD TV-50.
```

(<u>MUSIC: STING</u>)

(Courtesy of Jeffrey Stocker, Mars Advertising.)

Outlet Promos

Sometimes the assignment is to plug the station or network as a whole rather than a single personality on it. One way this task can be performed is by an image song's lyric copy. Because we discuss music earlier in this and the previous two chapters, little more need be said here. When both lyric and the tune that transports it (1) mirror the essence of the outlet's format and (2) repeat the "what we do for you" promise, the resulting promo will prove a marketing plus.

```
SUNG:   Move right on Q
        Go right to the top
        On Q107 the hits never stop.
        Yeah, 107---it's right on Q
        Less talk---more music
        comin' to you.
        So slide to the right
        'bout as far as you can
        the hits are just waitin'
        for a twist of your hand.
        Hits happening right on Q
        Q107
        Q107
        Hits happening right on Q
        Riiiii-ght!
```

(Courtesy of WRQX Radio.)

More often in today's radio world, the outlet promo is spoken rather than sung and uses ID liner-type techniques in a more extended form. "Liners alone are not enough to get the [station positioning] idea across," maintains promotion veteran Jim Teeson. "You should submit an order to your traffic department for a flight of sixty- or thirty-second announcements and produce commercials for your station. . . . Use your creative copywriting skills to embellish your basic positioning statement."[3] "The foundation of every station image," adds promotion executive John Follmer, "is its personality. It is what makes it indigenous to its locale, yet different from the other stations it competes with. A station's defined personality is what is used to focus an image campaign and, an image campaign, in turn, helps build on that personality."[4] This 30-second New England outlet promo wraps its image statement around a clear expression of specific listener benefits:

```
What makes country music great? People the world over,
people in New Hampshire, Southern Maine and Northern Mass
agree: country songs talk about real life. Real people. You
can understand the words. Above all, country songs are fun.
And out of all the conceivable songs we could play, the
WOKQ personalities are workin' hard to select just the best
songs---and put them together just right. On Country
Favorites---97.5 WOKQ.
```

(Courtesy of Ramsey Elliot, Fuller-Jeffrey Broadcasting Companies, Inc.)

As with program plugs, if the outlet is a network affiliate, the copywriter can draft a local-enhancing statement for a network talent to voice. Such network assistance is readily available—provided your script also promotes that personality's show.

```
BRUCE:  This is Bruce Williams from Talknet. Meet me right
        here on 590 K-I-D at 6, weeknights. Call me with
        your questions on taxes, lawsuits, financial
        planning and money problems in general. Keep your
        dial at 590 K-I-D, 24 hours a day, for the best in
        local news coverage, weather, major sports, and of
        course, great music and entertainment. 590 K-I-D,
        Idaho Falls. One of the West's great radio stations
        for 59 years.
```

(Courtesy of Richard Greenhut, NBC Radio.)

Another outlet promo method is to use a dialogue. Most often, the dialogue is between two station or network personalities. However, the danger with this approach is that you will not involve the public because this technique results in two seller surrogates and *no* buyer who could ask the key questions. (Review the section on dialogue writing in Chapter 8.) An alternative is to cast both voices as listeners—one who knows your station and the other who has yet to discover it:

JACK: Yes, I've tried to choose the best all my life. In food, friends, leisure, etc.

DICK: Really?

JACK: Oh, yes. Nothing mainstream about me. I trickle down my own river and so forth.

DICK: What radio station do you listen to?

JACK: Hmmmm?

DICK: They say the best programming is on KCRW.

JACK: Oh, yes. K-C- uh, yes. Love it!

DICK: Do you listen to KCRW?

JACK: I wouldn't go to any other place on the dial.

DICK: What program?

JACK: Well---I don't have a fav---, Everything!

DICK: Do you listen to Morning Edition?

JACK: Oh, yes. I---yes, I do.

DICK: All Things Considered?

JACK: All things concerned, yes.

DICK: Considered!

JACK: Right, Love it.

DICK: How about Phil's Polka Parade?

JACK: Very fond of it, never miss it.

DICK: You big phony! There isn't such a show on KCRW!

JACK: I don't know that? I know that! I sensed you were joshing me, you scamp you!

DICK: You don't listen to KCRW at all!

JACK: What?

DICK: Not the great music, the exciting drama, the commentary, the news---

JACK: I do too!

DICK: What do they do on <u>Morning Becomes Eclectic</u>?

JACK: They talk about---electricity.

DICK: What?

JACK: The plugs, the bulbs, the wires, and that's wrong, right?

DICK: Right, wrong!

JACK: <u>So</u>, you found me out for the phony fool I am. Well, I deserve a good smack!

          (SFX: SMACK)

JACK: Thank you.

ANNCR: If you're not a regular KCRW listener, you deserve a good smack too!

          (SFX: SMACK)

JACK: Thank you again.

(Courtesy of Dick Orkin, Dick Orkin's Radio Ranch.)

Lyric, straight copy, or dialogue, an outlet promo must be conceived with one overriding principle in mind. As radio consultant Ed Shane puts it, "a station has to market itself not from how it perceives itself, but how it best can serve the listener."[5]

Enhancers and Features

In striving to solidify their position in an ever more fragmenting marketplace, radio stations, syndicators, and networks are constantly developing new copy-driven format embellishments. Some of these offerings are straight news or commentary and are thus outside the scope of this book. But in many cases, these devices consist of comedic entertainment bits injected on a regularly scheduled (feature) or occasional drop-in (enhancer) basis. These enhancers and features are designed to brighten the listener's day and encourage that listener's continued loyalty to our audio service.

A typical example is this 60-second bit from The American Comedy Network, one of a number of specialty syndicators whose copywriters generate such short-form materials:

LI: Hi, I'm Lee Iacocca with a message for all you middle-aged guys who think you've got to waste money on an overpriced <u>foreign</u> car to recapture your lost youth.

(<u>MUSIC: UP-TEMPO AND UNDER FOR LI</u>)

ANNCR: Introducing the new 'Mid-Life Chrysler' and fuel-injected 'Dodge Responsibility'; high-performance cars made in America for the man who doesn't know who he is!

        (SFX: CAR IGNITION, BIG START-UP, REVVING)

ANNCR: These babies are as sleek and sexy as that new secretary you just hired, but not quite as fast!

        (SFX: HUM OF SUNROOF OPENING)

ANNCR: Open up the sunroof and let the wind race through your thinning hair---

        (SFX: CAR RACING THROUGH STREET)

ANNCR: Settle into an extra wide seat for <u>your</u> extra wide seat---

        (SFX: CAR CONTINUES RACING)

ANNCR: And look into a brilliantly designed rear-view mirror that lets you see everything you've just left behind, <u>except</u> your wife and children---

        (SFX: WOMAN'S VOX HEARD CALLING IN THE DISTANCE: 'Honey!!!')

ANNCR: All this, plus a fool-injected engine that lets you accelerate away from all your obligations in under 6 seconds!

        (SFX: BIG SCREECHING STOP; CAR IDLES)

```
ANNCR:  And both cars have our standard 7-year itch, 70,000
        mile warranty!

           (SFX: DOOR SLAM)

LI:     So, test drive the all-new 'Mid-Life Chrysler' and
        'Dodge Responsibility' cars that take you where you
        want to go---even if you have no idea where that is!
```

(Courtesy of Andrew Goodman, The American Comedy Network.)

One advantage of such spoof commercials is that they tend to increase attention paid to the 'real' commercials being aired. Because listeners never know when an entertaining put-on is coming, they give more heed to every spot cluster.

Local copywriters can be just as bountiful a source of enhancers and features as syndicated or network wordsmiths. Whoever creates the material, it must serve as an integral component of station format and image. No enhancer or feature, no matter how well-conceived, can effectively complement every format and station positioning. The following local bit would probably be inappropriate on many radio stations. But on a Los Angeles–area rock outlet that targets males age 18 to 34, it blends in well with the overall listener-attracting strategy:

```
GUY:    Hi, this is Tom Bodacious from Motel Sex, where you
        can probably tell I'm darn excited about something
        brand spankin' new. You can still get a clean,
        comfortable room by the hour or by the day. Heck, if
        you want to stay a whole week, that would make us
        happier than pigs in slop. But clean sheets will be
        a little extra. The new-fangled stuff is a shiny new
        KNAC Pure Rock bumper sticker to let everybody know
        where you stand, and where you stayed. Of course,
        you still get your regular goodies: whips, chains,
        an ice bucket. And if you struck out again, we'll
        even get you an inflatable date. But you'll have to
        do all the talkin'. Now you don't have to stay with
        us to get your sticker. You can send a self-
        addressed, stamped envelope to KNAC Bumper Sticker,
        100 Ocean State Boulevard, Suite B-70, Long Beach,
        California, 90802. But think of all the fun you and
        your date will be missin'. Just remember, no
        sharp objects, please. I'm Tom Bodacious from Motel
        Sex; we'll leave the red light on for you.
```

(Courtesy of Ron Russ, KNAC.)

Among the most numerous features on contemporary radio are personal enrichment and helpful hints series. These brief segments are styled and selected with the needs of each station's target universe in mind. When brightly written, as in the following car-care module, they provide easily digestible and informative entertainment—perfect for the listener-friendly requirements of today's radio formats. As with any continuity, the copywriter must keep the message focused, interesting, and unequivocally under-standable without talking down to the audience.

BRO. #1: If you've ever been stuck steaming by the side of
the road, then you've probably asked yourself the
question we've all asked.

BRO. #2: Why me?

BRO. #1: We'll tell you because---

BOTH
BROS: We're the Rhodes Brothers, with a minute about
your car!

BRO. #1: Now, the reason you're boiling over maybe is
because you didn't check your fanbelt.

BRO. #2: (Singing) Fan belt's connected to the water
pump---

BRO. #1: Which pumps cooled water from your radiator right
back into your---

BRO. #2: Engine.

BRO. #1: That's it!

BRO. #2: What're we doing here?

BRO. #1: Talking about checking maybe two or three belts
under the hood, is all.

BRO. #2: And a serious warning---

BRO. #1: Yeah, the engine must be off when you're checking.

BRO. #2: Well, if you'd like future use of your fingers.

BRO. #1: Now, the belt must be tight to do its job, so
press you thumb down on the middle of the belt---

BRO. #2: Just like this.

253

```
BRO. #1:   No, your thumb. If it yields more than a quarter
           of an inch, it should be adjusted.

BRO. #2:   You can do it, or ask your mechanic.

BRO. #1:   Your favorite auto supply can give you some
           advice, and show you the tools you need.

BRO. #2:   Tools? I use my teeth.

BRO. #1:   Which explains a lot about your face. Now the
           other thing you're checking for is cracks and
           frays.

BRO. #2:   That's right!

BRO. #1:   Now do this, because you remember how lonely it
           gets at the side of the road.

BRO. #2:   That's it! A minute about your car.
```

(Courtesy of Rene Crapo, RJ Programming.)

On/Off-Air Listener Participations

Another means of hooking audience ears is the station-promoting contest. Some of these games take place on air, some off air, and some combine both on- and off-air activities. The copywriter's job in these matters is to (1) build listener enthusiasm; (2) clearly explain the rules and prizes; (3) link the contest unmistakably with the station and its image; and (4) accomplish all of this within thirty or, at most, sixty seconds.

Off-air participation promotions are usually tie-ins with one or more retail outlets. Thus, the contest copy assumes the additional burden of identifying who the retailers are. If, as in the following WWWY promo, a large number of client stores are participating, it is best to prepare a number of interchangeable tags or pieces of hole copy. In this way, all retailers receive equal mention without forcing your announcement to sound like a recitation of the Chamber of Commerce membership roster.

```
           Production Note: She speaks in a nursery-tale voice;
           He in a not-too-bright, cynical voice.

SHE:       Once upon a time, there were thirty-three little
           bears.
```

HE: Excuse me, that should be <u>three</u> little bears.

SHE: No, it's <u>thirty</u>-three little bears and they're really not so little. In fact, they're almost 4 feet tall.

HE: Wow! So there's about 11 Momma Bears, 11 Papa Bears, and---

SHE: No, you see, they're <u>all</u> Christmas Bears and they're <u>all</u> super-soft, cuddly, and down-right adorable.

HE: Can I see one?

SHE: You can see all thirty-three. They're at stores all over the Y-105 listening area.

HE: You say they're almost 4 feet tall?

SHE: Yep, and each store will give its bear away on December 21st. No purchase is necessary. <u>You</u> could win one of these giant, super-plush Christmas Bears and---

HE: Live happily ever after, right?

SHE: Actually, I was gonna say, 'And have a Merry Christmas.'

ANNCR: Register to win one of the Y-105 giant plush Christmas Bears at:

(TAG #1) Lincoln Center, Ketchum's Kornucopia, Tovey Shoes, The Big Blue Store, and Folger's Four-Season Florist.

(TAG #2) Gary Davis Music Makers, Elsberry's Greenhouse, The Fourth Street Bar, The Cosco Shop, and Steve's Taxidermy and Bass Shop.

(TAG #3) National Video, Tom Pickett Music, Ray's Marathon, Bradbury's Christmas Wonderland, Hull's Office Supply, and Dag's on 46-West.

(Courtesy of James Ganley, WWWY.)

When a continuing off-air promotion garners a winner, a little advance preparation can enable you turn the triumphant moment into an excitement builder for other listeners. By bringing a tape recorder and a release form along, WKHQ's Prize Patrol staffer captured a live actuality from which the station's writer could later harvest 'people-interest' excerpts to be bumpered with announcer copy:

ANNCR: 106 KHQ's Prize Patrol takes you to the streets
         every week to find you listening to 106 FM at work.

VOICE: (Screaming) Randy---

ANNCR: We searched high and low for Randy Weeter at Boze
         Wood Products in Harbor Springs.

VOICE: (Still screaming) We won for 'Take Your Radio to
         Work!'

ANNCR: We tracked him down---

VOICE: (Still screaming, now even louder) Randy!!!

ROB: I'm Rob Hazelton, 'Take Your Radio to Work Day'---

RANDY: Great!

ROB: What do you do here?

RANDY: I'm foreman over next door.

ROB: What are you doing over here? We almost couldn't
         find you.

RANDY: Just helping out.

ANNCR: If it's 'Take Your Radio to Work Day' it's KHQ-Cash
         on the spot.

BOB: Hey! One hundred---one, two, three, four, five and
         six. One hundred and six bucks!

ANNCR: And that's not all---

ROB: You've just won an on-the-spot massage for one hour,
         that's just yours, good for up to three people in
         your work place.

ANNCR: Three certificates---three people---three one-hour
        massages.

RANDY: We sure can use that.

ROB: And the money comes in handy, too.

RANDY: It sure does, I'm getting married in 4 months, it's
        going to help out a lot.

ROB: Great! Congratulations!

ANNCR: Each week brings a new 'Take Your Radio to
        Work Day' from the Fun and Games Department of
        106 KHQ.

(Courtesy of Tim Moore, WKHQ.)

Combination on/off-air participation announcements persuade listeners
to take some action (usually at one or more of the station's advertisers) that
qualifies them for involvement in later on-air activities. Such *value-added*
campaigns give sponsors more customer traffic for their advertising buck and
enhance the station's sales efforts. However, the copy must be listener-ori-
ented. It must depict the ease of taking part as well as show the relationship
of the off-air errand to the on-air fun:

VOICE: A crossword puzzle on the radio?

RICH: You bet! And you can win free groceries for one year
        from P&C and Radio 57/WSYR, when you play along.
        Pick up your crossword puzzle entry form at your
        local P&C Store and listen for the on-air clues.
        Only on Radio 57/WSYR.

VOICE: I'm sharpening my pencil!

RICH: The fun starts on March 17th with the last word in
        crossword puzzles from P&C, the Prize Champion, and
        Radio 57/WSYR.

For this particular contest, the on-air copy clues were set up in this manner:

ANNCR: Sharpen your pencil. It's time for another
        clue in the Radio 57/WSYR and P&C crossword
        puzzle---

```
ONE ACROSS--Radio 57/WSYR is the blank Weather
Station; you can depend on it.

Keep listening for the next crossword puzzle clue on
Radio 57/WSYR.
```

(Courtesy of Yvonne Sacripant, WSYR.)

Figure 9–1 illustrates another version of the on/off air event. This direct mail piece echoes the on-air copy contest directions and also provides a mail-in card that establishes eligibility for an additional prize. The campaign, in the words of KHOP Promotion Manager Gary Demaroney, is "designed to stimulate longer and new listening habits within our established audience and in a conversion audience."[6]

The exclusively on-air participation event depends on the telephone to achieve its goal. Sometimes, the station will call out to potential players at random. But this can result in listener-boring busy signals, no answers, and other unusable reactions. You're ensured of a player, however, is the game is designed so that willing participants call *in*. Thus, the copy emphasizes how easy it is for anyone to play right now. The copywriter would also pen a second announcement as an on-air response to the caller as well as an encouragement for audience play in the future.

Notice that the following on-air contest makes no scripted provision for losers. That's because it was designed for initial off-air call answering. Only successful respondents were then fed onto the airwaves. This procedure, of course, makes the contest seem more winnable and exciting as long as the rules are not so difficult that few contestants ever get broadcast.

```
ANNCR:  It's time to catch the new wave across America!
        Identify the secret word from the following
        clue---and you could win a microwave oven.

HOLE:   Here's clue number two: I'm used as a greeting, when
        you move your hand. And live on the ocean, rather
        than land.

ANNCR:  That's the clue for this hour's secret word. A
        random caller now who can tell me the word wins a
        microwave oven. 3-3-3--W-E-E-P. What's the word?
        Call in your answer now at 3-3-3--W-E-E-P.

ANNCR:  We have a winner! Who are you---and what's the
        secret word?
```

Figure 9-1

(Courtesy of Ramsey Elliot, Fuller-Jeffrey Broadcasting Companies, Inc.)

```
                (CALLER RESPONSE HERE)

    ANNCR:  That's it! You've won a brand new microwave oven!
            Keep track of the answers, and you might win our
            grand prize: two round-trip tickets on American
            Airlines to the destination of your choice.

    HOLE:   Once again, secret word number 2 is 'Wave.'

    ANNCR:  The Campbell Microwave Institute---leading the way
            in microwave cooking. Listen for your next chance to
            win a microwave oven---tomorrow morning at 11:20 on
            10-80, W-E-E-P.
```

(Courtesy of Rita Lilly, Unistar Radio.)

Interviews and Semiscripts

It has been stressed that in order to survive, today's radio station must project a sense of active involvement in the lives of listeners. As we've discussed, participation contests contribute to this goal through concise continuity bursts. Radio interview programs, meanwhile, address this task in more lengthy segments. The community discussion show, consisting primarily of conversations between a station personality and pertinent guests, is a common mechanism for catering to audience interests. To service a local (or, for that matter, national) interview show, a copywriter must perform several duties. First, as in the creation of program promos, the writer must set up a vibrant sense of expectation.

Therefore, the interview introduction, although brief, entails three distinct functions: (1) arouse listener interest, (2) provide a tight capsule of information that puts the guest and host in perspective, and (3) make the guest feel comfortable and at home. The same attention-getting devices discussed in previous chapters can be used to accomplish the first objective. The writer might need to structure these opening lines in such a way that they can also be used as lift-outs that serve periodically to promo the interview for several days before its airing.

Second, the interview intro needs to trace the essential parameters of the subject without being deliberately evasive on the one hand, or giving away the discussion's main revelation on the other. To open a drug abuse show by saying, "Here is a man who was hooked on heroin but after ten months of the new megatherapy is healthy and free," would leave the listener with little reason to stay tuned.

Finally, because many guests are not professional communicators, the interview introduction must strive to put the individual at ease. In this context, overpraise is just as dangerous as unabashed derision. Too many guests have suffered through introductions that were so overzealous they hardly dared open their mouths for fear of destroying that image. Write a deserved compliment or two for the guest but refrain from using intimidating superlatives.

The interview's closing or "outro" also has three intertwined purposes: (1) re-identify the guest and his or her topic/qualifications for late tuners-in, (2) also re-identify the host and program as well as (3) briefly promo today's next guest or the guest on the series' next show. As in the intro, the third function is fraught with the greatest dangers. The audience must be sufficiently intrigued about the next guest that they will tune in or stay tuned. But at the same time, you cannot demean the contribution just made by the current guest. The outro that seems to imply, "Once we get this turkey out of here, there's a really great person we want you to meet," is an unintentional but unforgivable disservice to the guest who's just finished. The opposite extreme, which might be accidentally conveyed as, "Wish we could bring you back but we've already scheduled some city sewage guy," serves the future guest no better.

The body of the interview might also require the copywriter's attention. You may be asked to prepare a list of key questions that can be put to the guest and that are guaranteed to elicit more than one-word responses. Many program hosts do not have the time, and some do now have the brainpower, to read up on the topic on which the guest is going to expound. Carefully worded and prechecked questions make the host look suitably knowledgeable, keep the guest comfortable and self-assured, and allow the interview to harvest the expertise or point of view for which the guest was invited in the first place.

Particularly if accompanied by commercial and continuity inserts, this list of questions, together with the fully scripted intro and outro, could be said to constitute a *semiscript*—a skeletal framework that allows the show to be extemporaneous while still adhering to an established announcement schedule and preordained set of objectives. The continuity writer must therefore sketch in the essential subject, pace, and tone of the show while allowing persons actually on air to flesh out the program within those guidelines. In semiscripting, the writer succeeds when the show displays a structured spontaneity that keeps the listener unaware it was preplanned at all.

A more limited derivation of the standard semiscript entirely omits the question as well as most outros. It concentrates almost exclusively on carefully fashioned intros and tight transitions between the program and the commercial messages that punctuate it. Normally, this version of the semiscript is used when the interviewer is an experienced communicator/interrogator adept at drawing out guests without major reliance on a set of

261

preplanned questions. *FOCUS*, a daily talk/discussion show aired by Detroit's WJR, has just such a host. A composite *FOCUS* program is reproduced below:

```
PRE-REC.
CART:      From Studio D, this is J. P. McCarthy's Focus.


(MUSIC: THEME UP, UNDER AND OUT)


CART:      WJR presents an active view of life and living in
           the Great Lakes Area, a lively look at people,
           places, events and attitudes. Put into focus
           by---J. P. McCarthy.


J. P.:     Paul, thank you very much. In Focus today, the
           senior managing editor for the Detroit Free Press,
           Neal Shine, to give a postmortem on last
           year---what was interesting, what was significant.
           Also, an update on one of the major Detroit
           riverfront projects; Harbortown---how it's going
           this chilly Monday in January. All of that, in
           Focus, in just a minute.


CART:      Today's Focus program is being brought to you in
           part by the Oreck Excel---the famous 8-pound
           upright hotel vacuum.
           _____


           POS. #1 Oreck spot

           POS. #2 Detroit Auto Show spot
           _____


J. P.:     Our first guest in Focus today is a familiar face
           from the back page of the Free Press--Neal Shine.
           I'm told he's the father confessor to about 90% of
           the writers at the Detroit Free Press; probably
           because he hired most of them. They come to him
           with their problems, for his suggestions. Neals'
           been a chronicler of Detroit and Southeast
           Michigan since his triumphant return from those
           bitter wars at Camp Pickett, Virginia, back in the
           1950s. He's making his annual visit with us to
```

take a look at the year just past: the good, the
bad, and the awful. Good afternoon, Neal---

(INTERVIEW #1)

The Detroit Free Press' Neal Shine. One of the big
downtown riverfront projects that we referred
to--Harbortown--discussed with two principals in
just a moment.

POS. #3 Joe Muer Restaurant spot

POS. #4 Henry Ford Community College spot

CART: You're in tune with the interesting interviews
       of J. P. McCarthy's <u>Focus</u> show. On WJR,
       Radio 76.

J. P.: My next guests in <u>Focus</u> are involved in one of the
        most ambitious of the the Detroit riverfront
        projects---Harbortown. So for an update on how
        it's gone, how it's going, and where it's going,
        it's a pleasure to welcome the president of
        American National Resources, Larry Marantette, and
        the president of MichCon Development Corporation,
        Dan Kern. These two companies are joint owners of
        this enterprise. Are your two firms connected in
        any other way?

(INTERVIEW #2)

Danny Kern from MichCon Development Corporation
and Larry Marantette from ANR. We'll see you on
<u>The Morning Show</u> from 6:15 to 10:00 tomorrow.
And in <u>Focus</u> tomorrow, our special guest will
be Detroit Free Press columnist Robin Abcarian,
who will show us her tattoo right here on the
radio!

(<u>MUSIC: SNEAK IN THEME UNDER</u>)

```
CART:     Today's Focus program has been brought to you in
          part by the Oreck Excel, the famous 8-pound
          upright hotel vacuum.
```

(MUSIC: FEATURE TO TIME)

(Courtesy of Marilyn Gordon, WJR.)

Semiscripts for preproduced entertainment programs tend to be more lengthy because written continuity must be injected more frequently to segue the multiple musical and/or verbal segments. Each individual piece of copy, however, is usually relatively short. People want to listen to the tunes/personalities themselves—not to long stretches of announcer copy about them. The writer's job is to deftly establish essential flow and identifications and then get out of the way. Notice the conciseness of these excerpted continuity segments from a syndicated program entitled *The Beatles—Fifty Best*:

```
(1)   I Want to Hold Your Hand,, the Beatles first U.S.
      release, arrived three weeks before they did and the
      Americans loved it. It remained at the number one
      position on the U.S. charts a full seven weeks---a
      record that rivaled Elvis Presley's best
      accomplishments.

(2)   I Saw Her Standing There was the 'flip side' of I Want
      to Hold Your Hand. Like dozens of Beatles songs, it
      was competing with another Beatles' song at the same
      time for the top spot.

.................................................................

(17)  If I Fell was a behind-the-scenes version of something
      the Beatles had already done on-stage on THE ED
      SULLIVAN SHOW. That 'something' was John Lennon and
      Paul McCartney singing into one microphone. Until
      then, all four were separated in the studio by several
      feet. Close-up camera angles on TV required the
      staging that led to memorable vocals in later
      recording sessions.

(18)  I'll Cry Instead was one of six songs from the movie
      soundtrack of A HARD DAY'S NIGHT. It was recorded at
      the Abbey Road studios under the guidance of another
      Beatles' idol, Carl Perkins.
```

(19)   I'm Happy Just to Dance with You was one of three
       songs The Beatles recorded on their first-ever 'Sunday
       Session.' Since they were able to record three songs
       in three hours on Sunday, March 1st, 1964, they tried
       on several Sundays after that. They were never that
       lucky again.

(50)   The Long and Winding Road was first intended and
       recorded as a Paul McCartney solo in 1968. The
       original tapes, with just Paul and a piano, were
       enhanced---adding full orchestration and production by
       American pop legend Phil Spector. However, the effort
       became 'the straw that broke the camel's back.' Paul
       McCartney went to court to try to stop Spector and
       John Lennon from releasing the version that went to
       the top of the charts. That ended the band.

(Note: The following copy can be re-written by your station as a wrap-up.)

Trying to put a 50-song boundary on the limit of The
Beatles hits is like trying to lasso a bronco with dental
floss. Notoriously absent from this list are classics like
Michelle, Baby, You Can Drive My Car, Here Comes the Sun,
Fool on the Hill, A Little Help from My Friends and dozens
more. In all, they produced more number one songs than
anyone before or since: an incredible 21 top-of-the-chart
hits. Truly, their likes will never be seen or heard again.
Maybe the reason The Beatles are still so incredibly
popular comes from the old saying: 'There is nothing so
powerful as an idea whose time has come.' In the case of
The Beatles, their time came---and it has never left.

(Courtesy of Edith Hilliard, Broadcast Programming.)

Presentations like the above are known as BYO (bring your own) types. The
syndicator provides the script and the music. The local station uses (brings)
one of their own air personalities to voice the copy. This gives the finished
product a customized and station-enhancing flair.

Special Commercial Challenges

Before closing this chapter on additional radio endeavors—and our entire
three-chapter radio section—we need to examine three kinds of aural adver-

tising that present unique difficulties. To an extent, these problem categories overlap. But each category is discussed separately as a means of revealing its special requirements.

Retail Advertising

This category embraces all the copy generated for local outlets (both locally and nationally owned) that sell a variety of consumer goods and services directly to the general public. Traditionally wedded to newspaper advertising, these retailers have been one of the most overlooked but now one of the most important targets for radio sales departments. Unlike other clients, retailers are looking for *results today*—not just for general image building or brand awareness. They tend to measure these results in terms of (1) the traffic through their stores and (2) the goods moved out the door. Most successful retailers are good pitchmen—they know their products well and know how to describe them in order to consummate sales.

Radio copywriters are therefore well advised to gain a working knowledge of their respective retailing communities. This knowledge-gathering should include conversations with retailers, noting the lines that flow most glibly from their mouths as they talk about their products. The retailer has probably used these phrases on customers for years—and used them successfully or they would not be a continuing part of his or her persuasive arsenal. The copywriter who can encapsulate those statements in a spot is thus not only profiting from a consumer-oriented approach that has already demonstrated its worth but is also making the commercial more appealing to the retailer, who will have a personal affinity for radio messages that use those favored pitches. In the following station-written commercial, client-proven lines like "the professionals in residential and automotive glass," "specialize in auto insurance claims," and "the bona fide doctors of broken glass" dramatize the selling scenario for both the audience and the advertiser.

```
(SFX: STADIUM CROWD)

VINCE:   There's the pitch and---(CRACK OF BAT, CROWD ROAR)
         the kid hits it right outta the park and (DISTANT
         GLASS CRASH) right into a beautiful vintage '56
         Caddy out in the lot! What a gem the car was. And
         what a home run!

BUD:     That little league player better run home, Vince,
         and tell his Dad to call Van Koonse Glass. They're
         the bona fide doctors of broken glass.
```

VINCE: And what a great glass team they are, Bud. Just take
a look at the Van Koonse stats: in business since
1946 as the professionals in residential and
automotive glass.

BUD: They specialize in auto insurance claims, and
they'll help you out with the paperwork. That way
you can get back on the road fast.

VINCE: Sounds good, Bud. Okay, here's our next batter up.
Tommy Watkins, eleven years old and---(CRACK OF BAT)
what a slugger!

(LOUD GLASS CRASH)

BUD: Oowwwwh!

VINCE: Whew! Good thing Van Koonse Glass does specialty
items like the windows in this broadcast booth. Hey
Frank---call the bona fide doctors of broken glass
at 542-7432. Van Koonse Glass here in Santa Rosa.
That's right---542-7432. Uh, better call a doctor
for Bud too.

(Courtesy of Ramsey Elliot, Fuller-Jeffrey Broadcasting Companies, Inc.)

In spots for multiple-product retailers such as grocery and department or discount stores, the radio copywriter encounters an additional difficulty. Comfortable with and accustomed to newspapers, these merchants will want you to compress all the product pictures and price balloons from a half- or even full-page print ad into one grossly overloaded radio minute. The resulting laundry-list radio commercial makes little or no impact on the listener because not enough time can be devoted to any one item to have it properly situated on the stage of the listener's "mind's eye." The alternative is to find a strong central concept on which the listener can focus and from which individual products can be hung like ornaments on a well-proportioned Christmas tree. The following "what's in a K-Mart bag" idea embraces several months' worth of items without fragmenting the selling statement the spot is commissioned to register.

KID: 'What I Learned This Summer,,' by T. R. Knight.
This was my eleventh summer, and I've wised up
since my tenth summer. Now I can tell what's
going on by what my Mom brings home from K mart.

My Mom is smart. She always shops at K mart
because K mart always has what she wants on sale.
In June, she came home with a good K mart bag.
Tennis shoes, shorts, T-shirts, and a softball
glove. That's a good K mart bag. Later in the
summer she brought home another very good K mart
bag. Swimming suit and more jeans. Summer stuff.
Very good bag. But, a few weeks ago, I found a
bad K mart bag. It was full of Back-to-School
stuff from the Back-to-School Sale---notebooks,
lunch bags, school clothes. This is a bad K mart
bag. Keep your eyes on those K mart bags. And
watch out for one full of bad news Back-to-School
stuff. It means summer's almost over. It means
washing your hair a lot and wearing good shirts.

SINGERS: AT K MART.
           WE'VE GOT IT AND
           WE'VE GOT IT GOOD.

(Courtesy of Sheila I. O'Donnell, Ross Roy Inc., Advertising.)

It is vital that, no matter what (or how many) goods and services the local outlet is pushing, a distinct and stable personality is maintained in your copy. "Typically," chides station KHAT general manager Dan Charleston, "local retailers run four different spots, written and voiced four different ways on four stations. There's no consistency. Their image is a jumble, and awareness plummets."[7] Whether you're an in-station or an agency writer, you cannot allow this to happen. If radio doesn't establish clear marketplace identity for the retailer, stations as well as agencies will lose that retailer's patronage.

Make certain that your copy sells as consistently and as hard on the air as do those retailers back at their stores. Construct copy that is sales-oriented—copy that speaks directly, conversationally, and cohesively to the wants of both prospect and retailer. Good point-of-purchase salespeople don't just push a product, they solve a problem. They just don't persuade, they explain. And they seem to listen as much as they talk:

ANNCR: Alright, so you were hoping for some silky, sensuous
        lingerie for Valentine's Day---and he got you a
        subscription to The Betty Crocker Newsletter. So
        what are you gonna do? Bake a cake? NO! You're gonna
        go to Manhattan Unmentionables and treat yourself to
        an 'After Valentine's Day' present. And you're gonna
        save money. Because this Thursday, Friday and

```
Saturday only it's Manhattan Unmentionable's big
'After Valentine's Day Sale.' Prices are already
reduced at Manhattan Unmentionables---but this
Thursday, Friday and Saturday only, they'll be
knocking an additional five to twenty percent off
everything in the store. Save on stockings, baby
dolls, negligees, camisoles, teddys---by all the
best names. All five to twenty percent off the
already reduced prices. So go to Manhattan
Unmentionables this Thursday, Friday and Saturday,
on Kelly Road four blocks south of Nine Mile. And
get yourself something really sexy. Then, when he
asks you to model it, you tell him thanks for The
Betty Crocker Newsletter---but he can't have his
cake and eat it too. Manhattan Unmentionables.
```

(Courtesy of Rick Wiggins, WDFX.)

Co-Op Advertising

In a cooperative (co-op) enterprise, the manufacturer shares the cost of advertising its product with the local retailer. Thus, all the pitfalls associated with retail advertising per se can also be encountered in attempting to fashion co-op spots. In addition, the copywriter must wrestle with the problem of two co-equal clients who share a contractual right to co-star status. It is essential that the listener be able to discern which is the brand (manufacturer) name and which the retailer (store) name. If, for example, Gladstone's Shoe Store is featured in a co-op spot with Dexter Shoes, and the listeners are led by the copy to look for the Dexter Shoe Store, they might pass right by Gladstone's, to the long-term detriment of both clients.

As a general rule, it is usually less confusing either to (1) start and end with the brand name, focusing on retailer identity in the center of the spot or (2) devote the first part of the message to the product and the last part to where that product can be obtained. This doughnut commercial for Andersen Windows uses the first method—a practice very common when the manufacturer supplies the doughnut (and pays the bulk of the advertising costs).

```
SINGER:  Come home to quality. Come home to Andersen.
         Come home to quality. Come home to Andersen.

ANNCR:   Andersen introduces a double-pane insulating glass
         more energy efficient than triple-pane. It's their
         new High-Performance insulating glass---optional
```

in Andersen Windows and gliding patio doors from Miller-Zeilstra Lumber. It's good news for homeowners here in Western Michigan because its special transparent coating keeps radiant heat indoors where it belongs in winter---reduces heating costs---keeps you comfortable in cold weather, even next to windows. For specific details about the new Andersen option---High-Performance insulating glass---talk to the experts at Miller-Zeilstra. They've been serving Grand Rapids area homeowners for over 50 years. Miller-Zeilstra is at 8-33 Michigan Northeast, just east of Eastern. Open daily 'til 6, and Saturdays 'til 4.

SINGER: <u>Come home to quality. Come home to Andersen</u>.

(Courtesy of James White and Paul Boscarino, WOOD Radio.)

The second method of co-op spot construction is known as the dealer tag technique. It initially gives heavy stress to product benefits and then turns exclusive attention to the local retailer. The store may be promoted in the first portion of the spot but generally not by name in order to minimize the danger of listener confusion.

ANNCR: Wisconsin's got Summerfest, and Winterfest. Now the biggest fest of all---Recyclerfest. And you don't even have to wait until summer. It's going on now at every Toro dealer in town. During Toro's Recyclerfest, you'll save on every single Toro Recycler mower in stock. Get behind the wheels of a Toro Recycler and mow your way through the summer with ease. Now, during Recyclerfest, the Toro Recycler mower is more affordable than ever before. Toro Recyclers start at just $299. With a Toro Recycler, your lawn can have that just-manicured look without bagging. So don't just mulch. Recycle with a Toro during Toro's Recyclerfest. This is the one fest you can't afford to miss. Sensational sale prices and no payments 'til October make owning a Toro Recycler mower easier than ever. Visit one of these Toro dealers today:

```
TAG #1:   In Depere, see Ambrosius Sales and Service or
          VanEvenhoven Hardware.

TAG #2:   In Green Bay, see Mathu's Appliance and Power,
          Pamp's Outboard, or Paulson Hardware.
```

(Courtesy of Paul Boscarino, WNFL/WKFX.)

When either (or both) of the parties to the co-op is extremely familiar, the copywriter can intersperse their names more freely. Because everyone in the target universe knows what a Chevy truck is, the following agency-written spot is able to scatter the dealer's name throughout the copy without danger that the listener will confuse manufacturer and retailer identities.

```
ANNCR:   Which trucks can you lean on, really depend on? You
         guessed it: tough Chevy trucks. Through the years,
         more folks have leaned on more Chevy trucks than any
         other make. And right now, (DEALER NAME) has a good
         selection on hand. Choose from tough, full-size
         Chevy Pickups with eager-to-work Vortec V-6
         power---the most powerful standard six-cylinder
         engine put in a half-ton pickup. (DEALER NAME)
         features a good selection of Chevy S-10 Pickups,
         too. They're bigger trucks than most imports, so
         you really get your money's worth. And check out
         (DEALER NAME'S) supply of versatile S-10 Blazers.
         It's America's most popular sport utility. Finally,
         look over his supply of new Chevy Astro Vans. You
         get van-like convenience, station-wagon comfort, and
         driving ease. Trucks you can lean on. They're all
         here at (DEALER NAME) right now. And they're ready
         to go at prices that are downright appealing. Stop
         by (DEALER NAME, ADDRESS) soon. Chances are, he's
         got just the right truck for you to lean on for
         years to come.
```

(Courtesy of Frederick Gordon, Lintas Campbell-Ewald Advertising.)

Whatever technique is used, the co-op copywriter must recognize that the manufacturer plays a determining role in the copy approval process. Often, stations obtain approval by reading the copy directly to the manufacturer over the phone. Such precautions are essential. If the manufacturer does not believe its wares and name have been adequately showcased in the commercial, it will not reimburse the local merchant for a portion of the airtime. Because the merchant counts on such reimbursement, the copywriter had better make certain that the script fully justifies its payment—or risk losing a local client.

Everything discussed so far in this section is known as a *vertical co-op*—the joint marketing of the product/service creator and the local outlet that actually conveys that product/service to the consumer. *Horizontal co-op,* also known as *tie-in advertising,* is a little different. In this type of enterprise, two or more manufacturers or two or more retailers come together for a joint promotion. Thus, a cereal company and an orange juice producer may use spots extolling the merits of a nutritious breakfast—defined as a blend of cornflakes and o.j. In an example of the other breed of horizontal co-op, several stores may join forces to get you through their adjacent doors. This is quite common in downtown merchant or mall co-op spots like the following. As in any retail ad, the trick is to find a central concept strong enough to carry the weight of the individual pieces without dropping message clarity in the process.

```
(SFX: AUDIENCE APPLAUSE)

LAURA:    'Best Buys' for thirty, Bob.

HOST:     Alright---the answer is: 'Has 125 doors, six
          silver screens, up to 18 thousand wheels' (SFX:
          LOUD BUZZER)---the question, Laura?

LAURA:    What is---uh---the Capitol Building!

HOST:     Huh?

LAURA:    ---uh---and Cinema Six!

HOST:     Noooooo

LAURA:    ---on a very loooonnngg train!!???

HOST:     You're reaching, Laura---(SFX: BUZZER)---Richard,
          to steal.

RICHARD:  (Arrogantly) What is---Wonderland Mall.

              (SFX: AUDIENCE SCOFFS)

HOST:     What is Wonderland Mall---is correct!

              (SFX: BELLS RING, AUDIENCE APPLAUSE)

LAURA:    (Incredulous) Wonderland Mall???
```

```
HOST:       Tell 'em about it, Johnny!

ANNCR:      Bob, Wonderland Mall---conveniently located in
            Livonia at Plymouth and Middlebelt Roads---offers
            125 different stores. Six movie theaters. Nearly
            2-dozen food specialty shops and restaurants. And
            more. Including---The Miss Wonderland Pageant,
            coming Friday, January 29th, starting at 6 P.M.
            Why go to Dearborn or anyplace else; when your
            place to shop's only minutes away. Bob?

LAURA:      But what about this '18 thousand wheels' stuff,
            huh?

RICHARD:    (Haughtily) 18 thousand, divided by 4, yields a
            numerator of 45 hundred---the exact number of
            free, lit parking spaces available at Wonderland.

LAURA:      Hey---he's got it scribbled on his palm!

RICHARD:    (Defensive) Do not! It's---a birthmark.

HOST:       Uh---tune in again next time---

LAURA:      (Sarcastically) Oh! Didn't know birthmarks came in
            green ballpoint!

SINGERS:    WONDERLAND---WONDERLAND MALL!
```
(Courtesy of Christopher Conn, WHYT-FM.)

Notice one thing more about the Wonderland Mall commercial. The announcer's speech sets up a *verbal doughnut*. After he says, "Including—," the master spot goes to blank tape for several seconds so that Wonderland's current event can be specified without the need to recut the entire production. This particular 'hole copy' ends with "starting at 6 P.M.," and we are back to the permanent body of the commercial.

Direct Response Advertising

In DR (also known as *per inquiry*) advertising, there is no local merchant. Instead, the commercial itself must consummate the sale by having the listener call or mail in an order. Thus, the direct-response spot must not only create the desire to own but also achieve the decision to buy. While it is said that advertising in general is the process of "diverting the consumer past the merchant's door," the DR message must work as the functional substitute for that door and the point-of-purchase salespeople who normally stand behind it. This means, says Ketchum Direct's president, Maryalice Fuller, that "direct response has to be incredibly clear, incredibly precise. Far more so than with all other forms of advertising. And you don't just get that kind of clarity and precision without the highest attention to creativity."[8]

Because of the selling and delivery burdens imposed on it, direct response copy does not have the time to be artsy or allegorical. Every word must be directed not just to the sell, but also to the activation of the purchasing decision through dialing or writing in. What is more, with DR, it soon becomes unequivocally apparent whether you have succeeded or failed based on how many units of the product your copy has actually moved. "Everything we and our agencies do," reveals direct marketer Thomas McAlevey, "is designed, executed, placed and measured in terms of cost per lead, appointment, and finally, sale. I found out quickly that creative egos and Clio-seeking writers and art directors had no place in the direct business, where communication is only judged to be successful if the target prospect acts, *in a measurable way*, in favor of the product."[9]

One can't blame poor store location or limited shelf space for a failed direct-response campaign because the commercial *itself* is that store and that shelf as well as the emotional/rational selling appeal. Direct response "is a real challenge for creative people because it's a test of their skills," points out agency owner Martin Puris. "There's a direct relation between what you're doing and how the product is doing. You know immediately whether the commercial you wrote is or isn't working. That's scary for a lot of creative people."[10]

To cope with DR fear, familiarize yourself with the following seven DR-mastering principles. They, along with what we've already discussed about effective radio writing in general, should outfit you with the confidence you need to make the direct-response landscape less foreboding.

1. Prepare Them for Action at the Top of the Copy. Because listeners are going to be urged to call or write, provide advance notice for them to 'get pencil and paper ready,' or to 'listen for our toll-free number at the end of this message.'

2. Show How the Product Can Impinge on the Listener's Life. Like any effective piece of salesmanship, the DR spot involves solving problems for people. But because these people can't check the product out in the store first, the DR commercial must be a *demonstrated* problem-solver before a listener is willing to part with some money.

3. Make Product Exclusivity Unmistakable. Lines like 'This product is not available in any store' inform the listener there is no alternative to buying from our client. Direct response will never be direct if the audience feels they have the option to shop around.

4. Take Listener Objections into Account. You don't want to replace one prospect doubt with another. 'You pay nothing now,' or 'certified safe by Underwriter's Labs' are lines that show the listener you have nothing to hide and make the buying decision a less apprehensive one.

5. Clearly and Repeatedly State Product Cost. Listeners know there's a price to everything. So don't arouse suspicion by attempting to conceal it. If the initial mailing is 'free,' *free* becomes the price and should also be repeated. This does not, however, give you the right to obscure the cost of succeeding installments.

6. Stress the Need for Immediate Action—But Don't Make the Deadline Too Near. Just as we don't want our prospects to assume that there are in-store alternatives to buying from our client, we also don't want them to postpone their purchase or reply into the indefinite future. Furthermore, a radio DR commercial leaves nothing behind as does a newspaper coupon or a direct-mail piece. So even if the audience has written down our number, delayed action probably results in *no* action because there remains no printed reminder that details just what that phone number could bring. Sometimes, immediate response is facilitated through setting of a deadline for ordering. But if the deadline comes too quickly, you may be shutting the door on some prospect procrastinators as well as allowing insufficient time for the spot to generate a profitable return. The way around this is to offer an 'act now' bonus such as 'a second disc' or 'a special 10 percent discount.' You thereby keep the product availability window open indefinitely but still provide an additional stimulus to 'act now.'

7. Communicate the Specific Purchase Process. Whether it's the repetition of a mailing address or a toll-free number, you must clearly state the 'how-to-get-it' part of the message at least twice. Creating the desire to own and getting the decision to buy will be worthless achievements if you do not set the customer on the path to client contact.

The commercial below includes all seven of these ingredients required for a hard-working DR pitch. Try to detect each ingredient in your analysis of this 60-second spot:

```
DEEP VOICE:    Four ninety-five. Four ninety-five.

MARY:          Hello. We've asked a man with a very deep
               voice to say:
```

DEEP VOICE: Four ninety-five.

MARY: Over and over again.

DEEP VOICE: Four ninety-five.

MARY: That would normally cost you---

DEEP VOICE: Four ninety-five.

MARY: No, cable installation is normally about
                   <u>twenty bucks.</u> Plus, you can get a <u>second</u> TV
                   hooked up for---

DEEP VOICE: Four ninety-five.

MARY: Wrong! The second cable TV hook-up is <u>free.</u>
                   And, when you order a <u>premium channel package,</u>
                   we'll give you <u>grocery coupons</u> for Ralph's
                   worth---

DEEP VOICE: Four ninety-five.

MARY: No! The coupons are worth <u>forty bucks,</u> the
                   installation is---

DEEP VOICE: Four ninety-five.

MARY: Right. Now try it <u>lower.</u>

DEEP VOICE: <u>Three</u> ninety-five.

MARY: No, I mean the <u>voice</u> lower.

DEEP VOICE: (Lower) <u>Four ninety-five.</u>

MARY: Good. And the phone number to call?

DEEP VOICE: 1-800-Cable Up.

MARY: Beautiful. Okay, one last time, make me feel
                   it. Cable installation for---

DEEP VOICE: (BIGGER, REVERBED) <u>$4.95!</u>

MARY: just by calling

DEEP VOICE: (BIGGER, REVERBED) <u>1-800-Cable Up!</u>

MARY: Offer ends soon! You know, that's a very deep
                   voice.

DEEP VOICE: Thank you.

(© 1992 Paul & Walt Worldwide. Writer: Walt Jaschek. Producer: Paul Fey.)

Due to the increase of talk formats and dial-in promotional contests, listeners are becoming increasingly accustomed to the DR marriage of the radio and their phone. This, together with the precise demographic slivering engaged in by each station, makes radio an increasingly potent marketing vehicle. As telemarketing expert Harvey Mednick affirms, "Radio *is* a direct-response medium. . . . We have conditioned our listeners that the single mystical link to radio stations in both directions is the telephone."[11]

Such consumer conditioning can be a real boon to the radio industry. Because "by 1997," predicts advertising commentator Michael Schrage, "the world's ten largest advertising agencies will discover that more than one-third of their operating revenues—and more than 50 percent of their operating profit—come from direct-response advertising campaigns."[12] For their own well-being (and perhaps survival), radio copywriters and their stations must take advantage of this trend by refining the techniques of effective DR persuasion in particular—and aural communication in general.

Endnotes

1. Dennis Soapes, "Making Your Automation Sizzle," *Broadcast Programming Newsletter* (April 1990), 8.
2. Rob Balon, "How to Talk to Listeners," *Broadcast Programming Newsletter* (April 1990), 10–11.
3. Jim Teeson, "What's Your Programming Position?" *NAB RadioWeek* (March 13, 1989), 6.
4. John Follmer, "The Concept-Driven Image," *BPME Image* (August/September 1990), 13.
5. "Event Marketing Adds to Radio's Coffers," *Broadcasting* (January 17, 1991), 36.
6. Gary Demaroney, memo to Ramsey Elliot, July 16, 1992.
7. Andrew Giangola, "Station Production: A Valuable Tool," *NAB RadioWeek* (November 7, 1988), 6.
8. Richard Szathmary, "Direct Response Creativity at Its Most Accessible," *ADS Magazine* (November 1984), 27.
9. Thomas McAlevey, letter to the editor, *ADWEEK* (August 12, 1991), 26.
10. Joe Mandese, "Getting a Direct Unit Going," *ADWEEK* (October 20, 1986), D.M. 16.
11. "Putting Direct Marketing to Work for Radio Stations," *Broadcasting* (February 1, 1988), 59.
12. Michael Schrage, "The Call of Response," *ADWEEK* (January 6, 1992), 17.

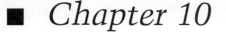
Key Elements of Television Writing

Though many of the communicative writing principles discussed in the previous chapters on radio also pertain to television, they are not reintroduced in this section. Instead, the next three chapters concentrate on concepts that apply mainly to the *visual* components of television continuity and commercial creation, or to the particular problems encountered in the interlocking of video and audio. Thus, if you have not already done so, the entire section on radio writing should be read before proceeding into the additional complexities of television.

Television Conceptual Vehicles

Three main instruments are used to capture and refine a television idea: the script, the storyboard, and the photoboard. Often, a given project will progress through all three as it wends its way onto the air. The characteristics of each vehicle are now explored.

The Script

As the following Hoover Hand Vac treatment demonstrates, television scripts are usually fashioned in the conventional two-column format, with video directions on the left and the corresponding audio directions on the right.

Video	Audio
OPEN ON FISHBOWL THAT HAS BEEN TIPPED OVER. GOLDFISH IS FLOPPING AROUND.	ANNCR (VO): Not long ago when the goldfish spilled
CUT TO CAT LICKING HIS LIPS.	this was the picker-upper.

Continued

Video	Audio
WET & DRY PICKS UP GOLDFISH WATER AND WE SEE FISH INSIDE VACUUM SWIMMING AROUND. CUT TO SHOT OF FISH AND WATER BEING POURED BACK INTO BOWL—FADE TO BLACK	Today the Hoover Dubl-Duty Wet 'N Dry Hand Vac picks up dry and picks up wet with ease.
HOOVER LOGO FADES UP <u>SUPER</u>: "THE DUBL-DUTY VAC. HOOVER INVENTED IT."	Pick up the Dubl-Duty Wet 'N Dry Hand Vac. Hoover invented it.

(Courtesy of Carol Skupien, Tatham-Laird & Kudner.)

Care is taken in spacing so that the audio indication is always directly opposite the visual it is intended to complement. To do otherwise would make the script very difficult to comprehend and would force the television director or film editor to read slantwise in trying to synchronize sound and picture properly. Note that video directions are in ALL CAPS form as, on the audio side, are character names (or VO for "announcer voice-over"). Should they be needed, sound effects and music cues are also in ALL CAPS with <u>MUSIC</u> underlined. Thus, the television audio side follows the same upper-case/lowercase conventions as the radio script.

An alternative script format ignores the left side/right side (dual column) separation in favor of a centered (single-column) approach. This format uses the right two-thirds of the page for the actual script, leaving the left one-third blank to accommodate notes by the director and other production people. As in the dual-column arrangement, all entries except dialogue are in CAPS. Hollywood writers have used the single-column format for years. It has the advantage of being clearer to read—especially by clients. With two-column script, the temptation is to read the entire audio side first—thereby distorting the spot's progression as well as underestimating the visual's importance. No such problem is encountered in the single-column format's chronological layout:

> OPEN ON HERO LEANING ON MODERN CAR.
> 'BRIDGEMAN' RESTAURANT SIGN IN
> BACKGROUND
>
>   HERO: I'm going back to my favorite
>   Bridgeman's, 1968.
>
> <u>MUSIC</u>: TEEN PSYCHEDELIC

```
                      HERO NOW BACK IN TIME, SEES FRIENDS

                        HERO:  Rejects!

                        GUYS:  Dirtball!

                        HERO:  My old girlfriend---

                      SHE TWISTS HIS NOSE. THEN BULLY
                      GIVES HIM SLOW NOOGIE WHILE HE
                      SAVORS FOOD

                        HERO:  M-mm; just like I remember it---

                      FRAME WIDENS TO REVEAL DESSERT

                        HERO:  And now, the Lallapallooza.

                      AS HE REACHES FOR DESSERT, A HAND
                      STOPS HIM

                        HERO:  Mom!

                        MUSIC OUT

                      HE SNAPS BACK TO PRESENT, NOTING WITH
                      SOME GLEE THAT HE STILL HAS THE
                      LALLAPALLOOZA

                        MUSIC: MODIFIED BACK IN

                        VO:    Bridgeman's. Stir up some
                               memories.

                      SUPER:   'STIR UP SOME MEMORIES'
```

(Courtesy of John Olson, Kruskopf Olson Advertising.)

A slight variation on the single-column format is sometimes used in corporate/industrial scripts when extensive narration occurs. To distinguish what happens on camera from what will be added later as narrative voice-over, the narrator's words are set in CAPS and moved to the right margin:

```
CLOSE-UP OF CHAIR LEG BEING FASHIONED
ON LATHE

              NARR:              MAPLE-RICH
                                FURNITURE
                                COMPONENTS
                                ARE
                                CUSTOM-MILLED
                                FOR SUPERIOR
                                FIT AND
                                FINISH.


STEVE IN HARDHAT STANDING IN PLANT

       STEVE:  Maple-Rich has never
               compromised on workmanship
               by forcing production
               speed-ups. My dad taught me
               that . . .
```

Whatever script arrangement is used, keep in mind that we usually double space within speeches and visual module descriptions and triple space between them. Our examples in this book, however, have been compressed to single and double spacing, respectively, to reduce the number of pages expended.

Either single or double columned, the professionally structured television script gives the copywriter the opportunity to probe visual concepts without having to draw the illustrations. Because many copywriters are somewhat the other side of cave paintings in their artistic abilities, the video script is a blessing for all concerned. It is used as one of the bases of consultation when the copywriter periodically gets together with an art director for the actual sketching of the proposed visual segments. Between these conferences, the script allows the writer to work alone in refining the treatment so that valuable artistic time is not wasted before the message concept has really jelled in the writer's mind.

The evolution of one spot's television script is distinctly focused in the following four versions supplied through the courtesy of Bruce S. Dunham, Jr., of W. B. Doner and Company. Though several more fine-tuning stages occurred between the creation of each script, the major copy refinements, which extended over eleven months, are well represented here. Clearly, television script maturation is neither a slap-dash nor an approximate business. Every word and every pictorial aspect must be scrupulously examined and evaluated in deriving the most cohesive and incisive treatment possible.

Read over these four scripts carefully. Note the progressive modifications made in both audio and video and try to discover for yourself what made these changes necessary and what they helped to accomplish in message clarification. As a television copywriter, you will soon have to make these same determinations about your own commercial and continuity material.

Version #1

Video	Audio
SPOT OPENS ON A PACKAGE OF AMERICAN TUBORG.	ANNCR V/O: This is Tuborg, the world famous beer of Denmark.
CAMERA GOES IN CLOSE TO LABEL TO SHOW THAT IT IS BREWED IN THE U.S.A.	As you can see, Tuborg is now brewed in America.
DISSOLVE TO WIDER SHOT AS HAND COMES INTO FRAME AND EXECUTES A LONG SLOW POUR. THERE IS AN UNUSUAL SIGNET RING ON ONE OF THE FINGERS.	Imported Tuborg used to be a very expensive beer. But now that Tuborg is also brewed in America---it is affordable by anyone who
THE DESIGN IS A COAT-OF-ARMS.	loves the flavor of good light Danish beer.
GLASS COMES BACK INTO FRAME.	(PAUSE)
CAMERA PANS TO COPY ON LABEL THAT READS "BY APPOINTMENT OF THE ROYAL DANISH COURT."	It is the only beer in America brewed by special appointment for the personal enjoyment of the kings of Denmark and Sweden.
CUT TO REGAL-LOOKING SPOKESMAN AS HE SMILES, REPOURS AND TOASTS THE VIEWER WITH A TONGUE-IN-CHEEK SMILE.	Now, if Tuborg is good enough to be a beer for Kings, shouldn't it be good enough for your next Saturday night beer bash?
SUPER POPS ON TUBORG.	
MANDATORY: Tuborg of Copenhagen, Ltd., Natick, Mass.	

Version #2

Video	Audio
OPEN ON MEDIUM SHOT OF BOTTLE OF TUBORG BESIDE RICHLY DESIGNED GOBLET.	ANNCR V/O: This is Tuborg, the famous beer of Denmark.
START ZOOM TO CLOSE-UP OF LABEL THAT IDENTIFIES THE BEER AS BEING BREWED IN THE U.S.A.	Now brewed in America
DIZ TO PART OF LABEL THAT IDENTIFIES APPOINTMENT TO DANISH COURT.	by special appointment to The Royal Courts of Denmark
BOTTLE ROTATES TO ALLOW VIEWER TO READ LABEL COPY THAT IDENTIFIES APPOINTMENT TO SWEDISH COURT.	and Sweden.
DIZ TO WIDER SHOT OF PACKAGE AND GOBLET.	Now you may think a beer brewed for Kings would be expensive.
HAND ENTERS FRAME AND GRASPS BOTTLE FOR POUR.	It was.
AS BEER IS POURED INTO THE GOBLET, ONE CAN SEE THAT ON THE MIDDLE FINGER THERE IS A RICHLY CARVED RING BEARING THE ROYAL COAT OF ARMS OR THE SEAL OF STATE OF DENMARK.	But now Tuborg is affordable by anyone who loves the authentic taste of good light Danish beer.
THE FILLED GOBLET IS HOISTED OUT OF FRAME AND CAMERA STARTS SLOW ZOOM INTO THE PACKAGE.	And for about the same money you've been paying for the king of beers---
THE DRAINED GOBLET IS THUNKED DOWN BESIDE PACKAGE AND CONTINUES TO ZOOM TO THE CROWN ON THE LABEL. TUBORG LOGO AND MANDATORY POP ON.	now you can get Tuborg, the beer of kings.

Version #3

Video	Audio
OPEN ON CLOSE-UP OF BOTTLE NECK, READING "Tuborg Gold."	ANNCR V/O: This is Tuborg Gold---
CAMERA TILTS DOWN ON BOTTLE, PICKS UP CROWN ON MAIN LABEL,	the golden beer of Danish kings---
AND PANS ACROSS TO READ:	
"By appointment to the Royal Danish Court/the Royal Swedish Court."	by appointment to the Royal Courts of Denmark and Sweden.
DISSOLVE TO CU OF LABEL ON BOTTLE BEING TILTED BY HAND FOR A POUR, AND READ, "Product of USA."	Tuborg Gold is now brewed in America---
DISSOLVE TO BEER BEING POURED INTO DANISH GLASS WITH RAISED IMPRIMATUR OF CROWN ON ITS FRONT.	and affordable to anyone
DISSOLVE TO HAND WEARING REGAL RING LIFTING GLASS UP AND OUT OF FRAME.	who loves the authentic taste of light, golden Danish beer.
DISSOLVE TO BEAUTY "STILL LIFE" OF BOTTLE AND FOOD ON A TABLE BEFORE BEAUTIFUL STAINED GLASS WINDOW, MOVING IN AS THE DRAINED GLASS IS SET DOWN BY HAND INTO THE FRAME, ENDING ON CU OF LABEL, FINALLY READING LARGE, "TUBORG GOLD."	So, for about what you'd pay for the king of beers ---now you can have Tuborg Gold, the beer of kings.
SUPER MANDATORY: Tuborg of Copenhagen, Ltd., Baltimore, Md.	

Version #4

Video	Audio
OPEN ON CLOSE UP OF BOTTLE NECK, READING "Tuborg Gold."	ANNCR V/O: This is our Tuborg Gold---
CAMERA TILTS DOWN BOTTLE, PICKS UP CROWN ON MAIN LABEL,	the golden beer of Danish kings---
AND PANS ACROSS TO READ:	
"By appointment to the Royal Danish Court/the Royal Swedish Court."	now affordable to anyone who loves the pure taste of light, golden Danish beer.
DISSOLVE TO BEER BEING POURED INTO DANISH GLASS WITH RAISED IMPRIMATUR OF CROWN ON ITS FRONT.	For Tuborg Gold is now brewed in America.
DISSOLVE TO HAND WEARING REGAL RING LIFTING GLASS UP AND OUT OF FRAME.	By appointment to the Royal Danish Court.
DISSOLVE TO BEAUTY "STILL LIFE" OF BOTTLE AND FOOD ON A TABLE BEFORE BEAUTIFUL STAINED GLASS WINDOW, MOVING IN AS THE DRAINED GLASS IS SET DOWN BY HAND INTO THE FRAME, ENDING ON CU OF LABEL, FINALLY READING LARGE, "TUBORG GOLD."	So, for about what you'd pay for the king of beers ---you can now have Tuborg Gold, the golden beer of Danish Kings.
SUPER MANDATORY: Carling National Breweries, Inc., Baltimore, Md.	

The Storyboard

This sequence of selected sketched stills in the proposed television treatment helps keep concept creation and evaluation visually oriented. In some situations, even the first attempt at an assignment is done in storyboard form by a copywriter/art director team. At other times, it is the copywriter who comes up with an initial script draft and perhaps even refines it before bringing the draft to the artist for visual workup. For reasons of economy and efficiency in conserving valuable artist time, several script rewrites may occur between each storyboard.

With a visual block on top and an audio box on the bottom, each storyboard frame or panel strives to illustrate the sequence of visual action, the camera settings, angles, and optical effects desired, and the dialogue, music, and sound effects being considered. Pads of blank storyboard sheets, with multiple frames per sheet, accommodate this task. Each frame is perforated for easy separation and rearrangement. Available from a number of suppliers (such as the Aquabee TV Pad by Bee Paper Company, Wayne, NJ), these pads provide ready-to-use storyboard layouts at a very low cost.

As it is being prepared, the storyboard provides the opportunity for good interplay between copy and art people. This interplay can be most effective when the two people involved are not afraid to make suggestions about the other's area and to accept suggestions about their own. Art directors *have* been known occasionally to come up with a better word or phrase than the copywriter had originally captured. And copywriters, in their own scattered moments of pictorial brilliance, do stumble on more compelling visual ideas than the artist at first had in mind. Since the professional well-being of both depends on their *collective* ability to derive a successful audio/visual communication, the copywriter and the art director each have something to gain from pooling rather than departmentalizing their knowledge and insight.

To be cohesively productive, the relationship between the two creatives should be a simultaneous rather than a consecutive enterprise, or the original concept may be lost. "Traditionally," laments commercial artist Alexander Molinello, "art directors or illustrators take copy and run with it and then come back with something that the writer never saw that way."[1] When artist and wordsmith physically work together on the board, however, you are much more likely to end up with one unified concept rather than with two mutually exclusive ones. Creating a unified concept takes active collaboration and the willingness to modify by both parties. Only partly in jest, copywriter Peter Kellogg warns, "If you walk into an art director's office with an idea and say, 'Here it is!' you're just asking to get your head chewed off. Art directors, you see, like to think that they have some part in the creative process, and you've got to convince them they do . . . Besides, sniffing spray mount and magic markers all day seems to affect their brains. So it's always wise to proceed with caution."[2]

The result of truly effective copywriter/art director partnership, the two storyboards that follow (Figures 10–1 and 10–2) illustrate intermediate stages in the maturation of the same Tuborg television production to which the four scripts pertain. From this pair of layouts, it is relatively easy to see how the script modifications determined and were themselves determined by refinements in the storyboard. With its self-contained audio/visual segments, the storyboard format also facilitates quick rearrangement of frames in the pursuit of more effective idea flow.

Technically, the first quick sketches, suitable only for showing to co-creators, constitute a *rough* or *loose* storyboard. Later versions (like Figures 10–1 and 10–2), which may be polished enough to exhibit to the client and more precisely delineate each frame, are *refined, tight,* or *comprehensive* boards. In short-deadline or low-budget projects, however, it is not uncommon to proceed directly from a *rough* into actual production—provided that the rough is definitive enough to motivate executive approval.

With modern computer technology, the distinction between rough and refined boards is narrowing. Personal computers and software programs such as IBM's *Storyboard Live* and Lake Compuframes's *ShowScape* (which even offers its own storyboard layout computer paper) now allow art directors to expand, contract, shift, and otherwise modify their frames on a video monitor before printing out their best effort as hard copy. Type style and size can be chosen and experimented with at will. When the client wants changes, the stored image can be retrieved, adjusted, and reshaped accordingly. These capabilities can cut the artist's time expenditure by at least one-third, with a much greater saving in art materials and photoprocessing. Perhaps even more important, the availability of computer-assisted storyboards permits artist and copywriter to sit down at the screen and manipulate images together— before anything gets locked into uncompromising ink!

The Photoboard

After the last-stage storyboards are prepared and approved, but before dubbing or distribution is authorized, a photoboard is often made up to give those people who have the final decision the clearest possible idea of the actual creative and production values present in the finished commercial, PSA, or piece of continuity. In many cases, the photoboard is constructed from selected stills lifted out of the tape or film footage from the completed message itself. In other situations, where reviewers want to see the photographic/telegenic effect earlier in the message's evolution, photoboards replace the later (refined) storyboards. In such instances, the still photographs themselves are shot and pasted up as board panels for scrutiny before final videotape or film production commences.

The photoboard in Figure 10–3 represents the culmination of the Tuborg "Label" commercial. You can see that it matches the copy called for in script version #4 but that the visuals have been further refined. The photoboard is also, in total affect, a good deal more polished than either of the stages represented in the two storyboards. In addition, because the visual component has already been shot as production *rushes* (total exposed tape/film footage

ANNOUNCER V/O: This is Tuborg Gold
the famous Beer of Denmark...

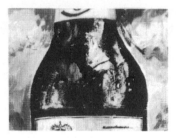

that is now brewed here in America.

that is brewed by special
appointment

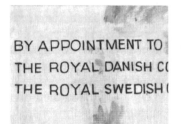

to the Royal Danish Court

for kings would be expensive.
It was.

But now that Tuborg Gold is brewed
here...it is affordable to anyone
who loves the authentic taste

Figure 10-1

(Courtesy of David R. Sackey, W. B. Doner and Company.)

from which the final version will be edited), a photoboard does not require the storyboard's verbal description of the pictures. (Check the second Tuborg storyboard to see how such verbal description at the top of the audio block is handled.)

It is the only beer

in the U.S.A.

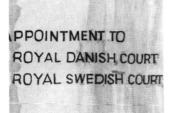

and the Royal Swedish Court.

Now you may think a beer
brewed

After final approval, the photoboard can also be used to provide stations and networks with a hard-copy record of the spot's submission to them for initial continuity acceptance and subsequent airing. Photoboards can also be sent to distributors of the product as a means of documenting the marketing efforts that the manufacturer is exerting on this commodity's behalf.

OPEN ON CLOSE UP OF BOTTLE NECK, READING
"Tuborg Gold."

- -

ANNCR V/O: This is Tuborg Gold --

CAMERA TILTS DOWN BOTTLE,

- -

the golden beer

"By appointment to the Royal Danish Court/
the Royal Swedish Court."

- -

of Denmark and Sweden.

DISSOLVE TO CU OF LABEL ON BOTTLE BEING
TILTED BY HAND FOR A POUR,

- -

Tuborg Gold

DISSOLVE TO HAND WEARING REGAL RING
LIFTING GLASS UP AND OUT OF FRAME,

- -

who loves the authentic taste of light,
golden Danish beer.

DISSOLVE TO BEAUTY "STILL LIFE" OF BOTTLE
AND FOOD ON A TABLE BEFORE BEAUTIFUL
STAINED GLASS WINDOW,

- -

So, for about what you'd pay for the king
of beers...

Figure 10-2

(Courtesy of David R. Sackey, W. B. Doner and Company.)

PICKS UP CROWN ON MAIN LABEL,

- -

of Danish kings —

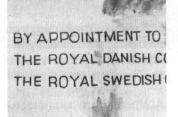

AND PANS ACROSS TO READ...

- -

by appointment to the Royal Courts

AND READ, "Product of USA."

- -

is now brewed in America...

DISSOLVE TO BEER BEING POURED INTO DANISH
GLASS WITH RAISED IMPRIMATUR OF CROWN ON
ITS FRONT.

- -

and affordable to anyone

MOVING IN AS THE DRAINED GLASS IS SET DOWN
BY HAND INTO THE FRAME,

- -

now you can have

ENDING ON CU OF LABEL, FINALLY READING
LARGE, "TUBORG GOLD."
SUPER MANDATORY: Tuborg of Copenhagen,
                 Ltd., Baltimore, Md.

- -

Tuborg Gold, the beer of kings.

ANNCR V/O: This is our Tuborg Gold . . .

the golden beer of Danish kings . . .

now affordable to anyone who loves the
true taste of light, golden Danish beer.

For Tuborg Gold is now brewed in America.

By appointment to the Royal Danish
Court.

So, for about what you'd pay for the king
of beer . . .

you can now have Tuborg Gold, the
the golden beer of Danish kings . . .

Carling National Breweries, Inc.
Baltimore, Md.

Figure 10-3

(Courtesy of David R. Sackey, W. B. Doner and Company.)

Additional Vehicles

Animatics are a way of bringing motion to a storyboard so that the concept can be presented to clients or tested on consumers before a commitment is made to full-scale production. In the past, animatics were constructed almost like inexpensive cartoons, with individual illustrated panels shot several times and then spliced together. Nowadays, computers have given the process much more fluidity and dropped the price of these movie storyboards as well. Using a basic software program called Hypercard, for example, advertising agency Jordan, McGrath, Case & Taylor has developed CLIP (Client Linked Idea Presentation). This animatic technique allows the agency to create moving pictures on the computer screen, add sound, transfer the result to videotape, and ship it to the client for a reaction. Using this procedure, a finished animatic can be produced in about ten hours. "That includes sending it out to a sketch man, recording time and edit time," says the agency's creative services director, Peter Farago. "With CLIP, I can take teenies [small sketches], . . . hand them to a guy who will scan them into the computer. You can do 16 frames in about two minutes, and the audio is digitized at the same time. By the time I get back to my desk, it's ready to be edited."[3] CLIP has dropped the price of an animatic from about $11,000 to $1,100,[4] making it feasible to take more promising concepts to the test stage.

More sophisticated animatics average about $10,000—still a fraction of the expenditure required to produce a conventional film or video test commercial. There is, however, a conceptual downside to these new computer capabilities. "Once you give those tools to creative people," warns Farago, "they get lost in the abyss of decisions. It's like giving an art director 10,000 typefaces."[5]

Photomatics also have been in use for some time and, like animatics, are being reinvigorated by the computer. The photomatic differs from the animatic only in that it uses photographs instead of an artist's illustrations. Now, these photos can be fed into a Macintosh that, using the right software, invests the subjects of the photos with flow and motion. When these photos are of real people rather than graphically created characters, the result is sometimes known as a *live-o-matic*. (Much less innovatively, *steal-o-matics* are made up of sequences pulled from other commercials that are quickly computer-assembled to suggest how the spot under development might look when completed.)[6]

Alternatively, and much more crudely by today's standards, the commercial prototype can be produced and presented as a 35-mm slide show. In this method, a still camera shoots drawings, graphic titles, and, perhaps, even the actual exterior scenes called for in the proposed commercial. For supervisor and client review, the resulting slides are then projected onto a screen to the accompaniment of a live voice-over read by the copywriter or a "rough cut" audiotape on which suggested music, sound effects, and talent voice elements have been recorded. Computers also can assist in this technique because they provide a ready means of enhancing and manipulating the content of the slides to give them more presence and clarity.

A Bubble about Animation

As our discussion above suggests, the rapid development of visual computer technology has increased the use and diversity of animated material in television spots and continuity. Certainly, through its ability to vivify concepts and events impossible in real life, the animated commercial provides the maximum in creative freedom and flexibility. In addition, the specially customized cartoon "spokesthing" can be an almost priceless asset to brand recall and a ready-made tie-in between the television message and such nonbroadcast media as print layouts, billboards, display cards, and direct mail pieces. Smokey the Bear and Tony the Tiger demonstrate that this phenomenon can work for both PSAs and commercials.

Sometimes, if a creative linkage with the product can be defined, and if the rights can be obtained, an *already popular* animated character may be recruited to promote your client. Such a character combines the elements of the celebrity testimonial with the inherent charm of cartoon characters who, unlike real people, are difficult for viewers to dislike. Animated characters also are able to demonstrate the product in ways real people can't, as in the Figure 10–4 Uniroyal spot that enlists a prominent inhabitant of the comic strip "B.C." The spot's effectiveness is further heightened by the appropriateness of using a caveman to demonstrate the fundamental necessity of the Uniroyal steel-belted radial, a snow tire seemingly second in importance only to the invention of the wheel itself.

Unfortunately, even if you can avoid "lease fees" for a popular animated character by creating your own, animation is still expensive. And if cartooning action must be matted (overlaid) onto footage of real-life scenes and characters, as in the kid-targeting Cookie Crisp spot in Figure 10–5, the cost can go through the roof. So if your account is on a small budget but an animated scene or spokesthing is considered essential, don't hire some art school dropout to animate the whole sequence simply because the price is right. Better to hire a top-notch artist to draw a few, well-rendered, single pics between which you can intercut and that lend themselves to use in several different messages or contexts.

In the spot for Ocean Spray Cranberry Sauce (Figure 10–6), a simple but concept-encompassing piece of cartooning is used to attract attention and set up the "cut-away" to the actual demonstration. All of animation's advantages are accrued without the necessity for cartoon/real life matting and without expensive end-to-end animation.

If you just *must* have a completely animated treatment, recognize that a 30-second television spot contains 720 film frames (24 frames per second). Full, Disney-quality cel animation would thus require the artist to produce 720 separate drawings. In practice, of course, this is rarely done. The eye will easily tolerate the same drawing in two consecutive frames—which cuts the number in half to 360. For really "limited" animation, one can reduce the number to as few as 6 drawings per frame (180 per 30-second spot), but this few will be disturbingly obvious unless the actions and characters are extremely simple.

There are, of course, an increasing number of computer-video alternatives to paying an artist to draw hundreds of acetate cel overlays. Through use of a computer-driven 'paint box,' a given cel can be *electronically* replicated and changes made only to the parts of the picture that move. Each perfected frame is then recorded on videotape or videodisc as the process continues. Depending

UNIROYAL
SNOW RADIALS
:30 Seconds T. V.
"Snows"

ORSON WELLES: "When man invented the wheel, he soon realized ...

... that wheels have an enemy.

The enemy is winter.

So to cope with winter, man invented ...

... the Uniroyal Steel Belted Radial Snow Tire.

On ice and snow, Uniroyal M&S Plus Steel Radials ...

... have proven they can turn the trick ...

... in man's annual contest with winter.

Uniroyal.

From the first man ...

... the last word ...

... in Steel Belted Radial Snow Tires!

Figure 10-4

(Courtesy of Barry Base, Base Brown Partners Ltd.; Copyright Field Syndicate Inc.)

Cookie-Crisp®

RALSTON PURINA
Cookie-Crisp
Cereal

:30 TV
Commercial
"Cookie Crook: Intro"

SFX: (CROOK WHISTLING
NONCHALANTLY.)
KIDS: Hey, Cookie Crook, whataya
doing?

CROOK: Uh…scratching my back!

GIRL: He's trying to steal our
Cookie-Crisp!

BOY: Where's the Cookie Cop!
SFX: (SIREN)

COP: Cookie Crook, you'll do anything

to get the real cookie taste of
Cookie-Crisp Cereal.

CROOK: I know, I know.

It even looks like little chocolate chip
cookies!

COP: But it stays (Tap! Tap!) crispy in
milk!

COP: (VO) And it's part of this complete
breakfast.

© Ralston Purina Company 1984

COP: Well, Cookie Crook, whataya have
to say for yourself?
CROOK: I guess I'm not such a smart
cookie, after all.

ANNCR: If you like cookies, you'll love
Cookie-Crisp.

Figure 10-5

(Reprinted with permission of Ralston Purina Company.)

Hi. I'm a turkey,...gobble,...gobble...

...You don't believe I'm a turkey, right?...

...That's why I can't get cranberry sauce. The turkeys get it all...

How about a cranberry glazed pork roast?...

The recipe's now on the Ocean Spray can...

Melt the cranberry sauce, stir in orange juice and brown sugar...

...and your pork gets cranberry excitement!

...Or, serve Cranberry Sauce with park chops...

With chicken? Go ahead...

...Serve it as a glaze...or in slices...

...Just don't forget me.

...Check the recipes on the Ocean Spray can...and gobble, gobble.
(SUPER) CHECK THE RECIPES.

Figure 10-6

(Courtesy of Irene Taffel, Kelly-Nason Inc.)

on the complexity of the image being rendered, some frames can be set down in less than a minute whereas others may require up to an hour. Because costs are figured on the basis of how much and what kind of computer time is needed to generate a desired effect, complexity automatically increases the price. "To render an image on a very large computer can take 20 or 30 minutes," reports computer marketing executive Gary Stump. "If you're doing 30 frames a second, that's a lot of minutes for 10 seconds of animation."[7]

Even the most sophisticated computers cannot replicate everything that is attainable via an artist's hand-painted cels. "Cel offers a softness and an artistic control that can only be obtained through a human touch," points out video production chief Tom Stefani. So today, "the video and film industries borrow from both worlds of animation to produce the desired effects in the most practical manner. . . . Even film directors are calling upon the computer to generate 3-D backdrops for primarily cel-animation productions. Disney's *Beauty and the Beast* is an example."[8]

Rotoscoping is another process that combines cel and computer techniques plus having video as well as film applications. With rotoscoping, either frames of live-action film are projected onto a table and traced by hand to make cels, or a video recorder feeds one frame at a time into the computer, allowing the artist's electronic tracings to customize it before recording the image and moving on to the next. In both media, rotoscoping permits the designer to (1) position animated characters in relation to live actors or (2) actually replace the frame space occupied by a 'real' person with an animated character to match. The effect can be dazzling, but only if it is laboriously carried through every one of film's twenty-four or video's thirty frames per second. "In a typical application," points out Digital F/X chairman Steve Mayer, "such as one commercial where the bags under an actress's eyes had to be painted out, the artist had to grab, paint and record 1,800 pictures."[9]

Claymation is no less expensive. In it, actual clay figures are physically positioned and a single frame is shot. The figures are reset and another frame is exposed. Figure repositioning is modeled after a reference tape on which live humans have acted out the movement the clay dolls are being positioned to replicate. As epitomized by the California Raisin Board's soulful raisins or the characters in the Figure 10–7 PSA, "claymation resembles live action more than it resembles any form of animation," says claymation producer David Altschul. "We're shooting and lighting in three dimensions, were blocking and editing sequences exactly as you would a live action piece of filmmaking."[10] However, at 1990 prices ranging "from $1,000 to $5,000 or more a second depending on the complexity of the piece,"[11] claymation is not an option when you are writing for small accounts.

In considering claymation or some other form of animation, the copywriter should ascertain whether or not it is really needed for the project at hand. Ultimately, there are six capabilities that justify animation's use. Stephen Wershing and Tanya Weinberger of Telesis Productions isolate four of these:

1. Such graphics can convey complex ideas in concise fashion.
2. You can portray processes not normally observable.
3. Dull subjects become initially more attractive.
4. A cartoon character, particularly a humorous one, can serve as a less intimidating spokesperson when addressing unpleasant subjects or possibilities.[12] (See Figure 10–7.)

OBESITY--WATCH OUT, ARNOLD Television Public Service Announcement :60 & :30

MUSIC...

DOCTOR: Listen to yourself, Arnold. You're totally out of breath because you're much too heavy. I'll give it to you straight.

DOCTOR V.O.: At this rate, you could be eating yourself into an early grave. But it's not too late to do something about it.

DOCTOR: Now first we give you a check up and work out a program of diet and exercise.

DOCTOR V.O.: And remember, Arnold, eat right and exercise. A healthy life is up to you.

Produced by
The Will Rogers Institute
in cooperation with
U.S. Department of
Health and Human Services
National Institute of Arthritis,
Metabolism, and Digestive Disease.

Figure 10-7

(Courtesy of Holly Holmes, Will Rogers Institute.)

299

Computer consultants Bob Bennett and John Javetski provide the final pair of rationales:

5. Given the attention span of the MTV generation, animation is more memorable than reality.
6. Animation is an ideal way to illustrate processes that flow over time and space, such as how to build a perfect hamburger.[13]

If these reasons are absent, it may be that animation, of whatever variety, is not right for the assignment at hand.

When some form of animation *is* to be pursued, agreement on an initial storyboard is essential so that art director, copywriter, computer artists/designers, and client all understand the message's destination and what it will cost to get there. Then, as production begins, the first thing to reach final form must NOT be the visuals but rather, the talent's voicing of the copy and production (if required) of the music track. From a synchronization standpoint, it is much easier for the cel or computer artist to fit the action to prerecorded dialogue and music than for talent and composer to fit their contributions to finished animation. Once voice track and music bed have been laid down, it is a comparatively straightforward job for the animator to create and polish the finalized 'cartoon' movements that will match verbal and musical accents.

Above all, remember that animation is never a substitute for a central concept. "A lot of unimaginative people try to mask their lack of skill with lots of effects," argues producer Randy Field. "You see everything spinning and twirling ad nauseum. It can become visual cotton candy. You wind up saying,'What was that?' I don't know, but it cost them $100,000."[14]

Basic Television Production Methods

Besides animation (which is a contributing agent to some of these more fundamental techniques) there are only five basic processes from which the television commercial, PSA, or piece of continuity is begotten.

Live

This is the quickest, cheapest, and also the most risky technique for producing anything for television. The annals of video are filled with sagas of refrigerator doors that refused to open, frying pans that wouldn't scour clean, and puppies who not only refused to eat the sponsor's dog food but also directed a socially repugnant comment at the dish that contained it. Still, if kept simple, the live message provides the most rapid turnaround time for copy changes and the greatest adaptability to specific events and conditions. Program promos and other forms of similar continuity are thus viable as live copy—especially when read on camera by a personality who is already well established on the individual show or station.

Slides and Flip Cards

This is the next least expensive method to on-camera, live presentation. It uses video obtained from 35-mm slides in the film chain, bits in an off-line computer storage system, or flip cards placed on easels in front of a studio camera. This series of still "pics" is then complemented by an audio message that can either be rendered live or recorded on an audio cartridge, perhaps with a complementary music bed. Station IDs, spots for small local clients, and local PSAs mesh well with this inexpensive but still visually flexible production method. The Designated Driver slide reproduced in Figure 10–8 is an example of this kind of device. It was provided by the National Safety Council to stations that could then voice-over this slide specific information about their locality's drunk driving prevention efforts.

For convenience, many stations and cable systems produce the entire slide or flip-card message on videotape so it can be cued up and run by the duty engineer without the need for additional announcer, studio, or film chain involvement. Slides can also be readily generated *from* videotape. Polaroid's FreezeFrame system, for instance, creates finished slides from a videotape recorder, laser disc player, or even television camera in just five minutes. If

Figure 10-8

(Reprinted with permission from the National Safety Council.)

the source picture lacks quality, the unit also "comes with five controls that let you enhance the contrast, tint, color intensity, brightness and sharpness of your image."[15] Kodak, meanwhile, is developing digital cameras that can inject high-resolution images directly into a production control room's computer hard-drive, thereby bypassing conventional slide film technology altogether.

Videotape

Since its industry entry in the late 1950s, videotape has replaced much of television's live fare and, with recent breakthroughs in economical electronic editing, is challenging film as the most-used medium for program material as well as for commercials and continuity. Tape provides live picture quality but with a safety net—you can reshoot that demonstration (studio time permitting) until it comes out right, and yet its visual quality will make it seem as spontaneous to the viewer as though it were done live. As noted above, with advances in solid-state technology and video cassette machines, even material originating as a slide/card presentation can be easily taped for later retrieval to free the studio cameras and personnel for other things.

If not provided as a service by a station on which you are placing commercials, video studio time or remote shooting can be expensive. Still, if your spokesperson does not talk on camera, even this cost can be mitigated by preproducing the audio track at a much lower cost-per-hour sound studio. Then you can use your rented video facilities for only as long as you need to "lay down" a good visual with which the previously finished audio can easily be linked.

Film Voice-Over

This same basic technique can be applied to film as well. If no one talks on camera, film can be quickly shot anywhere, stock footage can be rented as needed, and a nicely fashioned audio can be married to the result at the editing/assembly stage. Many producers still prefer the softer "look, tone, and mood" of film. So it will remain a viable if not a preferred medium for many PSA and commercial assignments for the foreseeable future. Because some stations, and most cable systems, do not have a control room film chain, the message is almost always converted to a video tape format prior to distribution.

Film Lip-Sync

Especially if outdoor location shooting is involved, this can be the most time-consuming and therefore expensive approach to message creation for television. Because the characters in the presentation talk on camera, great care must be taken to record their dialogue properly and synchronize it with the visual being captured at the same time. This process can become especially complex as the scene is consecutively reshot from several angles—each with its own sound bed—that must later be edited into a matching whole without visual or audio "glitches." Sometimes, later sound stage dubbing, in which the characters repeat their lines to match the previously filmed lip movements, must be scheduled in order to achieve acceptable audio quality and synchronization. Because indoor shooting normally allows for greater control of the sound environment than when filming outdoors, subsequent sound stage work can usually be avoided in the case of interior scenes, at least for the dialogue. Other sound sources like music may also have to be layered in, however, and unlike videotape production, this can seldom be done when the film cameras are rolling.

It is possible, of course, to mix and match elements from several of these five productional methods in order to achieve your television objectives within the available budget. Just keep in mind that whatever technique(s) is (are) employed, they should not call attention to themselves but rather, should help to articulate the central point of your spot, PSA, or continuity segment. And don't, whatever you do, try to use a production method that the budget really can't afford by cutting time and picture-value corners. The result will look shoddy and so, by implication, will whatever it is that your message is striving to promote. It is much better to employ a less expensive productional methodology and do it *right*.

Television Productional Terminology

As in the case of radio, the professional television copywriter must know and use the proper lingo if words and sketches are to be translated into desired moving and talking images. Directions for television audio are fundamentally the same as for radio so need not be reintroduced here. They are found in their entirety in Chapter 7. What does require cataloging at this point is the *visual* terminology writers must use in communicating their concepts to production crews. One cautionary note: Some copywriters, once they acquire a working knowledge of video jargon, tend to *overuse* it, to overspecify every visual detail so that the production personnel are entirely locked into what might not be the best visual treatment of the sequence in question. Give as many directions as needed to convey the main intent of your shot progressions but don't become so detailed that the hands of your video or film production experts are totally tied. Allow them some leeway to take advantage of opportunities that might present themselves on set or on location.

In this Montana Power Company message, the copywriter has clearly described overall effect and visual progression required while leaving subsidiary details to the best professional judgment of the director and other people responsible for creating the footage.

Video	Audio
WIDE ESTABLISHING SHOT OF WOMAN STANDING LOOKING OUT WINDOW, HER BACK TO CAMERA.	WOMAN: (Despondently) Empty promises! That's all I get! You promised to keep me warm. You don't. You made me think I'd live in comfort. I don't.
WOMAN TURNS SLOWLY AWAY FROM WINDOW	Instead, I spend all my time cleaning up after you. You just take, take, take.
SHE BEGINS TO SMILE	Well, enough is enough! (Proudly) Today, I bought a natural gas furnace.
CAMERA WIDENS TO REVEAL HER OLD WOODSTOVE	That's right! (Triumphantly) You're through!
SUPERS Montana Power Company 4.9% APR financing. You may qualify. Call for details.	VO: Get more than you expect with clean, comfortable natural gas heat. It's the smart choice.
	SFX: WOODSTOVE COUGHS, SIGHS

(Courtesy of Pam Lemelin, Wendt Advertising.)

We now turn to the specific pieces of visual terminology with which the television copywriter should be familiar. These designations can most easily be divided into four categories: (1) camera movements, (2) shot lengths and angles, (3) control room transitions and devices, and (4) other writer-used technical terms. As in our radio terminology discussion, it is not the intent here to cover the entire vocabulary of television and film production. Instead, attention is limited to words the copywriter is most likely to need in preparing the actual script.

Camera Movements

This category consists of directions that call for maneuvering of the camera and its base or some manipulation of the camera "head" alone while the base on which it is mounted remains stationary.

Dolly In/Dolly Out. When this movement is specified, the entire camera is pushed toward or away from the subject of the shot, who or which usually stays immobile.

Truck Left/Truck Right. This term specifies a lateral movement of the entire camera parallel to the scene being shot. Alternatively, trucking left or trucking right may be referred to as *tracking.*

Crane/Arc/Boom. These designations, which have become more or less interchangeable, require that the television or film camera be mounted on a long manual, hydraulic, or electric arm that allows for shots that demand smooth, flowing changes in height and/or semicircular sweeps toward and away from the scene. A much more restricted derivation of this type of movement is the *ped up/ped down,* where the camera is raised or lowered on its base without changing its angular relationship to or distance from the scene.

Pan Left/Pan Right. This is a more limited version of the truck since only the camera head turns to follow the action as that action modulates to one side of the set or the other. Because the camera's base does not move, the panning procedure also more graphically changes the shot's angle on the scene than does the *truck,* which keeps a constant parallel relationship with the scene and its elements. In the case of character movement, for example, a trucking shot would give the feeling of *walking with* an actor, whereas the pan would have the effect of following his approach to or departure from the viewer's psychological location at scene center.

Tilt Up/Tilt Down. If you stand in place and change the subject of your visual attention by the simple raising or lowering of your head, you will achieve the same effect created by the *tilt* as the camera head tips up or down on its base. The tilt allows television to change the altitude of the viewer's gaze without changing the perceived distances from the perimeter of the scene.

Shot Lengths and Angles

These designations refer to how close or how far the subject of the shot will seem to be in terms of the viewer's perspective as well as to the angular relationship between viewer and subject. The effects of shot lengths and angles are achieved by manipulation of available lens components and/or by the actual movement of the camera in any of the ways just discussed. The basic shot length continuum extends from the full shot (FS) to the extreme close-up (ECU). (See Figure 10–9.)

Full Shot (FS) or Cover Shot (CS). The entire scene is encompassed by this shot, which may thus include the whole set or even an outdoor epic's entire horizon. Because it often occurs at the opening of the message in order to acquaint the viewer with the total visual environment, the full shot/cover shot is also known as an *establishing shot.*

Long Shot (LS) or Wide Shot (CS). Long shots may or may not reveal the entire scene; if they do, they can be interchangeably referred to as *full shots.* In any event, long shots do encompass a comparatively wide angle of vision and would, in the case of the talent, show a character from head to toe. The term *wide shot* is also used to denote this same orientation.

Medium Shot (MS). This very broad category includes all visual fields too close or "narrow"to be called long shots and, on the other hand, perspectives too wide to be referred to as close ups. Though medium shots can thus vary widely depending on the scope of the scene in question, we generally think of them as framing only the upper two-thirds of a character and with minimal additional revelation of the set behind that character. When two or three characters are featured, a *medium two-shot (M2S)* or *medium three-shot (M3S)* can be requested. (Any more than three persons would require so wide an angle as to be called a long shot.) For more definitive designation, the terms *medium long shot (MLS)* and *medium close-up (MCU)* also refer to each end of the medium-shot spectrum.

Close-Up (CU). In the close-up, the specific character or prop fills most of the viewing screen. For example, only the head and shoulders of a person would be seen, and thus the CU may also be referred to as a *tight shot.* The *extreme close-up (ECU or XCU)* is the ultimate extension of this principle so that a pianist's hands or a single leaf on a tree can fill most of the picture area and engage the viewer's total focus.

For pictorial examples of the basic shot lengths, examine the Figure 10–10 photoboard. Here, the teacher is framed with a long shot in panel 1, medium

Figure 10-9
The Shot Length Continuum

shots in panels 3 and 9, close-ups in panels 5, 7, and 11, and an extreme close-up (part of her hand and the product) in panel 8.

TEACHER: Sometimes I wonder if I'm getting through to them.

Brian, am I getting through to you?

The only things that matter to them are Godzilla, basketball and chocolate.

BOYS: ARRRR!!

TEACHER: Not that I have anything against Godzilla or basketball.

(BOY SHOOTS BANANA PEEL INTO TRASHCAN)
BOY: Yes!

TEACHER: Or chocolate. I drink Yoo-Hoo.

It's a delicious chocolate snack

with vitamins and minerals.

BOY: Ready? Go.

TEACHER: It's the one thing we have in common. The only thing.

VO: Yoo-Hoo. The cool way to do chocolate.

Figure 10-10

(Courtesy of Rodney Underwood, Geer, Dubois Inc.)

Zoom In/Zoom Out.   Though it is technically a lens function to be treated under this section, the zoom in or out is functionally a technological replacement for the physical and comparatively awkward *dollying* of the entire camera. Through either manual or electronic changes in the lens's optics, a good zoom lens can smoothly bring viewer orientation from a full shot to an ECU and, if desired, back again without moving the camera base at all. In the case of outdoor productions, a zoom could traverse hundreds of feet—a much greater distance than the camera itself would be capable of moving within the TV spot's time confines.

In our discussion of shot lengths, we have tended to use the word *angle* to refer to the width of the resulting picture. This is because the closer we focus on a single object, the narrower our peripheral vision becomes. Thus, as already implied, long shots are also *wide* shots and close-ups are also *tight*. Writers of television commercial and continuity copy tend to use either or both of these descriptive sets, depending on what seems to depict most clearly the visual effect they have in mind.

Camera angles can also be designated another way in order to describe more graphically the spatial and psychological relationship between shot subject and viewer. A *point-of-view (POV)* shot, for example, looks at the scene through the eyes of a character or implement within it. In Figure 10–11, which is a frame from a promo for the Ontario Ministry of Industry &

Figure 10-11

(Courtesy of Carole McGill, Camp Associates Advertising Ltd.)

Tourism, the POV might be referred to as that of the gridiron's turf or (if you wanted to inject tragedy), POV DOWNED QUARTERBACK.

A similar effect is obtained when the writer calls for a SUBJECTIVE CAMERA, in which the on-camera talent addresses the lens as though it were a specific being. The Klondike commercial in Figure 10–12 uses this technique (SUBJECTIVE CAMERA: INTERVIEWER) to heighten audience involvement. Viewers are addressed by the man (frames 2–4) as substitutes for the off-camera interviewer and thus participate more directly in the good-natured goading of the on-camera victim.

Over the shoulder shots are another derivation in which one character is viewed by looking over the shoulder of the other. A *reverse angle* shot can then be used to give the viewer the scene from 180° away—looking "over the shoulder" of that second character back at the first. Either separately or in conjunction with any of these other techniques, *high angle* and *low angle* shots can draw special relationships or promote unique vantage points in order to illustrate more powerfully the message's main tenet. Notice how a variety of carefully linked shot lengths and angles helps convey the central concept and psychological involvement exploited for Paul Masson Champagne in Figure 10–13. In this classic photoboard, numbered Frame 7 is an OS PLAYER (over-the-shoulder shot, with the shoulder being that of the football player). The following numbered Frame 8 is then a reverse angle to complete the exchange. (Technically, Frame 8 is a ¾ REV ANGLE since we see the player from Gielgud's *side* rather than from directly behind his head. This is done here to enhance viewer participation by using the audience's rather than the product spokesman's frame of reference.) Notice too how a high angle shot such as Frame 7's seems to diminish the subject's (Gielgud's) size in relationship to the athlete and how Frame 8's low angle shot makes that athlete seem even more giantlike.

As a general rule, tighter (closer) shots tend to have more utility in television than do a preponderance of wider (longer) framings. According to Neil Kesler, president of Airfax Productions, this is because

> generally, television is viewed on a 19-inch color television set in a room that can have any number of distractions. The set itself is probably not a new one, and the colors often are not exactly right—the set might not be functioning properly, or it might not be tuned properly. The sound, too, is frequently no better than what emanates from the cheapest radio. . . . One certain way to reach that viewer—to make him sit up and pay attention—is with close, tight shots that cannot be ignored. . . . All this is not to say that all commercials should be continuously filled with close-ups (or that there is no place in advertising for big budget, elaborate commercials). The monotony would be disastrous. Instead, the close-up should be considered a major weapon in the creative arsenal, used selectively to focus the viewer's attention. Television is such an intimate medium that it's often a mistake to reject that intimacy.[16]

CLOWN
30 seconds

MUSIC: What would you do for a Klondike Bar?

V/O: Would you dress up like a clown?
MAN: Clown? Me? No, no, no, no.

ANNCR: Got the Klondike right here. Vanilla ice cream, sprinkled with Krispies, covered with thick chocolate ...   MAN: Well, okay.

ANNCR: First the nose.
MAN: Okay.

ANNCR: Then the wig.

ANNCR: That's the spirit.

SONG: For that chocolate coated ice cream loaded,

big and thick, no room for a stick ...

What would you do for a Klondike Bar?

MAN: Oh, hi boss. It's me.

Klondike?

Figure 10-12

(Courtesy of David R. Sackey, W. B. Doner and Company.)

COMM'L NO.: DSPM 2053

LENGTH: 30 SECONDS

(PLAYERS CHEER)

(PLAYERS CHEER)

JOHN GIELGUD: Gentlemen,

this is Paul Masson Champagne.
Supremely elegant

because it's made with the greatest
care.

And each bottle is vintage dated.

Can you read? **7.**

PLAYER: Vintage 1980. **8.**

JOHN GIELGUD: Remarkable.

Paul Masson Champagne.
(PLAYERS CHEER)

The civilized way to celebrate

Paul Masson will sell no wine before its
time.

Figure 10-13

(Courtesy of Melissa Wohltman, Doyle Dane Bernbach Advertising.)

Control Room Transitions and Devices

In television, video switchers and editing keyboards control the routing and assemblage of shots. This can be done either live (in real time) or by manipulating a number of pretaped sources. The lower the budget for the project, the more we strive for instant editing via a video switcher instead of extensive post-production work in editing bays. Either way, television uses a basic grammar of shot transitions that switchers and electronic editors execute. This grammar was borrowed from film—a medium that today is also edited electronically after transfer of its production rushes to videotape.

Fade In/Fade Out. Virtually all television messages "fade in" from "black" at the beginning and fade out or "fade to black" at their conclusion. Due to the abbreviated nature of television commercials and continuity, these fades are very rapid and may not even be specified in the script. For longer messages such as dramatic programs, varying the length of a fade can help to raise or lower more definitively television's version of the theatrical curtain.

Cut. This is the quickest and simplest method for changing from one shot to another. Today's visually literate audiences are so accustomed to this instantaneous transition that it often does not even impinge on their consciousness. Properly punctuated cuts can do a great deal to help the pacing of even very brief visual messages, and *intercutting* (rapid switching back and forth between two or more shots) has proven of significant utility when the creative concept requires an intense, pulsating delivery. *Cutaways* are a further variation on the term; they are especially prominent in certain types of commercials when we briefly replace the main scene with some laboratory or animated demonstration of a specific property the product possesses. Frames 7, 8, and 9 of the Klondike Bar photoboard in Figure 10–12 exploit the cutaway technique to illustrate the coating and wrapping of our luscious treat.

Because cuts are by far the most commonly used transition, a cut or "take" is assumed whenever any other scene or angle shift device is not specified in the script or at the top of the storyboard's audio block.

Dissolve. In this transition, one picture source seems gradually to "bleed through" and then finally replace another. Dissolves may be slow or fast and, in either case, provide a more fluid and gentle transition than the comparative punchiness of the cut. Visualize how Amtrak's 'California Zephyr' is invested with a smooth, motive impetus via the "through-the-train-window" dissolves called for in this script:

Video	Audio
OPEN MOUNTAINS	<u>MUSIC</u> <u>UP</u> <u>&</u> <u>UNDER</u>
DISSOLVE ELK	V/O: It was named
DISSOLVE MOUNTAINS	for the West Wind, the Zephyr.
DISS. MOUNTAIN TOPS	For the Zephyr takes you
DISS. TRAIN RUNNING THROUGH MOUNT.	where only the wind can go---
DISS. CU RACCOON	Through the
DISS. MOUNTAIN TOPS & SKY	high Rockies---
DISS. MOUNTAIN CANYON	into majestic canyons---
DISS. MOUNTAIN AT DUSK	and head long across
DISS. HORSES RUNNING THROUGH STREAM	the plains. From Chicago
DISS. TRAIN FOREGROUND, MOUNTAIN BACKGROUND	to the Pacific, ride Amtrak's California Zephyr.
DISS. OWL	By night
DISS. CLOUDS/NIGHT SKY	it will lull you to sleep---
DISS. MOUNTAINS, CLOUDS	By day, awaken
DISS. CU DEER & FAWN	your senses---
DISS. MOUNTAIN & CLOUDS AT SUNSET	And at sunset
DISS. SUNSET	it will blow you away.

Continued

Video	Audio
DISS. TRAIN COMING TO CAMERA	SONG: All aboard America
DISS. MOUNTAINS & SKY AT SUNSET	All aboard Amtrak
DISS. CU TRAIN RUNNING PAST CAMERA SUPER: LOGO: 'ALL ABOARD AMTRAK'	All aboard America
	All aboard Amtrak.

(Courtesy of National Railroad Passenger Corp. and DDB/Needham Worldwide.)

When the progress of the dissolve is stopped so that both picture sources remain discernible to the viewer, the result is a *superimposition*, or SUPER for short. *Matched dissolves* are hybrids in which we obtain a cumulative effect by dissolving from one similar or like thing to another. The old clock-face matched dissolves used to show passing time or the series of dissolves that make the pile of dirty dishes get smaller and the stack of clean ones get taller are both common (even trite) applications of this technique.

Contemporary solid-state electronics also makes possible a virtually infinite number of customized transitions that are programmed by the *special effects bank*, which works in conjunction with the video switcher or editor. Many of these effects are made possible by a *chroma-key*—the generic name for an apparatus that allows the removal of a given color from the original scene so a visual element from another source can be inserted in its place. Special effects terms, such as "split screen," "sunburst dissolve," and "checkerboard transition," are quite descriptive of the function each provides.

A standard cluster of special effects devices are known as *wipes*. Instead of one picture "bleeding through" the other, as in the dissolve/superimposition, a *wipe* allows one picture visually to push the other off the screen. Common direction-denoting varieties are *vertical, horizontal, diagonal, corner,* and *iris* (circular) wipes. A *split-screen* is simply the midpoint of a vertical, horizontal, or diagonal wipe. *Squeeze-zoom*, meanwhile, is a manufacturer-derived term referring to the namesake device's ability to compress, expand, and manipulate individual elements within a frame.

Squeeze-zoom and other proliferating electronic special effects phenomena use auxiliary terminology that is much more obscure because many of these state-of-the-art effects owe their existence to a computer. This marriage of television switching apparatus and computer hardware/software systems begets an almost bewildering array of tools from which to choose and an equally bewildering jargon all its own. For the copywriter, however, it is best to stick to a commonly understood phrase when attempting to specify some rarefied piece of special effects wizardry. The production and graphics people can put in their own parlance later, but they will at least start out with an accurate conception of what you want.

One overriding admonition must be heeded about special effects. Keep in mind that you are not selling, promoting, or identifying the transition or effect itself. Any technique that calls attention to itself at the expense of your subject is to be studiously avoided. If you should find yourself concentrating on what jazzy electronic explosion you can shoehorn into your next television spot or promo, it's time to stop and reexamine your priorities. "Special *defect* is my term," says Grey Advertising's executive vice president Richard Kiernan, "for a totally inappropriate use of special effects. Things like using a laser beam to create an apple pie when the strategy calls for old-fashioned-like-Grandma-used-to-bake. That kind of special effect not only doesn't reinforce the strategy; it undermines it. Or the bank that uses computer graphics in the attempt to dramatize warm, friendly, personalized service. . . . The magic, I maintain, is in how organic the solution is to the selling proposition. If you lose sight of the objective, then special effects can become special defects."[17] Any truly appropriate visual device will evolve naturally out of whatever you are trying to say in your message. The message's selling concept, not the effect, must come first. Leave the extraneous kaleidoscopes to the entertainment programs, which have thirty or sixty *minutes* to play with and can afford to be occasionally irrelevant.

"Advertising agencies should be in the business of selling *ideas*—not production values or the latest executional techniques of a trendy director," avows award-winning creative Ron Sandilands. "The ideal is to develop something substantive that can be stated simply and communicate a strong selling message to the consumer."[18] Or, as creative director Pat Burnham bluntly reminds commercial creators:

1. The production budget can't buy you an idea.
2. The director can't give you an idea.
3. You can't polish a turd.[19]

Other Writer-Used Technical Terms

Here are a variety of additional visual production designations common to television and often used on a script or storyboard to communicate the writer's intent to those who will pick up the project from there:

A/B ROLL: *editing procedure in which scenes/sounds on two videotape recorders (recorder A and recorder B) are intermixed onto a third machine (recorder C).*

ABSTRACT SET: *a plain and neutral background that uses only a few scattered implements to suggest the message environment. A single gas pump might represent a complete service station or a few framing tree branches simulate an entire forest. Though the abstract set is certainly not realistic, there is also less visual clutter in which the viewer might lose the product or central point of your message.*

ANIMATION: *drawing/cartooning that is sketched and photographed in a sequence that gives motion to a series of still pictures. May be computer-generated.*

ASPECT RATIO: *the constant three units high by four units wide dimensions of the television screen. The copywriter should keep this in mind when planning the television message since aspect ratio will circumscribe every visual idea funneled through the television medium. (Emerging* High Definition Television *uses an aspect ratio of nine units high by sixteen units wide.)*

BACKGROUND PROJECTION OR REAR PROJECTION (RP): *throwing a still slide or motion picture from behind a translucent screen so performers can use the result as scenery and stand in front of it without blocking the projector's illumination beam.*

BACKGROUND WASH: *a visual effect in which the matte color gradually changes in darkness/lightness or from one color to another.*

BACKLIGHT: *illumination from behind a subject in order to distinguish it more clearly from the background area.*

BEAUTY SHOT: *still picture of the product set in an environment that heightens its appeal, prestige, or appearance.*

BG: *commonly used abbreviation for the* background *of a scene.*

BLACK: *the condition of a video screen when it is processing no video information.*

BUMPER: *a graphic, slide, or brief animation used before or after a program or commercial segment.*

BUST SHOT OR CHEST SHOT: *a more specific designation for the Medium Close-Up (MCU) calling for a picture of a talent from the chest to just above the head.*

CAMEO: *lighting a foreground subject against a completely black background.*

CAPTION: *words/titles that are inserted onto other pictorial information.*

CHARACTER GENERATOR (CG): *computer keyboard apparatus that can electronically produce letters, symbols, and simple lines and backgrounds on the screen. Also permits these elements to move horizontally* (crawl) *or vertically* (roll). *Sometimes referred to as* Chyron, *after one of the original manufacturers of the device.*

CROSSFADE: *a pictorial transition in which the first scene dissolves to* black *and the next scene then dissolves from* black.

CYC (CYCLORAMA): *a U-shaped, stretched curtain that provides a neutral background for a television set.*

DEFOCUS: *a purposeful blurring of the picture.*

DEPTH OF FIELD: *that swath of territory in front of the camera lens in which all objects and subjects are in focus.*

DIGITAL VIDEO EFFECTS (DVE): *blanket term encompassing all the specialized computer techniques that allow images to expand, contract, spin, stretch, contort, or be otherwise manipulated.*

DOWNSTAGE: *the area nearest the camera lens; seemingly closest to the viewing audience.*

DROP: *a piece of scenic background, normally painted on canvas.*

EDGE WIPE: *wipe in which picture fringes are manipulated to give the central subject more prominence.*

FG: *commonly used abbreviation for the* foreground *of a scene.*

FILM CHAIN: *equipment linked together to permit the showing of 35-mm slides and motion picture film on television and normally consisting of the slide and film projectors plus a multiplexer and a specially adapted television camera.*

FILM VO: *script indication that a piece of film includes the copy set forth on that script.*

FISHEYE LENS: *lens that delivers an extremely wide angle picture to provide a field of view of up to 180°.*

FLASHBACK: *quick return to an earlier time/scene to show how the current scene evolved and/or graphically to contrast conditions portrayed in each.*

FLIP CARDS: *pieces of cardboard, cut into proper aspect ratio, that contain credits or other simple visual information. Flip cards are also known as* super cards *(from "superimposition") or* camera/studio/easel cards *and come in* lower one-third *(for names and subtitles) and* full-frame *varieties.*

FOLLOW SHOT: *use of a single, stationary camera to follow the action of a moving subject or object.*

FOLLOW SPOT: *high intensity, narrow-beam light used to illuminate subjects in motion.*

FREEZE FRAME: *stopping the motion of a film or tape so a single frame can be viewed as a still picture. Also called* Stop Action *and, particularly when it occurs at the end of a spot, may result in a* BEAUTY SHOT *(see above).*

GRAPHIC TABLET: *device on which the artist draws with an electronic pen (light-pen) to produce an image on the associated video screen.*

HARD LIGHT: *a strong directional beam from a spotlight that produces sharply defined shadows.*

HEADROOM: *area between the top of a subject's head and the upper edge of the TV screen.*

HIGH KEY: *relatively even illumination with few discernible shadows.*

IN MORTISE: *literally, "in a box"; placing the subject within a graphically rendered frame—often to set it off from "supered" titles that appear on the border this frame creates.*

JUMP CUT: *a disturbing or unnaturally abrupt transition between two pictures.*

KINESCOPE (KINE): *a comparatively poor quality film recording of a live television program or segment made by making a motion picture from the image on a television monitor.*

LIMBO: *a perfectly neutral and empty background.*

MATTE SHOT: *a portion of the picture is blanked out and replaced by a separate picture or pictures of any of a variety of sizes; often accomplished via chroma-keying.*

MONOCHROME: *a picture consisting solely of shades of gray.*

MONTAGE: *composite picture created from many separate images or a series of rapidly intercut visuals designed to create a certain association of ideas.*

MOS: *abbreviation for "Mit Out Sound," thus signifying a silent piece of film or tape footage.*

MULTIPLEXER: *special optical sampling device that allows one television camera to service several slide drums and/or movie projectors (see FILM CHAIN).*

NEGATIVE IMAGE (REVERSE POLARITY): *electronic manipulation that makes the "white" parts of a television picture appear "black" and vice versa.*

NI: *old but occasionally still-used abbreviation for "network identification."*

OC: *abbreviation for "on-camera"; person speaking is shown in the shot. Generally used to cancel a previous "voice-over" direction (see VO).*

PIXILLATION: *frame-by-frame animation technique using live actors or actual props rather than cartoon characters. When projected up to standard speed, pixillation makes talent/subject movements comedically jerky and abrupt.*

REACTION SHOT: *any picture designed to reveal the emotional response of a character to some previously shown, or about to be revealed, event.*

SHARED ID: *in television, commercial material that is placed on a flip card, slide, or film together with some graphic representation of the station identification.*

S.I.: *a sponsor identification line.*

SOF: *abbreviation for "sound on film"; a motion picture with its own synchronized sound track.*

SOFT FOCUS: *a slight defocusing of the picture resulting in a hazy effect indicative of dreams or semiconsciousness.*

SOT: *same as SOF when the medium is videotape rather than film.*

SPECIFIC ILLUMINATION: *lighting of highly localized and discrete areas.*

STOCK SHOT/STOCK FOOTAGE: *still or motion pictures of subjects that can be used in many different messages. An urban street scene, picture of a jet-liner taking off, or view of a charming old castle can all constitute stock footage.*

SWEETENING: *adding elements to a signal such as captions, pictorial inserts, and enhancing sound information.*

SWISHPAN: *an extremely rapid camera pan that is perceived on the screen as a blur.*

TEASE: *very brief promo for an upcoming program segment or the opening "grabber" in a long-form commercial.*

TELECINE: *equipment for projecting film and slides on television (see FILM CHAIN).*

TIGHT CLOSE-UP (TCU): *more precise delineation of a close-up in which we deliver a forehead-to-chin view of the talent.*

UNDERCUT: *changing the background of a scene without modifying foreground subjects—usually accomplished via matte or keying.*

UPSTAGE: *the area farthest from the camera lens; seemingly the most distant from the viewing audience.*

VECTOR: *process of creating pictures on a video screen through use of a light-pen (see GRAPHIC TABLET).*

VO: *abbreviation for "voice-over"; words spoken by someone not shown in the shot.*

VTR: *abbreviation for "videotape recorder" or for the recording it makes.*

X/S: *abbreviation sometimes used to designate an over-the-shoulder shot.*

The Audio-Video Coalition

All of these video techniques and terms must not be allowed to obscure the importance of audio to the successful television communication. Many new television copywriters find it difficult to grasp the fundamental principle that their soundtrack must enhance, not be merely an after-thought echo of, the picture. Effective television audio neither distracts from nor duplicates what that picture is striving to present.

Some writers rebel at this concept. Either they don't believe television audio is that important or they have never learned to write effective audio in the first place. That is why a solid grounding in radio copy creation is so valuable for the television writer. Given a large shooting budget and high-priced production personnel, a lot of visually adept copywriters can come up with a fairly interesting, even relevant piece of pictorial continuity or advertising. But let an assignment come along that for budgetary or conceptual reasons demands a relatively basic and unadorned picture, then many of these same visual artistes will fall flat on their eyeballs because their audio is only good enough to stash behind the scenery. Associate creative director Martha

Holmes maintains that "there isn't any reason to think that words are less interesting in commercials—as long as the words are not advertisingese, and don't have a list of client strategies in there. People's interest is not necessarily visual . . . what's important is a synergy between what's spoken and the film technique."[20]

Certainly, television is a visual medium. But it is also a frantically competitive one in which every possible advantage must be exploited to break through the clutter of the tube into the listener's consciousness. If the audio in your message is only "no worse than anybody else's," you are throwing away an immense opportunity to stand out from the crowd. Think the sound track of a television communication really doesn't matter? Then imagine:

```
shots of various mouth-watering delicacies available at
your local ice cream emporium---and a soundtrack consisting
of a bunch of pig snorts
```

or

```
action footage of a new pick-up truck bounding across rough
terrain---with an audio that features a tinkling music-box
rendition of 'Twinkle, Twinkle, Little Star.'
```

Just now, even with the imperfect conveyance of print, were you able to keep concentrating on the ice cream after the audio barnyard was called up in your mind? Could you maintain your focus on the ruggedness of the pick-up truck once its delicate little aural counterpoint impinged on your consciousness? Obviously, most television sound tracks are not this incongruous, but the power of the audio portion of the television message to confuse as well as to complement must always be respected because that power is present in every video assignment you face.

The Michigan Bell script that follows demonstrates how well-selected audio can complement and embellish the visual without making that visual dependent on it. This is very important because the basic point of a good television message should be capable of viewer discernment from the visual alone. The audio then serves to amplify that point. A high-interest visual (something every television message should possess) naturally arouses audience attention toward the audio that augments it. It is then up to the audio to fulfill the expectations that the visual and thence the viewer have set up for it. In this Yellow Pages commercial, the picture alone fully conveys the hassles of random, unorganized shopping. Yet, it is the audio that encapsulates the problem into supportive catch phrases and fully identifies these with the classified solution:

Video	Audio
MAN IN CAR BACKS OUT OF DRIVEWAY.	(SFX: TIRE/BRAKE SQUEAL)
	V/O: A simple shopping trip,
CAR BACKS UP TO THE PLUNGER OF PINBALL MACHINE AND STOPS ABRUPTLY.	(SFX: PINBALL DROPPING IN SLOT)
	without the Ameritech Michigan Bell Yellow Pages---
PLUNGER LAUNCHES CAR INTO PINBALL GAME.	(SFX: PLUNGER RELEASE)
	---could be an unforgettable experience.
CAR SPIRALS AROUND PINBALL BUMPER.	(SFX: BOING! BOING!)
	You could end up in circles---
CAR THROWN RAPIDLY BETWEEN PINBALL GAME BUMPERS.	(SFX: BUZZER)
	or going no place fast---
PINBALL FLIPPER SENDS CAR INTO "CLOSED" SIGN.	(SFX: DING! DING! DING!)
	---and getting there too late.
	(SFX: GENERAL PINBALL MACHINE MAYHEM)
CAR IN FRONT OF "WRONG AGAIN" SIGN AT END OF ALLEY.	Going down one blind alley after another---
CAR COMES TO A HALT IN FRONT OF OWN GARAGE.	---why go through that?
CU OF YELLOW PAGES BOOK ON TABLE NEXT TO PHONE AND DARK LAMP IN FRONT OF WINDOW.	---when you can go through Michigan's most complete shopping guide, before you leave.
SAME TABLE SHOT SHOWING SHAKING MAN THROUGH WINDOW.	

Continued

Video	Audio
CU OF MAN'S HAND TURNING ON LAMP OVER BOOK AND PHONE.	The Ameritech Michigan Bell Yellow Pages. Next to the phone, there's nothing better.

(Courtesy of Sheila I. O'Donnell, Ross Roy Inc., Advertising.)

We have just mentioned that the visual alone should be capable of attracting viewer interest in the message as well as giving a basic understanding of what that message is about. In fact, a good test of a piece of television continuity or advertising is to view it, or imagine it, with the sound off. Does the central point of the message still come through? And further, does it make us *want* to turn up that audio so we learn more?

Because a television announcement must *be* vision to attract viewer attention, it is general practice to write your pictorial descriptions first. Let the sense of sight carry as much of the revelation task as possible and then supplement as needed with SFX, music, and last, with spoken words. In creating television impressions, your best and most extensive writing will not be heard by the audience but instead will be *seen* by them through the produced result of your verbal video design.

This necessity of capturing pictures before words is as true in TV copywriting as it is in TV news. Both journalists and copywriters are inherently storytellers. "In doing a television story," declares CBS News Correspondent Charles Kuralt, "you must always know what picture it is you're writing to. That is, you never write a sentence without knowing exactly what the picture is going to be. I will say that again. My philosophy is that you must always know what picture accompanies the words you write. You cannot write for television without knowing what the picture is."[21]

Tonight, try turning off the sound on the television announcements and news stories to which you are exposed. How many of these messages convey the main point with the visual alone? And of these, how may tempt you to turn up the audio to get more information? Finally, did the audio actually deliver that information? Was that aural information relevant and meaningful? The results of this experiment should give you a general idea of the percentage of television messages that really exploit the audio-video coalition to its full potential.

It is through this coalition that television communication becomes a cohesive rather than a fragmentary discourse. Scripts, storyboards, camera movements, shot lengths, flip cards, videotape, and the other devices introduced in this chapter are all complementary or alternate means to the same end. Use them as needed to produce the most effective copy concepts possible.

Don't let them use you lest you become a purveyor of *hardware* instead of *ideas.*

No matter how state-of-the-art or costly the technique, it is irrelevant when not motivated by the strong, central selling concept that you, the copywriter, must engineer. As creative director Jim Dale cautions, "It all keeps coming back to the idea. Being forced to have one. And having everything riding on the idea being great. When you have it, there's always a way to bring it off. When you don't have it, all the techniques and tricks and hot songs and New Wave and blah blah blah aren't enough. And the funny thing is, when you do have a strong idea, finding a way to pull it off isn't even as hard as you thought anyway. Because people *want* to work on a great idea. They can smell it on a storyboard or a script and they start pulling rabbits out of hats from the beginning."[22]

Endnotes

1. "Storyboards That Really Control Production and Save Money Too," *ASAP* (May/June 1988), 12.
2. Peter Kellogg, "Artful Deception Fills a Copywriter's Day," *ADWEEK* (April 16, 1984), 38.
3. Betsy Sharkey, "Software Lets Thrifty Clients 'CLIP' and Save," *ADWEEK* (November 7, 1988), 36.
4. Ibid., 38.
5. Cathy Madison, "Desktop Video Editing Has Ad Makers Clicking," *ADWEEK* (March 11, 1991), 47.
6. Warren Berger, "Video Feeds the Hype Machine," *Corporate Video Decisions* (February 1990), 30.
7. Martin Levine, "The Computer Animation Shift: Champagne at Beer Prices," *Corporate Video Decisions* (August, 1989), 44.
8. Tom Stefani, "Cartoon to Boardroom: Animation for All Audiences," *Video Systems* (February 1992), 36.
9. Steve Meyer, "Effects Solutions," *Video Systems* (July 1992), Sup. 16.
10. Ron Gales, "Fateful Attractions: Rollicking Raisins and a Manic Noid, *ADWEEK* (October 12, 1987), 54.
11. Jeanette Salvito, "Gumby Is Alive and Well in America," *Audio Visual Communications* (September 1990), 17.
12. Stephen Wershing and Tanya Weinberger, "Corporate Communications Come to Life with Animation," *Educational & Industrial Television* (March 1986), 42–43.
13. Bob Bennett and John Javetski, "Automated Animation," *Video Systems* (January 1991), Sup. 14.
14. Jeffrey Cohen, "Are Corporate Graphics Losing Their Punch?" *Corporate Video Decisions* (November 1988), 32.
15. *FreezeFrame Product Brochure,* Polaroid Corporation, May 1988.
16. Neil Kesler, writing in "Monday Memo," *Broadcasting* (August 20, 1984), 12.

17. Richard Kiernan, writing in "Monday Memo," *Broadcasting* (August 15, 1983), 24.
18. Ron Sandilands, "Sandilands' Creative Review," *Winners* (February 1988), 9.
19. Cathy Madison, "Midwest MVP: Pat Burnham," *ADWEEK* (February 20, 1989), 19.
20. Barbara Lippert, "The New Terseness," *ADWEEK* (February 1985), C.R. 1.
21. Charles Kuralt, speaking at the Writing for Television Seminar, Center for Communications, Inc., 12 November 1985, New York.
22. Jim Dale, "Budget TV," *ADS Magazine* (June 1985), 96.

■ *Chapter 11*

Television Commercials

In proportion to the number of words expended, television commercial writers probably get more money per word than do wordsmiths for any other medium—even when the vital but unspoken words on the script's video side are included in the computation. These high-priced words are also key to career advancement. "People like to do TV," admits advertising veteran Peter Cohen, "so they can go to another agency and ask for more money."[1]

Just as important, from a psychological standpoint, TV spot writers experience the fun of dealing with a communications vehicle that is more flexible than any other channel human beings have contrived—a vehicle that is becoming *more* flexible all the time. The danger, however, is that we become so captivated by television's technological possibilities that the ads we create become too diffuse. All of our efforts, therefore, must be directed to focusing our message and to employing only those tools that are necessary to that message's realization in the minds of our target viewers.

TV Commercial Noncopy Data Block

In television, message focusing is typographically initiated, as it is on radio, with a well-organized noncopy data block such as the one Table 11-1 illustrates.

Because the television script must direct simultaneous attention to both audio and visual elements, and because of the expense of television as compared to most radio production, the TV data block requires a specific articulation of the commercial's objective. This precise goal statement is a constant reminder of the project's reason for being. It provides an unblinking quality control mechanism for the copy and pictorial elements that follow this objective on the page. Thus, in the Table 11-1 spot, the objective is not "to sell gum." That any spot is supposed to "sell" its product goes without saying. Rather, this commercial's written objective specifies (1) a universe (subteens), (2) the precise product characteristic being promoted (blackberry taste), and

Table 11-1
TV Commercial Data Block

AIMED-WRITE ADVERTISING
(television copy)

CLIENT <u>Simmons Gum Company</u>   SUBMIT DATE <u>Sept. 30, 1994</u>
JOB # <u>V-SG-31</u>   LIVE _____ FILM _____ VTR <u>XX</u>
PRODUCT <u>Tooth-Treat Gum</u>   SLIDE _____
REVISION # <u>3</u>   ISCI # <u>SIGC-1411</u> LENGTH <u>:30</u>
CLIENT APPRV DATE <u>10/9/94</u>   TITLE <u>Tooth-Treat Troll</u>
    AS PRODUCED <u>Oct. 31, 1994</u>

<u>OBJECTIVE:</u> To demonstrate to subteens that the blackberry
   taste of Simmons Tooth-Treat Gum is so enlivening that it
   brightens the disposition of almost anyone.

<u>PRODUCTION</u> <u>NOTE:</u> The locale is a picturesque though
   sinister-looking bridge spanning a forest ravine. A
   sharp-featured, scowling dwarf appears from under the
   bridge. Young (7-10 year-old) boy and girl who encounter
   him are of contrasting types---one a dark brunette, the
   other a light blond.

Video	Audio
1. OPEN ON ESTABLISHING SHOT OF RAVINE	<u>MUSIC:</u> LONELY, EERIE 'STORY-BOOK TYPE' THEME
2. TROLL APPEARS STAGE LEFT	<u>TROLL:</u> I hate people--

. . . .

---

(3) the viewer benefit flowing from the characteristic (the brightening of a person's mood/disposition). Every well-honed objective statement must cover all three of these elements.

    In addition to the objective's prominent display, the data block features several other noteworthy items. Working from the top, the block sets forth the client's corporate name and the SUBMIT DATE of this particular script to them. The JOB # (V–SG–35) is the agency's own filing designation for this project. In this case, 'V' means it's a video assignment for (SG) Simmons Gum and is the 35th television spot created for that client. Because VTR is 'XX-ed,' the spot is a videotape production for (PRODUCT) Tooth-Treat Gum.

The ISCI # is an abbreviation for the Industry Standard Commercial Identification System. ISCI (pronounced 'iss-key') was created in 1970 to, in the words of its chief administrator David Dole, "answer the need for a standard-length, standard-format, computer-compatible identity code for television commercials. . . . ISCI's capability as a worldwide 'identity' standard includes 17,000-plus agency prefixes (7 percent used), each capable of coding 100 commercials for each of 100 advertisers, 33,000 advertiser prefixes (10 percent used) and 175,000,000 program codes."[2] ISCI prefixes are assigned without charge to qualifying agencies and advertisers because the system is underwritten by the major networks as well as by broadcast and advertising trade associations. If you look carefully, you will find ISCI numbers on several of the photoboards appearing in this book.

Reading on, the data block also tells us that this is a 30-second spot in LENGTH, and that the script to follow is its third major REVISION. The treatment's TITLE is Tooth-Treat Troll (recall the importance of title development in our Chapter 8 radio discussion), and it was given final approval by the client on October 11. Actual videotape production was then completed on October 31.

Below the OBJECTIVE, to which we already have referred, the PRODUCTION NOTE sets forth the commercial's major scene and casting requirements so these are prominently called to the reader's attention while not cluttering the body of the actual shooting script.

Compulsory Demonstrability—The D.D.Q.

In constructing the actual body of the commercial script, focusing the television commercial means focusing on the product/service demonstration. Through its simultaneously moving audio and video discourses, television is the real "show and tell" vehicle. Your viewers have come to expect a demonstration from the products they see on the tube, and your client is paying big money to put it there. So as a copywriter, it is incumbent on you to use this costly capability to the fullest. The television commercial that does not demonstrate does not belong on television.

Can all products or services be demonstrated? Yes. Provided you are willing REALLY TO ANALYZE the assignment in front of you. The best way to structure this analysis is via the following five-step question/answer process that we label *The Demo-Deriving Quintet (D.D.Q.):*

1. What is the subject's key attribute?
2. What benefit flows from that attribute?
3. What implement(s) make(s) the benefit most tangible?
4. What scene best showcases the implement(s)?
5. What happens in that scene? (What's the pictorial progression?)

1. What Is the Subject's Key Attribute?

You may recall our previous focus on "key attributes" in conjunction with the Chapter 7 discussion of *Poetic Packaging.* There, the emphasis is on isolating this prime component of our product so the proper radio *sounds* could be enlisted to describe it. Here, we are seeking to cull out the same key attribute as the first step in determining which *pictures* will best delineate it. Most often this key attribute is, by itself, intangible, as in the "locally grown" core of the Michigan Department of Agriculture commercial in Figure 11–1.

2. What Benefit Flows from That Attribute?

The important word in this second-level question is, of course, *benefit,* benefit in relation to the viewers at whom the commercial is directed. It is one thing, for example, to use slow motion and freeze frame to show tennis players that your client's ball stays on the racket longer. But unless this attribute is unequivocally translated into the greater *control* that is thereby brought to your game, the viewer will be unimpressed. Similarly, we can expend 60 seconds or more in illuminating the coarse texture of our breakfast cereal. This will be wasted effort, however, if our geriatric universe isn't able to comprehend the digestive advantages this texture provides. In the Figure 11–1 spot, the isolated benefit is "fresh variety." Viewers get a return on their home-state patronage.

3. What Implement(s) Make(s) the Benefit Most Tangible?

Now, with the frustratingly nonvisual initial two steps decided, and with the indispensable framework they provide in place, we can proceed to carve out the concept at which a camera can point. We can choose a pictorial referent for that product-derived and consumer-related benefit. In Figure 11–1, the Michigan farmer in frame 5 and the Michigan produce in frames 6, 7, and 9 epitomize the freshness and variety that is contrasted with the random commodities being haphazardly transported in frames 1–4 and 8. In the Kendall Oil script below, meanwhile, an unmarred ring of gold is used to substantiate the product's impressive maintenance benefit.

V/O: Do you know where your last meal came from?

From out of the blue?

...Across the river?

...Across the border?

Or from more familiar ground?

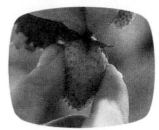

Michigan produces and processes

enough delicious variety for three different meals a day for a year

So why eat food that's better traveled than you are?

Buy Michigan. There's nothing like the great taste of home.

Figure 11-1

(Courtesy of Brogan & Partners Advertising.)

Video	Audio
KENDALL CAN AND GOLD RINGS IN FOREGROUND	ANNCR. (VO): Kendall Motor Oil protects engines from friction.

Continued

Video	Audio
HAND PICKS UP RING.	To prove how well.
ECU OF ANNCR. AND RINGS.	ANNCR. (OC): we plated ordinary piston rings with pure gold.
CUT TO: MED, SHOT ANNCR. AND ENGINE	and ran them inside this engine for 5,000 miles.
HOLD UP CAN.	Kendall friction fighters are better than car makers demand---
CUT TO HAND REMOVING RIM RINGS.	but can Kendall protect even soft gold?
ECU ANNCR. AND RINGS.	Look---No visible wear! That's protection!
BEAUTY SHOT OF CAN AND RINGS. TITLE: 'Protection worth its weight in gold.'	Friction Fighting Kendall Motor Oil---for protection worth its weight in gold.

(Courtesy of Ken Merrit, Al Paul Lefton Company, Inc.)

It should be clear by now that the range of benefit-illustrating implements from which you, as a copywriter, can select is as broad as the ever-widening technology of film and tape can provide. Today, small, local accounts can obtain productional services that, until recently, were available only to the costly, nationally distributed commercials of the largest companies in the land. But this does not mean you select a pictorial implement simply because it's now within budgetary reach or because a lot of other commercials are using it. That is nothing more than "me-too" advertising; a dangerous practice because it only invites more imitation with consequent loss of identity. And "in those cases where 'me-too' advertising has led to 'me-three' look-alikes," reports commercial testing expert Dave Vadehra, "anything short of innovative will surely be as boring to the viewer as it is confining to the advertiser."[3] If, on the other hand, your chosen benefit implement is a natural and inevitable outgrowth of the conclusions reached in the Demo-Deriving Quintet's first two levels, that implement's intrinsic relationship to your product will make copying attempts by others counterproductive.

4. What Scene Best Showcases the Implement(s)?

In some assignments, this aspect is decided almost simultaneously with the third step above. To endanger a gold piston ring, for instance, it immediately follows that we need an engine in a service garage. To locate "fresh variety," a spectrum of foods situated in from-the field wooden baskets (Figure 11–1's frame 7) makes obvious sense—and contrasts markedly with the in-transit alternatives.

In other circumstances, such as the classic Big Banana approach in Figure 11–2, the selected benefit implement may mandate placement in more than one environment. To make Shakespeare a credible modern "expresser," therefore, he and the benefit he represents jump from the Elizabethan court to a contemporary coffee house. Even though people fail to understand him in the former environment, he connects in the latter through the simple addition of our product.

5. What Happens in That Scene? (What's the Pictorial Progression?)

Finally, after carefully thinking through the first four levels of D.D.Q. analysis, we are in a position to determine the scenario, the actual storyline of our commercial. It is important that the tale we are spinning unfold in a manner that continues to hold viewer attention while, at the same time, keeping the product benefit at center stage. The story that is so dominant that the mission it serves gets lost is a story that should never have been told. Fortunately, if the first four levels of *Demo-Deriving* have been scrupulously and honestly dealt with, the resulting scenario should be so product/benefit actuated that it is difficult to separate the story from the goods in whose support it evolved. After the rigors of quality-deficient travels in Figure 11–1's first four frames, it is a relief to "come home" to fresh Michigan produce. Similarly, in the Figure 11–3 GTE commercial, the life-perpetuating journey of a dandelion seed becomes an allegory for the company's communication-extending services.

The GTE spot also conforms to what advertising industry spokesman John O'Toole years ago isolated as the need for *commercial tension:*

> It seems to me that something has to happen very quickly in a commercial, much as in a print ad, to engage and hold the prospect. I suspect it must occur in the first five seconds.
>
> It also seems to me (and again, this is not dissimilar to the print experience) that the commercial must establish a tension, a sort of magnetic field compelling enough to overcome the viewer's natural tendency to discuss the preceding program material, to listen to someone else do so, to go to the bathroom or to simply disengage his mind.
>
> In addition, it seems to me that the tension must center on, or lead quickly to, some question the viewer might want answered, some need or

Wells, Rich, Greene, Inc./767 Fifth Avenue/New York, N.Y. 10022/Plaza 8-4300

CLIENT: Bic Pen Co.	CODE NO.: WBBM 3327
PRODUCT: Bic Banana	TITLE: "Shakespeare"
	LENGTH: :30

V.O.:   For years, Shakespeare struggled to express himself.

And today, there are still people trying to figure out what he was talking about.

"To be or not to be."

What does it mean?

If he had a Bic Banana, he would've written: "I am.   Take it or leave it."

(SFX: Pleased sounds from people in coffee house) Because you can express yourself with a Bic Banana.

You could write, sign, draw, mark, and mainly go crazy! You don't find that kind of expressiveness in a ballpoint.

In a ballpoint you find: "Wherefore art thou, Romeo"

In a Bic Banana you're gonna get,

"Romeo, you keep yourself nice. Let's get married."

Get a Bic Banana.

It comes in ten expressive colors!

Figure 11-2

(Courtesy of Kenneth Olshan, Wells, Rich, Greene, Inc.)

want or problem he suddenly recognizes or acknowledges, some insight into the reality of his life. Whichever, it must relate logically to the product or service that is being advertised.[4]

A spot need not depict a life-threatening situation to achieve a storyline that both demonstrates a benefit and possesses the O'Toole-advocated ten-

ANNCR: Mobile communication. It is the power to hold your world together.

At GTE we can put that power at hand

to take with you where it has never gone before.

Into the skies.

Down endless highways

Beyond all past limitations.

At GTE we give you the freedom of personal communication and the power of new opportunities.

Because at GTE, the power is on.

Figure 11-3

(Courtesy of GTE and DDB/Needham Advertising.)

sion. Nor must it feature a wealth of special effects and shot changes. Sometimes, the simplest environment and scenario project tension best. As evidence of this truth, consult the landmark Broxodent Automatic Toothbrush message featured in Figure 11–4. This is a demonstration, a story *dramatization*, that additional props and characters would only clutter.

1. ANNCR: During the next 60 seconds, this toothbrush will brush 200 up and down strokes.

2. About as fast as you brush your teeth by hand.

3. Now let's try the Broxodent Automatic Toothbrush.

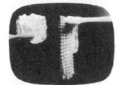
4. This is how long it takes the Broxodent to brush 200 up and down strokes.

5. There. 200 in less than 4 seconds.

6. So if you take a minute to brush your teeth, instead of 200 ...

7. up and down strokes with an ordinary toothbrush, you get 3,600 with a Broxodent.

8. Because you brush with an ordinary toothbrush, ...

9. but you brrrush with a Broxodent, ...

10. the automatic toothbrush from Squib.

11. That just about sums it up. But we can't end this commercial ...

12. till we've finished doing 200 up and down strokes by hand ...

13. as promised.

14. (SFX).

15. (SFX).

Figure 11-4

(Courtesy of Robert Levenson, Doyle Dane Bernbach Advertising.)

Despite the obvious differences among the clients and treatments presented in the preceding pages, they all share and exhibit a persuasive demonstrability that flows unstoppably from the central attribute of each product being advertised. Notice that nowhere in the *Demo-Deriving Quintet* have we mentioned camera angles, special effects banks, or fancy superimpositions. Instead, applying the DDQ allows the subject itself to determine what should be done and the visual components that most naturally should be called to do it. There is plenty of time to worry about specific production techniques once each of *Demo-Deriving's* five questions has been successfully met and, in order, perceptively answered. To "think production" any earlier is to sell a video technique rather than a client's wares.

The reason that people with no experience in video production often make better television copywriters than those who come out of the television industry is that the former lack the background to concentrate on anything but the *message concept.* The broadcast or film veteran, on the other hand, has spent so much time with the machinery of the medium that questions of execution keep getting in the way of much more central questions of content. "I see a lot of commercials where there is a good idea, but it's buried in production values or too many benefits," observes star TV copywriter Bruce Bildsten. "The spot can still be beautiful and richly produced, but it's more the simplicity of the idea itself. You have to make it work so that the idea comes through."[5]

If you possess, or are acquiring a video or film production background—fine. That knowledge will help you polish your finished scripts and boards so that they will more easily jump the gap between the creation and production phases of a commercial's development. Just don't let your technical expertise clutter up your mind and your advertisement any earlier in the process. Don't, whatever you do, let the production run away with the message in the conceptual stage or it will invariably run away with the message once it gets "on the tube."

Keep structuring your commercial development process via the *Demo-Deriving Quintet.* The D.D.Q. will not only keep your television creations "on track" but will also make you a more focused and disciplined visual writer. And just to review the Quintet's five steps, and the progressive interaction of each of those steps on the others, let's follow the labors of one trainee group as it tried to evolve a spot for a hypothetical Terry Cuff Ring campaign.

The Terry Cuff Ring (an actual though largely unadvertised product) is an oval-shaped and open-ended, flexible metal band, imported from England. Cyclists clamp it above their ankle to keep pants cuffs from snagging in the bicycle chain.

What is the Terry Cuff Ring's key attribute? After unproductive forays into aspects of "protection" and "safety"—forays that broke down in later steps—the trainees (in some unjustified panic) clutched at the idea of *convenience.*

What benefit flows from convenience? Most obviously, quickness of use. The Terry Cuff Ring can be slipped onto one's leg in far less time than it takes to position and tie a lace or small piece of rope.

What implement(s) make(s) the benefit most tangible? This too is very obvious in this case and, with a little fine-tuning, the trainees decided on a trouser leg that sported a substantial cuff.

What scene best showcase the implement? To determine this answer took some time and seemed to present several possible ways to go until one of the trainees perceptively pointed out that (1) the product was English-made; (2) English-made goods have a positive reputation for quality; and (3) there were American-made versions of the Terry Cuff Ring from which it must be distinguished. An English motif seemed to be the natural response to these factors, and what is more English than a bobby (English policeman)? Whose trouser leg more appropriate than his?

What happens in that scene? Whatever the event, it was crucial that it set up an episode in which the previously selected "quickness of use" benefit could prominently be showcased and that it be the bobby who derived this benefit. After more trainee discussion the scenario took shape.

```
A typical British crook (complete with little tweed cap,
black eye mask, and turtle neck sweater) bursts out of a
village thatched-roof bank carrying a bag of money. He runs
toward his cycle but, enroute, sees and is seen by our
stalwart bobby who is standing down the street near his own
bicycle that sports a "Constable" sign on the handlebars.
The nervous robber, after some obvious disconcertion,
jumps on his bike but his heavy trouser leg is already
enmeshed in the chain. Frantically, he pulls the string off
the bag of money and attempts to lace it around his cuff. A
view of the bobby then displays his exquisite poise and
confidence as he pulls a Terry Cuff Ring out of his pocket
and effortlessly places it on his trouser leg. The robber
is still tying his lace with money falling out of the
now-open bag as the bobby rides up and arrests him. The
Terry Cuff Ring triumphs again.
```

Visual technology and, in fact, the determination of the entire sound track, could come later. What the trainee group had succeeded in doing was to shape a compelling demonstration that possessed flow and tension, held interest, and clearly defined both the specific product and the benefit that the viewer would accrue from using it. If you want to write television that *is* truly television, go ye and do likewise. Provide your video treatments with benefit-centered demonstrations that are so intrinsic, so relevant, that you never need to call on some overexposed announcer to scream those viewer-alienating words: "Here's proof."

Getting Recognized and Remembered

As you concentrate on demonstration display, don't forget that the product name must come through loud and clear. The viewer has to be made aware (and be able to *recall*) that the *Terry Cuff Ring* helped the bobby, that the *Broxodent* beat the ordinary toothbrush by 56 seconds, and that *GTE* is where "the power is on." Brand recall is as important in television as it is on radio and should be promoted as part and parcel of the benefit-depicting demonstration.

The same *identity line* formulation principles that were presented in the chapter on radio commercials can also be applied to television—but with the additional requirement that the ID line have conspicuous *visual* relevance to the demonstrations being featured. Thus, to succeed on television, the commercial must let the viewer *see* that Kendall Motor Oil's protection is "worth its weight in gold"; *see* that you brush with an ordinary toothbrush but you "brrrush with a Broxodent"; *see* the smile on the little Michigan girl's face that come from experiencing "the great taste of home."

As in radio, the television ID line that is also *categorical*—that signifies its production classification—usually has a longer and more functional life expectancy. Here are some video identity lines that helped the spots that demonstrated them to drive home category/brand recall:

```
Tuborg: The golden beer of Danish kings.

Check-Up Gum: When you can't brush, chew.

Joy cleans down to the shine; and that's a nice reflection
on you.

Krylon Paint: no runs, no drips, no errors.

Head and shoulders hates your dandruff but loves your
hair.

Arm & Hammer---a nice little secret for your refrigerator.

The Michigan Bell Yellow Pages; next to the phone there's
nothing better.

Miracle Whip: the bread spread from Kraft.

Nothing sparks like a Champion.
```

Getting recognized and remembered means writing a spot that doesn't just *attract* attention, but also *converts* attention into robust brand recall at the point-of-purchase. This is becoming an increasingly formidable task as more and shorter spots crowd the airwaves. Arbitron reports, for instance, that the number of weekly commercials on broadcast networks rose from fewer than 3,000 in 1971 to well over 6,000 by 1990.[6] It is no surprise, then, that "according to day-after recall tests by Burke Marketing Research, the percent of adults recalling commercials dropped from 24 percent in 1978 to 21 percent in 1988," reveals media research executive Gerard Broussard.[7]

Certainly, the zipping and zapping made possible by VCRs and remote controls is a contributing factor to this worsening recall situation. That is why astute marketers, like Buick's Jay Qualman, use fast-forward viewing as a test to make sure that spots provided by his agency have a clear and straightforward storyline that can be fundamentally understood even at high speed. Roger Sarotte, Qualman's counterpart at Chrysler, takes a similar approach. "We try to make sure people can catch the key things, so they grab the idea of the ad," Sarotte reveals.[8] In a zipping environment, the graphic demonstration—enhanced by an aurally and visually articulated ID line—can be the copywriter's best chance of engineering a recall breakthrough.

The Oh Henry! spot in Figure 11–5, for instance, focuses initial attention via a compelling little cartoon man whose diminutive size lets the original product take over the frame. The product is then unmistakably shouldered aside by the *line extension* item (a new variation on the brand). Recall is reinforced by continuous portrayal of the mouth-watering qualities for which O Henry! has long been recognized. The original candy bar and its new "ice cream cousin" thus cross-reference each other, with this interrelationship visually reemphasized in the final frame's audio/visual expression of the featured ID line. Even in fast-forward, it is doubtful that the product name or ice cream category will be missed.

Video DR, Infomercials, and Co-Op

Television direct response (DR) commercials require an additional recall element, of course—registration of the contact phone number or mailing address. In fact all the tenets of radio DR introduced in Chapter 9 also apply to its television execution. That is, the TV direct response ad should (1) prepare viewers for action at the top of the message, (2) show how the product can impinge on the viewer's life, (3) make product exclusivity unmistakable, (4) take viewer objections into account, (5) clearly and repeatedly state product cost, (6) stress the need for immediate action, and (7) communicate the specific purchase process.

INTERVIEWER:
This is the big one!

He's one of Canada's
biggest bars! One of
Canada's best selling bars!

Famous for nuts!
Famous for caramel!

Hey, is it cold in here?

VO: Meet Oh Henry's cousin,
the Oh Henry Ice Cream Bar!
INTERVIEWER: Yikes! He's freezing!

VO: Introducing the
Oh Henry Ice Cream Bar.

Same big peanuts!

Rich chocolatey coating!
Creamy caramel!

Singles or eight-packs!

INTERVIEWER:
You're cool, kid.

But you're gonna be the
hottest thing in the freezer!

VO: Meet Oh Henry's
Ice Cream cousin!
He lives in the grocer's
ice cream cabinet!

Qualicolor
Systems

Figure 11-5

(Courtesy of Barry Base, Base Brown Partners, Ltd.)

Because television has both sound and picture available to accomplish these objectives, the copywriter enjoys greater flexibility in message design. Phone numbers can be supered on the screen, for example, thus freeing the soundtrack for other information. Remember, in most television DR messages, you are, in direct marketer Freeman Gosden's words,

> selling the offer, not your product. This is especially true in lead generation programs where you are trying to get people to identify themselves as someone who might be interested. Once you have enticed them with the offer, you can sell them in person, by phone or by mail much more easily. . . . State your offer prominently. If you bury your offer, you might as well not even use one. People are used to seeing offers prominently displayed. They also want to learn all they can about the offer—because that is what they are responding to. . . . State your offer's benefit clearly. People are not buying your product and they are not really buying your offer. They are buying the benefits of your offer. Offers are not perceived to be good unless you tell the audience they are good. Benefits, benefits, benefits.[9]

In fashioning a benefit statement, the copywriter must decide whether to strive for a *maximum* response or a *qualified* response. A maximum response may generate a significant number of leads—but are all of these leads in a position to obtain the product? A qualifed response will result in fewer inquiries—but virtually all of these inquiries will be from prospects whose financial and lifestyle position makes product purchase feasible. In addition, if your offer includes a premium, make certain it is a freebie that will appeal to your client's customers. Prospective users of a discount brokerage house probably already own a pocket calculator—so holding it out as a gift will be insufficient motivation to call.

From its opening frame, the following DR message zeros in on qualified amateur golfer prospects. It offers a premium that is a natural extension of the main product's benefit plus frequent 800-number 'supers' to stimulate how-to-get-it recognition:

Video	Audio
OPEN ON WIDE SHOT OF GOLF TOURNAMENT. LARGE BANNER ESTABLISHES "GOLF DIGEST PRO-AM". CROWD WATCHES AS TOM WATSON AND PARTNER WARM UP WITH PRACTICE SWINGS.	
	A.V.O.: What would it be like to play in a Pro-Am with Tom Watson?

Continued

Video	Audio
THEN, STILL GLANCING AT TOM, HE TAKES STANCE, THEN ADJUSTS STANCE. THEN ADJUSTS GRIP.	PARTNER (TRYING TO STAY COOL) If you see anything I can improve, Tom, just (ha ha) speak up.
CAMERA MOVES IN ON TWOSOME AS TOM INTERRUPTS PARTNER AT TOP OF SWING TO SHOW HIM HOW TO TURN HIS BACK MORE.	TOM (FRIENDLY AND PATIENT): Remember Andy, you have to turn your back on the target---
MOVE IN ON PARTNER, STILL POISED AT TOP OF SWING, AS HE ADJUSTS BACK, AND COMPLETES SWING.	---every time you make a full swing. SFX: CLUB HITS BALL.
A FRAME IS FROZEN AND PERHAPS TRANSFORMED INTO AN ILLUSTRATION. PULL BACK TO REVEAL IT AS PART OF A MAGAZINE SPREAD OF AN INSTRUCTIONAL ARTICLE. APPROPRIATE HEADLINE COPY IS INCLUDED. 800 NUMBER IS BRIEFLY SUPERED.	
QUICK SHOT OF AMAZED PLEASURE ON AMATEUR'S FACE	
CUT TO TOM DEMONSTRATING MOVEMENT OF KNEE	TOM: On chip shots around the green, start the forward swing by
WIDEN SHOT TO SHOW THAT TOM AND PARTNER ARE IN A NEW LOCATION AND THAT THE LATTER IS AGAIN EMULATING TOM AND AGAIN COMPLETES THE SWING.	---moving the right knee toward the target.
	SFX: CLUB HITS BALL

Continued

Video	Audio
A FRAME IS FROZEN AND PERHAPS TRANSFORMED INTO AN ILLUSTRATION. PULL BACK TO REVEAL IT AS PART OF A MAGAZINE SPREAD OF AN INSTRUCTIONAL ARTICLE. APPROPRIATE HEADLINE COPY IS INCLUDED. 800 NUMBER IS BRIEFLY SUPERED.	
QUICK SHOT OF TOM AND AMATEUR'S FACE REVEALS SUCCESS OF SUGGESTION.	
CUT TO AMATEUR ON GREEN, CONCENTRATING ON PUTT. WATSON KNEELS BEHIND HIM, COACHING,	TOM: When you're putting in the wind, widen your stance and
HE ADJUSTS HIS STANCE PER TOM'S INSTRUCTIONS.	crouch a little.
AND COMPLETES PUTT.	SFX: GENTLE APPLAUSE FROM CROWD
A FRAME IS FROZEN AND PERHAPS TRANSFORMED INTO AN ILLUSTRATION. PULL BACK TO REVEAL IT AS PART OF A MAGAZINE SPREAD OF AN INSTRUCTIONAL ARTICLE. APPROPRIATE HEADLINE COPY IS INCLUDED. 800 NUMBER IS BRIEFLY SUPERED.	
TWO SHOT. ELATED AMATEUR WITH SMILING TOM	PARTNER: Wow, Tom! Got any more tips?
FOCUS ON TOM AS HE PULLS GOLF DIGEST MAGAZINE FROM HIS GOLF BAG	TOM: Yep. Best one of all: a lesson every month,

Continued

Video	Audio
TOM DISPLAYS MAGAZINE	along with tips from guys like Jack Nicklaus, Tom Kite, and Sam Snead---
CUT TO ECU OF <u>GOLF</u> <u>DIGEST</u> NAME ON FRONT OF MAGAZINE AND PULL OUT TO REVEAL COVER FEATURING TOM WATSON AND PARTNER SMILING AND HOLDING TROPHY WITH HEADLINE ANNOUNCING VICTORY	
	<u>A.V.O.:</u> Golf Digest is like playing with the champs, 12 times a year.
CONTINUE TO PULL OUT TO REVEAL THAT SPREAD IS PART OF A DISPLAY OF 12 ISSUES PLUS BOOK "GOLF LESSONS FROM THE PROS". LAID OUT ON GREEN AROUND HOLE WITH BALL IN IT. <u>SUPER</u> <u>PHONE</u> <u>NUMBER.</u>	Call 800-_____ for a full year of <u>Golf Digest</u> for only $12.77. 46% off the cover price.
	Order now and also get <u>Golf Lessons From The Pros</u> free. Call 800-_____.
ADD SUPER 12 ISSUES--- $12.77	

(Courtesy of Lawrence Butner, Lawrence Butner Advertising, Inc.)

Especially when they provide a substantial amount of instruction (like the above Golf Digest message), DR spots of 2 minutes or more also qualify as *infomercials*. Extending up to a half-hour in length, these descendants of the old newsreels and PR films provide significantly more time to register the subject and specifics of your message. Many DR experts enlist infomercial lengths mainly to expand attention to "how-to-get-it" data. The one-minute spot, for example, allows only ten to twelve seconds for such information, whereas the two-minute pitch usually permits twenty to twenty-two seconds.[10] DR authority Francie Barson advocates, therefore, that you write a 120-second spot to carry your main campaign and supplement this with a sixty to enhance the number of impressions achieved with your target audience.[11]

As its name implies, however, the *info*mercial decrees that more than just offer/benefit/purchase process be discussed. The viewer must also be given specific and tangible *information* that can be of interest and value *in its own right*. The following Grocerama message, for example, provides enlightenment on nutrition as well as on the economics of food distribution. It also has time to dramatize much more extensively how Grocerama can impinge on the viewer's life. Spots of this length (and, indeed, all infomercials) owe much of their increasing popularity and exposure to cable television networks, which have the scheduling flexibility, available time, and more specific "narrowcast" audience to accommodate the infomercial's needs and the sponsor's market requirements.

PRODUCTION NOTE: Talent is mid-thirties woman. She's attractive but not gorgeous and dressed in skirt and blouse equally appropriate to secretary, teacher, or homemaker.

Video	Audio
OPEN MLS TALENT W/SHOPPING CART AND STOCKBOY	TALENT: Excuse me, where do you keep your olives?
	BOY: Huh?
	TALENT: Your olives.
	BOY: I don't work on <u>that</u> side of the store, lady.
DIS M2S TALENT AND CASHIER; CASHIER HOLDING 4-PACK OF BATHROOM TISSUE.	CASHIER: There's no price on this.
	TALENT: It's a dollar thirty-nine.
	CASHIER: (yelling into mike) Toilet paper price check on 11, Al!

Continued

Video	Audio
WIPE TO MS SPOKESMAN STANDING IN FRONT OF FREEZER.	SPOKES: You don't have to put up with supermarket battles any longer. Not with Grocerama in your corner.
SPOKESMAN STEPS ASIDE TO REVEAL GROCERAMA LOGO ON FREEZER DOOR	Grocerama is the new shop-at-home food plan that lets you order all your grocery needs by phone.
HE PULLS FREEZER DOOR OPEN TO REVEAL, NEAT, WELL-STOCKED FREEZER	Yes, steaks, chops, vegetables, frozen fruit, ice cream, and all kinds of canned and paper goods for your cupboard.
ZOOM IN, PAN ACROSS FOOD	You name it. Grocerama gets it for you and brings it to you every week.
DIS MS SPOKESMAN AT DESK, HOLDING UP CHECKLIST	Plus, this exclusive Grocerama food analysis system was prepared by nutrition experts to ensure that what you buy is not only what you want, but what you need for healthy living.
DIS "BASIC 4" CHART	SPOKES (VO): We've all heard of the Basic 4 food groups: dairy products; meat, fish

Continued

Video	Audio
	and eggs; vegetables and fruits; and bread and cereals. But do you always remember them when you shop?
DIS "CALORIES SOURCES" CHART	And how about the sources of calories? Fats, carbohydrates and protein? Do you know how each of these contributes to health?
DIS BACK TO SPOKESMAN	<u>SPOKES (OC):</u> Well, Grocerama's patented nutritional analysis takes all of these dietary needs into consideration in helping you create the tastiest, healthiest meal plan imaginable.
LS TALENT IN KITCHEN	<u>TALENT:</u> But I can't afford all of this.
SPOKESMAN WALKS INTO SHOT	<u>SPOKES:</u> Not only can you afford it, but you'll probably <u>save</u> money over what you're spending at the supermarket now. That's because Grocerama buys in bulk from distributors and delivers the groceries direct to you. Grocerama

Continued

Video	Audio	
		eliminates the middleman's profits to put more money in your pocket.
MCU TALENT	TALENT:	Can I check this out?
MS SPOKESMAN. SQUEEZEZOOM SPOKESMAN IN MORTISE, SUPER LOCAL OR 800 NUMBER HERE	SPOKES:	You certainly can. Just dial this number for a free, no obligation booklet on Grocerama services. Discover just how easy it is to eat healthier for less.
GROCERAMA LOGO ON BLUE BACKGROUND RE-SUPE NUMBER	VO:	Why waste any more time or money shopping the old way? Call this number now and learn how Grocerama can start working for you. Grocerama. Better food. Better nutrition. Better prices.

Given the multiplicity of channels in a cable world, and the sales successes that many infomercials have already posted, these long-form commercials are likely to become a more and more significant segment of television copywriting assignments. Consumer sales generated by infomercials are estimated to have increased from $250 million in 1988[12] to $800 million four years later.[13] Infomercial telecasts grew from 2,500 per month in 1985 to more than 21,000 per month by 1991. This escalating activity is occurring because well-conceived 'long-forms' *work*---and in a cost-effective manner. A 30-minute ad for a Kitchenmate handmixer cost just $125,000 to produce, for example. But its producer reports that it generated $55 million in sales.[14]

Though television *co-op* efforts occasionally assume infomercial form, they most often consist of conventional 30-second efforts. The essence of co-op, after all, is to attract customers to a local point-of-purchase. Infomercials, in contrast, require more time because they must consummate the sale on a DR basis. In addition, thirties are much more likely to be affordable for local dealer participation. The basic structure and function of effective co-op spots is covered in our Chapter 9 radio discussion. But by adding the visual, television gives the copywriter more ways to register manufacturer and local distributor names.

Most of the time, the manufacturer is featured in the body of the spot, with audio and video tagging occurring in the thirty's last five to eight seconds. In end-to-end local/national messages, such as the Champion commercial in Figure 11–6, however, dealer referents can be sprinkled throughout the ad.

Because this is a much more involved and expensive procedure than a simple tag at the end, the dealer must usually make a greater budgetary commitment to the project in order to make the co-op cost effective for the manufacturer. Note, for example, that the Champion photoboard contains a box requiring dealers to purchase enough airtime to accumulate 100 gross rating points before the message will be customized for them. Note also that in frame 4, this spot provides four different hole-copy options from which the dealer can choose.

Retail and Business-to-Business Pitches

In so-called pure retail advertising, the dealers are on their own, with no manufacturer dollars to create the spots or to help underwrite the cost of airing them. Some retail outlets are, of course, mammoth enterprises fully capable of mounting major national and regional television campaigns. Other retailers and service providers, however, are one-store operations. Attracted by local cable's extremely low rate-card prices, such businesses are just now toying with the idea of television exposure.

Especially during the last decade, the commercial television industry, led by its sales promotion arm, the Television Bureau of Advertising (TVB), has attempted to show local and regional retailers that television is an effective and affordable advertising vehicle for them. TVB's Retail TV Commercials Workshops and its various sales clinics strive to provide industry copywriters and salespersons with extensive assistance in courting retail clients. The Cabletelevision Advertising Bureau (CAB) and the Radio Advertising Bureau (RAB) provide similar services to their industries. But, even though local dealers have long been accustomed to the fact that radio is at least an option as one of their marketing tools, the idea of television still appears daunting—obscured in the ominous fog of the super-production mystique.

As a copywriter, you will probably not be directly involved in the television salesperson's task of persuading that department store, beauty parlor, or

1) VO: Why get Champion Spark Plugs from Hometown Auto Parts?

2) Imagine you're on a dark and lonely road . . .
SFX: OWLS
at midnight in a blizzard . . .
SFX: BLIZZARD

3) And your car . . . won't start. Then the dam breaks . . .
SFX: FLOOD   MAN: Help!

4) (See individual copy below)

5) I'll just spend winter in a warm place.
ANNCR: You're in a desert.

6) SFX: HOT WIND
ANNCR: Miles from water.
SFX: GRINDING
MAN: OK, I'll get 'em.
ANNCR: Nothing sparks like a Champion from Hometown Auto Parts.

4) PRICE
Help is at (STORE NAME). Where Champion's Copper Plus Spark Plugs, uniquely designed for great performance in winter, are just (PRICE) each.

4) NON-PRICE
Help is at (STORE NAME). Where right now, you can get Champion's Copper Plus Plugs at a special low price.

4) TUNE-UP
Help is at (STORE NAME). Where you can get a complete tune-up with Champion's Copper Plus Spark Plugs for just (PRICE).

4) DUAL
Help is at (STORE NAME). Where Champion's Copper Plus Spark Plugs are just (PRICE) each, or (PRICE) with a tune-up.

A minimum 100 G.R.P. schedule must be purchased to qualify for FREE T.V. spot customization.

Figure 11-6

(Courtesy of Dan Nelson, W.B. Doner and Company.)

lumberyard to use video. You may, however, be called on to assist in the pitch by designing a sample (spec) commercial that showcases the prospective client in an effective, yet frugally produced manner. And, should the retailer make an initial commitment to try television, you, as an in-station or agency wordsmith, must be the prime person to satisfy the local business's expectations for a penetrating and cost-efficient production—expectations that the station, system, or agency sales folks may have uplifted to a disturbingly high level.

Fortunately, one inherently persuasive charm of local television advertising accrues when it *looks* local. As Louisville Productions' President Richard Gordon once told a convention of the National Retail Merchant's Association:

> Whether you are Bloomingdale's or Bacon's, May Company or Belk, you are still local and should appear that way. Your spots should stand out from the impersonal national spots. This does not mean a sacrifice of image or quality, but they should be different. . . . The spot should say that here's a local store with the fashion and items the customers want. Don't try to be national when being local is an advantage.[15]

In this spot for a local grocery, customer values are well articulated by both the audio and video. Just as important, the commercial has been constructed to have a long life and yet still be seasonally, even weekly adaptable. Try to discern how this adaptation could most simply be accomplished.

OBJECTIVE: To demonstrate that Townsend's produce is so fresh that mothers can let their children shop for it and still be certain of good quality.

PRODUCTION NOTE: Johnny is 6-8 years old. Mother's voice featured exclusively throughout.

Video	Audio
1. M2S IN KITCHEN. MOTHER GIVES LIST AND SMALL CHANGE PURSE TO SON JOHNNY AND SENDS HIM OFF.	MOTHER: Run down to Townsend's and get what's on this list, please.
2. WHEN JOHNNY EXITS FRAME, SHE FACES CAMERA.	I send Johnny to Townsend's Market because---
3. MLS OF TOWNSEND'S EXTERIOR. FEATURE "TOWNSEND'S MARKET" SIGN ON STOREFRONT.	(V.O.): at Townsend's, I'm sure of getting the best produce for my money.
4. MCU SLIDE OF LARGE SHINY RED APPLE DISPLAY IN FG, WITH JOHNNY'S FACE OVERLOOKING IT.	Townsend's apples, like their fruits and vegetables, are the freshest apples in town.

Continued

Video	Audio
5. MCU OF JOHNNY AT CHECK-OUT COUNTER. CASHIER'S HANDS GIVE HIM GROCERY BAG OF UNDISCLOSED CONTENTS; DROP CHANGE BACK IN HIS COIN PURSE.	And this week, they're at especially low prices.
6. LS OF TOWNSEND'S EXTERIOR TO INCLUDE ENTIRE STREET CORNER DIS. TO---	Townsend's Market on Hillcrest and Dale is nice and close, too.
7. M2S AS JOHNNY ENTERS KITCHEN AND IS GREETED BY MOTHER	(END V.O.) My, that was quick.
8. MOTHER LOOKS DOWN INTO BAG AND SMILES	Townsend's Market---mmmmmmm.

If you weren't able to ascertain the modular nature of this script, re-examine module 4. In this particular ad, Townsend's is using apples to generate next day (or even *same day*) traffic. But merely by substituting a slide of a different display, and changing the fruit-specifying module 4 voice-over, the treatment can become a promotion for Townsend's oranges, tomatoes, bananas, or any other produce item. The spot thus has the capability of an almost unlimited number of modifications—and at virtually no additional cost beyond that required to produce the initial commercial "bed." Expenditures can be further reduced by using slides rather than film/tape footage for segments 3, 5, and 6. And, if Townsend's is in a four-season climate zone, these slides could even be shot to reflect the different times of the year. Because we never see Johnny outdoors, the footage of him and his mother at home (segments 1, 2, 7, and 8) could be used year-round as long as telltale costuming like a snowsuit or bathing togs was not used in the kitchen scene.

For a retailer with a somewhat larger budget, another way to vary the product pitch is to produce a series of fifteens, each of which features a different product category. It is important, however, that the same basic concept and retailer identity be maintained in all spots making up the campaign. Each of the four Snyder's commercials in Figure 11–7, for instance, begins with a categorical question, follows this with a comedic illustration of the resulting problem, and concludes with the client logo and promise.

Remember that retailers measure advertising success by how many customers come through the door. Long-term image building is fine—but not if it gets in the way of stimulating same- or next-day traffic. Placing

SNYDER'S
"Chisel", "Baby", "Hairdo", "Slapping" :15's

AVO: Out of stationery?

Snyder's has a department full of
writing paper and greeting cards.

AVO: Out of diapers?

Snyder's has 4 top brands of diapers.

AVO: Out of hairspray?

Snyder's has 28 brands of hairspray.

AVO: Out of mosquito repellent?

Snyder's has 11 different kinds of
protective sprays and lotions.

Figure 11-7

*(Martin/Williams Advertising, Incorporated. Creative Director: Lyle
Wedemeyer; Creative Supervisor/Copywriter: Emily Scott; Art Director:
Pam Mariutto; Director: John Kump Zurick; Production Company: Setterholm
Productions, Minneapolis.)*

items on sale is a long-standing retail practice to lure people to the store. Yet, a sale is hardly a breakthrough idea on which to center your copy. In their work for Bayless Markets, however, Rubin Postaer and Associates prove that a sale—even on very prosaic items—can stand out in the viewer's mind if you give it a neat little twist. And the twist need not require super-production expenditures.

Video	Audio
SHOT OF HAND PLACING BATHROOM TISSUE.	V.O.: Ladies and Gentlemen---
SHOT OF BATHROOM TISSUE ROLL.	Bathroom tissue. Right now for a limited time only, on sale at Bayless.
HAND REACHES TOWARD INSIDE BATHROOM TISSUE.	And inside every roll of bathroom tissue---
HAND PULLS OUT CARDBOARD TUBE AND SETS IT DOWN.	you'll get a cardboard tube.
SHOT OF TISSUE AND TUBE.	Absolutely free.
SUPER: BAYLESS	The new Bayless.

(Courtesy of Robert Coburn and Gary Yoshida, Rubin Postaer and Associates.)

Though we don't stop to think about it, sports franchises also are local retailers with an irrevocable need to get traffic through the stadium door *all at once.* Unfortunately, that door opens a very limited number of times, so prospects must be channeled to take very specific action. Finding a concept that will convert a 'coming event' print piece into a true television scenario is not easy, but it is nonetheless vital in moving a viewer to action. J. Walter Thompson/Toronto created just such a concept in a series of fifteens for the city's major league baseball team. Here are two of the scripts:

Video	Audio
OPEN ON ANIMATED WATER.	SFX: (ROWING)
	SFX: ("Stroke, STROKE . . .")

Continued

Video	Audio
BOAT ENTERS FRAME, AS MEN ABOARD ROW, THE BOAT SINKS.	SFX: (BUBBLING, GURGLING, ETC . . .)
FADE	
SUPER: SEE THE JAYS SINK THE MARINERS	
SUPER: JUNE 1, 2, AND 3	
BLUE JAY FLIES OUT OF FRAME AND CATCHES BASEBALL.	
SUPER: BLUE JAYS BASEBALL. CATCH IT LIVE.	
CALL 595-0077.	

. . . .

Video	Audio
OPEN ON ORIOLE.	SFX: (BIRD WHISTLING)
BLUE STREAK RUFFLES ORIOLE.	SFX: (2ND BIRD WHISTLING)
BLUE JAY LANDS.	SFX: (BIRD CRIES. FLUTTERING WINGS)
A FEATHER ENTERS FRAME. IT SLOWLY FALLS TO THE GROUND.	SFX: (BIRD SQUAWK)
SUPER: SEE THE JAYS RUFFLE THE ORIOLES. JUNE 5, 6, AND 7	SFX (BIRD WHISTLING)
BLUE JAY FLIES OUT OF FRAME AND CATCHES BASEBALL.	
SUPER: BLUE JAYS BASEBALL CATCH IT LIVE. CALL 595-0077	

(Courtesy of Rea Kelly, J. Walter Thompson/Toronto)

With the loosening of restrictions by their professional associations, legal and medical service providers are also now in the same local commercial mainstream as other small businesses. Because the concept of service is an intangible, however, television commercials written for such clients must always demonstrate specific *executions* of that service on behalf of people with whom target viewers can identify. Once again, as in all video spots, clear and relevant scenario construction is the key. Notice the drama unwinding in this message created by a copywriter at a local cable system.

Video	Audio
MAN ON PAY PHONE, ACCIDENT	SFX: ENVIRONMENT NOISE SCENE
WOMAN ANSWERING PHONE AT HOME	SFX: PHONE RING
MAN ON PHONE	<u>MAN:</u> Marge, this is Tony. Listen: I've been stopped by the police. And I need the number for Lee Steinberg, the lawyer.
WOMAN SEARCHING FOR NUMBER	<u>WOMAN:</u> Oh, Tony---here it is. Lee Steinberg. 356-6250.
DIZ MAN NOW IN POLICE STATION ON PHONE	<u>MAN:</u> ---I don't know. But I need a lawyer, and fast!
LAWYER ON PHONE IN OFFICE, SLEEVES ROLLED UP, EXUDES BUSINESS-LIKE CONFIDENCE	<u>LAWYER:</u> Are you okay? We'll send legal counsel right away. So rest a little---we'll take care of you.
POV LAWYER, MAN LOOKS UP FROM JAIL CELL COT THROUGH BARS	<u>LAWYER (VO):</u> Tony? <u>MAN:</u> Hi, boy, am I glad to see you.
GRAPHIC: Lee Steinberg	<u>ANNCR.</u> <u>VO:</u> For 24-hour legal help, call Lee Steinberg, 356-6250.

(Courtesy of David Clements, United Cable Television of Oakland County.)

Just like professional services advertising, *business-to-business* messages have also been attracted to cable television due to the medium's low costs and well-delineated audience slivers. This activity, in turn, has further stimulated business-to-business use of broadcast television, too. Corporations once content to communicate to each other via trade magazine and financial newspaper layouts are now trying new marketing options. "In this age of instantaneous communications," argues A. Scott Hults, president of Infomedia, "there's got to be a better way for a b-to-b advertiser to get its messages across than being stuck on page 44 of a newspaper."[16] "Now," adds Martin/Williams Advertising's creative director Tom Weyl, "[advertisers] realize that business consumers are people, too. They see TV like anyone else and still need to be talked to."[17]

But writing business-to-business television does not mean merely committing a print layout to videotape. Everything we emphasized in regard to the D.D.Q. and the importance of Getting Recognized and Remembered also applies in business-to-business activities. "We're moving away from the old get-the-name-out-there approach," reports National Business Network director Walter Johnson, "to very bright, user-oriented, user-benefit advertising that reaches out with the same tools formerly exclusively used in consumer advertising."[18] In the Figure 11–8 Continental Bank message, for example, we see the same strong benefit-centered demonstrability that we could prize in any general consumer spot. Other ads in the flight featured identical copy, but with different—and equally visual—metaphorical solutions.

Business-to-business advertising is expanding in all media, including television. In fact, states trade writer Andrew Jaffe, it "has been growing at roughly twice the rate of consumer advertising."[19] With both broadcast and cable television hungry for new ad dollars, b-to-b is an attractive field and will remain attractive as long as video copywriters apply the same proven communicative principles to its execution as they use in fashioning advertising for traditional consumer accounts.

The Storyboard Presentation

No matter what category of television commercial we're composing, a major hurdle is the securing of acceptance of our concept. For most major clients and production budgets, getting approval for a television spot is not, like radio, simply reading copy to someone in an office or over the phone. Rather, whole teams of people with the diffuse power of group decision-making will want to see your video concept early, and in detail. Under these circumstances, the storyboard is most often the central focus of attention and main creative battleground. Since both writer and art director sink or swim by what is on that 'board as well as by how well they *present* what is on it, you must know

"HOLE" :15

(Music under)
AVO: At Continental Bank,

we try to get to you

with solutions

before you realize you need them , , ,

. . .

. . .

Continental Bank.

Anticipating the needs of business.

Figure 11-8

(Courtesy of Dana Bromwich Howe, Fallon McElligott Advertising.)

how to handle yourself and your multiframe offspring in the review sessions, where its fate is ruthlessly determined.

First, it must be made unequivocally clear that a good presentation won't save a bad 'board, but a bad presentation can certainly kill a good one. If you are as glib of tongue as you are of pen the fates have shone kindly on you. But don't come to rely on your gift of gab as a substitute for disciplined and well-ordered preparation of your assignments. Water-cooler mythology notwithstanding, client representatives, creative directors, and account supervisors do not hold their seats in those storyboard review sessions because they are easily duped.

By the same token, the best 'board still needs some well-fashioned promotion to transform it from a static piece of cardboard into a dynamic, breathing story. Even walking in with an approach in which you are supremely confident, you must be aware that the storyboard review session requires you to perform three simultaneous selling jobs on its behalf:

1. You are selling yourself as an articulate, knowledgeable product-wise copywriter. Your art director is normally there to help you with the presentation, but your creative judges expect the most precise treatment defense to come out of your mouth. You, after all, are supposed to be the duo's wordsmith.
2. You are selling your 'board as an appropriate, even heaven-sent answer to the client's marketing needs. Once you've shown yourself to be a competent professional, you must then prove that you've fully applied this competence to the 'board at hand.
3. You are selling the product or service being featured in that 'board. This, of course, is the ultimate task of advertising, but your approach will never get a chance to accomplish it if you have not surmounted the previous two selling barriers.

Assuming that, as a backdrop, you understand the tri-leveled, persuasive role you are expected to play, let's proceed with the five-step unveiling that constitutes the review session's usual liturgy:

1. State the specific purpose, the defined objective, that the spot is intended to achieve. Depending on the situation, this may also involve an explanation of *why* television is required to meet the objective, why (if television commercials for the product are already being run) this additional treatment is needed, and how it will fit in with the style and orientation of all other advertising the client is currently running or planning to run on behalf of this product. This may include a discussion of print as well as of electronic campaign material and strategies.

    Don't slight this first step just because it appears more a marketing than a creative concern. Copywriters today are as involved in writing copy platforms and strategies as they are in penning commercials. Modern competitive forces no longer permit writers to be oblivious to the dynamics of the marketplace. The evolution of VALS and other psychographic targeting systems discussed in Chapter 5 indicates just how extensively copy styling and market delineation must now intermesh. Only after you have justified your proposed orientation in terms of business realities can your storyboard presentation proceed to the subsequent explication of creative values.

2. Unveil your treatment's video properties slowly. Do this via a frame-by-frame progression that serves to put the picture in your reviewers' minds. Explain any technical terms and effects quickly and simply. You don't want your presentation to become a telefilm production seminar any more than you want your finished commercial to submerge the message in the medium.

   Even in an informal review session, a pointer is helpful in directing attention to the proper frame without blocking anyone's view. A collapsible antenna from an obsolete transistor radio makes it easy always to have a pointer in your pocket and is another indication that you're in well-prepared command of the situation.

3. Next, with pointer at the ready, go through the entire commercial again, now articulating the audio as you direct attention to each succeeding picture. Read dialogue in a style as similar as possible to the way in which you expect the talent to read it. If the music background is important, you may also want your art director to hum along or, especially if your partner is tone deaf, a cassette recorder can be called on to suggest the general musical effect you have in mind. Above all, keep your portrayal of the audio clear so everyone knows exactly what the soundtrack is saying.

4. Now present the entire storyboard again, combining both audio and video descriptions. This is your chance to make that whole greater than the sum of its parts—and your audience's opportunity to put the complete communication into interlocked perspective. If the reviewers (who are handsomely paid to pay close attention to your proposed spot) don't understand the concept by this time, the bored and listless consumers on the other side of the tube will never get it. Step 4 should pull everything together with all the assurance of a steel trap springing shut.

5. Last, close with a solid and meticulously prepared summary statement that reemphasizes the storyboard's objective, the mechanism by which it meets that objective, and the indispensable way in which the television medium is enlisted to serve the project's needs. At this juncture, the meeting is normally opened for questions and follow-up discussion. You answer these questions in a resolute and nondefensive manner that spotlights the 'board rather than your proprietary interest in it.

"The presenters," warns consultant Tony Lacitignola, "cannot be condescending, patronizing or even vaguely arrogant. The ideas can be superb, but the client has to feel comfortable and at home with them."[20]

For practice, take the Figure 11–9 storyboard and stage your own five-step exposition of it to your favorite full-length mirror. This procedure should familiarize you with the presentation process without the additional con-

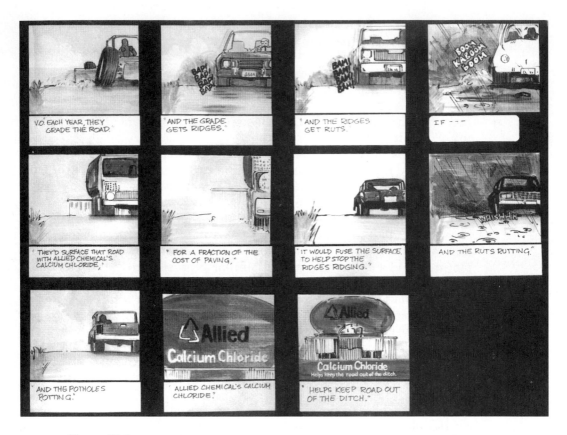

Figure 11-9

(Courtesy of Barry Base, Base Brown Partners Ltd.)

founding variable that comes from ego-involvement with a 'board that you have created. This exercise will also force you to dig out and articulate the spot's central objective and the manner in which it's portrayed. Once you're satisfied with your handling of "Bumpy Road," you should be ready to attempt a storyboard demonstration of one of your own creative concepts.

No matter how experienced you become, intensive practice sessions are an essential prelude to successful storyboard pitches. As advertising consultant Helene Kalmanson warns, "Lack of rehearsal is painfully obvious to clients. It results in a visible lack of teamwork (such as presenters contradicting each other) and produces presentations that run too long. Few of us can afford the luxury of looking unprepared, uncoordinated or out of sync with our co-workers. Rehearsal allows you to fill in the holes, enliven the boring bits, clean up the logic flow, turn stilted tech-ese into memorable sound bites and focus on the client instead of your next line."[21]

Once you enter the actual presentation, corporate communications expert Phillip Stella urges adherence to what he labels his ten Fast Tips:

1. Stay calm. You're the boss on stage.
2. Smile and the whole world smiles with you.
3. Be aware of on whom and what to focus your line of sight.
4. Gesture clearly at the audience members or visual media.
5. Don't pace the floor.
6. Don't jingle change.
7. Don't answer questions too quickly.
8. Be patient with the audience asking questions.
9. Don't drink too much coffee before a presentation.
10. Watch the clock.[22]

Finally, here are the *Seven Deadly Sins* that copy trainees are especially tempted to commit in the zealous fostering of their own 'boards. Mending your ways now will prevent your concepts' damnation later:

1. The objective is clearly stated—but is never really linked to the treatment being proposed. Reviewers are thereby left to wonder whether they misunderstood the objective or whether the advocated approach is at all compatible with it.
2. The consumer benefit is stated in negative terms ("this spot for the Futzmobile is intended to keep people from buying an imported car"). Audiences seldom remember what they *shouldn't* do—especially if you haven't really bannered what they are *supposed* to do.
3. The overall presentation lacks flow. Instead of each step smoothly segueing into the next, reviewers are assailed with such stop/start lines as: "That completes step two. Now let's move on to the audio." Your oral transitions, in short, should be as fluid and graceful as your written and pictorial ones.
4. The presentation is projected into the storyboard rather than out to the reviewers. This gives the impression that you are self-conscious about the approach being proposed—and sets up a reviewer suspicion that you may have a right to be. Use the aforementioned pointer and a few inconspicuous notecards so you can talk to the people rather than the props. This avoids blocking the line of sight and doesn't force you into the awkward contortions required to read audio blocks off the storyboard itself.
5. Production costs are totally ignored. Saying, "I don't care what this costs because it's a zowie approach" will never stretch a ten-thousand dollar budget to thirty thousand—or a fifty-thousand limit to seventy. Do some prior research to obtain at least an approximation of your 'board's shooting price tag. And, if no one bothered to tell you, find out the budgetary

range that the particular account has devoted to video production in the past.

6. Brand recall is advanced as the commercial's objective. Yet, as you should be aware by now, brand recall is useful and feasible only when it is tied to a specific, consumer-related benefit. It is the articulation of this benefit that constitutes the core of your spot's objective and through which brand recall can be implemented. People don't remember names that mean nothing to them.

7. Inadvertently, or out of an acute sense of frustration, the client or assignment is belittled in an attempt to make the treatment look more praiseworthy: "This is a terrible product to try to do anything with on television but—." To paraphrase a famous theatrical truism, there are no terrible products, only unimaginative copywriters.

Most important of all, you must be careful not to assume your 'board is yourself. Put some distance between you and it—not physical distance, or professional distance, but *psychological* distance. All advertising review sessions, and storyboard presentations in particular, can generate a lot of sometimes heated discussion and often pointed criticism. If you see your 'board as a total projection of your psyche—if you can't separate attacks on it from attacks on you—real psychological damage can result. Serena Deutsch of Riverside Psychotherapy Associates, who treats a number of patients from the advertising community, warns that a creative person's strong identification with his or her work can be dangerous. "If they so identify with their work and the work is attacked, then they feel attacked," Deutsch observes. "Sometimes they have trouble seeing the difference."[23]

Avoiding the Storyboard

Now that you've absorbed all the whys and wherefores of storyboard presentations, let it be said that there are people in the industry who would circumvent their use altogether—not the use of presentation sessions but the use of storyboards *in* them. Such a situation makes the review arena all the more rigorous for the copywriter because there is now nothing to capture that judgment panel's attention except your words on paper and in the air. It is as though you are back pushing a radio concept but, due to the cost factor, with stakes that are much, much higher.

More that a quarter-century ago, advertising veteran Alfred L. Goldman made one of the strongest cases on record for *not* using storyboards, a case that revolves around these key points and that is still used as anti-'board ammunition today:

We discovered that beyond the selling of words, pictures, and ideas, there was a "fourth" dimension: a kind of total impression that not only underscored the words, pictures and ideas, but which turned out to be an experience in itself; a kind of "cathedral effect" (thank you Mr. McLuhan) that spread its wings over the entire commercial and helped win friends and influence sales.

Second only to the basic selling idea, and far more vital than isolated words and pictures, this total impression is something that no storyboard can deliver.

In fact, the storyboard tends to kill it. We are looking at a print interpretation of a motion picture idea. And we are looking at in a logical series of pictures with captions on a frame-by-frame basis. What's more, we are forced to accept what a talented artist can do with a drawing pencil in the suffocating confines of a little box measuring a few inches wide by a few inches deep.

Neither the artist nor the still camera can capture the essence of the idea as it will emerge on a fluid piece of film. There is a distortion of values, too, because we illustrate "pretty girl goes here" and "pretty package goes there" and it has nothing to do with the true dimensions of time and space as they will occur in the finished commercial. . . .

So how can you beat the storyboard booby trap? . . .

Go to the client with a script. Let your creative people play it out by creating a movie in the client's mind. They can explain, describe, act out, flash pictures, use sound effects and do whatever they must to set the stage and position the players just as if they were describing a feature film they had seen. Then, read the script against this background and the whole reel will unwind in the client's mind and he'll get the full "cathedral effect" of your commercial. When he "buys" the idea, he is buying a *tour de force* rather than meaningless isolated pictures and words as they appear in a storyboard.[24]

Much more recently, producer Linda Tesa argued that the storyboard can present problems at the production stage as well. "Sometimes," she observed, "a storyboard is just too stiff and it's better to let the spot evolve through discussions between the creative team and the director. However, I want to say that there is a big distinction between an arrangement like this out of choice versus being forced into it by the client. One way is productive, but the other way is scary and out of control."[25]

In the event that you someday find yourself in a "no storyboard" ballpark, prepare now to erect the "cathedral effect" of which Goldman spoke. And even if you never have to face a television review session without your trusty 'board, the communication dexterity that comes from successfully presenting pictures without pictures will stand you in good stead in describing radio treatments, too. Words are words whether scrawled on paper or gliding through your dentures. Particularly in the advertising business, you must learn to string them together effectively in both contexts.

As an exercise to hone your oral abilities, take the following Australian spot script and "play it out" for a friend. Then evaluate your effectiveness by having that friend tell it back to you. Did the commercial's objective survive the retelling? If so, you're on your way. If not, if the point of the spot got lost between A and B, you really didn't comprehend the objective yourself or you lost sight of it in your efforts to convey pictorial brilliance and snippets of sound track. Strive to make your oral presentation as much a cohesive, *demonstrative* totality as is the commercial concept on which that presentation is based.

Video	Audio
OPEN ON WIDE HORIZONS SHOT OF TYPICAL OUTBACK STATION HOMESTEAD. SUPER: NO FLIES ON BAKKABURK STATION	MUSIC: MORTEIN THEME UNDER THROUGHOUT.
DISSOLVE TO DROVER APPROACHING SCREENED FRONT VERANDAH OF HOMESTEAD TRAILED BY A CATTLEDOG. HE SPEAKS TO CAMERA AS HE ENTERS THROUGH SCREEN DOOR AND DROPS HIS SADDLE IN A CLOUD OF DUST ON THE FLOOR.	DROVER: You think you've got flies. Out here we've got more flies than a zipper factory.
CUT TO CU OF DROVER AS HE DELIVERS LINE WITH LACONIC GRIN.	And big---they're big enough to shear!
CUT WIDER AS HE APPROACHES HIS WIFE WHO IS SITTING IN AN OLD ROCKER AT THE END OF THE VERANDAH SHELLING PEAS IN MECHANICAL MANNER. SHE IS CHEWING AND STARING INTO SPACE AND HARDLY NOTICES AS THE DROVER APPROACHES HER AND PICKS UP A CAN OF MORTEIN FAST KNOCKDOWN FROM A TABLE BESIDE HER. HE HOLDS CAN UP CLOSE TO CAMERA.	So, the missus got this can of Mortein Fast Knockdown and those flies went down quicker than cold beer in a dust storm.

Continued

Video	Audio
CUT TO FRONT ROOM OF HOMESTEAD AS DROVER ENTERS THROUGH FRONT DOOR WITH CAN IN ONE HAND AND HAT IN THE OTHER. HE PLACES HAT ON PEG AND SPRAYS SOME PRODUCT INTO THE AIR. HE SNIFFS THE SPRAYED PRODUCT.	And it's a new formula--- doesn't smell like sheep dip.
CUT TIGHTER ON DROVER. AS HE SPEAKS A GUST OF WIND BLOWS HIS HAIR AND HE LOOKS UP. QUICK INTERCUT OF CATTLEDOG LOOKING AROUND WARILY. THE DROVER SPRAYS UP INTO THE AIR.	Good for blowies, too. Here's one now---
CUT WIDE TO SEE DROVER REACT TO THUNDERING CRASH OFF CAMERA. GREAT CLOUDS OF DUST RISE FROM THE FLOOR, TABLES AND CHAIRS CLATTER AND BANG. QUICK INTERCUT SHOWS DOG HIGH-TAILING IT OUT OF THE WINDOW WITH A WHIMPER.	SFX: VARIOUS CRASHING FX, WHIMPERING OF DOG.
CUT TIGHTER ON DROVER AS HE REGATHERS HIS COMPOSURE.	DROVER: and that was just a baby!
ONE OF THREE FLYING DUCKS ON WALL BEHIND FALLS TO GROUND IN FINAL PROTEST.	
CUT TO PACK SHOT---MORTEIN FAST KNOCKDOWN CAN IN FOREGROUND ON TABLE IN HOMESTEAD FRONT ROOM. SUPER: AUSTRALIA'S FASTEST FLYSPRAY. ON WALL BEHIND WE SEE SHADOW OF THE DROVER HUMPING OUT THE HUGE "BLOWFLY."	ANNCR VO: Mortein. Australia's fastest flyspray. DROVER OFF CAMERA: Get the door, luv!

(Courtesy of Kilner Mason. McCann-Erickson Advertising Pty Limited.)

365

You may wish to ask yourself whether the trial presentation of the Mortein script was easier or more laborious than your practice unveiling of the Allied Chemical 'board. The answer to this question will help reveal for you the unique differences between script and storyboard "selling" as well as your own presentational strengths and weaknesses.

If you found both exercises difficult, remember that this difficulty will be ego-compounded when it's your own creations that have to be pitched. Nevertheless, whether boosting a 'board or selling a script, you must strive to make your approach stand out—and stand out in a credible, relevant way. If it can't attract favorable attention in a session called specifically to debut it, you can't expect your message to survive in the wilderness of television air schedules.

Agency consultant Chuck Phillips urges that your review presentations, like your video spots, "must get the prospect: (a) to like you; (b) to think you're smart; (c) to feel you're enthusiastic about their business (or life); (d) to believe you do terrific ads!"[26] This task is not insurmountable. You can count on the fact that your client or consumer audience "carries around in its dustbin of a mind just about every reference you're capable of dredging up," emphasizes creative director Barry Day. "TV sees to it that nothing gets thrown away and everything is in a constant present tense. All that matters is that you treat the references with reverence, style and wit."[27]

Endnotes

1. "Quips, Quotes, Gripes, Swipes," *Winners* (April 1989), 64.
2. David Dole, writing in "Monday Memo," *Broadcasting* (February 12, 1990), 17.
3. Richard Morgan, "The Decline of Me-Too Advertising," *ADWEEK* (February 1984), C.R. 8.
4. John O'Toole, writing in "Monday Memo," *Broadcasting* (April 17, 1978), 14.
5. "Adweek's Creative All-Star Team," *ADWEEK* (February 4, 1992).
6. "Higher and Higher," *ADWEEK* (October 1, 1990), M.O. 9.
7. Gerard Broussard, writing in "Monday Memo," *Broadcasting* (October 23, 1989), 33.
8. Theodore Roth, "Buick Says Its Ads Outsmart Zappers," *ADWEEK* (July 16, 1990), 1, 4.
9. Freeman Gosden, "Marketing and Making an Offer," *ADWEEK* (April 30, 1984), 68.
10. "Teleshopping Nothing New Under Broadcasters' Sun," *Broadcasting* (September 1, 1986), 90.
11. Francie Barson, panel comments at the Direct Marketing Day, Chicago Association of Direct Marketers, 5 June 1986, at Chicago.
12. All Jaffe, "Show and Tell," *Channels* (September 24, 1990), 10.
13. Richard Zoglin, "It's Amazing! Call Now!" *Time* (June 17, 1991), 71.

14. Ibid.
15. "From Down Louisville Way: Some Shrewd Advice on Selling While Keeping the Local Image," *Broadcasting* (January 16, 1978), 55.
16. Rich Zahradnik, "Turning to the Tube," *ADWEEK* (May 23, 1988), B.M. 20.
17. Andrew Jaffe, "The Big Guys Get Serious," *ADWEEK* (May 23, 1988), B.M. 6.
18. Ibid., B.M. 4.
19. Ibid.
20. Tony Lacitignola, "Pitching New Business: More Grit Than Glamour, *ADWEEK* (September 19, 1988), 38.
21. Helene Kalmanson, "Call to Attention," *ADWEEK* (August 10, 1992), 23.
22. Phillip Stella, "Communicating to Your Audience," *Audio Visual Communications* (December 1990), 33.
23. Debbie Seaman, "Creatives Take Their Problems to Creative Therapy," *ADWEEK* (September 24, 1984), 50.
24. Alfred Goldman, writing in "Monday Memo," *Broadcasting* (May 1, 1967), 20.
25. Tarquin Cardona, "Are Directors Overshadowing Agency Art Directors?," *ADWEEK* (October 19, 1987), C.P. 8.
26. Chuck Phillips, "Pennant-Winning Pitching," *ADWEEK* (June 22, 1987), 55.
27. Barry Day, "'84's 10 Best," *ADS Magazine* (December 1984), 32.

 *Chapter 12*

Additional
Television Endeavors

Beyond commercial construction, a copywriter's other video challenges closely, though not exactly, parallel the additional tasks encountered by radio wordsmiths—tasks dissected in Chapter 9. Differences between the radio and television situations are due primarily to two factors: (1) television program structure, which permits fewer ID and promo interruptions than do radio's brief music and information modules; and (2) video's popularity as a medium for a number of nonbroadcast/cable applications in the corporate, industrial, education, and human services areas.

In-House Noncopy Data Block

As with radio, when a script for an outside commercial client is written in-house, the conventional commercial data block is used. For TV outlet self-promotional scripts, however, a heading very similar to that used for radio in-house projects is adopted as shown in Table 12–1.

The only significant departure from the radio continuity format is the addition of a line (*Air Sked*) that permits insertion of the times in which the piece is slated to air. Because television time is expensive and generally less flexible than radio availabilities, scheduling decisions require documented executive approval. This and other items left blank in Table 12–1 are usually inked in after announcement production. Depending on the number of staffers involved and the complexity of the project, the OBJECTIVE and PRODUCTION NOTE may or may not be employed.

Outlet IDs and Promos

Television station and cable system IDs and promos are just as important in the visual media as they are on radio. And, as in radio, each ID or outlet promo must compete with a lot of other continuity. The growth of new television

Table 12-1
Television In-House Data Block

TV-61 CONTINUITY PRODUCTION ORDER	
Subject: Al Slick Intro Promo	Order #: 1621
Date Ordered: 5/30/94	Length: :15
Format: Slide/VO	Start Date: 7/1/94
Ordered By: Jerry Gazette	End Date: 7/15/94
Written By: Paula Prompter	Scripted: 6/8/94
Accepted By:	Produced:
Air Sked:	Approved:

OBJECTIVE: Position Al as the weatherman who can make
  meteorology enjoyably concise.

PRODUCTION NOTE: All slides must center on Al with plenty
  of head room for weather scene registration.

services and delivery systems via cable, microwave, satellite, and home video has propelled both mature and fledgling television enterprises to unprecedented efforts to establish an identity with the viewing public. Younger multichannel enterprises are seeking ways and means to achieve recognition in an arena long-dominated by single-channel broadcasters. "Most cable systems still don't have a local identity," observes promotion company executive Bob Klein, "even though they offer 40 to 60 channels. A few MSOs [multiple system operators] are beginning to recognize the importance of cross-channel promotion and are now setting aside 15 percent to 20 percent of their on-air time for local promotion."[1]

This outlet identity is comprised of two parts: (1) the image of the transmitting entity (station, network, or cable service) itself and (2) the sum of the programmatic appeals encompassed in that entity's offerings. In short, today's viewers need to be constantly reminded of who you are, what you did for them yesterday (*proof of performance* promotion), and what you *will do* for them both today and tomorrow.

Similar to sound medium procedures, video IDs and outlet promos can occur separately or as a single thing. A station identification may simply give the governmentally mandated information in audio and video form and then apply the remaining eight seconds to a commercial pitch (see the "Shared ID" definition in the "other technical terms" section of Chapter 10). In this case, the audio copy is not much different from that found on a radio billboard spot with the slide/flipcard or computer graphics accentuating the station call letters, channel number logo, and corporate symbol for the parent company or participating sponsor.

But as the competition for viewers and the dollars they bring has everywhere intensified, more and more facilities are preferring to reserve this ID for self-promotional purposes. Many television outlets now boast their own "signature slogans" that come complete with moving graphic and music bed over which the announcer can read customized and timely promotion copy. Frequently, as in Figure 12–1, these ID enhancement devices are prepared by an outside production or consulting firm.

The music beds that often back up these graphics reflect many of the same style and copy characteristics used to showcase IDs on radio. But, because television stations do not have a single well-delineated music format to which they must adhere, most TV identification music and lyrics tend to reflect a "safe" though up-tempo, middle-of-the-road orientation. The average broadcast channel's viewing audience is comprised of a more heterogeneous mass than the usually segmented groups to which most radio stations strive to appeal. Thus, though the ID stylings may vary somewhat from one part of the outlet's viewing day to another, the music and the copy are seldom allowed to wander too far from mainstream acceptability. "Be very leery of trendy music," warn industry experts John Locke and Hal Brown. "*Trendiness* and *longevity* don't normally appear in the same sentence!"[2]

Locke and Brown also offer guidance on the four qualities that effective video ID music *should* possess: memorability, quality of sound, flexibility, and accurate identity.

1. Memorability. It is very important that you utilize audio to its maximum promotion capability. Every time your four-to five-note musical ID or :30 image spot hits the radio or television, people must associate that sequence of notes with your station. It's very simple. If people can't remember the tune easily, they'll never have the chance to make the association needed to establish your identity. . . . (If it gets in your head and drives you crazy that's a very good sign).

2. Quality of sound. . . . Your promos are being sandwiched between national commercials and super station spots. It may be unrealistic financially to match that quality, but you owe it to yourself to obtain the best sound for the dollars available. . . .

3. Flexibility. Your music must have key elements for you to work with day in and day out. Three to five second workhorse IDs, rhythm mixes, tag sings and donuts are a *must* in any effective music package. No matter how great it may initially sound, the music will die in six months if it's not designed to meet the variety of production needs within a television station. . . .

4. Accurate Identity. All the above is very important; however, none of it matters if you misrepresent your station's identity musically. . . . People will form an impression from your music. Make sure it's targeting your

Figure 12-1

*(Technical Director/Animator: John Berton;
Data Generation: Maria Palazzi; Technical
Director/Software Developer: Shaun Ho; Art
Director: Ron Tsang; Hardware: Marc
Howard. For NBC Sports: John Schipp, Mgr.
of On-Air Promotion and Advertising.
Courtesy of NBC Sports and Cranston/Csuri
Productions, Columbus, Ohio.)*

audience and supporting your benefits rather than satisfying a personal fetish for 'the hippest sound around.'[3]

Most often in the form of lyrics, the copy for video promotional IDs is not markedly different from that used in the counterpart continuity on radio. (Turn back to Chapter 9 to review radio samples.) The main difference between television and radio promos may be that, since we now have a visual to occupy center stage, the lyrics and music should lend themselves to a variety of pictorial treatments. It should be possible to create a multitude of visual spots that project the same theme via a unified soundtrack. Thus, the "hometown pride" idea expressed in the following lyric could be reiterated with more station-oriented pictures in subsequent promos.

Video	Audio
UMBRELLAS WALKING	<u>SINGERS:</u> Today's a new day
ZOOM, LEE LOOKS UP	In the Heart of Illinois

Continued

Video	Audio
KIDS ON "SONAR TIDE"	Better than ever
CU TWIN TOWERS IN SUNGLASSES	The Pride of Illinois
NEWSPEOPLE AT WILDLIFE PRAIRIE PARK	Peoria's back now On the right track now
PLANE PULLING OUR BANNER	Stand up and tell 'em You're from the Heart.
CATERPILLAR FACTORY SHOT	We build it better Share the hometown Pride.
BLOOMINGTON/NORMAL MAYORS 'HIGH-FIVE'	Bloomington-Normal Working side by side.
MALOOF, MENOLD, CHUCK SHERMAN WITH CARRIAGE	The world is ours to Reach out and turn to
CHUCK STANDS UP	Stand up and tell 'em You're from the Heart.
TERI PUSHING BIKE GIRL RIDING	You've got the spirit Tell 'em you're from the Heart.
HEART IN FIELD FROM PLANE CUT TO BOB MOWING	Come on, let's hear it Tell 'em you're from the Heart.
GIRLS JUMPING ROPE	We're a team of hometowns
OLD PEOPLE FROM BALCONY	There's no town like your town
PAN PEORIA AT NIGHT	Peoria's the Heart of it.
DIZ IN FIREWORKS	19's a part of it.
PEOPLE ON BUS BENCH	Stand up and tell 'em You're from the Heart.

(Courtesy of Pam Lovell, Moss Advertising, Inc.)

Network IDs and promos, of course, exhibit most of the same characteristics as do those for local outlets but with the additional advantages of bigger budgets and larger in-house staffs. Nonetheless, network lyric copy must pay just as much attention to image positioning and theme-bolstering repetition as do lyrics at the local level.

Meanwhile, the promo writer at the local affiliate must be careful that his or her spots don't clash with network image elements. "The challenge," points out promotions consultant John Chavez, "is how to effectively integrate the network theme into the station's overall promotion effort to create a single, unifying on-air look."[4] To accomplish this task, NBC promotions executive Martha Stanville would urge the affiliate to rely on the customizable vehicles provided by the network. "In the face of growing competition," she says, "using the network package eliminates conflicting positioning lines and delivers more bang for your buck."[5]

But should the local in-station writer *always* rely on network-derived material? Bob Klein believes that "It's best to be selective. If there is a question, go it on your own. If your promotion is strong, it will do a lot more for you and the network than the network can do for you." If you decide on a separate and distinct local campaign, then, as a general rule, use network-derived image builders solely around network shows and your own image package at times that are locally programmed. If a logical link cannot be found between the network thematic package and your own, then keep them mutually isolated to avoid confusing your own viewers on your own air. At the least, you should be able to design or acquire some ID graphics that bridge the gap between the two themes at times in the program day when network and local features abut.

Just like its radio cousin, the television ID/promo package must reflect how your outlet's sales, promotion, and programming departments view the operation of which they are all a part. Any continuity, no matter how brilliant, that does not mesh with the organization's overall programming promise and sales orientation is only worth its weight in ulcers. Creative director Karl Sjodahl advocates asking yourself ten key questions to test the viability of your ID/promo concept. If these questions cannot be answered unequivocally, or if different people in the outlet answer them differently, then it's time to rethink the whole project.

1. So what? Who cares? Is it clear *why* you are doing the piece at all?
2. What's in it for the viewer? Is there a specific viewer benefit?
3. What *results* do you expect from the campaign? (Short *and* long term?)
4. How do you want the viewers to *feel* about the station after the campaign? And how is that feeling *different* from the way they feel *now*?
5. Is "impact" important to achieving your objective? If it is, does the statement reflect that?

6. Is it do-able? Given staff capabilities, time, and budget, is the objective within your reach?
7. Is the objective *specific* to the strengths of your station and your current position in the market?
8. Will it set you apart from your competition—or could anybody run it with equal success?
9. Does everyone involved with the project *agree* that it is possible to meet the objectives and the statement is accurate and complete?
10. Is everybody involved willing to *actively support* the achievement of the objectives?[7]

Ultimately, points out marketing agency president Bruce Bloom, "Audiences tend to be more comfortable spending their time with stations they know and trust. Stations they perceive as better able to meet their viewing needs."[8] Successful IDs and promos make those acquaintances, isolate those needs, and build that trust by showing how their video service's benefit statement has taken those needs to heart.

Because television can deliver dynamic analogies for an outlet's character, radio stations increasingly are turning to television to promote their own unique identities. The same visualizable stylings that are used to distinguish a video channel from its competitors can also be employed to register a radio outlet in the eyes of its target audience. Examining the Figure 12–2 photoboard, what kind of personality does WJLB project? To what prime audience is the projection designed to appeal?

Program Promos and Trailers

Just as radio stations can use television to promote their essence, so television can exploit radio as a "barker" for its programs. Often, this can best be accomplished by writing radio spots that lift compelling sound bites out of the TV program you're pushing. When properly selected and showcased with wrap-around copy, these bites make the listener want to watch in order to experience the visual scene they have just overheard:

```
ANNCR:  Captain Benjamin Franklin Pierce. Nickname:
        'Hawkeye.'

BITE:   Just last night I pasted a new liver in my scrapbook.

ANNCR:  A dedicated surgeon---

BITE:   Even as a proctologist, I'd be seeing new faces all
        the time.

ANNCR:  With high standards of conduct---
```

V/O: WJLB FM 98.

Pumping out strong songs.

WJLB FM 98.

Working out

strong songs.

WJLB FM 98.

Detroit's strongest songs.

WOMAN: Now is that strong enough for you?

Figure 12-2

(Courtesy of Brogan & Partners Advertising/Public Relations.)

```
BITE:   I don't care how drunk you make me, I'm not going
        home with you.

ANNCR:  And a deep concern for personnel relations.

BITE:   You should forget about your mind, and pay more
        attention to your body. Or if you don't have the
        time, let me do it for you.
```

ANNCR: He's Hawkeye Pierce. On M*A*S*H.

LOCAL   (Channel, time and outlet slogan)
TAG:

(Copyright 1991. Twentieth Century Fox Film Corporation. All Rights Reserved. Courtesy Twentieth Century Fox Film Corporation.)

    Television promos are also effective on the radio when they use radio-friendly jingles to isolate a program series' key characteristics:

                <u>PRODUCTION NOTE:</u> In the style of a serious country & western ballad. The deep-voiced cowboy talks over the hum of back-up singers.

COWBOY: He sits in <u>judgment.</u> He stands for the <u>law.</u> Kinda looks like a <u>hero</u>---and sounds like your <u>Paw.</u>

SINGERS: <u>Wapner!</u>

COWBOY: He smiles 'n' he <u>laughs,</u> his voice tinged with gravel---but the bad guys just <u>gasp</u> when he bangs his <u>big gavel.</u>

SINGERS: <u>Judge Wapner!</u>

COWBOY: When <u>neighbors</u> brawl, when <u>lovers</u> refute.
When <u>suppliers</u> and <u>buyers</u> and <u>liars</u> dispute---
Wapner won't let those <u>law-books</u> get dusty.
Got a buddy named <u>Doug</u>---and a side-kick named <u>Rusty.</u>

SINGERS: <u>Rusty!</u>

COWBOY: With Wapner.

SINGERS: <u>Judge Wapner!</u>

COWBOY: He doesn't do it from <u>towers,</u> doesn't do it from steeples---
He does it in <u>court:</u> a court called <u>'People's.'</u>

SINGERS: <u>People's!</u>

```
COWBOY:     People's Court.

SINGERS:    With Wapner!

COWBOY:     Call him---your honor.

SINGERS:    Song over!

COWBOY:     Song over.

SINGERS:    (HUM A FEW MORE BARS, THEN OUT TO TIME.)
```

(© 1992 Paul & Walt Worldwide. Writer: Walt Jaschek. Producer: Paul Fey.)

Even sports telecasts can be effectively promoted on radio when the copy allows the listener to conjure up and anticipate pictures that are more self-involving than any highlights film:

```
ANNCR:  To the uninitiated it's a swirling mass of confusion.
        Anarchy on ice.
        Impossible to follow.
        But for anyone who has ever put a doke on an opponent
        or a puck in a net,
        hockey is not only easy to follow,
        it's easy to love.
        And when such a person watches the professionals play,
        he may groan at their clumsiness
        and boo at their mistakes.
        But deep down he knows how much skill and
        how much courage is needed---
        to play the world's fastest game
        in the world's toughest league.
        Hockey Night in Canada on CBC.
        Co-sponsored by Molson Canadian.
        What Beer's All About.
```

(Courtesy of Stephen Creet, MacLaren: Lintas Advertising Ltd.)

Notice, too, that because the above promo strives to be like a poem in its imagery, it is typed on the page as a poetry stanza.

National Program Promos

Most television programed promos, of course, are written to appear *on* television and to air on the outlets actually carrying the show. Promos for network and syndicated series are usually prepared by their network or syndicator source with provision made for local channel tagging at the end. Series promos can either be *generic* (in support of the show as a whole) or *topical* (selling a particular episode). CBS promotion executive Joe Passarella believes that the generic or "image" ads create "a receptivity to your show which you then follow up with the more 'retail' [topical] ads geared toward a program's specific episodes."[8]

The *M*A*S*H*, *People's Court,* and *Hockey Night in Canada* promos above all are generics for nationally distributed shows. Television versions of these radio generics would similarly emphasize elements common to *every* telecast of the respective series. In choosing the exact elements to spotlight, Warner Brothers Television's Jim Moloshok reveals that "we conduct preliminary promotional marketing research on our new entry. Our goal is to define what we call a show's 'hot spots' and 'cold spots.' The 'hot spots' are those areas that attract potential viewers to the program, and conversely, as you can easily guess, 'cold spots' are those points that may turn off an audience if not properly treated in all advertising."[10]

This same approach carries over to topicals. "With so much competition, every promo counts and each one needs to hit the nail (i.e. target audience) right on the head," asserts King/World creative services director Frank Brooks. "Creative needs to grab a viewer's attention in the first few seconds and hold their attention over and over again. Even daily topical spots deserve some 'kick.' "[11] In the following topical, for example, the key characters and turning points are isolated to convey a feeling of the episode's "heat" without revealing its outcomes. The numerical designations on the script's video side indicate where the featured liftouts can be found in the actual show.

Video	Audio
OPENING GRAPHIC	<u>VO:</u> Next on <u>A Different World:</u>
WHIT, DWAYNE & JULIAN AT TABLE 3:09	<u>WHIT:</u> Do I sound like I'm getting a cold?
	<u>JUL:</u> You sound like you're getting an F.
WHIT DEMONSTRATES HER ON-COMING COLD 3:17	<u>VO:</u> Midterms are here and so is Whitney's cold.
	<u>WHIT:</u> I'm definitely nasal.

Continued

Video	Audio
DWAYNE 3:23	<u>DWAY</u>: I suggest you work more on this math and less on that cold.
WHIT IN BED, SICK	<u>VO</u>: But Kim has the real problem.
KIM ON PHONE 5:48	<u>KIM</u>: He's been shot?!
	<u>WHIT</u>: Your daddy?
	<u>KIM</u>: I love you so much.
TAIL GRAPHIC/RUNOUT	<u>VO</u>: A special episode.

(Courtesy of Laurie Zettler, Viacom Entertainment.)

Local Program Promos

Promos created by local outlet copywriters also make use of both generic and topical approaches. The following KXAS-TV generic, for instance, was designed, in the words of the station's promotion director, Annette Fanning, "to position our late news as different from our earlier 5:00 and 6:00 reports as well as different from the competition's news."[12] The promo lets the viewer conclude how much *fresh* work (with consequent audience-informing benefit) is involved in the KXAS late news by showing night happenings and how station staff apprehends them.

<u>PRODUCTION NOTE:</u> All shots are night except as otherwise indicated.

Video	Audio
FADE IN TO PAVEMENT-LEVEL SUNSET SHOT OF FREEWAY	<u>MUSIC: SENSUOUS SAXOPHONE THEME THROUGHOUT AND FEATURED BETWEEN VO SEGMENTS</u>
DOWNTOWN SKYLINE (DUSK)	<u>WOMAN (VO):</u> Night falls

Continued

Video	Audio
CU FEMALE ANCHOR	on the city
FS DUSK SKYLINE TO FEATURE HYATT GLOBE	
KXAS 'COPTER LIFTING OFF	And there is
SEQUINED-DRESSED WOMAN LEAVING RED SPORTSCAR	a difference
'FLYING HORSE' NEON SIGN AGLOW	
DEFOCUS SHOT OF CAR HEADLIGHT	
FOCUS TO REVEAL IT'S KXAS NEWS VAN	in the
DALLAS COP TURNS TO CAMERA WITH HAND NEAR HOLSTER	way
ECU MAN'S HANDS LIGHTING CIGARETTE	things
ECU BLACK CAT'S FACE	look.
DIZ CU SAXOPHONIST WAILING IN FRONT OF FOUNTAIN	
CU MAN'S MOVING SHADOW ON WALL	A difference in the way they feel.
DIZ KXAS VAN AS REFLECTED IN OFFICE BLDG. WINDOW	A difference
POLICE CAR WITH FLASHERS BLAZING	in the way they sound.
OS SHOT OF MAN USING WANDS TO DIRECT JET TO RAMP	
DIZ SHOT OF KXAS DIRECTOR IN CONTROL ROOM TO FEATURE ANCHORS ON MULTIPLE MONITORS	All newscasts are not alike.

Continued

Video	Audio
DIZ AERIAL SHOT OF KXAS VAN	The Channel 5 Night Team.
DIZ CU OF MALE ANCHOR CROSSING TO NEWS SET	
CU WEATHERMAN AT HIS DESK	
OS SHOT OF SHADOWY FIGURE SPRAY-PAINTING 'Nite' ON A BRICK WALL	The difference is like day
FIGURE FLEES IN FRONT OF PAINTING	and night.
QUICK FADE TO BLACK	

(Courtesy of Annette Fanning, KXAS–TV. Produced by Kathi Devlin, shot and edited by Pattie Wayne.)

Newscasts are certainly the main, and sometimes the *only* programming produced by a local outlet. Thus, news promos become the chief way of distinguishing your facility from the competition. And because a person is more tangible than a program, some of the most successful news generics are built around the people who comprise the local news team. In creating these *personality promos,* the copywriter must make certain that each spot answers four questions for the audience: (1) Who is this person? (2) What makes this person unique? (3) What viewer benefit flows from this uniqueness? and (4) On what channel is this person to be found? Note how all four of these questions are covered in the following personality promo for a station meteorologist:

Video	Audio
BOYS COME UP OVER CREST OF HILL CARRYING KITE	MUSIC: LIGHT WOODWIND AND STRINGS UNDER
	VO: Even when Eric Nefstead was a kid, his head was in the clouds.
TWO SHOT, FRONT, BOYS LOOKING UP	BOY ERIC: You know what kind of clouds those are, Tommy?

Continued

Video	Audio
	TOMMY: (Sarcastically) White ones!
CU BOY ERIC POINTING AT THE SKY	BOY ERIC: They're fairweather cumulus clouds. That means it's great kite flying weather.
TWO SHOT FROM BEHIND BOYS, SEEING KITE IN TREE	TOMMY: If we ever get it out of the tree.
CU KITE IN TREE	MUSIC: STINGER; THEN SNEAK IN EYEWITNESS NEWS DITTY UNDER
DIS. TO KITE: ZOOM OUT TO SEE IT IS UNDER WEATHER DESK WITH MAN ERIC SITTING AT DESK. HE TURNS TO CAMERA AND SMILES.	VO: Meteorologist Eric Nefstead, down-to-earth weather reporting from a forecaster who knows what he's talking about.
SHOT FREEZES AND EYE-NEWS LOGO IS SUPERED.	Weeknights at 5:30 and ten on 19 Eyewitness News.

(Courtesy of Charles E. Sherman, WHOI–TV).

Topical news promos are often accomplished by blending an inventory of past specific successes (proof of performance) with a spotlighting of at least one current story or series. In this KTVN topical, three past scoops help give credence to this week's bannered live coverage from San Diego. At the same time, viewers are also reminded of the uniqueness of the station's hourly voice-over updates:

Video	Audio
'DOESN'T WAIT' GRAPHIC	VO: News doesn't wait.
FEMALE REPORTER IN DESERT; MIDDAY	That's why NEWS SOURCE 2 instituted news updates,
REPORTER; DAWN OUTDOOR BKG	on the hour, seven days a week.

Continued

Video	Audio
OTHER REPORTER AT NEWSDESK; WIPE TO:	Since then, NEWS SOURCE 2 has brought you:
OAKLAND FIRE PIC WITH REPORT IN FG	the first live coverage of the Oakland fire;
CRASH PIC	breaking coverage of the Thanksgiving Day CareFlight tragedy;
JOHNSON NEWS CONFERENCE	the first coverage of the Magic Johnson story;
CHRIS AULT ON SCENE	and this week, live coverage of Chris Ault in San Diego.
PLANE LANDING MINUS NOSEWHEEL: SPARKS FLYING	You <u>heard</u> about these stories before you <u>saw</u> them on our newscasts. On our <u>UPDATES.</u>
REPORTER IN MORTICE, COP CARS BY SIDE OF HIGHWAY	For live, up-to-the-minute coverage, wherever, whenever news happens,
CAR SPEEDS PAST ACCIDENT	count on NEWS SOURCE 2.
SLOGAN GRAPHIC ABOVE STATION LOGO	Because breaking news doesn't wait.

(Courtesy of Ruth Whitmore, KTVN.)

Network offerings also provide solid opportunities for promo exploitation on behalf of local outlet talent. As a means of showcasing their own stars, networks often make these stars available for cross-pitch messages to be aired by their affiliates. Copy for these spots may be supplied either by the network or by the outlet with network approval. The following promo, was one of four dozen produced at Turner Broadcasting System's Atlanta headquarters that paired *Headline News* anchor Don Harrison with the anchors of *Local Edition* inserts on 48 participating affiliates. In this instance, the local anchor was Suzanne Shaw from KRON-TV, San Francisco:

Video	Audio
M2S OF HARRISON AND SHAW AT ANCHOR DESK WITH KRON/HEADLINE NEWS COMBO SLIDE GRAPHIC BEHIND	HARRISON: Count on CNN Headline News to bring you the top news, sports, and business stories from around the world every 30 minutes---24 hours a day.
	SHAW: And at 24 and 54 past the hour, count on NewsCenter 4 to keep you up to date with the latest breaking news throughout the city.
	HARRISON: Whether new breaks around the world or around the corner, count on CNN Headline News and Newscenter 4's City Edition to bring it home to you on Viacom Cable Channel 43.

(Courtesy of David Talley, CNN.)

Affiliate copywriters who know the options open to them and who can carry out the advance planning required for proper coordination with network or syndicator promotions people gain a wealth of extra resources to make their outlet look prestigious.

End-Credit Voicers

One additional topical device that can be exploited by both networks and individual outlets is the end credit voicer. With this continuity technique, an audio-only promo for the following program is read over the visual credits of the show that has just concluded. Networks and local outlets may use this technique at the conclusion of their own or each other's shows in an attempt to hold their audience for the next event and inhibit channel switching.

Because the video is unrelated, however, the voicer itself must be especially compelling to break through this pictorial irrelevancy and entice the audience into sticking around. Attention-getting skills learned in radio copywriting thus are put to good use in end-credit voicer exploitation. Notice how the following ABC voicer leads with a powerful hook calculated to attract female demographics to the upcoming program.

LEA: So, Deena, have you found a man yet?

DEANA: No, they're all so <u>boring.</u>

LEA: (Teasing) I know where to find funny men.

DEANA: Really? Funny men! Where? How? When?

LEA: I'm not telling.

GARY   But I am. You'll find lots of funny men and
OWENS: women on the Sixth Annual American Comedy Awards.
          Next.

DEANA: He sounds funny.

LEA: Yeah, for an announcer.

(Courtesy of ABC Affiliate Marketing Services and Andrew Orgel, Video Jukebox Network, Inc.)

Trailers

These long-form program promos traditionally use both voice-over narration and audio/video clips from the show being pitched. The term *trailer* comes from the old movie house practice of having the teaser for the next week's serial episode follow or "trail" the current week's installment. Thus, today's video trailers mirror this "come-back-into-the-tent" heritage. They exploit several short, attention-riveting cuts to overcome home distractions and register the appealing essence of an offered full-length feature.

Trailers continue to be used in movie houses and on television to preview upcoming films, and the form has been diversified to cross-promote video and motion picture industry releases on each other's screens. Many home video cassettes are also bumpered with trailers for separate projects being released by the same media company. Even though trailer technique hasn't changed much over the years, the form's multiplying promotional applications now include *commercial trailers* as well—two- to four-minute spots that pitch a product or company.

Whether they are actually promos or commercials, trailers should follow the same communicative principles as do other video copywriting assignments. Even though they are more extensive than 30-second spots, trailers must still capture a target audience via words and pictures that lead to a single demonstration-based sell. In a fragmenting media marketplace, the copywriter must be prepared to adapt old forms such as the trailer to entirely new tasks.

The following trailer script, for example, is intended for conventional movie house distribution. It does not promote a feature film or other video product, however, but innovatively hawks a radio station. The promo thus reflects the flexibility that copywriters must use in pioneering novel technique/medium pairings to accomplish the marketing objectives of their clients. As this script also illustrates, trailers are often written in the centered (single-column) format that reflects their Hollywood heritage.

FADE UP

1. TITLE SEQUENCE-RATING DISCLAIMER   1.

                        ANNCR (V/O)

    The following motion picture has been rated PG,
    'pretty good,' by the Motion Picture Association
    of New York.

2. TITLE SEQUENCE-STATION LOGO.   2.

                        ANNCR (V/O)

    Power 95 presents---

3. EXT. MORNING-LARGE EXPENSIVE HOME.   3.

Dan, The Potty Man arrives in his van. He makes his way to
the front door carrying a toolbox and looking like the
ultimate geek.

                        JINGLE
                Dan, Dan the potty man,
              He's a sink and sewer fan.
               In a hurry, in a rush?
            Dan can make things swirl and flush.

He rings the door bell and takes a moment to run a comb through
his Brylcreamed hair. Suddenly the door opens and he finds
himself face to face with VICTORIA, an absolutely beautiful woman
of considerable money. He's speechless.

VICTORIA

Hi, you must be Dan. Come on in.

4. INT. LARGE EXPENSIVE HOME.   4.

Dan follows Victoria into a large room that's obviously being
remodeled---dropcloths and ladders are everywhere.

DAN
(gaining his composure)

Okay. Just movin' in, huh? From what you told me on
the phone, it's probably just some sheet rock dust or
something in your trap. Construction workers. Maybe
it's a beer can---

VICTORIA

Can I get you something to drink?

DAN

Yeah, sure, Buttermilk if you got it. Hey, a radio. Is
is okay if I listen?

Victoria smiles, seeming to know a great deal more than she's
willing to tell.

VICTORIA

Oh sure, go ahead. It might change your life.

She exits as he gives it a flick and Power 95 starts playing. We
HEAR a deep rumbling sound as the furniture begins to shake and
bright lights begin moving throughout the room. A fog moves in
around Dan and a mighty wind comes up strong enough to move his
plastered hair. Within a matter of moments he's supernaturally
changed into a tuxedoed prince charming. Victoria rushes in
wearing an evening gown and carrying two glasses of buttermilk.
She's overwhelmed.

VICTORIA

Dan, are you all right?

                         DAN
                  (very deep voice)

    Hi.

Dan pulls out a roll of black electrical tape and tears off a
strip long enough to put around his neck and tie into the perfect
bowtie.

                       VICTORIA
                  (soft and casual)

    Hi.

                         DAN

    You called for a plumber?

                       VICTORIA
                  (approaching---very sexy)

    I called for Dan, The Potty Man.

Victoria marvels at the black and silver 'Dan' patch on his lapel.

                         DAN

    That's me. Dinner tonight?

                       VICTORIA

    And maybe more.

Dan slides an arm around her waist as their mouths rush toward
one another, but pauses just before meeting.

                         DAN

    Great station.

                       VICTORIA

    I know.

```
Victoria cups her hands behind Dan's neck. She draws his mouth to
hers, and just as their lips meet we---

                                                         CUT TO:


5. TITLE SEQUENCE-STATION LOGO.                              5.

                         ANNCR (V/O)

     Power 95-FM. New York's hit music, free money station.
     Listen and it could change your life.

                                                         CUT TO:


6. TITLE SEQUENCE-NOW PLAYING                                6.

                         ANNCR (V/O)

     Now playing at 95.5 FM

                                                    CUT TO BLACK
```

(Courtesy of RadioFilms/RadioWorks, Inc.)

As bizarre as this trailer might seen, it deftly characterizes the irreverent, young-male appealing personality of Power 95-FM. When placed in front of movies attracting this same target universe, the promo communicates what it wants to exactly whom it wants—a key requisite for any successful promotions effort. As Gary Taylor, president of the Broadcast Promotion and Marketing Executives (BPME) reminds us: "Faced with an audience that's into channel-flipping, grazing, button-pushing and skim-reading, today's multimedia marketing professional has the extremely difficult task of targeting more accurately—'micromarketing' to a highly segmented, specifically defined listener/viewer, whose orientation is based on perceptions."[13] Wisc promotions copywriters exploit every possible avenue and technique for shaping those perceptions to the branding of their outlet or network.

Interviews and Semiscripts

Interview programs, particularly at the local level, are at least as prominent a part of television public service schedules as they are on radio, and for the same community relations-related reasons. (See the section on "Interviews" in Chapter 9.) From a structural standpoint, the television interview's intro and outro each should accomplish the same three purposes as their radio cousins but with some added dimensions that must be taken into consideration.

Arousing audience interest about the television interview, for example, may prove more difficult given the comparatively undynamic but nevertheless prominent visual of two or more people sitting and looking at each other. Film clips, tape segments, or selected still pics that relate to the guest's subject can help overcome the initial talking-head doldrums. If this is not possible, the opening of the program itself should be visually scripted and produced in such a way that viewers' attention is grabbed long enough for a compelling statement of the topic to sink in and, hopefully, keep them watching.

Making the guest feel at home, the third function of any public interview intro, is even more difficult on television, where bright lights and moving cameras can cause nonmedia visitors to feel especially isolated and uncomfortable. Thus, the continuity writer's well-chosen words of welcome are probably even more crucial in this environment than they were on radio, where the guest had only to contend with a blind and stationary microphone.

Other aspects of the television interview in particular, and of television semiscripts in general, tend to follow much the same procedures and possess much the same requirements that these forms entail on radio. The one unblinking overlay, however, is the presence of the visual dimension that the continuity writer may need to embellish subtly via suggested props or graphic bumpers. The following continuity bed for the opening portion of a *Good Afternoon Detroit* program from WXYZ-TV is indicative of the semiscripts used by many successful interview and magazine shows. In this script, the term *homebase* refers to the standard in-studio conversation set.

ITEM 1. STUDIO TEASE HOMEBASE	JOHN: Greenfield Village is a place for family fun and we'll be finding out what's going on this Fall---
	MARILYN: And Perry King, will be telling us about the latest twists in his career---next!
ITEM 2. END BREAK. VTR SOT. FLASH CAM.	

Continued

ITEM 3. STUDIO COLD OPEN. HOME
BASE
<u>SUPE.</u> John Kelly

<u>JOHN:</u> Good afternoon, Detroit.
Handsome actor Perry King was
one of the starts of the TV
adventure series---<u>The Quest.</u>
Today, Perry is joining us to
talk about what it's like to
be an actor who's more
interested in acting than
being a star.

ITEM 4. HOMEBASE
<u>SUPE:</u> Marilyn Turner

<u>MARILYN:</u> Sylvia Glover is on a
shopping trip to learn how to
get away from it all---anytime
she wants.

<u>JOHN:</u> We'll have a look at
elegant back-to-school
fashions for the mature
student---

<u>MARI:</u> And we'll find out that
the folks at Greenfield
Village are gearing up for a
great Fall season---

<u>JOHN:</u> Good afternoon, Detroit!

ITEM 5. ANIMATED OPEN

ITEM 6. HOMEBASE.

<u>JOHN:</u> Good afternoon, Detroit.
It's Friday, we're heading
into the weekend.

(AD LIB---GAIL PARKER---
LETTING GO KIDS)

(Copyright Capital Cities/ABC Inc.)

Sometimes, as in Figure 12–3, a semiscript takes the form of a rough storyboard. In this commercial concept for Toronto's Ontario Place amusement park, suggested dialogue has been written for Dad in frame 1, Mom in frame 3, Girl in frame 4, Boy in frame 6, Grandma in frame 7, Boy in frame 9, and Dad in frame 10. The actual comments to appear in the final spot, however, will depend on what real people extemporaneously say when asked leading questions on-camera at the park.

30' Ontario Place
General spot
②

SINGER Ontario Place!

MUSIC: upbeat, percussive,
continue under.

Cut to a Dad with his family
outside the Cinesphere.

DAD: Ontario Place is one place
where we can all have fun
together.

Cut to MCU Mom with the lake
behind her.

MOM: We love the Cinesphere,
the Waterfall Showplace . . .

Cut to little girl at Children's
Village.

GIRL: moon bounce . . .

Cut to boy in same position.

BOY: waterplay . . .

Cut to Grandma sitting on a bench
at Children's Village.

GRANDMA: I love just watching
the kids play.

Cut to family playing together
at Mini Greens.

Cut back to boy.

BOY: Dad won't play Mini-golf
'cause I always win!

Cut back to Dad..

DAD: And it doesn't cost that
much at all!

Cut to signature Graphic.

ANNCR: Come to the place where
the whole family can have fun
together, Ontario Place.

SINGER: Ontario Place. It's more
fun every day!

Figure 12-3

(Courtesy of Barry Base, Base Brown & Partners Ltd.)

Such a preplanned approach avoids wasted time while accommodating the spontaneity of what happens during sequence gathering. Whether in script or storyboard form, this blueprint keeps the project on-target and within budget. "In any situation, there's any number of things you could be shooting, or in an interview, any number of things you could ask," points out producer Christina Crowley of the Kenwood Group. A semiscript vehicle "narrows your focus, so you don't ask unnecessary questions. You come back with what you need, rather than what you need plus another 10,000 feet of videotape."[14]

Trade and Consumer Presentation Events

Though primarily for conference room, exhibition hall, or closed-circuit delivery, the *presentation* event (or "dog and pony show" as it is known in our industry) is simply an extended and fully fleshed-out cousin of the TV semiscript. In writing a presentation aimed at other businesspersons or consumers, you may be integrating still pics and slides into a live speech or preparing narrator/presenter wraparounds to relevant pieces of film or tape footage. Because the presentation thus uses the same materials as conventional television continuity writing, and since presentations are vital aspects of decision making in our own and our client's businesses (recall Chapter 11's discussion of the storyboard presentation), dog-and-pony-show design should be well within the television copywriter's area of expertise. In fact, corporate communications experts Chris Petersen and Guillermo Real argue that in all formal business pitches, "The mission must be to stop creating lengthy, laborious industrial sales, corporate image and training programs. Instead, we must produce 'cluster-of-commercials' films which utilize the thinking and creative style that govern the production of advertisers' TV announcements."[15]

As in any radio and television writing, the aim here must be to keep the copy conversational so the presenter seems to be talking *with* rather than lecturing *to* the audience. Clean, clear interlock between script segments and their illustrative visuals is also of pre-eminent concern. Nothing short-circuits a dog and pony show faster than when the dogs and ponies get out of sync: when the pics are scripted in such a way that they come too fast or too slow for the meaning and style of the presenter's aural delivery and perceivers' comprehension. A well-formatted outline combined with language that clearly relates to the on-stage action are essential properties here.

Several other considerations also impinge on the presentation-sculpting process. First, make certain you and the client know and agree on the objective for the piece. Second, you should not write meandering copy even though more time is available than in a 30-second commercial. Granted, it is possible to register several related points in a presentation script—but not if you allow tangential material to creep in. Third, conserve your time, both in terms of how much of it you use and how well you use it. Eight to ten minutes is an ideal presentation length for most purposes, and twenty minutes is the absolute limit if you expect to command audience attention and subject-matter retention.

As in any effective commercial, use your opening to get attention—but don't place the heart of your message there. People are still settling into their seats at the top of a presentation and may not apprehend the first moments of your material. Provide rewards for early listening and viewing but don't make immediate attention a prerequisite to later understanding. Similarly, because you have several minutes rather than a few seconds at your disposal, take time (before writing) to plot out the internal variations that propel your script forward. Don't think in terms of a 12- or 15-minute speech; think instead of a string of 10 to 20 modules that will build viewer involvement and comprehension but will also provide momentary relaxers and pace changers.

Further, it is essential to consider equipment needs carefully. Radio/television copywriters are especially prone to recruit a more sophisticated delivery system, or more glitzy productional effects, than the show's objective can profit from. Public relations experts Lawrence Nolte and Dennis Wilcox have observed that

> large amounts of money have been wasted on audio visual materials because someone leaped into production without considering the purpose to be served, the audience to be reached and the aid which could be most effective. Motion pictures are produced when a slide production would do the job. Costs are overlooked and budgets wrecked because decisions are made without thinking about the need and values of the various aids.[16]

In short, don't become an equipment junkie and overindulge in hardware.

Moderation is important when it comes to music's use as well. Music can create impact and stimulate audience involvement if it is correctly selected and planned for early. "Too often," declares Omni Music's Sam White, "music is tacked on after everything else is done. This tends to force the music into the background of the track, eliminating interaction of the music with the visuals to create the desired effect."[17] As White also points out, the style of the music must be dependent, not on the copywriter's or client's personal taste, but on the intended audience:

> A corporate image video with a score that's heavy on big orchestral themes may do well among potential investors because the music tells the audience that the company is solid as a rock. However, it may not fare as well among young potential recruits, who will hear the music as old and stuffy. And that guitar and harmonica theme that makes a big agricultural company seem friendly to the farming community may foster a negative company image to a Wall Street audience.[18]

Finally, never surrender the power and responsibility that as a copywriter you are paid to exercise. "When copywriters get the feeling that they're doing nothing but transcribing what the client has told them then they should take a vacation," advises producer Eric Larson. "When they're fresh they have a little more fight. And they realize that what they do is an art and is crucial."[19]

What follows is the opening of an Auto Show presentation that Visual Services, Inc., prepared on behalf of the Chrysler Corporation. Note that in more complex stage presentations such as this, the actual script is preceded by a Scenario Summary that concisely yet graphically sets forth the essential set details and general flow of the pitch. In this way, the client gets a clear idea of the overall presentational environment before examining the actual words and actions that the copywriter has employed.

<u>Scenario Summary</u>

A 1992 Plymouth Voyager is positioned onstage opposite a
4-ft.-tall Olympic Gold Medal, leaning back slightly as if
resting on its ribbon, which is coiled behind it.

The show begins when the model/narrator takes the stage. The
Voyager and the gold medal are elevated on their rotating
circular stages. The Voyager then descends to eye-level where
noted in the script.

As the narrator moves onto the stage, midway between the
Voyager and the Olympic gold medal, special lighting and a
<u>musical fanfare</u> (on the show's videotape soundtrack) draws
the attention of passers-by, alerting them to the fact that
a show is about to begin. This happens for approx. 18
seconds.

Special lighting enhances the luster of the gold medal and
highlights the van---and the narrator, whenever appropriate.

During the show, the "live" narrator's presentation is augmented
by video on monitors suspended above the stage, showing the
features or components the narrator is describing.

Throughout the show, the circular stage on which the Voyager is
positioned will be lowered, for better viewing of its interior
and components. The Voyager will be programmed to slowly revolve,
or to remain stationary during the presentation, in keeping with
the requirements of the script. The Olympic Gold Medal will
revolve slowly throughout the presentation.

(:18 FANFARE & SPOTLIGHTS AS NARRATOR/MODEL ASCENDS STAGE)

:00 LIVE NARRATOR (OVER FOOTAGE OF 1984 VOYAGER):

395

When it was introduced in 1984, the Plymouth Voyager set a <u>new</u>
<u>standard</u> by giving <u>birth</u> to the mini-van market! Voyager quickly
became a leader in resale value and owner loyalty, often imitated
but <u>never</u> duplicated.

:14 "GOLD STANDARD" TITLE SLIDE W/OLYMPIC RINGS AND GOLD MEDAL

Today, Chrysler Corporation is a proud sponsor of the U.S.
Olympic Team, as American athletes compete for the <u>ultimate honor:</u>

(NARRATOR SWEEPS HER ARM TOWARD, WALKS TOWARD, GOLD MEDAL)

the <u>gold medal.</u> At the Olympics, athletes from all over the world
strive to reach the performance standards set by <u>previous</u> gold
medal winners and record-holders. In much the same way, <u>mini-vans</u>
the world over are trying to reach the standard set by Plymouth
Voyager. But even now, eight years after its introduction,
Voyager <u>continues</u> to set a gold medal pace the competition just
can't match.

(NARRATOR SWEEPS HER ARM TOWARD VOYAGER, AS IF "INTRODUCING" IT)

Ladies and gentlemen, Chrysler-Plymouth <u>proudly</u> presents the
'Gold Standard of Mini-Vans,' Voyager for 1992! Witness the
<u>evolution</u> of the mini-van!

:54 'METAMORPHOSIS' COMMERCIAL RUNS, IN ITS ENTIRETY, WITH
FULL SOUND. FOLLOWING COMMERCIAL, THE MONITORS GO BLACK FOR
9 SECONDS AS NARRATOR SAYS:

(1:24) <u>Now,</u> ladies and gentlemen, let's take a <u>closer</u> look at the
1992 Plymouth Voyager, and see why it <u>continues</u> to set standards.

1:32 FRONT OF THE VAN IS ANGLED TOWARD THE NARRATOR, AND THE
<u>MALE V/O NARRATOR</u> (PRE-RECORDED ON THE VIDEO'S SOUNDTRACK),
TAKES OVER.

<u>Video and Stage Action</u>	<u>Male V/O Narrator</u>
OPENING OF 'METAMORPHOSIS' SPOT, FOLLOWED BY FOOTAGE FROM S.E.T. VIDEO	For 1992, The Gold Standard of Mini-Vans is identified by its unique aerostyling, including a low, sloping hood and curved fender corners for greater visibility.

1:43 VAN BEGINS SLOWLY ROTATING ON TURNTABLE	And for '92, a unique <u>Gold Decor Package</u> is available on both the Voyager and Grand Voyager SE models.
TWO SLIDES SHOWING NEW GOLD DECOR PACKAGE	The package includes 15-inch, gold-finish, cast-aluminum lace wheels, 15-inch front disc and rear drum brakes. Wide, 205-series tires. Choose from a variety of available exterior colors, all with twin, gold-finish body stripes.
2:14 NEW '92 FILM FOOTAGE	Voyager's handling? It's good as <u>gold</u>,, thanks to innovations like a gas-pressurized front suspension that enhances your 'feel' of the road.
2:22 WHEELS ARE HIGHLIGHTED WITH CHASING FIBER OPTICS, WHICH ROTATE AROUND THE WHEEL AS AWD AND ABS ARE COVERED	You get sure-footed front-wheel drive with <u>every</u> Voyager. And, the <u>added</u> safety of <u>All</u>-Wheel Drive is also available. It provides . . .

. . . . script continued . . . .

(Courtesy of Jerry Downey, Visual Services, Inc.)

Although the full Voyager presentation runs 7:28, it nonetheless, like any effective thirty-second spot, projects and develops a single theme. In this case, the theme exploits an Olympic tie-in of "being first/getting gold." When you write your own dog-and-pony scripts, make sure that they are grounded in a single-concept base as well. Even in a full-length presentation, scattered ideas and techniques make for fragmentary audience impact.

Specialized Venues

The continued expansion of video in the corporate and consumer sectors has provided new options and opportunities for television copywriters. Although we lack the space to explore these in detail, such variegated tasks can all be met by applying the basic principles for effective visual communication that we have introduced in Chapters 10, 11, and 12.

Video News Releases

Usually referred to as VNRs, these video press handouts combine the techniques of journalism and public relations to publicize events and developments that are of substantial interest to a corporate client. A 1990 Nielsen survey conducted for Medialink, the Video News Release Network, discovered that almost 80 percent of television stations used a VNR in their newscasts at least once a week. Two years later, VNR producer and former CBS correspondent Larry Pintak found this use increasing. "The news industry has been so gutted over the years," Pintak observed, "that they don't have a choice."[20]

Essentially, the VNR gives television news directors a press release in a format adapted to their needs—just as the printed handout has met the needs of newspaper editors for almost a century. "When I was a television news reporter, the assignment editor had a stack of newsletters," recalls VNR production house owner Nancy Herr. "He'd have to have a reporter like me turn it into a form we can use. That's what a video news release is: a press release in a form that's *usable*."[21] The VNR writer has "got to think in terms of news producers looking for pictures, features, and angles," adds Medialink senior editor Nick Peters. "If it's a good story, with a good hook, *somebody* will use it."[22]

This hook, and the story as a whole, must be honest and accurate, of course—the same ethical burden that a copywriter bears when preparing a commercial. But because the VNR is neither a paid spot nor identified as commercial matter, extra care must be taken to ensure that the piece provides audience-helpful information first, and client-serving impact second. "I have an ethical problem of taking a lightweight story and going to the trouble and expense of producing it," states Hill & Knowlton's George Glazer. "If the story doesn't justify it, we don't do it. We've got our name on it. We don't want stations saying 'Here comes more Hill & Knowlton s---."[23]

The following VNR for GM Hughes Electronics is topical because it ties into the upcoming Indianapolis 500 auto race. It presents interesting information both visually and via the soundtrack and possesses highway safety implications as well. The fact that it also promotes the technological expertise of its corporate sponsor does not detract from these positives because the device being profiled was, in fact, a GM/Hughes innovation. Like many VNRs, the piece is packaged in such a way that each station's own talent can voice the intro and subsequent narration.

(Suggested introduction)

Even before the green flag waves, starting the 72nd
running of the Indianapolis 500 race, one driver will
be using technology that was originally developed for
use in military aircraft---

Video	Audio
MS DRIVER IN PACE CAR	SUGGESTED VO NARRATION: The driver will be behind the wheel of the Oldsmobile Cutlass Supreme pace car and he'll be seeing
LS HEAD-UP DISPLAY	a projected image of his speed which will appear to be floating out over the front bumper of the car. It's called a Head-Up Display and it's designed to keep the driver's eyes on the road ahead.
LS TWO FIGHTERS IN FORMATION	Because of the complicated instruments and controls in a modern jet fighter, the original Head-Up Displays have been a boon to fighter pilots who can't afford to take their eyes off their instruments for even a split second.
LS HEAD-UP DISPLAY, INDY TRACK	Developed by GM Hughes Electronics, the down-to-earth model is expected to make a positive contribution to driving safety.
MS HARRY KING Suggested Super: Dr. Harry King GM Hughes Electronics	KING SOT: Particularly in collision avoidance situations where you may be looking down at the dashboard working on the controls,

Continued

Video	Audio
PROFILE DRIVER, PAN TO WINDSHIELD	if an emergency occurs and you're looking up through the windshield, you're certainly
HEAD-UP DISPLAY, TURN SIGNAL	going to pick that up more quickly in your field of view and respond to it more quickly.
CONTINUE HEAD-UP DISPLAY SCENE	SUGGESTED VO: In addition to speed, the Head-Up Display in the pace car shows low fuel, high beam headlights and turn signals.
LS FOLLOW PACE CAR ON PIT ROAD	KING SOT: We can also put other displays there, possibly allow you to tune your radio or set heater controls or have other
LS 3/4 FRONT RUNNING SHOT	temporary displays that you could use to make the driver's life easier as he drives the car.
CONTINUE RUNNING SHOT	SUGGESTED VO: Although the Head-Up Display is now only in the limited production Oldsmobile Cutlass Supreme replica pace
LS PAN PACE CAR DOWN PIT ROAD	cars, it is expected to be available in a number of General Motors cars in the near future.

TOTAL RUNNING TIME: 1 MINUTE 24 SECONDS

(Courtesy of Jim O'Donnell, NTN Film & Video Productions.)

In-Flight Spots

Several advertisers are making a concentrated effort to reach prime business prospects via the highly targeted avenue of airline programming. Commercials are now being sold by the airlines as wrap-around material to the movies and news shows that they feature on longer flights. Initially, these sky spots were used mainly by travel-related companies such as hotels, luggage manufacturers, and car rental firms. Later, computer companies, credit-card services, and auto manufacturers joined the mix. In the highly captive environment of an aircraft cabin, on-screen advertisements reach upscale individuals who are among the lightest users of conventional television.

From a copywriting standpoint, in-flight messages tend to be shorter, more sophisticated, and less reliant on voice-overs than are their grounded counterparts. "I don't think you're going to sell them [business travelers] with someone barking at them like in a carnival," asserts airline in-flight entertainment manager Judy Oldham. "This kind of person doesn't want to be hammered at that way."[24] And when the visual rather than voice-over carries the essential information (a style that land-based TV would do well to emulate), even those passengers who don't rent headsets are likely to be exposed to the essence of your pitch.

In-Store Commercials

Seeking new revenue sources and ways to promote the products they carry, stores are now making use of video selling as well. In 1990, for example, Sears placed monitors in the young men's fashion, activewear, and seasonal departments of more than 500 of its stores. Running a mix of music videos, sports highlights, and movie clips with the ads, Sears sought to increase the time young consumers spent in their stores while providing a video forum for product manufacturers. Although many of the spots are for goods carried in the store, others promote such items as soft drinks, cars, and new movie releases. For a charge of $33,660 for a one-month package, an advertiser's 30-second spot ran every thirty minutes.[25]

Two years later, both Turner Communications and NBC were in various stages of rolling out video services for grocery store check-out lanes. Programming for these projects includes brief clips of self-promotional material prepared by their parent networks plus 15-second spots for packaged goods sold in the store. Turner also launched a similar effort in key airports (The Airport Channel) and another designed for display inside McDonald's restaurants.

All of this "place-based" media activity is in recognition of the fact that while traditional advertising expenditures increased from 4 to 6 percent annually between 1987 and 1992, in-store advertising/promotion dollars ex-

Figure 12-4
A Place-Based Media Installation

*(Photo by David Darst, Graphic Production,
LIR, Central Michigan University.)*

panded between 10 percent and 15 percent each year during the same period. As marketing information specialist Ross Blair explains, "Now there's such a plethora of products, so many messages, so much clutter, that mass messages don't work so well anymore. It's much more cost-effective to target in-store than nationally. And it is this marketing dynamic that will drive much more micromarketing and geodemographic clustering—targeting consumers by life style, income and education."[26]

"Television" copywriters of the future thus are likely to be crafting fewer messages for a conventional broadcast environment and more commercials for point-of-purchase display. This means coming up with concepts that are even more visually riveting while pairing down the idea to its most graphic and unmistakable essence. It also means that we need to target our spots even more precisely for the specific store venue and time of day. The demise of Turner's Checkout Channel in 1993, for instance, was due, argues Paine-Webber media analyst Alan Gottesman, to the fact that it "simply recycled and didn't craft programming for the environment. It had nothing to do with the environment of a supermarket. NBC [on-Site] avoids most of these problems. It's tailored and silent, designed to be almost a sign."[27]

In light of all of these new and maddeningly distinct marketing situations, many advertising agencies are creating special departments to take another look at consumers. Saatchi & Saatchi/New York's Betsy Frank, whose title is Director of Television Information and New Media, affirms that "There's no doubt the consumer world is becoming more cluttered and fragmented and there is more of a need to break through the clutter and find solutions that weren't used, or even available, 10 or 15 years ago."[28] Many of these solutions, of course, will be expected to come from the keyboards of today's and tomorrow's copywriters. The basic principles of television communications we've explored will remain the same—but your application of these principles must be more flexible than ever.

Casting and Voice-Over Considerations

Whatever the environment for which you are preparing a television message, the people who deliver that message will significantly impact its appeal and palatability. Because video announcements that show people tend to be more interesting *to* people, casting is an important issue most of the time. Although the copywriter might not make the final casting decisions, the writer's specifications, when translated via the art director's sketches, form the blueprint from which the producers choose their talent. This selection process deserves as much of your input as possible because if the audience does not like the people who appear in your message, they will apply this distaste to the message itself. Take some time to write a vivid and compelling production note that clearly delineates the type of person you had in mind during script creation. Then, read over that description to make certain it describes the sort of individual who would most likely be found in the environment in which your vignette transpires. (Or, if you want comedic incongruity, do just the opposite.) When multiple roles are required, particularly to suggest our message's universal relevance, well-chosen, differentiated casting can be effective in the same way the multivoice technique functions on radio.

A fundamental casting decision involves whether to use (1) real people, (2) pseudo-real people, or (3) celebrity people. As the Figure 12–3 Ontario Place concept suggested, real people possess a charm all their own. If you have the time and budget to shoot and edit their random activities and unpolished commentaries, real people help keep the spotlight squarely on your message because as viewers, we have no prior association with them to distract us. The people-interest emotional pull is thus exerted without the people becoming the central point of our message. Instead, they are tools for the spot's goal attainment and can sometimes bring extemporaneous touches to our message that a professional actor would never have devised.

Pseudo-real people, like the man cast in Figure 12–5, are professional but anonymous talent. They should be able to convince the viewer that they're 'just folks' without expending the shooting/editing time required to make authentic real people palatable. These unknown actors or actresses need not be imported from New York or Los Angeles. They are available throughout the country and can deliver compelling performances at no more than scale rates. Youngsters, oldsters, and people at every age in between can bring a polished credibility to your message without making it too glitzy, on the one hand, or too untutored on the other.

PRODUCT: TURFBUILDER PLUS 2
TITLE: "WHAT DANDELIONS"

LENGTH: 30 SECONDS
COMM'L NO.: ITOM 2330

(MUSIC UNDER)
MAN: Gentlemen, it's curtains.

I told you dandelions not to come back again.

But you didn't listen, did you?

No more Mr. Nice Guy.

ANNCR: (VO) Turfbuilder Plus 2 Weed and Feed from Scotts

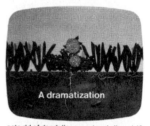

gets rid of dandelions, root and all, and 40 other weeds,

while it helps thicken your lawn with Turfbuilder fertilizer.

MAN: See, I told you I meant business.

WIFE: (VO) Ralph, are you out there

talking to those dandelions again?

MAN: What dandelions? You see any dandelions?

ANNCR: (VO) Say goodbye to dandelions.

Figure 12-5
(Courtesy of Melissa Wohltman, Doyle Dane Bernbach Advertising.)

Celebrities are individuals already well-known to viewers. Celebrity pitches work best when there is a natural tie-in between what is being discussed and the reason for the celebrity's fame. Lee Iacocca could talk about cars because we knew he had spent his career in the automotive business and at more than one company. A famous scrambling quarterback can visually attest to the fit and flexibility of a pair of slacks by demonstrating his continued dexterity while wearing them. But a teenage rock idol lauding a detergent's power or an insurance company's dividend record savages credibility because that idol is in no position personally to authenticate either. "When I first started in the business," confessed casting director Ellen Golden, "it was very popular, both in public relations and advertising, to get celebrities. Sometimes celebrities have been used only for sex appeal or shock value or awareness . . . but it's not necessarily the way to go. The fit has to be right . . . and I think the days are over when you just buy a celebrity and assume it's going to work."[29] "We had a celebrity in the White House in the '80s," points out creative director Donny Deutsch. "In the '90s, there's a swing away from celebrities in advertising unless it's part of the big creative idea."[30]

In their study of consumer perception, persuasion, and processing of celebrity advertising, Professors Abhilasha Mehta and Clive Davis found that "Celebrities trigger past connection in viewers' minds, so use celebrities that would evoke positive connections. Thoughts related to the celebrity dominate the processing. Thus, it appears that if the celebrity in the ad is well matched with the product and highly involved with the product in the ad, thoughts about the celebrity may evoke product-related thoughts which may help promote favorable attitudes."[31] An example of affirmative and effective celebrity employment is found in the Figure 12–6 spot for Weight Watchers. Lynn Redgrave's movie-certified poundage problem, to which she refers in the commercial's first frame, gives her a hefty touch of credibility. She then converts this credibility into plentiful product sell by exhibiting how the client's entrees satisfy a "fat taste" without inducing a fat figure.

Voice-overs present the option of casting a video message without worrying about the subject's physical appearance, mannerisms, or the prior associations these might conjure up in the mind of the viewer. Unless you want the voice to be recognized as someone specific, it can remain anonymous because audiences have long ago become accustomed to the unidentified aural being. Use of the voice-over even allows you to cast a role two ways. In the Figure 12–7 commercial, for example, our young tuba player never speaks on camera. Thus, you could cast one child based on his visual appeal and use another child to portray that same character's voice. In fact, because we never have to show the articulator of the copy, you might recruit a young female or even an adult talent for the voicer if the delivery better matched your conception of what this bespeckled munchkin should sound like.

In selecting voice-over talent, the general trend today is toward conversational deliverers and away from what are called "voice of God" proclaimers.

WEIGHT WATCHERS FROZEN MEALS
"RED DRESS" :30

CLIENT: FOODWAYS NATIONAL, INC.   COMM'L NO.: HZWO 3003

LYNN REDGRAVE: This is the size dress I wore when I was in the movie, "Georgy Girl".

With steely determination, I got myself down to a size 10.

But you know what stayed fat?

My love for good food.

Like Pizza peppered with sausage.

Lasagna layered with . . . rich ricotta.

Even southern fried chicken.

LYNN (VO): I still eat all these delicious things. I can.

They're Weight Watchers Frozen Foods.

LYNN REDGRAVE: They're why my fat taste . . .

for good food . . .

doesn't show!

Figure 12-6

(Courtesy of Melissa Wohltman, Doyle Dane Bernbach Advertising.)

"TUBA"

CAMPAIGN: "HOME RUN FAMILY"
COMM'L. NO.: HZOG 7120

LENGTH: 30 SECONDS

VO: Mom teaches the violin . . .

. . . but the tuba is my instrument.

I think it sounds great . . .

. . . when I practice outside.

The bird's don't.

Playing the tuba takes lots of energy.

So does carrying it.

When I get home, I'm *hungry.*

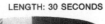

So mom makes me great dinners with lots of crinkly Ore-Ida fries.

I told her that if every tuba player had Ore-Ida fries after practice . . .

. . . there'd be a lot more tuba players.

Mom said, let's just keep this to ourselves.

Figure 12-7

(Courtesy of Ore/Ida and DDB Needham Worldwide.)

"The use of naturalistic, pleasant-sounding, warm and energetic voices furthers an effort to make the corporation appear more human—and accessible—to its audiences," writes industry observer Stephen Barr.[32] "An effective narrator," adds producer Ken French, "conveys the *attitude* behind the information. He or she must be versatile enough to infuse the appropriate personality into your words, yet still be sincere and accurate."[33]

Barr's recognition of the "he/she" option is important. For years, clients and copywriters assumed that male voices were more authoritative and effective. Then, in 1986, the Women's Voice-Over Committee of the Screen Actors Guild's New York branch commissioned a McCollum-Spielman study of the subject. The research results indicated that "those consumers tested found commercials equally persuasive when they had a female voice-over as when they had a male voice-over."[34] Gradually, "people are starting to use women more," reports casting agent Don Pitts. "A few years ago 1 out of 13 calls would be for women; today that's shifted to 1 out of 9."[35]

When you have the opportunity to indicate the kind of narration you want for your spot or script, give careful consideration to both male and female options. As copywriter/voice-over artist Laura Stigler points out, "A spring 1990 survey by Mediamark Research, Inc., unveils these amazing facts: Women buy more than 50 percent of new automobiles. Women buy more than 50 percent of household cleaning supplies, cereals, pet foods, soap, cameras, and movie tickets."[36] Therefore, can't a female voice be at least as persuasive as a male in describing and validating the merits of these and related products?

One final casting caution. Whether on-camera or voice-over, male or female, don't employ a look- or sound-alike substitute for a celebrity whom you can't afford. If the imitation is inept, it will make your sponsor look cheap or shady. If the imitation is skillful, it invites an infringement suit from the celebrity being mimicked.

Endnotes

1. Mike Freeman, "Cable-Friendly in Seattle," *Broadcasting* (June 15, 1992), 39.
2. John Locke and Hal Brown, "Music for Television—The Tempo of Your Marketplace," *BPME Image* (March 1987), 22.
3. Ibid.
4. John Chavez, "Network/Affiliate Packages," *BPME Image* (January 1989), 13.
5. *Ibid.*, 18.
6. Bob Klein, "Survival Guide to Station Image Development," *NATPE Programmer* (January 1986), 124.
7. Karl Sjodahl, "The Station's Image," *BPME Image* (March 1988), 17.
8. Bruce Bloom, writing in "Monday Memo," *Broadcasting* (October 6, 1986), 24.
9. "The Inside Story: John Larkin," *BPME Image* (January 1991), 4.
10. Jim Moloshok, writing in "Monday Memo," *Broadcasting* (October 2, 1989), 30.

11. Frank Brooks, "Maintaining the Leading Edge in Syndication/Promotion," *BPME Image* (October 1991), 15.
12. Annette Fanning. Letter to the author, 12 August 1987.
13. Gary Taylor, "Gob Management," *BPME Image* (June 1992), 4.
14. Fred Cohn, "Getting It Down on Paper," *Corporate Video Decisions* (June 1989), 25.
15. Chris Petersen and Guillermo Real, "Muster Your Clusters," *Audio-Visual Communications* (November 1987), 53.
16. Lawrence Nolte and Dennis Wilcox, *Effective Publicity: How to Reach the Public* (New York: John Wiley, 1984), 281.
17. Sam White, "The Power of Music," *Video Systems* (August 1988), 48.
18. Ibid., 46.
19. "Orchestrating the Commercial," *ASAP* (January/February 1988), 17.
20. David Lieberman, "Fake News," *TV Guide* (February 22, 1992), 16.
21. Fred Cohn, "PR Enters the Video Age," *Corporate Video Decisions* (March 1989), 34.
22. Ibid., 36.
23. *Ibid.*
24. Pat Hinsberg, "In-Flight Advertising Hits New High," *ADWEEK* (July 17, 1989), 48.
25. Kathy Brown and Richard Brunelli, "Sears OKs Ads on In-Store Video," *ADWEEK* (May 21, 1990), 3.
26. Lorne Manly, "Selling in the Stores of the Future," *ADWEEK* (January 20, 1992), 12.
27. *Ibid.*, 13.
28. Richard Brunelli, "Malls to Walls: Needham Examines Placement Options," *ADWEEK* (January 1, 1990), 10.
29. Karen Singer, "SpokeSearch: Matching Messengers with Messages," *ADWEEK* (December 14, 1987), 20.
30. Iris Selinger, "Celebrity Overexposure," *ADWEEK* (March 4, 1991), 13.
31. Abhilasha Mehta and Clive Davis, "Celebrity Advertising: Perception, Persuasion and Processing." Paper presented at the 1990 Association for Education in Journalism and Mass Communication Convention, 14–15, at Minneapolis.
32. Stephen Barr, "Voiceover Talent Turns Warm and Fuzzy," *Corporate Video Decisions* (August 1990), 18.
33. Ken French, "Producing an Effective Voice-Over," *AVC Music Mart* (April 1990), 47.
34. Debbie Seaman, "Voice-Over Study Shouts Down Male-Superiority Notion," *ADWEEK* (September 22, 1986), 58.
35. Kathy Brown, "Hearing Voices," *ADWEEK* (July 1, 1991), 16.
36. Laura Stigler, "I Am Woman; Hear My Voice," *ADWEEK* (September 24, 1990), 41.

Chapter 13

Radio/Television Campaign Construction

Up to this point, our concern has focused on the prewriting analysis, script creation, and postdraft evaluation of individual pieces of radio and television copy. Now it is time to view the process in compound form, to examine how an entire campaign is constructed and the individual messages within it coordinated into a mutually reinforcing whole. Even though the discussion in this chapter centers primarily on *commercial* strategies, keep in mind that the same basic steps and procedures can, and usually should, be followed in forging well-aimed outlet promotion, program promotion, and PSA packages as well. It should be noted, too, that cross-media campaigns in which both print and electronic media are employed would also conform to the same basic mode of operation.

Isolating Brand Character

Any product, service, media outlet, or community institution has a name. And, as marketing professor Terance Shimp points out, a good brand name can evoke feelings of trust, confidence, security, strength, and many other desirable associations.[1] What the copywriter must do is to tap into the essence of this brand identity to discover *brand character*—the unique property that this name now reflects or could reflect given proper campaign exposure. An effective way to zero in on current brand character—and to ascertain whether it needs reinforcement, amplification, or transformation—is to construct a paper-and-pencil inventory of the existing marketing situation. Not only will this inventory process acclimate you to the client's world, but it will also make you feel more a part of it because you have injected some of your own words into this world, if only in list form. Making lists starts you grappling with campaign strategy and the brand character that this strategy is calculated to sculpt and promote.

Of course, before you can construct any list, you have to find out as much as possible about your subject. There are many ways to do this. After his agency acquired the Texaco account in 1934, Jack Cunningham, one of the founders of Cunningham & Walsh, "spent two weeks wearing the Texaco star, pumping gas, greasing axles and changing oil. From his time at the point of sale, Cunningham learned that customers cared more about the cleanliness of a service station's restrooms than they cared about the gasoline sold there. For several years to follow, it was clean restrooms that sold Texaco's petrol."[2]

Much more recently, Goldsmith Jeffrey staffers spent a thirteen-hour shift riding the New York subways to develop ideas for a Metropolitan Transportation Authority campaign. DDB/Needham creatives (male and female) were given makeovers using new client Maybelline's beauty products, and Ayer employees spent a week behind the counters to acquaint themselves first-hand with their Burger King account. That fast-food experience "made us much more knowledgeable and realistic, and more sensitive to the crew person," testified Ayer senior vice-president, Lee Rubin. Among the Ayer staff, added vice-president Peter Varvara, "the universal response was that this [fast-food serving] is incredibly hard."[3] Even more intensively, copywriter John Stingley and art director Nark Johnson spent three weeks in Germany after their agency won the Porsche account. During this time, they "immersed themselves in Porsche culture, spending three weeks in the Stuttgart plant and engineers' homes."[4]

On projects to which you are assigned, you may not always have the time to go to such lengths. But all of these examples illustrate just how central acquired product/market knowledge is to brand character isolation. Once you have gained an understanding of brand and market specifics, by whatever means, the list-making process can proceed in the assurance that it is based on fact.

1. List the Positive Attributes

The first and most obvious portion of your inventory should encompass all the reasons that someone [or different groups of someones] would want to utilize/patronize the product or service. Set down each of these in a consumer-benefit form and include at least one for each of the SIMPLE rational motivations discussed in Chapter 4. Keep an entirely open mind at this point, for you can never predict which benefit may, once the total analysis is completed, exhibit the greatest success potential. Write down every conceivable product merit, no matter how bizarre, and allow the process to isolate the *most* meritorious later.

2. List the Weaknesses

The perfect product or service never existed in this imperfect world, and don't assume yours will break the pattern. The honest and ultimately triumphant campaign always takes its client's drawbacks into consideration and proceeds accordingly. As you may recall from Chapter 1, the in-house agency sometimes lacks the capability or willingness to view corporate output in this light. Such self-imposed blinders too often ignore marketplace realities and substitute management's hallucinations for public attitudes. A weakness glossed over in the campaign planning is almost certain to surface like a dead, bloated whale in campaign execution. Get all the product or service drawbacks out on paper, where you can see and deal with them *in advance*.

3. Retrieve the Exploitable Weaknesses

Once you've made a candid appraisal of product limitations, see if you can't transform them into positive attributes by casting them in a new light. This process can harvest the most persuasive brand character because it shows consumers that what they thought was a negative factor is really, on closer examination, a laudable characteristic. Thus, for a certain candy mint, "you pay a few cents more, but for a breath deodorant it's worth it." Similarly, an insurance company's inability to contact personally every household is explained away by the popularity of the policies that are keeping its agents so busy. And, as revealed in the 10-second spot below, lack of a lounge may save both your ears and your wallet some pain:

Video	Audio
OPEN MS MARTIN MULL SITTING IN OVER-DECORATED LOUNGE. HE'S LEANING ON BAR NEXT TO SEQUIN-DRESSED WOMAN WHOSE BACK IS TURNED. BEHIND MULL IS MALE SINGER WITH GREASED HAIR AND TASTELESS BLUE-PLAID DINNER JACKET	MULL: You know, you'll always pay less at Red Roof Inns because you don't have to pay for extras like a lounge.
	SINGER: (Off-key) Uh, uh, goo goo face---
	MULL: Aren't you glad?
LS STANDARD OF RED ROOF INN EXTERIOR AT DUSK WITH CAR PULLING IN	VO: Next time, hit the roof, Red Roof Inns.

(Courtesy of Ed Klein, W.B. Doner and Company Advertising.)

In fact, retrieving an exploitable weakness might even save the business itself. The story is told of the small salmon packing plant that gradually was losing more and more share of market because its steam-based canning processes turned the naturally pink salmon meat to *white*. Though the process was just as hygienic as the methods employed at bigger plants, and though the steaming did not adversely affect taste, new consumers were suspicious of white salmon. The plant did not have the money to install another process, and all seemed lost until an astute copywriter unearthed the perfect exploitable weakness theme:

(Company name) Salmon---the only salmon guaranteed not to turn pink in the can.

In one stroke, the conventional became the unacceptable and the regional market for *white* salmon jumped to an all-time sales high.

4. Amalgamate the Benefits and Excuses

Next, take all the positive attributes from list #1 and all the feasible excuses from list #3. Merge them into one composite slate and condense this to the fewest possible essentials. You want to have a comprehensive catalog of benefits related to your product or service without a confusing and potentially replicative overlap. At this juncture, you should now have before you the total range of differentiated options, each of which may conceivably be selected as a main branding theme, depending on the demographic/psychographic profile of your client's target audience. This comprehensively sets the stage for the winnowing process that follows.

5. List the Client's Past Approaches

Since we began with the assumption that you are planning a new campaign, it must also be assumed that the current approach is not working or has run its course, as did the other approaches that might have preceded it. Generally, it is deemed undesirable to reharvest a previously abandoned theme from which all the usable fruit has already been picked and consumed. Thus, list #5 serves to eliminate items from #4 that have been stressed in the past. Should you *want* to resurrect an earlier theme, however, cross-checking it with list #4 should ascertain whether there is a solid and readily identifiable current benefit from which that theme can issue. It may be discovered that the particular approach failed to work before because it really didn't relate to true brand character or mismatched an advantage with an inappropriate target audience, such as pitching a tire's durability to high-income types who only buy tires with a new car attached.

413

6. List What the Competition Is Stressing

This particular catalog may be long or short depending on how many major competitors there are and how many different campaigns each may be running. In our own campaign, we usually attempt to emphasize some aspect that the "other guys" are not reflecting in order to differentiate more effectively our character from theirs. Nevertheless, if your product is unequivocally and demonstrably superior to a competitor in terms of the element that competitor is currently stressing, you may want to take him on at his own game. In either event, list #6 gives you an inventory of what tunes the others are singing. It can therefore serve to eliminate their approaches from your composite list of options or it can alert you to the fact that encroaching on any of these "occupied" themes may set up doubtful brand recall and/or perilous comparative advertising considerations.

7. Weigh the Options That Remain

After crossing off those benefit approaches from list #4 that are (1) undesirably replicative of past campaigns or (2) dominated by the competition, you are left with a final and residual slate of possibilities. From this slate, and in conjunction with client representatives and their target audience specifications, the benefit-expressing campaign theme must be selected. For maximum effectiveness, all subsequent advertising for the product, service, program, or station should be expressed in terms of this theme. Otherwise, you run the risk of advertising against yourself—of seeming to promote two separate and competing characters rather than a single, consistently portrayed identity.

8. Pick a Product Personality

Based on your theme and the benefit it conveys, a product personality, expressed in a consistent and meticulously tailored writing style, should be allowed to emerge. Product personality is the ultimate manifestation of brand character. It will come through in your spots whether you want it to or not, so take the initiative to fashion one that is most appropriate to the campaign, the client, and the target audience that client is attempting to reach. Too many campaigns are afflicted with vapid or even schizoid image traits because, though the benefit theme has been carefully determined, the verve and style of the words conveying that theme have not been scrupulously monitored from spot to spot. In such cases, the product or client may, for instance, sometimes come across as somber, at other times appear simply businesslike, and on still other occasions appear downright dictatorial.

Product personality is the single most perplexing concept for a novice writer to grasp because, though certain personalities seem generally associated with particular benefit themes or product categories, there are now lighthearted insurance companies as well as deadly serious breakfast cereals. Like an old friend whose actions have a comfortable and reassuring predictability, a product personality's familiarity flows from a distinctive yet elusive way of saying and doing things.

Copywriters need to "dimensionalize brands like people," argues Ayer marketing executive Fred Posner. "If you're describing a friend, you don't say she has a head, two arms, and two legs. You say, she's reliable, sincere, trustworthy, warm. The brands that will have staying power in the 1990's are the ones with similarly identifiable and affective personality traits."[5]

Sustaining this trait portrait usually becomes so second nature to a copy group, in fact, that major personality modification can in most cases be accomplished only when the account changes agencies. "Good advertising people believe," observes veteran ad creator Malcolm MacDougall, "that each product is born with a special purpose, endowed with a unique personality and blessed with a soul. They believe that their advertising is a part of that soul."[6]

If you still don't understand the dynamics of product personality, take a look at the photoboards in Figures 13–1 and 13–2. Imagine if the personalities were reversed. Could a spot projecting a multipurpose liquid treat for kids do so with a unblushing evocation of allurement? Would a premium-priced fruit drink from France want to stress the juvenile wholesomeness of its ingredients and ignore its status as a French import with all that heritage implies? Probably not. Instead, the visual exploitation of the neighborhood "treat cart" works better as an alternative to more conventional kids' beverages. The trendy European bounce of Orelia, on the other hand, requires an approach that spotlights the kind of people who exemplify these qualities. Ocean Spray Cran-Grape, in short, benefits from a mantle of hometown goodness whereas Orelia profits from a continental aura of sex. By epitomizing key product attributes and their most closely associated consumer rewards, product personality becomes an irreplaceable mechanism for campaign cohesion.

Summing it all up, Grey Advertising's Richard Kiernan relates product personality to the larger concept of brand character via the following equation and explanation:

Product + Positioning + Personality = Brand Character.

A totality that expresses how a brand looks and feels to the consumer.
What its unique character is that distinguishes it from its competition.
That lifts it above the crowd.
A television campaign that helps create that strong character has a look,
a sound, a feeling as personal—as identifiable—as those characteristics
which distinguish one person from another.

KELLY . NASON
INCORPORATED
Advertising

Client: OCEAN SPRAY
Product: GRAN-GRAPE/CRAN WAGON

Title: LEMONADE STAND
Comm'l. No.: OGSG-6013
Length: 30 SECONDS

FRANK: Cranberries!!!
KIDS: Hi Frank!

FRANK: How's business?
KID: Too much competition.

FRANK: Sell Ocean Spray Cran-Grape...
sweet juicy grapes and tangy cranberries-
all natural flavor.

Try it with ginger ale...

and even ice cream.

KIDS: Wow!!

FRANK: There are lots of ways to use
Ocean Spray...Cran-Grape, Cranberry
Juice Cocktail, and Ocean Spray
Cranapple.

KIDS: Cran-Grape! Ocean Spray
Cran-Grape!

FRANK: Cranberries!!!

Figure 13-1

(Courtesy of Irene Taffel, Kelly-Nason Inc.)

And, like the character of a person, it endures. The brand with a strong character is recognizable from commercial to commercial, from campaign to campaign over the years. Just as a person is recognizable over the years no matter how much weight they have put on (or taken off), what clothes they are wearing or how they've changed hair styles.[7]

We've already examined the product and personality ingredients of Kiernan's Brand Character equation, of course. *Positioning* and its roots are explored in the following section.

MUSIC AND SFX

MUSIC AND SFX

MUSIC AND SFX

MUSIC THROUGHOUT
VO: Orelia.
Smooth. Sparkling...
Bubbly...

Bouncy...Sensational...
Satisfying...
Refreshing...

Orelia
Sparkling orange.

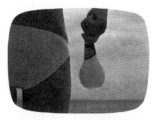

So deliciously natural the pulp needs a
shake.

Orelia.
The second most popular thing in
France.

Figure 13-2

(Courtesy of Mimi Rydre, Brugnatelli & Partners Inc.)

Concept Engineering—Fashioning the Campaign Proposal

Frequently a senior copywriter is called on not only to compose a radio/television treatment but also to take a hand in the vital preliminary preparation that leads to the development of a *campaign proposal* (for a new client or campaign) or *copy platform* (for a particular spot or flight). Unlike Brand Character Isolation's previously discussed lists, which remain the copywriter's private working sketches, campaign proposals and copy platforms are

417

themselves submitted to a variety of other people within the agency and client organizations. The quality of these submissions must be high because the scripts may never be produced, the account never won, if the platform or proposal lacks clarity, precision, and persuasiveness. Writing solid proposals is especially crucial since they are the prerequisite to attracting entire accounts—entire accounts that may bring in the means to pay your entire salary. Proposal realization is normally the sum of five component steps:

1. Client analysis
2. Competition analysis
3. Advertising Objective (AO) development
4. Creative Selling Idea (CSI) construction
5. Sample message creation

Let's take a careful look at each phase of the process.

1. Client (Internal) Analysis

The more you know about the firm whose products you're seeking the opportunity to sell, and the more you know about each of those products, the larger will be the range of options that open themselves to you. The comprehensive client analysis shows the firm you are courting that you have taken the trouble to learn a lot about its operation and have compiled all the relevant information needed to marshal a proper campaign response. Thus, the client analysis stage comprises the gathering of the raw data out of which those brand character-isolating lists of positive attributes and weaknesses can easily and accurately be assembled.

Even though clients themselves can usually be counted on to supply a great deal of information about themselves, smart campaign creators have learned not to rely exclusively on such materials. This is because client-originated dossiers may be flawed or incomplete for either of two reasons:

1. Clients are so close to their business that they fail to take note of elements that, though mundane to them, may be of unusual appeal to lay consumers. One brewer, around his firm's copper tanks all his life, was surprised that a touring creative team took such interest in them. When exploited in a "gleaming copper kettles" approach, however, this client-dismissed aspect became a successful and tangible referent for the beer's fire-brewing benefit. As writers, we are (fortunately) as initially ignorant of the operations of most of the businesses for whom we write as are the consumers at whom we aim our messages. We, sometimes better than the client, can therefore isolate those methods and modes of operation that are of greatest potential interest to current or prospective customers. We can spotlight an implement or process that, while unremarkable to the

client, can be of great benefit-illustrating significance to us and the audiences to whom we are writing.

2. Client-orginated information may also be deficient because top management, or those who work for them, are afraid to lay bare product/corporate weaknesses. Management (or more often, management's nervous hireling) tries to "gild the lily" and treat the copywriter or agency as just one more consumer of its public relations plaudits. Then they wonder why the subsequent advertising blows up in their faces because the public wasn't told about the mandatory eight-week delivery delay or that the additive didn't help pre-1989 engines. Experienced copywriters and market-wise clients have discovered that the firm's public relations department is usually *not* the best liaison with its advertising agency. To do its job, the agency needs the ugly truth rather than the rosy glow that emanates from the PR office.

Take the data that the client or prospective client provides and thoroughly evaluate them as filtered through your own appraisal of client/product strengths and weaknesses. If you can, visit the firm's office, store, or plant. Take note of everything, for you can never tell when a seemingly insignificant on-site discovery can later be the key to a blockbuster campaign. Above all, cautions marketing consultant William Bartolini, be certain you have honed in on your client's "real business as determined by the consumer who uses your product. For instance, Black and Decker is not in the business of selling drills, they sell 'easy holes.' Similarly, you may work for a station but the station's real 'business' is probably entertainment."[8]

2. Competition (External) Analysis

Once you have briefed yourself and *been* briefed on all available account data, you are in a position to define and scrutinize the competition's scope and character. Putting it another way, you are ready to complete a broadened framework for Brand Character Isolation's list #6.

The first requisite of a functional competition analysis is the *competition yardstick*, a definitional framework that separates the real from the imagined rivals. Because the client analysis has already provided you with a clear portrait of your own account, it is relatively easy to isolate its main wares and use these as discriminatory criteria. If you client's restaurant caters to the cocktail crowd, you probably should not worry too much about threats posed by family eateries and diners, for example. In short, your client's key activities become the central qualities that any other firm must possess in order to constitute real competition. Here are some sample yardsticks, each of which would usually be preceded by the phrase "Competition for (client/product name) would include. . . ."

> any gas station within eight miles that also features complete engine repair service;
>
> any store that sells shoes for the whole family;
>
> every all-seasons sporting goods establishment whether self-contained or part of a department store;
>
> every presweetened cereal intended primarily for consumption by children;
>
> any residential plumbing and heating contractor that handles both installation and maintenance.

Once yardsticks such as these ferret out the *primary* rivals, a work-up statement on each rival can be prepared. Such statements are not required to have the depth of the original client analysis but instead need concentrate only on describing each competitor's condition *relative to the strengths and weaknesses of your own account.* Hopefully, a pattern will at this point begin to emerge and you will discover that your client or product is consistently superior (or, at least, *different from*) all competitors in regard to certain specific qualities or ways of doing business.

It might be that your firm has longer hours, a more convenient location, or more years of experience than any of its rivals. Or, your product may be less expensive, faster to use, or easier to store than those manufactured by other companies. Whatever the case, such distinctive advantages have now been identified as potential prime agents for the total campaign strategy.

As the last part of our competition analysis, it is necessary to uncover which advertising vehicles the competition is using and what approaches they are taking via these vehicles. Your responding creative may qualitatively and stylistically vary a great deal depending on whether your opponents are exploiting radio and television in a significant and high-profile manner. You can't, for instance, outspend a much larger rival, so you may want to consider capitalizing on that very size discrepancy through copy that orchestrates your benefit to the tune of an underdog motif (we're the little company that does more for you because we need your business more).

3. Advertising Objective (AO) Development

With the completion of steps 1 and 2, all the results are in; it is now time to make the unequivocal choice of the central theme that all advertising for this particular product will be designed to promote. Bolstered by an incisive and, we trust, unblushing appraisal of marketplace realities, we are now in a position to adopt an approach calculated to achieve the most positive recognition possible for the client whose aims we are serving.

From a workability standpoint, the AO must be narrow enough to delineate your client clearly from the competition yet broad enough to encompass several related subthemes that may later evolve in campaign fine-tuning. We want to provide growing room for our overall approach without making the AO so vague that we lose the sense of client uniqueness. If, for example, that same Advertising Objective could be put to use by a rival, it should never have been selected. As in the following classic examples, the AO usually includes a specification of target audience (universe) and a delineation of our key client benefit or benefit complex:

Assure women forty-five and over that Second Debut moisturizing lotion is an effective cosmetic ally for the good and productive years that lie ahead.[9]

Persuade the soft-drink-user spectrum that Dr Pepper is neither a root beer nor a cola but a popular beverage for every occasion.[10]

Convince blue-collar males that Miller Beer possesses the traditional American attributes of "value, worth and quality."[11]

Convince middle-aged and older blue-collar workers in the tristate market that Buick is an affordable as well as a desirable car.[12]

Tell physically active women that Pretty Feet & Hands is indispensable as an all-around skin care/repair application.[13]

Demonstrate to men and women ages eighteen to forty-five that, unlike the competition, Supercuts will give you the great looking haircut you want, with no surprises.[14]

Help consumers age fifty and up understand that the Guardian Plan is the sensible way to complete funeral arrangements so that loved ones won't be burdened.[15]

Communicate to above-average-income families with children that Pizza Hut restaurants employ dedicated people whose primary responsibility is to serve customers.[16]

Show kids that Milk Duds is America's long-lasting alternative to the candy bar.[17]

Introduce women ages twenty-five to fifty-four to Snuggle's *low-priced* fabric softening and static-cling reducing capabilities.[18]

The selected advertising objective is then recast into a *positioning statement* that allows the essence of the AO to be articulated in the spot. You would never want to use the above Pizza Hut objective as copy, for example, but the positioning statement "our people make our pizza better" expresses its central tenet in a more abbreviated and conversational form that easily lends itself to script inclusion. Likewise, "when a candy bar is only a memory, you'll still be eating your Milk Duds" is a swingy, copy-ripe translation of the necessarily clinical AO whose cause it promotes. And "snuggly softness that's really less expensive" deftly works in the Snuggle product name as a benefit adjective while still mirroring its AO motivator.

Carelessly selected positioning statements can be at least as meaningful—but in a client-maiming way. Imagine the consumer reaction to this copywriter-created line on behalf of a bank whose embezzling vice president had skipped the country only months before:

```
Your money goes farther at the ____ National Bank.
```

Or the derision that greeted this TV news positioning statement:

```
If it happens in (town name), it's news to TV-6.
```

Positioning statements must be fashioned so as to bolster their parent AOs. An undisciplined line will inevitably turn on the client it's supposed to be servicing.

As an overall marketing strategy, *positioning* itself is defined by its co-founder Al Ries as the culmination of "looking for a hole that doesn't belong to someone else."[19] Once this hole is discovered via the analytical procedures we've been exploring, the copywriter sculpts a perceptual brand shape to fill it. Looking at positioning from a related perspective, DDB Needham CEO Keith Reinhard believes that "the essence of positioning is sacrifice—deciding what's unimportant, what can be cut away and left behind; reducing your perspective to a very sharp point of view. Once that's done, you have to apply all of your energy, talent, heart and resources toward making your point of view a guiding star for your people."[20]

Positioning, therefore, is what all of our earlier-mentioned lists and proposal steps have been geared to facilitate. We are trying to find what might be called the high ground of advantage—the consumer-benefit orientation toward our product or service that clearly and auspiciously sets it apart from the competition. According to Mr. Ries's long-accepted tenets:

> The first rule of positioning is this: You can't compete head-on against a company that has a strong, established position. You can go around, under or over, but never head-to-head. The leader owns the high ground.
>
> The classic example of No. 2 strategy is Avis's. But many marketing people misread the Avis story. They assume the company was successful because it tried harder. Not at all. Avis was successful because it related itself to the position of Hertz. Avis pre-empted the No. 2 position. . . .
>
> Too many companies embark on marketing and advertising programs as if the competitor's position did not exist. They advertise their products in a vacuum and are disappointed when their messages fail to get through.[21]

The associated technique of *re*positioning entails the application of a prime product characteristic to a new consumer-use benefit. With so few people baking from scratch anymore, the Arm & Hammer people may have foreseen ever-deepening sales problems for their baking soda. But through repositioning, the anachronistic baking ingredient became the modern "nice little secret for your refrigerator." To heighten further its benefit as a deodorant for closed spaces, the advertising that flowed from this repositioning also was set up to demonstrate how, once its refrigerator days were over, the stuff could be used to freshen a drain or kitty's "drop-box."

Similarly, Sara Lee offset a big decline in frozen dessert sales by moving from an image of plebeian pound cake convenience to that of purveyor of "Elegant Evenings" cheesccakes and croissants, hawked by a Parisian-sounding actress who queried, "Zis Sarah Lee, she is French, no?" For its part, the hair-dyeing Miss Clairol was also saved by the studied repositioning repetition of the "Does She or Doesn't She?" question. "Previously," recalls marketing consultant Faith Popcorn, "the only women who dyed their hair had been blue-haired or of questionable reputation. Clairol's repositioning of hair coloring made it a legitimate option for self-respecting proper American women of any age."[22]

Positioning/repositioning statements, and the Advertising Objectives that mandate them, are obviously of extreme importance for both old and new products and use-benefits. They are also the prime indication that today's copywriter must be part creator and part market strategist, a professional at home in both worlds. In fact, David Ogilvy has observed that campaign mastery depends less on "how we write your advertising than on how your product is positioned."[23]

4. Creative Selling Idea (CSI) Construction

From the AO, and the positioning statement that mirrors it, are spun a number of related, more detailed, and more focused applications. Each application can, in turn, form the skeletal idea for a spot or flight of spots. Definitionally, a CSI is:

a consumer-related *benefit*

(+)

a *technique* for presenting it

(as applied)

specifically to this product or service.

CSIs must be very carefully constructed if they are to contain all of the above ingredients as well as relate unmistakably to their parent Advertising Objective.

Frequently, a novice writer will construct CSIs that are long on technique but in which the benefit is buried if not missing altogether; or the benefit may be there but its execution is vague or unworkable within the creative and budgetary confines of the campaign. Worst of all, the benefit and technique may show real labor and promise but fail to showcase the product properly or be totally outside the parameters set by the coordinating AO. This last defect, of course, would result in the sort of campaign fragmentation that all the previous stages of proposal development have worked so diligently to preclude.

Advertising executive Paul Goldsmith warns,

> When a creative person sits down to conceive an advertisement, he will often find it tempting to wander away from the agreed-upon strategy. Clearly, a desired quality is the discipline to keep the work within the confines of the product positioning. A scintillating piece of copy for a new car that highlights the fact that you need never carry a spare tire, when the strategy talks about better mileage, is a flop no matter how clever or brilliantly executed. "That's brilliant!" "That's funny!" "Beautifully done!" All are wasted words when the client says, "This is not the strategy we agreed upon."[24]

On the other hand, here is an Advertising Objective for Marlene's Dress Shop and three *disciplined* CSIs that flow from it. Notice how each includes all three components of a good Creative Selling Idea and how each relates back to the umbrella AO. Note too that each CSI could constitute the basis for a single spot as well as for a whole series of closely related spots that would thereby comprise an *integrated flight:*

Advertising Objective:
Attract over-40 women to Marlene's by stressing the shop's concern for sensible fashions.

Creative Selling Ideas:
1. Multivoice spots featuring female school teacher(s) who find(s) Marlene's blouses are comfortable to teach in and still look smart.
2. Husband univoice testimonials to the economical altering service Marlene's provides to "tailor-make" their clothes---even after the sale.
3. Marlene talks to the ladies about her fashionable yet adaptable headwear.

As another example, here is how an eatery might be positioned through AO/CSI framing:

Advertising Objective:
Establish for area lower-income families and singles that Taco Heaven is the place to go for inexpensive and appealing Mexican food.

Creative Selling Ideas:
1. Multivoiced spots of teens enjoying an after-school snack at Taco Heaven---affordable munchies even on an allowance budget.
2. Testimonials by blue-collar and clerical workers that eating at Taco Heaven converts lunchtime into a mini Mexican vacation.
3. Dialogue spots in which one homemaker tells another how Taco Heaven's menu entices her children to eat fresh vegetables, and for a lower-than-grocery-store cost.

5. Sample Message Creation

As the final step in your proposal development, you are ready to engage in what most copywriters (vocationally, at least) like best. You can now create a sample series of announcements that reflects all the market data and decision making with which the first four stages of the proposal are preoccupied. The messages constructed and presented at this, the final, stage of the proposal, may either all relate to a single CSI—and thereby constitute an integrated flight—or they may derive from several different CSIs in order to demonstrate the range of campaign possibilities that exist within the framework of the advocated AO.

The coordinating objectives for the Jiffy Lube campaign showcased in Figure 13–3, 13–4, and 13–5, for instance, is to *show busy white-collar men and women that Jiffy Lube's Pennzoil-using 14-point service will have them back on the road coast-to-coast in 10 minutes' time.* CSI 1 (Figure 13–3) focuses on the high performance of the shop's employees, CSI 2 (Figure 13–4) stresses the availability of this service nationwide, and CSI 3 (Figure 13–5) illuminates Jiffy Lube's responsiveness to the schedules of working women. The campaign's integrating positioning statement is always VO-expressed in frame 11—"Coast to coast, come to Jiffy Lube for complete 14-point service."

Well-designed promotional campaigns likewise are built via Concept Engineering principles. In the following radio spots for Nickelodeon's Saturday night line-up (dubbed "SNICK"), the cable channel's objective is *to convince eight-to-fifteen-year-olds that "Snick is a better alternative to ANYTHING you could do on a Saturday night."*[25] Or, as the positioning statement puts it, "On Saturday night, its SNICK. Or it'snot." Each CSI selects a different pubescent activity for humorous and negative comparison. The alternatives torpedoed in the CSIs represented by the spot on pages 429–432 are school dances, video rentals, and hanging out at the mall.

Figure 13-3

(Courtesy of George Lois, Lois U.S.A.)

jiffy lube **Coast to coast/Pennzoil** :30 TV

Announcer V.O.:
From California…

to New York…

From Minnesota…

to Texas…
Jiffy Lube has America's team—

Man 1:
The J-Team!!!

Man 2:
In 10 minutes with no appointment
we'll change your oil with Pennzoil.

Man 3:
Replace the oil filter,

Man 1:
and check and fill every fluid!

Man 2:
And Jiffy Lube's 14-point service is
honored by every J-Team
all across America!

J-Team:
That's J-Teamwork!!!

Announcer V.O.:
Coast to coast, come to Jiffy Lube
for complete 14-point service!

Jimmy The Greek Snyder:
In my book, the J-Team's
a 14-point favorite!

Figure 13-4

(Courtesy of George Lois, Lois U.S.A.)

Figure 13-5

(Courtesy of George Lois, Lois U.S.A.)

ANNCR: It's Saturday night, and there's a big school dance. Only you get there late and there's no girls left to dance with except old Mrs. Peabody, your Latin teacher.

MRS. P: Yoo Hoo, Todd---

ANNCR: Your friends are watching your every move.

MRS. P: Would you like to dance?

ANNCR: Just your luck, The next song is---the Lambada.

(LAMBADA MUSIC BEGINS AND UNDER)

MRS. P: Ooooo.

ANNCR: You do your best, but as you dip her backwards, her beehive goes into the punch bowl (SFX: SPLUUSH) and as you spin her she sprays punch all over everyone. (SFX: SPRAYING)

CROWD: AAAGGGHHHH!

ANNCR: You toss her to the right.

(SFX: SPRAYING AND PEOPLE SCREAMING)

ANNCR: You toss her to the left.

(MORE SPRAYING AND SCREAMING)

ANNCR: You toss her a little too high.

MRS. P: WOOOOOO

(SFX: THUD)

ANNCR: As you help her up you step on her hem and rip off the bottom half of her dress.

(SFX: RIIIPPPP.)

CROWD: EWWWWWW!!!

ANNCR: Now, you wish you had stayed home and watched
          SNICK. Saturday night on Nickelodeon from 8 to 10.
          Four juicy shows, including the all-new <u>Are You
          Afraid of the Dark</u>. But you had to go and piss off
          Mrs. Peabody.

MRS. P: Todd, I think you need to spend another year in the
          8th grade.

TODD: AAAGGHHHH!

ANNCR: On Saturday night, it's SNICK.

              (SFX: LAUGHS)

ANNCR: Or it'snot.

              (SFX: GROANS)

_____
_____

(SFX: WILD WIND)

ANNCR: It's a hot muggy Saturday night, Hotter and muggier
          than it's ever been. And you're on your way to
          the video store, as a dirty wind shoots through
          your paper-thin T-shirt like a knife---or a
          meat hook. (WIND GETS WILDER) Or a knife with a
          meat hood attached to the handle in some crude
          and hideous fashion.

              (SFX: HAIL BLOWING AROUND)

ANNCR: And you're blinded by the blowing soot and the
          dirt and the dirty soot. And the soot blows
          through your clothes (HAIL GETS WILDER PLUS
          LABORED BREATHING) and you start to itch---
          like nobody's ever itched before. So you start
          to scratch (SFX: SCRATCHING) like nobody's
          every scratched before. (SFX: SCRATCHING GETS
          FRANTIC; RIPPING CLOTHING) And then comes the
          rain.

              (SFX: HARD WET RAIN AND LIGHTNING)

ANNCR: A hard wet rain that turns your paper-thin T-shirt into a human aquarium. (SFX: SQUISHY WET CLOTHES) Then it stops. Like the twist of a faucet.

   (SFX: WIND, HAIL, RAIN STOP SUDDENLY, WITH A LOUD SQUEAK OF A FAUCET)

ANNCR: And out come the waterbugs.

   (SFX: ARMY OF CREEPY CRAWLING SOUNDS)

SNICK: You shoulda stayed home and watched SNICK. Saturday night on Nickelodeon, from 8 to 10 with four juicy shows, like <u>Ren and Stimpy</u>. So Saturday night, it's SNICK (SFX: WILD LAUGH) or it'snot. (SFX: GROAN).

ANNCR: It's Saturday night and everyone's going to the mall. 'Cept when you get there, nothing's really happening so you cruise through this department store and some crazy perfume lady---

LADY: Free gift today!

ANNCR: ---spritzes you.

   (SFX: SPRAY)

You: Hey!

ANNCR: So now you smell like your Aunt Edith or fruit salad or something. So you head for the fountain and start scooping pennies out and throwing 'em back in. (SFX: PLOOP, PLOOP) and Amy says---

AMY: Oooh, get that quarter.

ANNCR: But it's kinda far out there and (SFX: SPLASH) you're sucking fountain water. So you go to the restroom to dry off. 'Cept all they have are those hot-air driers (SFX: WHIRRRR) so when you come out your hair's sticking straight up, but you seem to

```
                 be pulling it off 'cause you're getting those big
                 smiles from the girls---

      GIRLS:     Tee-hee-hee.

      ANNCR:     ---and you're starting to feel pretty good and
                 Kevin says:

      KEVIN:     Look at your foot, dude.

      ANNCR:     And you look down and you've got toilet paper stuck
                 to your shoe.

      ALL:       Hahahahahahahaha!

      ANNCR:     And you're thinking---I coulda stayed home and
                 watched SNICK. Saturday night on Nickelodeon from 8
                 to 10. Four twisted shows, including Clarissa.
                 Because on Saturday night, it's SNICK (SFX: LAUGHS)
                 or it'snot. (SFX: GROANS)
```

(All of the above courtesy of Arthur Bijur, Cliff Freeman and Partners.)

Looking at our total five-stage proposal process in retrospect, it schemati-cally suggests an hour glass, such as that diagramed in Figure 13–6. We start off as broadly as possible, gathering and analyzing client data from every conceivable source and perspective. This leads to developing a discriminatory competition yardstick and a consequent narrowing of focus to encompass only those other firms and products that meet the yardstick's specified criteria. From this we taper the process even more in the construction of an Advertis-ing Objective and associated positioning statement. Together, these set the boundaries within which our product can be discussed and revealed to its greatest advantage. Several applied Creative Selling Ideas or subgoals branch out from this coordinating AO. These CSIs and subgoals, in turn, can each give birth to several closely associated spots and series of spots.

Through it all, the AO functions as central controlling agent. The first two stages of proposal development are devoted to its careful sculpting and the last two stages to its preservation and attainment. The Advertising Objective, in short, constitutes the *synergism* [look that up in your Noah Webster] between broad-based market research and multifaceted creativity.

But whatever you do, don't assume your spots will automatically conform to your AO blueprint. *You* must apply the mental discipline to enforce this conformance. In campaign execution, "Where do people go wrong most often?" radio executive Mike Fenley asks. "Message! By concentrating on

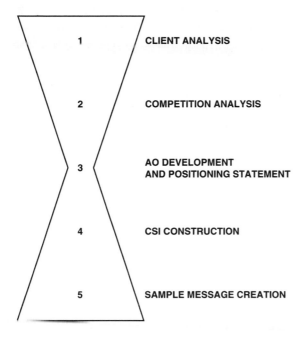

Figure 13-6
Concept Engineering's Proposal Hour Glass

things that aren't important to the target consumer, over use of unnecessary information, and failure to focus on the real goal, we set ourselves up for failure of the campaign."[26] To avoid such failure, make sure the same conceptual sand flows undiverted from the top to the bottom of your own proposal hourglass.

Proposal-Related Activities and Implements

Particularly as an in-station or cable copywriter, you may never be called on to construct a full-scale proposal of the type just described. Your local accounts may have long since been presold or attracted by a special price structure or ratings report that your outlet's salespeople are pushing. Under such circumstances, your main responsibilities will be to write the copy for these local paying customers in the manner to which they and/or your sales staff are accustomed. If, for instance, client merchants simply like to see/hear themselves on the air, you accept the fact that they are spending money to sell themselves rather than their businesses and showcase these people as best you can.

Prospects File

There comes a time, however, when even the most prosperous station/system needs to solicit some new accounts or, due to changing marketing or client management conditions, to revamp existing copy strategies. Perhaps a new competitor has emerged for your client or that client has moved into a new line or area of endeavor that presents a whole new slate of competitors. Under such conditions, the *prospects file* becomes a crucial resource—and one for which you, the copywriter, may be responsible.

Simply put, the prospects file is made up of profiles of area businesses that are either potential clients or potential or actual competitors of current clients. Each profile usually consists of a somewhat abbreviated version of proposal stage #1 (client analysis) plus a semistandardized stage #2 (competition analysis).

Since you don't have the time, nor the immediate need, for truly comprehensive client analyses in this prospects file resource bank, each sketch will normally just set down the main characteristics of each business and any advantages or weaknesses for which it is particularly noted. The limited depth of these profiles, in turn, makes it impossible to draw up *detailed* and customized competition analyses from them. Because the prospects file is an initial familiarizer rather than a finalized product, however, *individualized* competition analyses for a bunch of businesses that may never become your clients would be a waste of effort.

Instead, certain categorized competition surveys can be written in such subject areas as restaurants, financial institutions, auto repair shops, and so on. Copies of these surveys can be placed with each prospective client profile belonging to that category. If the classification is an especially large one given the market situation, you can also break down these categories into subunits. Restaurants, for example, can be divided into fast-food places, pizza parlors, and formal dining establishments, with separate competitive summaries written for each division.

For purposes of illustration, let's say that one of your station's sales personnel is trying to woo business from a furniture emporium that has not previously advertised on your outlet. This salesperson should be able to obtain from the prospects file a prewritten, generic competition analysis covering local furniture stores as a whole. This can be supplemented with the individual sketches on each of the stores, including, of course, the profile on the store being courted. As that store becomes more interested and requests more detailed advertising suggestions, its abbreviated profile can be expanded and updated on the basis of the information to which it now gives you or your sales staff access. The generic competition analysis can also be customized to take into account the particular strengths and activities of this store and, if necessary, the other three stages of a full-dress proposal can now be prepared.

If the furniture stores joins your list of clients, the preresearch will have immediately paid off. But even if the store decides to forgo business with your outlet or through your agency at this time, all the effort has not been wasted. For, in the courting process, you have acquired a great deal more information about that store and, therefore, about the furniture business in your market. This information can help you serve that firm more quickly in the future. And even if the store *never* signs a contract with you, your prospects file has still been enriched by much more specific and comprehensive material about it—material that can be very useful in constructing pitches or formal proposals for that store's competition.

Spec(ulative) Writing

A closely allied procedure in which the copywriter may be involved is called *spec writing.* In spec writing, you prepare sample spots for businesses that are not yet your clients. Technically, the last stage of formal proposal development can be labeled spec writing but, more commonly, the term is applied to the creation of a catalog of generic spots for each of the prime business categories from which your outlet or agency would expect to draw clientele.

In this latter use of the term, spec writing can be an extremely frustrating experience for the copywriter since, in many ways, you are writing in a vacuum. If you have access to a prospects file, you at least have a general idea about the competitive arena in which your sample spots must function and a broad outline of the advertising approaches being used in it. Nonetheless, you are still forced to create prototype advertising for an as yet unnamed product or business, advertising that your station's sales or agency's account force might use to entice several different firms in that same classification.

Worse yet, you may find yourself in a regional or national spec writing situation in which you have only the broadest of market data to guide you. And, in a few cases, you may even be ordered to prepare a *general spec spot inventory*—a series of treatments that could be auditioned by prospects in a wide variety of business categories to show them the advantages of radio or television or the type of creative styling your firm can use to showcase them.

Under such circumstances, you can only, like Charles M. Schulz's poor old Charlie Brown, bull your neck and grit your teeth and swing. Use whatever product classification parameters and data are available to you in orienting your hypothetical approach to the very real marketplace consumers at which this approach is supposedly aimed. Even if you have been given only the broadest description of the types of business or services to which your spec spots are expected to appeal, you can, at the minimum, make sure each announcement you write includes a rational appeal, an emotional appeal, a consumer-involving benefit, and the other main qualities we discuss in the previous twelve chapters. Since even the most vaguely assigned piece of spec writing still has to have some sort of product or service in it in order to *be* a spot, you can at least formulate a workable benefit approach common to the general product classifications to which your spec spot can be applied.

The following spec spot has been adroitly created by master copywriter Dick Orkin to promote virtually any economy furniture store anywhere in the country. The underlined sections can be removed and replaced with another emporium's name without in any way compromising the integrity of the concept. That is spec writing at its finest and most challenging.

WIFE: Charles, it's not necessary for you to build all our furniture yourself!

MAN: But where could you find a couch like this?

WIFE: This is not a couch!

MAN: What is it then?

WIFE: This is a lot of bleach bottles stapled together and covered with an old shower curtain.

MAN: But think of all the money we're saving!

WIFE: <u>There's a better way to furnish our home! Brandon Furniture! They're inexpensive, but they have a wide selection of quality furniture.</u>

MAN: Like our coffee table.

WIFE: This is just an old tire.

MAN: So?

WIFE: So where do you put stuff on it?

MAN: I didn't say it was perfect.

WIFE: <u>Take me to Brandon Furniture so we can get rid of this junk!</u>

MAN: This dining room table you call junk?

WIFE: Because it's our old worn out screen door balancing
        on two garbage cans---

MAN: But think of the money we're saving!

WIFE: It's nothing compared to what we'd save at Brandon
        Furniture.

        For example, this lamp you're making out of tuna
        fish cans. What's it costing you?

MAN: Um---well, let's see. 500 cans of tuna fish, at
        $800, plus two kitty cats to eat the tuna---

WIFE: Charles---

ANNCR: Think how much farther your money will go during
        Brandon Brothers Fall Clearance. Everything on the
        floor is up to one-half off now through the end of
        the month. Save now during Fall Clearance prices at
        Brandon Brothers Furniture. Jupiter Road at Kingsley.

(Courtesy of Fran Sax, FirstCom.)

Unless anchored by a particularly strong category concept (like the above Orkin spot) spec-written spots usually are not capable of getting any actual airplay. Indeed, one of the strongest objections to spec work is that even account-winning creative seldom sees the light of day. This is because clients never *fully* brief the prospective copywriter on business details until after they are certain this copywriter will be working for them. From everything we have said in this and previous chapters, it should be clear that the most successful radio/television advertising arises from careful scrutiny of a *particular* product with *particular benefits for a particular* target audience, and possessing *particular* advantages over a *particular* list of competitors. The speculative spot, conversely, is intended to evince creative selling technique. Except when constructed by an outstanding copywriter with a multimarket use plan firmly in mind, the spec spot's sole priority is to sell *itself* and the station or agency that is using it to attract new clients. Once the spec spot has blazed the trail, the custom-tailored message get the public exposure.

Despite all of these drawbacks, spec spots are becoming an even more important element in the winning of new business. "The trend is toward more and more spec work," writes industry analyst Cathy Madison, "both because strapped agencies are willing to do it, and because clients want proof that agencies can solve specific problems. . . . These days, anywhere from half to two-thirds of reviews include creative."[27] As a copywriter, therefore, be prepared to take whatever information is made available and to endure the mixed emotions of birthing messages that may never mature into finished commercials. Renowned creative director Ed McCabe even argues that "like boys and girls living together instead of getting married, it [spec writing] sort of works but seldom produces wonderful children."[28]

Four Case Studies

A discussion of radio/television campaign construction and its motivating creative strategies would not be complete without the presentation of some classic illustrative examples of campaign development in action. The cases that follow do not articulate every step in proposal evolution. That would require an entire book in and of itself. Instead, they collectively serve to exemplify the interaction of market factors and analyses with creative design and development.

Case #1: Riceland Rice[29]

When Noble-Dury & Associates acquired the Riceland Rice account, the Nashville agency knew the campaign task from the start. It had to demonstrate to heavy users of rice—to people who are already virtual rice experts—that Riceland was the brand for them. As the largest selling brand of regularly milled rice in the United States, the Arkansas-based farmer-marketing organization that *is* Riceland knew that reaching heavy users of rice was essential to sales growth since only 36 percent of all households use rice once a week or more. But this market is further complicated by the fact that it is divided into two segments: those who use precooked rice (like Minute and Uncle Ben's), and those willing to take the extra ten or twelve minutes to use a regular milled variety such as Riceland. Thus, Noble-Dury had to devise an advertising position that had merit for both precooked and regular-milled users in the half of the country in which its client's product was distributed.

Through further client analysis, the agency found that Riceland was already the leading regular-milled brand and that it was served in the most popular restaurants in the heaviest rice-using states (Arkansas, Louisiana,

South Carolina). From these marketing data, a two-pronged Advertising Objective was derived:

```
To show users of precooked rice that Riceland offers better
flavor for the extra few minutes of cooking time needed.
```

(and)

```
To illustrate for users of regular rice that Riceland
offers constantly good flavor.
```

Out of this dual AO came the single positioning statement:

```
Riceland Rice---for people that know about rice.
```

Neither an elegant nor a particularly glossy line, it nonetheless succeeded because it was on-target with the style and preferences of the heavy-user universe at which it was aimed. The commercial executions struck this same responsive chord. Shot in popular restaurants located in heavy rice-consuming areas, each spot used music indigenous to the pictured locale to bolster further the credibility of the visual testimonials and make the positioning statement come alive for rice lovers. Photoboards of these spots are featured in Figures 13–7, 13–8, and 13–9.

Case #2: Calavo Avocado Guacamole[30]

A carefully directed radio campaign can have just as much impact in its own way as can a television plan—even in cases where the product itself is in basic need of defining. Such a definitional problem was met head-on and solved by the old Anderson-McConnell agency in an historic campaign on behalf of its client, the Calavo Growers of California.

The product to be marketed was Calavo's guacamole—a frozen avocado dip which, though one-of-a-kind as to its ingredients, had to compete with the much better known dip flavors manufactured and promoted by much larger corporations.

With a small budget that made radio the only feasible broadcast delivery system, the Anderson-McConnell creative group went about their analytical work. Given the uniqueness of the product and its name, an extensive client and competition analysis was unnecessary. The Advertising Objective, after all, was virtually automatic:

```
To identify and introduce to party-givers what guacamole is
and who makes it.
```

439

MUSIC
ANNCR: Maybe it's crazy to drive hundreds of miles

for chicken 'n rice.

But not when it's Mrs. Beardsley's chicken 'n rice.

MUSIC

She runs the Stockholm Restaurant

in Heber Springs, Arkansas. And the things

Mrs. Beardsley does with her Riceland Rice

you've just gotta taste to believe. It always cooks up tender

and tastes terrific.

Do like Mrs. Beardsley:

Get Riceland Rice for some good eatin'.

Riceland Rice. For people who know about rice.

Figure 13-7

Because avocados were still a fairly exotic item in most parts of the country, it was doubtful that consumers would make that key original purchase simply for their own snacking as they would, say, a new brand of potato chips. Rather, special foods are purchased for special occasions—for parties, in other words—so people whose social and economic status

440

MUSIC

MUSIC

ANNCR: Here in Pierre Part, Louisiana,

people come to the Rainbow Inn

for a good Cajun band

and Jimmie Cavalier's shrimp creole.

Jimmie knows the freshest shrimp and
the tastiest peppers

deserve the tenderest, fluffiest rice.
Riceland Rice.

If you want the best shrimp creole on
the bayou . . .

or in your own home . . .

use the best rice!

Riceland Rice.
For people who know about rice.

Figure 13-8

enabled them to give parties became the campaign's target audience. And since parties are supposed to be fun, a light, humorous approach seemed not only natural, but almost mandatory—as long as the humor did not decrease the attention given to product definition. Here are two of the spots that executed this concept.

441

MUSIC: (VO) Charleston, South Carolina.

Where you can ride back through the Centuries.

And here at Perdita's Restaurant,

you'll be tempted with entrees like Crab Remick....

prepared with fresh seafood...

and Riceland Rice.

Nothing compares to Riceland's texture and natural flavor.

If you can't spend a day in Charleston and Perdita's, spend 14 minutes preparing the world's finest rice.

Riceland Rice. For people who know about rice.

Figure 13-9

(Courtesy of Noble-Dury & Associates, Nashville, Tennessee. CLIENT: Riceland Foods, Stuttgart, Arkansas. CREATIVE DIRECTOR: Bill Mostad. COPYWRITER: Don Wirth. PRODUCER: Don Wirth. PRODUCTION COMPANY: Morrison Productions, New Orleans. DIRECTOR: Hobby Morrison.)

<u>Spot #1 (30 secs.)</u>

(MUSIC: COCKTAIL DANCE-BEAT BEGINS)

(SFX: INTERMINGLE PARTY SOUNDS)

WOMAN: Would you like to try the avocado dip?

MAN: Sure, is it anything like the tango?

(<u>MUSIC: UP AND STOPS FOR:</u>)

MAN: Do you realize that Calavo is the only one in history to successfully freeze a ready-to-serve avocado dip?

2ND MAN: Holy guacamole!

(<u>MUSIC: STARTS AND STOPS FOR:</u>)

WOMAN: Listen---if <u>she's</u> serving this jazzy avocado dip, it <u>must</u> be easy to serve. Why, it takes her two hours to make instant coffee.

(<u>MUSIC STARTS WITH FOLLOWING VOICES OVER IT</u>)

MAN: GWA-ka-mole, eh?

WOMAN: <u>WA</u>-ke-mole. Calavo Avocado Guacamole.

MAN: (In rhythm) Calavo Avocado Guacamole (BEAT) Dip.

ALL: (In rhythm) Calavo Avocado Guacamole (BEAT) Dip.

              (Fading off) Calavo Avocado Guacamole (BEAT) Dip.

              (Repeat to fade out at time.)

. . . .

<u>Spot #2 (60 secs.)</u>

(<u>MUSIC: COCKTAIL DANCE-BEAT BEGINS</u>)

(SFX: INTERMINGLE PARTY SOUNDS)

(<u>MUSIC: STOPS FOR:</u>)

MAN: (Pompous) It's a scientific breakthrough, do you hear? Frozen avocado dip, fully prepared and ready to release its provocative flavor at the touch of a can opener. What do you say to that, eh?

2ND MAN: What <u>can</u> I say? Holy guacamole!

(<u>MUSIC: STARTS AND STOPS FOR:</u>)

443

WOMAN: Calavo Avocado Guacamole, Roger?

3RD MAN: You're talking my language, Elaine.

                (<u>MUSIC: STARTS AND STOPS FOR:</u>)

MAN: Honey, did you know that this avocado dip is
                frozen at 300 degrees below zero?

2ND WOMAN: Speaking of that, dear, did you notice I'm the
                only woman at this party without a mink coat?

                (<u>MUSIC: STARTS:</u>)

2ND MAN: GWA-ka-mole, eh?

3RD WOMAN: <u>WA</u>-ka-mole. Calavo Avocado Guacamole.

3RD MAN: (In rhythm) Calavo Avocado Guacamole (BEAT) Dip.

ALL: (In rhythm) Calavo Avocado Guacamole (BEAT)
                Dip. (Repeat to fade out at time.)

Definition, boisterous brand memorability, and continuing universe-oriented interest make this Calavo campaign a classic low-budget success story. As it unmistakably proves, careful campaign planning can bring significant dividends to small as well as large accounts.

Case #3: Nationwide Buying Group[31]

Registering a single brand is one thing. But it is quite another task to promote a client whose outlets are known by different names and sell multiple products.

That was the situation Lawler Ballard Advertising faced in creating a campaign for the Nationwide Buying Group. Nationwide is a purchasing consortium comprised of six different chains. Thus, the task became one of deriving a single, generic approach that each entity could use in its own marketing area as a distinctive and cohesive campaign.

Lawler Ballard knew that clients of this type require a number of low-cost commercials rather than one or two blockbusters. Further, flight cohesion would have to be maintained over a long string of season-oriented ads while still keeping production costs down. Videotape seemed the obvious budgetary choice and, when thinking about genres usually shot on tape, soap operas came to the creatives' minds. Out of this brainstorming gradually emerged

"Monica," a continuing soap opera that propelled the title-role heroine through a number of pun-raising spots in which the advertised sale was the payoff to each dramatic episode. Monica's exploits were so campy, and the puns they motivated so shameless, that the campaign "serial" soon acquired a loyal following among audiences in Norfolk, Virginia, where the Nationwide stores bore the name Northeast. As advertising critic Barbara Lippert observes, "Ad serials make sense because they mimic the TV medium, and they provide an opportunity to add texture and dimension by building interest on what's already familiar."[32]

In each "Monica" installment, the tag frame was easily customizable via a single graphic and voice-over that identified the particular chain found in each respective market. Because so much retail advertising looks like it was created on a Xerox machine, "Monica" truly stood out as a high-profile and easily extendable concept that raised viewer attentiveness and sale awareness levels. Three of "Monica's" sequenced episodes appear below.

Video	Audio
FALL CLEARANCE SALE	
MONICA ENTERS LIVING ROOM, SETS DOWN BAG, TURNS ON ANSWERING MACHINE	SFX: BEEP GRANT (VO): Hey, Monica. This is Grant. Can't wait till tonight.
SHE TAKES OFF HER COAT AS SHE LISTENS	SFX: BEEP RODNEY (VO): Hey baby, it's Rodney. I had a cancellation tonight. You're on.
MONICA MOVES CLOSE TO MACHINE	SFX: BEEP DADDY (VO): Hey you little filly, Sugar Daddy here. I'm at the airport and on my way!
MONICA TURNS OFF MACHINE. WE SEE GUY COMING OUT OF KITCHEN WITH WINE AND GLASSES. HE'S WEARING A BATHROBE.	GUY: Surprise, Monica!

Continued

Video	Audio
ART CARD: 'Over-Stocked Sale'	<u>VO</u>: Too much of a good thing---selected appliances, color TVs, stereos, VCRs and more. 10 to 50 percent off.
ADD NORTHEAST TITLE	The Overstocked Sale, at Northeast.

THANKSGIVING SALE

MONICA AND JASON AT FRONT DOOR; HE TURNS AS SHE HELPS HIM ON WITH HIS COAT	<u>JASON</u>: That was some Thanksgiving dinner, Monica.
HE ADMIRES HIMSELF IN MIRROR	But you know what really made the meal? The wine I brought.
	SFX: CAB HONKS
	<u>MONICA</u>: There's your cab.
JASON OPENS DOOR	<u>JASON</u>: Oh, if my Christmas plans fall through, maybe I'll give you a call.
GIVES HER PECK ON CHEEK; SHE CLOSES DOOR WITH SHOCKED DISGUST.	SFX: DOOR CLOSE
ART CARD: 'After the Turkey's Gone Sale'	<u>VO</u>: Now that the turkey's gone, we've trimmed our prices to the bone.
ADD NORTHEAST TITLE	The After the Turkey's Gone Sale at Northeast.

Continued

Video	Audio
CHRISTMAS SALE	
MONICA AND NOEL ON COUCH, TOASTING WITH WINE GLASSES	NOEL: Forever, Monica.
	SFX: PHONE RINGS
MONICA LEAVES ROOM; NOEL PICKS UP PHONE	Hello? Oh, hello! (Nervous whisper) Tiffany, I can't talk to you right now---Monica's here. What??? You left them here???
NOEL LOOKS UP TO SEE SCOWLING MONICA IN DOORWAY HOLDING UP A NYLON STOCKING	
ART CARD: 'Stocking Stuffer Sale'	VO: Anything you can stuff in a sock---from cordless phones to video tape. Now 30 percent off.
ADD NORTHEAST TITLE	The Stocking Stuffer Sale, Northeast

(Above scripts courtesy of Marlene Passarelli, Lawler Ballard Advertising.)

Case #4: SelectCare[33]

Nationwide Buying Group had to establish multiple identities. SelectCare, a new Detroit-area health care insurance plan, needed to register just one name—but it had to accomplish this recognition attainment in a market that had long been dominated by advertising for Blue Cross/Blue Shield.

To promote its client, Whitmore Communications realized that targeting employees would be just as important as reaching employers. If workers wouldn't sign up for SelectCare, employers would not offer it as a health plan option. To reach these employees, radio and television became key players in the resulting campaign.

Whitmore's market research discovered that Blue Cross/Blue Shield enjoyed a 70 percent penetration of the Detroit market. Yet, as a group, the 'Blues' cardholders were very antagonistic toward it, with many complaints

about claims servicing. These people felt, however, that there was no financially stable alternative so, for security's sake, stuck with this long-estab-
lished monolith. These consumer interviews also showed Whitmore that
financial stability concerns about SelectCare were allayed when prospects
were told the names of the owner hospitals who formed SelectCare. The
agency further discovered that copy points about "new ideas," "worldwide
coverage for emergencies," and "more coverage than traditional insurance"
strongly appealed to younger participants in the interview groups.

These findings became the basis for the resulting radio and television
advertising. The campaign began with a full-sing radio spot that introduced
SelectCare to the airwaves in a soft-sell, identity-raising manner:

SOLO SINGER: When you get the best out of life
                       And make the most of your health
                       then you know you're living well
                       And that's an art all by itself.

                       You want to go the distance
                       Getting better every day
                       And the people at SelectCare
                       Are with you all the way.

SOLOIST & CHORUS: SelectCare for the way you live
                       SelectCare anywhere
                       Worldwide
                       SelectCare
                       The New Standard in Health Care.

SOLOIST BRIDGE: You like to live the way you choose
                       Select a plan that you can use.

SOLOIST & CHORUS: SelectCare for the way you live
                       SelectCare anywhere
                       Worldwide
                       SelectCare
                       The New Standard in Health Care.

Three weeks later, the first television spot debuted—a spot so successful
that one of the named member hospitals was deluged with phone calls that
very first day. This happened despite the fact that no phone number appeared
in the commercial! The next day, the agency added a super of SelectCare's
master 800 number to divert calls to the proper office.

Video	Audio
SHOT OF BLUE CROSS/BLUE SHIELD BUILDING (EXACTLY AS SEEN DOWNTOWN). INTERESTING SKY IN BG; ROCKY CLIFFS BEHIND.	VO: Health care coverage used to be so simple.
PULL BACK FROM BUILDING TO REVEAL WAVES LAPPING AT ITS BASE.	Some people think it still is.
WAVES WIPE OUT A LUMP OF THE BUILDING, REVEALING THAT IT IS MADE OF SAND.	But health care coverage has changed. Some forms of insurance may not measure up.
CU OF MORE AND MORE OF THE BUILDING DISSOLVING, EVEN THE BLUE CROSS/BLUE SHIELD EMBLEM WHICH SPILLS BLUE INK DOWN ITS SIDE AS THE WAVE HITS IT.	
A LUMP OF SAND ON THE BEACH IS ALL THAT'S LEFT. A MIX OF BLUE INK SPILLING INTO THE MEDITERRANEAN BLUE WATERS.	One company has new ideas you should know about. This company was founded by Beaumont, Oakwood, Providence and Saint John Hospitals.
CAMERA PANS UPWARD TO THE ROCKY CLIFFS, WHERE THE SUN HITS THE ROCKS IN SUCH A WAY AS TO SPOTLIGHT ('ANOINT' AS IT WERE) THE WORDS CARVED IN MONUMENTAL STYLE ON THE FACE OF THE CLIFFS.	It'll cover you in an emergency, anywhere. Worldwide.
CAMERA CENTERS ON WORDS, SELECTCARE	This company is called SelectCare.
SUPE LOWER THIRD: The new standard in health care.	It's the new standard in health care.
ADD SUPER: 1-800-334-3122	

Continued

Blue Cross/Blue Shield felt so threatened by the announcement's impact that the company's executives began phoning complaints about it to the board members of SelectCare's owner hospitals. Having established SelectCare's visibility so powerfully, the company and the agency therefore replaced the contentious commercial with one called "Silence." In this spot, nothing was said about the 'Blues.' In fact, nothing was said on the audio track at all! Instead, the visual carried a starkly written "believe what you read" crawl that now presented SelectCare as though there were no real competition worth mentioning:

Video	Audio
WORDS APPEAR OVER BLACK, REVERSED OUT IN WHITE, UNDERNEATH STONE LOGO OF SELECTCARE WHICH REMAINS ON THE SCREEN FOR ENTIRE :30	MUSIC: THEME FIRST 5 SECONDS
ROLL: We're sponsoring a few seconds of silence so you can consider something new in health care.	
	MUSIC OUT
WORDS CONTINUE TO APPEAR, SLIDE UP UNDERNEATH LOGO AT WHAT WOULD BE NORMAL SPEAKING RATE IF VOICED. ROLL: SelectCare, founded by Beaumont, Oakwood, Providence and Saint John Hospitals offers a family of health plans. By design, our plans provide more coverage than traditional health insurance. We cover 100 percent of outpatient services such as X-rays and lab work. In many cases, physicians' office visits are fully covered. With one of our plans, you can keep your present doctor.	

Video	Audio
SelectCare also covers you worldwide in emergencies. We think this is something to think about. SelectCare. AS FOLLOWING WORDS APPEAR, THEY HOLD ON FRAME UNDERNEATH THE STONE LOGO AND THE 800 NUMBER DISSOLVES IN: ROLL: The New Standard in Health Care. 1-800-334-3122	

(All of the above courtesy of Ruth Whitmore. Whitmore Communications, Inc.)

About one month after the campaign's run, an independent research firm hired by SelectCare found that an unusually high 47 percent of the people surveyed still recalled the campaign, with 77 percent of those expressing that they either "liked it" or "liked it very much." Even more dramatically, name awareness of SelectCare, which had been 6 percent in the target group before the broadcast campaign, now registered a whopping 66 percent. There is no better testament to the power of strong copy backed by pertinent objective-honing research.

A Campaign Conclusion

Having studied Brand Character and Concept Engineering, and after your exposure to four separate case studies, you should have developed a working sensitivity to the components of radio-television campaign construction. It should be clear by now that successful campaigns are neither generated by, nor aired in, a vacuum. Rather, they are the outgrowth of a great deal of laborious research and step-by-step intellectual analysis. As advertising agency chairman Paul Harper once remarked at a seminar for his staffers:

> It is the right combination of shoe leather and scholarship that eventually leads you to a key fact about the market that everyone else has overlooked. It is only by separating truths from half-truths, straw from chaff, that you

eventually find the shining needle—a competitive weakness, a proprietary strength—that nobody perceived before in quite the same way.

That is the beginning of advertising victory.[34]

Much of this "shoe leather and scholarship" moves beyond the specifics of any single marketing problem and embraces your total awareness of the environment in which you, your clients, and your target consumers reside. So to become a truly great campaign copywriter, advises creative director Helayne Spivak, you must

keep reading, keep watching television, keep aware of the world around you. Stay in touch with popular culture; know what people are reading, seeing, thinking. You can't isolate yourself. Watching public television isn't enough. You need to be immersed in the culture of our times. It's not enough to be obsessed with advertising. You need to be obsessed with *life*.[35]

Endnotes

1. Terance Shimp, *Promotion Management and Marketing Communications*, 2nd ed. (Hinsdale, IL: Dryden Press, 1990), 67.
2. Chuck Reece, "Admen Remember Jack Cunningham," *ADWEEK* (March 4, 1985), 2.
3. Casey Davidson, "Client to New Agency: 'Walk a Mile in My Shoes,' " *ADWEEK* (August 29, 1988), 17.
4. "Founder and His Philosophy Star in Unconventional Porsche Ads," *ADWEEK* (September 11, 1989), 10.
5. Debra Goldman, "Study: Advertisers Aren't Talking to Consumers," *ADWEEK* (August 27, 1990), 25.
6. Malcolm MacDougall, "How to Sell Parity Products," *ADWEEK* (February 13, 1984), 30.
7. Richard Kiernan, writing in "Monday Memo," *Broadcasting* (August 25, 1980), 24.
8. William Bartolini, "Market Planning as a Team Effort," *BPME Image* (April/May 1989), 8.
9. Mel Rubin, writing in "Monday Memo," *Broadcasting* (July 9, 1979), 10.
10. Frank DeVito, writing in "Monday Memo," *Broadcasting* (February 16, 1981), 24.
11. William Meyers, "The Campaign to Save a Flagging Brand," *ADWEEK* (April 1985), F.C. 22.
12. Don Ferguson, writing in "Monday Memo," *Broadcasting* (May 28, 1973), 14.
13. John Muhlfeld, writing in "Monday Memo," *Broadcasting* (August 21, 1978), 16.
14. Extracted from materials courtesy of Kathy Kane; Foote, Cone & Belding/San Francisco.
15. Lisa Paikowski, "Funeral Marketer Breaks New Ground in Traditional Trade," *ADWEEK* (August 3, 1987), 17.

16. Sam Moyers, writing in "Monday Memo," *Broadcasting* (July 21, 1975), 10.
17. Al Ries, writing in "Monday Memo," *Broadcasting* (August 26, 1974), 11.
18. Merri Rosenberg, "Snuggle: A Hard Sell in a Cuddly Package," *ADWEEK* (April 1985), F.C. 36.
19. Ries, 11.
20. "Keith's Beliefs," *ADWEEK* (May 29, 1989), 14.
21. "Do's and Don'ts of Broadcast Promotion Star at BPA Seminar," *Broadcasting* (November 26, 1973), 30.
22. Faith Popcorn, "Repositioning with Real Sell," *ADWEEK* (December 12, 1983), 42.
23. Craig Tanner, "Taking a Leaf from Ogilvy's Book," *ADWEEK* (March 7, 1983), 32.
24. Paul Goldsmith, writing in "Monday Memo," *Broadcasting* (September 22, 1980), 12.
25. Arthur Bijur. Letter to the author, 14 September 1992.
26. Mike Fenley. Letter to the author, 29 June 1992.
27. Cathy Madison, "Spec-tacular Successes: Clients Now Demand—and Use—More Spec Work," *ADWEEK* (July 15, 1991), 1, 36.
28. Ed McCabe, "Spec Pitches: A Substitute for Reality," *ADWEEK* (July 16, 1990), 21.
29. Extracted from Don Wirth, writing in "Monday Memo," *Broadcasting* (July 4, 1977), 8.
30. Extracted from Clinton Rogers, writing in "Monday Memo," *Broadcasting* (June 10, 1968), 18.
31. Extracted from materials courtesy of Marlene Passarelli; Lawler Ballard Advertising.
32. Barbara Lippert, "DuPont Serves Second Helping of Rich and Food Stained," *ADWEEK* (April 1, 1991), 10.
33. Extracted from materials courtesy of Ruth Whitmore; Whitmore Communications, Inc.
34. Paul Harper, *Victory in Advertising* (New York: Needham, Harper & Steers, 1980), 4.
35. "Helayne Reigns," *ADWEEK* (March 23, 1992), R.C. 11.

■ *Chapter 14*

Public Service Campaigns

Several examples of successful public service announcements (PSAs) in previous chapters illustrate various copy-creation principles. As these examples amply demonstrate, public service messages need not be any less skillful or appealing than their commercial counterparts. Yet, too many writers approach the PSA assignment with self-imposed blinders. Because the client is a church, a charity, or a governmental institution, these scribes construct dignified, straitlaced, and totally boring messages that are too bland to enlist anyone's interest or attention.

If anything, PSAs must be even more creative, more vibrant than commercial copy because:

1. the "product" is often an intangible (safety, love, patriotism), which must be made concrete for the audience;
2. this "product" often asks more of the audience (give, join, call) with a less immediate or less specific benefit to be gained in return;
3. since they receive no money for airing them, outlets are free to select for airing whichever PSAs they wish.

The importance of this last point cannot be overstressed. As long as a *commercial* is not libelous, obscene, or in violation of continuity acceptance policies, we know it will be transmitted because the outlet is being paid to do just that. Thereafter, it is a matter of whether the advertisement is appealing enough for consumers to give it heed. In the case of public service announcements, however, we cannot even take airing for granted. Instead, the PSA we write must contend with those prepared by dozens of other copywriters and organizations equally dependent on making a favorable impression on outlet personnel before they will even have the opportunity to make a favorable impression on that outlet's audience. "Many PSA directors are finding it increasingly tough to choose among the many well-intentioned public-service campaigns," reports *ADWEEK*'s Joe Mandese. "And for every national campaign vying for time and space, 'you have to figure that there are tens of thousands of little local groups out there doing something,' [the Advertising Council's Eleanor] Hangley says."[1]

The Ad Council itself, which coordinates national nonprofit campaigns through volunteer advertising agencies, gets from three to four hundred requests for assistance each year—even though it is hard pressed to handle more than three dozen.[2] In light of this "good cause glut," it is unreasonable to expect that a dull or format-incompatible PSA will have much chance of being aired. Therefore, all the copy techniques and appeals we've previously mentioned should be considered and, as appropriate, exploited when it comes to fashioning a PSA campaign.

The Three Hallmarks of Successful PSAs

Whatever your chosen approach, you should evaluate the result via these three key questions:

1. Do the PSAs break the intangibility barrier?
2. Do the PSAs appeal to *enlightened self-interest?*
3. Do the PSAs make the outlet want to air them?

Breaking the intangibility barrier means coming up with a pictoral concept that encapsulates the essence of your message in a manner that can easily be visualized. Many people have difficulty dealing with subjects that lack a concrete dimension. By providing them with an easily comprehendable symbol for what we are talking about, we make our PSA much more accessible. This, after all, is why Jesus used parables. By building his lessons around mustard seeds, stray sheep, and lost coins, he was able to communicate complex philosophical principles to a largely uneducated populace. Even for modern and well-schooled media audiences, a central, concrete referent (like the following spot's checker game) helps the PSA 'lesson' break through to memorability.

> Production Note: Relaxed, warm conversational tones.
> Periodic sounds of checkers on game board and
> background street activity. BG is elderly black
> gentleman; WG is elderly white gentleman.

BG: Beautiful day, just playin' checkers on the porch with my buddy.

WG: Your neighbor,, since open housing.

BG: Been better 'n twenty years.

WG: Since you won a game? Jumped your king.

BG: Since open housing. No race; no handicap; and no national background standing between someone and a place to live.

WG: <u>And</u> no more going crosstown just to teach <u>you</u> the checkers game.

BG: Well, we sure covered a lot of ground to get open housing.

WG: Wonder if we'll be neighbors in the great beyond?

BG: Why not? Beyond the pearly gates, open housing's always been the game plan. Your move.

BOTH: (Chuckle)

ANNCR: A message from the Wayne/Oakland County Community Housing Resource Board.

(Courtesy of Susan Montgomery.)

Appealing to 'enlightened self-interest' is a two-part process. As they move through life, most people like to think of themselves as reasonably "good," as doing the right think when confronted by choices and temptations. That is the 'enlightened' part of human nature. At the same time, however, it is also human nature, when confronted with a task or an option, to ask "What's in it for me?" That is the less noble but no less common component of the human equation. By appealing to enlightened self-interest, therefore, we try to cast our spot in such a way that both virtue and meaningful audience benefit flow from the action or belief that our PSA is advocating. Never make a "we need your help" appeal without also demonstrating what the listener or viewer will obtain by providing that assistance. Thus, this multivoice PSA showcases the "right" thing to do by testifying that such enlightened action is simultaneously good for business:

<u>Production Note:</u> Owner is casual, Voice is matter-of-fact, without emotion.

OWNER: I'll be honest with ya. At first, I wasn't really enthused with the idea of hiring a disabled person.

VOICE: Mid-Michigan Industries is a private, non-profit corporation for training handicapped adults.

OWNER: I guess I didn't think they could handle the work.
VOICE: An M-M-I job coach helps the client to completely master the job.

OWNER: I mean, I'm a businessman. I didn't want to
         jeopardize my place. And I also didn't want to put
         someone in over their head.

VOICE: Clients are entered into the job placement program
         only when their skills completely meet job needs.

OWNER: But ya know? Everything turned out great. Ted's one
         of my best workers. And he gets along really well
         with everybody.

VOICE: If you want trained workers for your business, call
         Mid-Michigan Industries at 773-6918. That's
         Mid-Michigan Industries. 773-6918.

OWNER: Looking back at it. I'm glad I called Mid-Michigan
         Industries. Come to think of it. So is Ted.

(Courtesy of John Schroeder and Mid-Michigan Industries, Inc.)

Making the outlet want to air your PSA involves careful handling of two elements: content and form. The content of the message must be entertaining and compelling enough that it will keep the audience tuned and attentive to the channel presenting it. The nonprofit organization wants people to perceive their spot actively, and the outlet wants its audience to stay rather than leave. Therefore, both the organization and the outlet depend on the copywriter to make the PSA an interesting "tune-in" rather than a boring or repulsive "tune-out" program segment. For instance, while there is no dialogue in the following spot, the writer's involving visual storyline is calculated to engage audience notice and participation in the unwinding drama.

Video	Audio
VIEW OF ONE LANE OF ASPHALT ROAD THRU A WINDSHIELD	MUSIC: SPACIOUS ORCHESTRAL 'HORIZON' SCORE CONTINUES THROUGHOUT, KEYED TO ACTION
DIS. REVERSE ANGLE OF CHROME-LESS 'MUSCLE' CAR COMING TOWARD US ON THE COUNTRY TWO-LANE WITH MAJESTIC SNOW-CAPPED MOUNTAIN IN BG.	

Continued

Video	Audio
CAR OUTFITTED WITH FOUR IMPOSING ROOF LIGHTS AND COVERED WITH BACK COUNTRY DUST	
MS CAR'S INTERIOR. HANDSOME, YOUNG LEATHER-JACKETED DRIVER IS SMILING AT ATTRACTIVE BLONDE IN PASSENGER'S SEAT WHO'S WIPING HER LIPS WITH TISSUE	
REVERSE ANGLE TO FEATURE GIRL TOSSING TISSUE OUT OPEN WINDOW	
DOG IN REAR SEAT LOOKS BACK AT TISSUE BLOWING ONTO ROADSIDE	<u>DOG:</u> Growls
ECU MAN'S DISGUSTED FACE	
ECU WOMAN REACTING NERVOUSLY TO HIS DISAPPROVAL	
ECU MAN'S FACE; DETERMINED	
ECU HIS BIKER BOOT AS IT HITS BRAKE	
LS OF CAR FROM REAR AS IT SCREECHES TO HALT: WE SEE TISSUE IN FOREGROUND GRASS	SFX: TIRES GRABBING TO A STOP
MS TWO PEOPLE AS HE SHIFTS CAR INTO REVERSE; SHE SLAMS BACK INTO HER SEAT	
CU DOG HUNKERING DOWN, PAWS OVER HIS HEAD IN FEAR	<u>DOG:</u> Whimpers
ECU BIKER BOOT HITTING ACCELERATOR	

Continued

Video	Audio
PREVIOUS SHOT OF TISSUE IN GRASS AS CAR BACKS TOWARD IT, STOPS	
ECU BOOT BEING RAISED, SEEMINGLY TO KICK WOMAN OUT OF DOOR	
ECU WOMAN POUTING	
ECU MAN SMILES, SHAKES HEAD 'NO'	
MS DOG GETS OUT OF CAR, RACES PAST TWIN EXHAUST PIPES, RETRIEVES TISSUE	SFX: CAR ENGINE RUMBLING
MCU WOMAN, STILL WITH POUT, NOW IN BACK SEAT	
ECU MAN'S HAND PUTTING TISSUE IN GLOVEBOX-HANGING LITTERBAG NEXT TO DOG NOW IN FRONT SEAT	
MLS CAR PULLING AWAY WITH DOG HAPPILY LEANING OUT OF RIGHT FRONT WINDOW; GIRL SULKING ALONE IN DOG'S PREVIOUS BACK-SEAT LOCATION	SFX: CAR ENGINE ACCELERATING
UPPER-THIRD SUPER 'Don't Waste Utah' AS WE WATCH CAR DRIVE OFF TOWARD A CURVE WITH MOUNTAIN BACKDROP	
ADD LOWER THIRD SUPER 'Utah Department of Transportation'	

(Courtesy of Bruce Jensen, Fotheringham & Associates.)

While the content of the PSA must be enticing to the outlet, that is only half the battle. The spot must also be cast in a *format* that makes it as easy as possible for the broadcaster/cablecaster to move it out of the mailbag and onto the air. Here are several guidelines to secure the best possible reception for your free-airtime-requesting message. In the case of submitted radio scripts:

1. Triple-space all copy on standard 8 $\frac{1}{2}$ × 11-inch paper, leaving ample margins at the sides and bottom. Copy should start one-third of the way down the page, preceded by the proper noncopy data block (discussed in the next section of this chapter). Remember, because PSAs are freebies, those that enter a station's copy book in script form will probably be read 'cold' without talent rehearsal. So give this talent every typographical assistance to pick it up easily.
2. For this same reason, make sure the copy is cleanly typed on reasonably heavy, noncrackly paper. A clean, well-inked impression on the page is a must.
3. Type (MORE) at the bottom of a page when another page follows and '30' or the symbols # # # at the end of your copy. The reader should not have to guess whether a second page exists. Also, never break a spoken line over a page turn.
4. If your PSA is not being provided in prerecorded form (and many radio stations prefer recordings to scripts they would have to produce themselves), always give the station an ample number of script copies to meet its legal and productional requirements. The outlet will want at least one file copy of the script and one copy for each of what might be several continuity books used in its control rooms and announce booths. Anywhere from five to ten copies may be required. If your PSA is being prepared for taped distribution, provide the recording studio with several scripts so costly time is not wasted when some minor functionary demands a personal copy. And even if you are sending recordings to the stations, be certain to include at least two copies of the script for their previewing and record-keeping purposes.

The engineering and productional functions required in creating and transmitting *television* content are considerably more complex than those demanded by radio. Consequently, the personnel and equipment at the television station or cable system can seldom accommodate material that does not come ready for airing. At the optimum, this means that PSAs should arrive in finished 16mm sound-on-film or broadcast quality (not home camcorder) videotape. Each tape or film should be accompanied by a script and a postage-paid reply/evaluation card that can be mailed back as a record of when the spot was aired or why it was rejected. If 16mm sound film or broadcast quality videotape is totally beyond the resources of the agency for whom you are preparing the announcement, a silent 16mm film with a preproduced audiotape sound track would be the next best, but much less desirable, alternative. Only in the case of a local organization whose message really helps address a fundamental community need should 35mm slide or flip card formats even be considered.

For the moment, let's assume that your copy is communicating a local message the station/system is interested in addressing and that still pics, if properly prepared, will be accepted. In that case, the following procedures should be followed to avoid the channel's having to go any farther out of its way to serve the needs of the community and your client organization:

1. Take the visuals that have been selected for the PSA and have them all made into 35mm slides. Flip cards are much more trouble to handle than slides since they require actual studio production. Slides, on the other had, can be taped or aired directly from the control room's film chain. The minimal expense that slide creation entails is an investment that any media user should be prepared to absorb in order to make everyone's life easier.

2. Provide one slide for every six seconds of running time (five slides for a thirty, ten slides for a sixty). This is, if not a "happy" medium, at least a livable one that promotes some visual interest on the one hand, but does not demand rehearsed and split-second intercutting on the other. No station has the time to produce a technical extravaganza that comes disguised as a 30-second "freebie" kit.

3. Keep the copy "spacious"—don't pack the message so tightly that the technicians have trouble catching each slide's cue line or don't have time to check the monitor for proper word/picture matching. This means, of course, that multiple copies of your PSA script must be provided along with the preproduced audio tape. If they like your message, the channel will probably transfer it to videotape and then simply replay the tape whenever the PSA is scheduled. Thus, it is especially important that your copy and script allow for a "clean" and trouble-free taping the first time so as not to antagonize any of the technicians who may be involved in its replay.

4. Make certain that the visuals selected are intrinsically related to the central point of your PSA and are necessary to the realization of that point. Too many low-budget public-service announcements try to use pictures because they are conveniently lying around rather than because they are appropriate to the message itself. If highly relevant and meaningful illustrations are not available, and if resources don't permit their procurement, then fashion the communication for radio, where it can have positive rather than negative impact.

Tape, film, or slide, if your PSA has been cast in 60-second form, be sure to prepare and distribute a half-minute version as well. Only a thirty has a chance to be aired during a broadcast television's more lucrative hours, but the sixty is potentially playable at the fringe times and on local cable systems anytime. To provide stations with maximum flexibility, radio PSAs should be submitted in 30- and 60-second lengths, too. Television 15-second messages may also be appropriate; but many video outlets like to reserve such slots for paying customers exclusively.

PSA Noncopy Data Blocks

The other component of an outlet-friendly format is use of the proper noncopy data block to identify your creation. Table 14–1 sets forth a standard radio PSA heading. Even though some of this information might be rearranged into other patterns, it should all be included somewhere in the block. Of course, if the PSA source generates a good deal of radio copy, much of these data will be cast as preprinted letterhead or logohead.

This format sample in Table 14–1 clearly provides the outlet with information as to the source of this material, a code number in order to identify unmistakably this particular message, an indication of how contemporary this announcement is, and a specification of total message length. Particularly when PSAs arrive from small or relatively obscure organizations, the word count/length data lets the station know that this 30-second message will, in fact, fit into thirty seconds. Thus, the outlet has the assurance that it will not

Table 14-1
Radio PSA 'Release' Data Block

From:	For release:
Committee for Field Mouse Preservation	Wednesday, November 21, 1994
George Doorstop, Director, Public Relations	Message No.: CFP-64R-94
613 Kane Street	
Meritorious, Maine 04651	
(207) 339-6085	
Time: 30 seconds	
Words: 72	

. . . .

ANNCR: As cities annex more farmland, and developers put up
new subdivisions, a little one's rights . . .

end up giving more free time to the announcement than it will be able to get credit for.

A slightly different data arrangement is used when the subject of the radio PSA is a limited-duration event. In such a case, it is vital that neither the outlet nor the copywriter be embarrassed by the airing of event promotion *after* that event is over! Consequently, the use dates will begin before the actual start of the observance and will end on, if not slightly before, the event's conclusion. Event PSA scripts also begin with a "headline" to further highlight the name of the activity and its time frame. Table 14–2 provides an example of such a data block.

Because many television PSAs are produced by advertising agencies, they use the same data block as in their commercial scripts. An ISCI number might even be assigned if the PSA is on behalf of a national organization. On the other hand, if the nonprofit group itself is supplying the script, the standard heading is often preceded and modified by additional entries in order to reflect more clearly the noncommercial source and nature of the communication to follow. Table 14–3 illustrates such a situation.

Table 14-2
Radio PSA 'Event' Data Block

                                   BANTAM HOCKEY LEAGUE WEEK

From: For Use: September 18, 1994
Eddie Shack, Coordinator,   to
Sudbury Bantam Hockey League   September 24, 1994
65 Imlach Lane
Sudbury, Ontario L9G 2K1
705) 774-7279

                  BANTAM HOCKEY LEAGUE WEEK
             September 18 to September 24, 1994

Time: 60 seconds
Words: 148

. . . .

ANNCR: As pucks hit the ice all over Ontario, it's time to
       pay tribute to the leagues that give our children a
       start in the noble sport of hockey. Here in Sudbury,
       this means skating into the Bantam League fundraiser
       at full speed . . .

Table 14-3
TV 'In-House' PSA Data Block

```
                 A PUBLIC SERVICE MESSAGE FROM:
                 The League of Community Orchestras
                 1291 Cadenza Avenue
                 Rosin, Rhode Island 03212
                 (401) 598-6763
FOR RELEASE: July 11, 1994
             (or)
FOR USE: February 1, 1995 to February 15, 1995

JOB/ISCI # SYMP-8816           LIVE___FILM_xx_VTR___SLIDE___
SUBJECT   Composition Contest  LENGTH    :30
REVISION      4                TITLE       The Winning Chart
APPRV DATE  4/30/94            AS PRODUCED  5/21/94
```

OBJECTIVE: To encourage college-age composers to submit
overtures that are playable by volunteer/community
orchestras throughout the country.

PRODUCTION NOTE: The entire scene takes place in the lobby
of a nondescript bus station. STUDENT is young
(19-22-year-old) woman. Three passengers she encounters are
all over 50; two males and one female.

VIDEO	AUDIO
OPEN ON ESTAB. SHOT OF STATION LOBBY	ATMOSPHERE SFX
SLOW ZOOM INTO STUDENT ON BENCH, SCRIBBLING ON MANUSCRIPT PAPER	VO: Inspiration can strike at any time--

. . . .

PSAs, of course, are aired free. Therefore, no written contract specifies the running schedule, and the noncopy data block must clearly indicate any time-frame limitations to the message's usability. In addition, radio and television PSA copy arrives at the outlet totally unsolicited and from people who may be completely unknown to the outlet's staff. Public service scripts thus, must sell *themselves* every step of the way—beginning with their professional introduction at the top of the page.

Ten Public Service Postulates

In constructing what comes below the data block, try to be as fluid in your PSA conceptions as you are in writing your commercial assignments. Far too many otherwise uninhibited copywriters seem mentally to put on black suits and high starched collars when given a public service task. Their resulting scripts sound like somber sermons rather than engaging conversations—and somber sermons are *not* what most people want when they turn on their TV or radio. All the successes and techniques that you've established in the writing of commercials and promos should be brought to bear on the PSA pitch. In addition, here are ten postulates to keep in mind in order to maximize your PSA's chances of being aired by the media outlet and profitably attended to by your target audience.

1. Cultivate Bizarre Thinking

One way to prevent "good-cause dullness" and PSA predictability is to draw relationships that are out of the ordinary—if not downright creative. Veteran PSA producer Jim O'Donnell gives this example of what he means by bizarre thinking:

> An insurance industry client wants a PSA that urges car owners to lock their vehicles to make it tougher for car thieves. Conventional thinking would produce pictures of people locking their cars and pocketing the keys, etc., accompanied by a droning narrative about the importance of locking your car. Bizarre thinking would open with a shot of a briefcase lying in a parking space in a crowded parking lot. A suspicious character would approach, open the unlocked briefcase stuffed with $100 bills, close it and disappear. The viewer's first question is likely to be: "How absurd—who, in his right mind, would leave 15 grand in cold cash lying unprotected in such a place?" Here, straightforward narration would remind the viewer that people do it every day by not locking their cars and pocketing their keys. The final exhortation might do a play on the words "lock-it" and "pocket."[3]

Bizarre thinking allows both the writer and the audience to explore an insight rather than merely contemplate a command.

2. One Concept to a Cause, Please

Presenting a PSA in a clear and compelling manner also means sticking to one main image/idea. Given the usually intangible or remote nature of the PSA's audience benefit, every sound and picture must help flesh out the one key conclusion that our message was commissioned to communicate. Even in the

465

case of television's audio and video capabilities, multiple copy points only guarantee that, no matter how much information is originally taken in, little if any will be retained. Notice how the Figure 14–1 spot registers one terse observation, even while sweeping the viewer across thousands of years.

3. Bolster Believability

The single-concept PSA also makes it easier for the audience to grasp how the issue impinges on their own lives. Like an involving short story or an engaging commercial, the believable PSA is one whose simplicity enables people to put themselves in the picture—to participate mentally and emotionally in the little vignette being spun out before their eyes and/or ears. Thus, Figure 14–2's PSA expresses the dangers of AIDS transmission not in remote statistical terms, but in terms of highly proximate choices and people.

PSA believability is enhanced by the presence of three key factors: (1) sincere-sounding copy; (2) trustworthy testimonials; and (3) for television, comfortable yet contemporary photographic values.

Sincere-sounding copy is the element over which the copywriter obviously has the greatest control. Sincere copy can make unknown talent seem just as familiar as (and perhaps more believable than) the famous folks who are usually beyond a public service's budget. The sincere message *makes honest sense,* and makes it in a way that strikes the audience as neither pompous nor patronizing:

```
WOMAN:   I'll never forget my best friend Lanie's wedding. It
         was right before the ceremony and I walked into her
         bathroom without knocking because like I said, she
         was my best friend. And there she was in here
         gorgeous white lace dress, leaning over the sink
         with a straw up her nose. I says, 'Hey, what are you
         doing?' She jumps up and says, 'Shut the door, shut
         the door.' Then I see the white powder and I froze.
         She says, 'Hey, it's cool.' Then she leans over the
         sink and I say, 'Move it off or I'll blow it off.'
         She says, 'You do and I'll kill you.' Then she
         started to cry. And I started to cry. And we held
         each other real tight. Then I blew the coke off the
         sink and bolted outta there. I sent her a silver
         flower bowl, but she never wrote to thank me. I felt
         bad; so after three months, I broke down and called
         her. I thought maybe we could bury the hatchet
         because like I said, she was my best friend. But it
         was too late. They already buried Lanie.
```

"Evolution" :30 (CNFF–2130)

(MUSIC UP)

Long ago, in a place where there was nothing,

something incredible began to happen.

As the centuries passed,

a beautiful forest blossomed.

And all was well.

Then one day a man was careless.

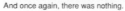

And once again, there was nothing.

ONLY YOU CAN PREVENT FOREST FIRES

USDA FOREST SERVICE AND YOUR STATE FORESTER

SMOKEY

A Public Service Campaign of the Advertising Council
On behalf of the U.S.D.A. Forest Service and the State Foresters
Volunteer Agency: Foote, Cone & Belding, Inc.

Ad Council
192

Figure 14-1

(Courtesy of Suzanne Holeton, The Advertising Council, Inc.)

SFX: SOUNDS OF A MOVIE
THEATRE

ANNCR (VO): So you're thinking
about sleeping with Steve.

WOMAN NODS YES
ANNCR (VO): Of course you know
you'll also be sleeping with Steve's
ex-girlfriend, Beth.

And both of her old boyfriends.

And all eight of their old girl-friends.

In effect you'll be going to bed with
hundreds of people tonight. So if
you're not going to say no, at least
use a condom, AIDS will sleep with
anyone.

PROTECT YOURSELF.
1-800-872-AIDS
EN ESPAÑOL
MICHIGAN DEPARTMENT OF PUBLIC HEALTH
AIDS PREVENTION PROGRAM

Figure 14-2

(Courtesy of Marcie Brogan, Brogan & Partners.)

```
ANNCR:  If you think you can't live without drugs, don't
        worry. Pretty soon you may not have to. Partnership
        for a Drug-Free America.
```

(Courtesy of Joy Golden, Joy Radio.)

As the above message also demonstrates, *trustworthy testimonials* add credibility to your PSA when the individuals who deliver them speak from experience. Particularly in the life-enveloping subjects with which many PSAs deal, average people rather than celebrities beget much more realism—unless the celebrity has demonstrated personal involvement in the problem or cause you're discussing. Even then, some audience members may still doubt the veracity of the spot and perceive the star merely to be playing some phony, self-serving role. The man in Figure 14–3 is authentic, and the sense of human drama he brings to the plea could not easily be replicated by an actor.

Our final believability element, *comfortable yet contemporary photographic values*, positions the television PSA in a productional middle ground. The effective nonprofit pitch does not exude an institutional coldness in direction and pacing of its shots. Nor, on the other hand, are its cinematic techniques so hotly avant garde that only spaced-out video freaks understand them.

For years I never had a reason to get up in the morning.

No one would hire me.

But then a friend told me about Goodwill Industries

and their job training programs.

Now I go to work just like my neighbors.

I'm making a real contribution and the people here respect me and my ability.

I'm still disabled, but I'm lucky. Because of Goodwill Industries, I've not only learned to live with my disability, I've learned to work with it.

Goodwill Industries. Our business works. So people can.

Figure 14-3

(Courtesy of DDB/Needham Advertising.)

Unfortunately, the tendency of some PSA writers is to swing from one extreme to the other in their visual stylings. They try either to respect some assumed propriety mandate from the sponsoring organization or, on discovering that to be an imaginary constraint, go wild in a self-indulgent attempt to out-hip the most outlandish commercial treatment around. It is as though a public service announcement must be either more straitlaced or more radical than anything else on the tube in order to command viewer attention. This, of course, is anything but the case. Provided the central concept has been well-honed, a PSA can compete with any other commercial or continuity fare on television—and compete in the productional mainstream rather than on the uptight or far-out fringes. In the Figure 14–4 photoboard, the central

VO: While the popularity of cocaine has been on the rise over the last five years, so have some other things.

Cocaine-related emergency room treatments — up 300%

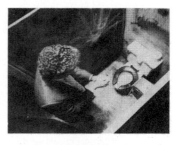

Cocaine-related deaths — up 323%

And thousands of lives down the drain.
Now, if for some reason you weren't aware of all this . . .

welcome to the glamorous world of drugs.

Figure 14-4

(Courtesy of Rose Marie Ialapi, McCann-Erickson/Detroit.)

concept is given full rein through an imaginatively angled, but by no means disorienting, pictorial progression.

4. Liberate the Visual

However they are shot and amalgamated, PSA pictures must not be smothered by excessive soundtrack verbiage. Unfortunately, some television copywriters are like once-a-month preachers trying to jam four sermons into each appearance.

Granted, the subject of your piece is laudable, humane, and vital. And it may be aired quite infrequently. But packing it with so much copy that the viewer must become primarily a *listener* throws away television's unique advantage. The perceptive PSA writer knows that the silent speech of gestures, facial expressions, and other camera revelations can have much more impact when not weighted down with wall-to-wall dialogue or voice-over copy. Certainly, the PSA's point is more difficult to delineate than a soft drink, cereal, or tennis shoe. But talking your script to death is no way to exploit video's potential. In all your television writing, and particularly in PSAs, where the tendency to pontificate is so strong, write copy as sparingly as a compelling visual will allow. In this way, the words you *do* use will possess special force and significance. For the 30-second treatment in Figure 14–5, any more words would intrude on the visual and blunt the resounding quality of the copy that *was* employed.

5. Tag with Discretion

As with commercials, the most resounding element of a radio or television PSA is often the tag line. Further, in order to be accepted for airing, public service tags must usually identify their sponsoring institution. This tag ID need be neither extensive nor detailed, but it should include the name and (in television) the logo of the originating institution.

If your intention is to have audience members write or call, then ample time must be allowed to permit registering and repetition of the mailing address or phone number. On radio, if the number or address is not mentioned at least twice, there is little or no chance of listener recall. On television, this 'supered' information should be held for at least 5 seconds.

Conversely, if you don't expect people to write or call, don't bother with an address or phone number. Fundraising appeals, for instance, are normally successful only when conducted via direct mail or telemarketing (phone calls to prospects). In such cases, your PSA's goals should be to pave the way for recognition and favorable response when the actual mail or phone solicitation later is received.

471

American Medical Association

"Teen Suicide/Portrait" :30
ID# PSAS1870

MUSIC BEGINS—
PLAYS IN BACKGROUND
THROUGHOUT SPOT...

ANNCR: This year 5000 of our
children

will take their own lives.

One way to prevent suicide is
listening...

...Are you?

A PUBLIC SERVICE MESSAGE FROM
THE AMERICAN MEDICAL ASSOCATION

Figure 14-5

(Courtesy of Shari Wolk, American Medical Association.)

Whether a short or long tag is used, there is no need to waste valuable time and audience attention with the words "This message is brought to you by. . . . " Simple verbalization or graphic conveyance of the organization's name will cue in today's consumers to the source of the piece.

6. Localize to Your Advantage

Stations and cable systems are more likely to select PSAs that address local needs because airing such spots shows these outlets to be more community-responsive. Therefore, anything the copywriter can do to bring a local slant to the subject increases the message's chances of outlet as well as audience attention. Even if the campaign is regional or national in scope, our just-mentioned discrete tagging should be designed to permit a customized conclusion:

```
ANNCR:  Can you use an extra monthly paycheck? Would you
        like a headstart on job responsibility and
        leadership? If you're seventeen or older, and
        qualified, the Naval Reserve Sea and Air Mariner
        Program can give you all this and more. SAM offers a
        part-time job, close to home, that you don't need
        experience to get. Find out more about SAM.
        Contact_____, your local Naval
        Reserve recruiter in _____ or call
        _____. Naval Reserve. You are tomorrow.
        You are the Navy.
```

(Courtesy of Naval Reserve Recruiting Command.)

Television can accomplish the same localization through basic end-frame supers. All that is required in the Figure 14–6 Red Cross spot is the addition of a dark-character phone number at the bottom of frame 12.

7. Instruct—Don't Intimidate

Whether PSAs are local or national, research has shown that they face an uphill battle in trying to convince people to alter certain counterproductive behaviors. However, evidence from the Stanford Heart Disease Prevention Program found that behavior change *can* be attained "if public service messages instruct audiences how to cease their negative practices."[4] A Washington State University study suggests further that "a skills-training PSA can help people learn how to dissuade their friends from driving drunk—especially when the skills are demonstrated by a person typical of the target audience."[5]

30 SECONDS (with :15 and :10 lifts.) CC (CNRC-8130/8115/8110)

ANNCR. (VO): When Friend fell, he called for Help.

But the only ones there, were: Ignorance,

Incompetence,

Indifference.

Friend called for Help again—

Confusion came instead.

At last Help came.

Help knew what to do.

In times of emergency, are you Help?

Learn Red Cross First Aid where you work—

American Red Cross

or call your local chapter.

And 30 SECONDS (:25/:05) and 10 SECONDS (:06/:04) versions which may be localized (or may be run without addition of local address or phone number). (CNRC-8230/CNRC-8210)

Volunteer Advertising Agency: J. Walter Thompson Company
Volunteer Coordinator: Bruce Wilson, Eastman Kodak Company

PO-000-148   688

Figure 14-6

(Courtesy of Suzanne Holeton, The Advertising Council, Inc.)

In other words, spots that provide simple, direct instruction on how to modify harmful conduct are much more effective than scare-tactic pitches. This holds true for both older and younger people—as long as they can identify with the PSA character doing the demonstrating:

Production Note: Man and Woman are both elderly but NOT feeble-voiced.

(SFX: ESTABLISH SHOPPING MALL SOUNDS AND UNDER)

MAN: Didn't I see you get out of the bus in front of the mall?

WOMAN: That was me.

MAN: Where's your car?

WOMAN: I haven't been driving lately. I'm getting too old.

MAN: C'mon Jennie. I'm older than you and I'm still driving. I took a refresher course and just changed my driving habits a bit.

WOMAN: What do you mean?

MAN: Well, our eyes and hearing and reflexes change as the years go by. It's natural. So it's best to drive during daylight and avoid heavy traffic and bad weather. Just a few adjustments and we can stay on the road. Give it a try.

ANNCR: A public service message for Cedarton seniors from KTRE and the Motor Vehicle Manufacturers Association.

(Courtesy of James O'Donnell, NTN Film & Video Productions.)

8. Don't Rewage the Crusades

Few PSA copywriters set out to intimidate their audiences. But because they believe so strongly in their client's cause, writers often become much more strident in their public service scripts than they would ever think of being when selling a tube of toothpaste or a liquid breath freshener. As a London *Times* reviewer once observed about media content in general, "Good causes do not automatically beget good programs." Assaulting the consumer with shrill self-righteousness only invites that consumer to retaliate by tuning out.

Imagine the understandably defensive reactions of San Diego residents if a water conservation message snarled like this:

ANNCR: Unless you want sand coming out of your faucets, you had better stop wasting water. Selfish people are indulging themselves and their manicured lawns at

the expense of the welfare of everyone in the
county. In just the last couple of hours, you
probably squandered gallons of water---water that
could have been conserved for more vital purposes.
It's time you economized to preserve our fragile
environment. Call 297-3218 to learn how you can stop
being a water waster. That's 297-3218 to find out 24
simple ways to reform your water use practices. Only
hoodlums squander H-2-O.

Such a pronouncement virtually begs the listener to counter with clever
rejoinders like "Who says?" "How do you know?" "Go douse yourself!" or
several more colorful and unprintable responses. Certainly, the listener would
be energized by such a message—but toward all the wrong actions. In the
actual PSA below, on the other hand, the copywriter covered much the same
ground on behalf of the San Diego County Water Authority, but in a much less
combative, much more positive manner:

ANNCR: This (SFX: THREE FIRM TAPS ON METAL BUCKET) is a
bucket. And this (SFX: ONE DROP HITTING BUCKET
BOTTOM) is a drop in the bucket. And if I asked you
to promise me to cut back the water you use each day
by 10 percent, well, you'd probably think that all
you'd be doing is (SFX: ONE MORE DROPLET). But now
that San Diego County, and other parts of
California, are in a fourth year of drought, if you
(ANOTHER DROPLET) and I (ONE MORE HIGHER-PITCHED
DROPLET) and everyone else (MULTIPLE ACCELERATING
DROPLETS) in San Diego County---. Hey, in 1977, we
faced a similar water shortage, and during that
summer we all pitched in and voluntarily cut water
usage by 15 percent, (ONE DROPLET) one drop at a
time. So find out 24 simple ways to save water by
calling 297-3218. That's 297-3218. And don't worry.
We didn't waste any water making this commercial. It
was all done with sound effects. (ONE VERY TINNY
DROPLET). Your San Diego County Water Authority.

(Courtesy of James R. Melton, San Diego County Water Authority.)

Arriving through the extremely personal electronic media, the PSA is a
guest in people's homes, or a rider in their cars. It must behave as a guest is
expected to behave or the consumer has every right to kick it into the street.
Don't push your cause with waving banners and blazing eyeballs. Don't try to
rewage the Crusades in your copy or you'll just be as futile as they were.

9. Remember That Stodginess Stinks

Conducting a Crusade is not the only way to defeat your public service purpose. Another surefire method for producing PSAs that fail is to use tedious word arrangements. Copy traits that are merely moldy in commercials can reek in PSAs where we generally start out with a subject that is harder to freshly package than a commercial product pitch. Thus, the following three limpish writing tendencies are especially to be avoided: *'five-dollar' words*, *redundancy*, and *periodic sentences*.

As a class, PSAs have acquired a reputation for a certain, ponderous, bureaucratic copy style. Using *'five-dollar words,'* bigger words than we require, will reinforce rather than counter this stereotype:

```
ANNCR:  The voluntary expropriation of your hemoglobin is a
        matter of unquestioned importunateness as Municipal
        Hospital endeavors to replenish its sorely depleted
        inventory.
```

Besides the use of some inaccurate terminology, why couldn't the copywriter just say the hospital was badly in need of blood? Overblown prose doesn't make the appeal seem more official—only more unapproachable.

Redundancy, our second stodgy stink, differs from aromatic *emphasis* chiefly because of word placement. Both devices use the same word or phrase several times. But redundancy also puts it at the same place in a number of recurring sentences and thereby saps listener interest. Emphasis, conversely, varies the placement so the word or phrase is exposed at novel and unanticipated junctures. In its deft juxtaposition of "wait" and "waiting," the following PSA illustrates beneficial emphasis:

```
ANNCR:  Waiting for some things is a part of life. We wait
        in line at stores, gas stations, movies; waiting is
        simply a fact of life. Except when you're hungry.
        Except when you're poor, jobless, under-employed.
        Then waiting destroys. The Campaign for Human
        Development believes in people working together to
        solve their common problems so that no person in
        America must wait to live a decent life. The
        Campaign for Human Development, United States
        Catholic Conference.
```

(Courtesy of Francis P. Frost, United States Catholic Conference.)

Redundancy, on the other hand, would negate this cumulative sense of suspense by giving the repeated phrase an all-too-predictable and monotonous position:

> ANNCR: Waiting for some things is a part of life. Waiting
>   in line at stores. Waiting at gas stations and
>   movies. Waiting is simply a fact of life. Waiting is
>   endurable except when---

Another mechanism for repeating a point with emphasis rather than redundancy is to split it between several voices, as in Figure 14–7. In reinforcing the premise for/to each other, the characters multiply our chances of successful communication with the audience.

Beyond varying word placement and speaker, redundancy also can be avoided by checking your writing for such 'double statements' as:

VO: Three popular myths about old age:

VO: Getting old means getting sick.
MAN: Hogwash. Today the majority of older Americans are healthy.

VO: Most old people live in nursing homes.
WOMAN: No, no, no. Only 5% do.

VO: Old people shouldn't exert themselves.
WOMAN: Wrong. Some exercise is good for you, no matter what your age.

WOMAN: Just because you're sixty-five you don't have to retire from life.

VO: For your continuing good health from the American Medical Association.

Figure 14-7

(Courtesy of Shari Wolk, American Medical Association.)

most favorite	accidental disasters
informative news	excess waste
giving charity	sad tragedy
the thrill of excitement	unwanted embarrassment

Periodic sentences, the final contributor to overripe discourse, are constructions that force the audience to hold several phrases in mind while waiting for the main verb to give it all meaning. Pretentious even for print, the following periodic sentence is pure torture on radio or as a TV voice-over. The receiver must juggle long clauses with one ear and strain for the verb with the other:

```
ANNCR:  The need for help, for donations of time and money,
        for the tools of farming and hygiene education,
        for a care that negates the neglect of the past
        and the abject futility of the future, all of
        these needs can be met with a Community Chest
        contribution.
```

In contrast, observe the craftsmanship in this Michigan Department of Health PSA. Here, the copywriter has placed the verbs near the front of compact idea units rather than burying them at the rear of overextended ones. This technique gives the message more impact—and more clarity.

```
VICTIM: I didn't know I had AIDS until I saw it on my baby's
        death certificate. I did drugs for 20 years and I
        never thought I'd hurt anyone but myself. But I gave
        it to my wife, and she gave it to our daughter. I
        got AIDS by sharing my friend's works. He had it in
        his blood. Sure I'm scared of dying, but what's
        worse is that I destroyed my baby and my wife.

ANNCR:  Don't share a bed with someone who shares a needle.
        Michigan Department of Public Health AIDS Prevention
        Program.
```

(Courtesy of Marcie Brogan, Brogan & Partners.)

Five-dollar words, redundancy, and periodic sentences release obscuring fumes that do not emanate from copy that is fresh. They simply confirm people's worst suspicions about PSAs' mustiness. In short, such stodginess stinks.

10. Banish Commercialism

The final Public Service Postulate reminds us that true PSAs serve nonprofit causes exclusively. Never use a public service announcement as a Trojan horse for some commercial pitch. At the very least, that practice incurs the understandable animosity of the outlet, which you have duped into airing an *advertisement* for free. At worst, it flagrantly deceives the listening/viewing public. Avoid copy like the following, and you'll similarly avoid such dangers and damage:

```
ANNCR:  The Greencrest Brownie Troop is hosting its
        semi-annual bake sale at the Selkirk Hardware store,
        Cherry Street and Main. That's Selkirk's
        Hardware---where you can also obtain the finest
        selection of tools, lumber, and all-round building
        supplies available anywhere in the area.
```

Everything occurring after the street address constitutes commercial copy. If Selkirk wanted a pitch, he should have sold a few more nails and *purchased* the airtime himself.

Campaign Case Studies

Despite their nonprofit motive, however, PSA campaigns should be developed via the same Concept Engineering procedure we discuss in Chapter 13. Below is the objective for the United States Catholic Conference's Campaign for Human Development, together with a sample spot to illustrate how each of this objective's *subgoals* is to be realized. Because of the intangibility and breadth of their subjects, public service organizations often fashion subgoals rather than creative selling ideas (CSIs) to flesh out the various components of the belief or action they're advocating. By defining the parts, the subgoals therefore help collectively to characterize the campaign as whole.

```
Objective: To heighten adult awareness of the problems of poverty
as well as to illuminate some of the solutions such as (subgoals)
community organizing, caring, and working together.

            Subgoal #1---Community Organization

              30-Second TV spot
```

Continued

Video	Audio
CONVENTION SCENE CAMERA MOVES DOWN CENTER AISLE	<u>VOICE OF MEETING CHAIRMAN</u>: The Third Annual Convention of the Northeast Community Organization is hereby called to order.
CU, SIGNS: Trinity United Methodist, NE Mothers for Peace Our Lady of Lourdes	<u>ANNCR. (VO)</u>: A convention---but a different kind.
WOMEN WORKING AT TABLE	The elderly, the poor, the little people getting together
MAN STANDING AT MICROPHONE SIGN: Strength in Action	to stand up against big wrongs in their neighborhood. Wrongs like industrial pollution,
CU: INDIVIDUALS SPEAKING INTO MICROPHONES	Landlord abuse---wrongs they didn't think they could change until they got together. (SOUND OF APPLAUSE)
CU: PEOPLE APPLAUDING	
CUT TO FULL SCREEN: Campaign for Human Development U.S. Catholic Conference Washington, D.C. 20005	Campaign for Human Development

. . . .

Subgoal #2---Caring

60-second TV spot

Video	Audio
TWO INDIAN WOMEN WITH AN INFANT WALKING IN A BARREN FIELD	<u>MALE VOCALIST WITH GUITAR (VO)</u>: It's the same old earth It'll always be.
OLD INDIAN MAN	With a newfound worth, and dignity;

Continued

Video	Audio
QUICK CUTS OF PEOPLE, INCLUDING:	Livin' with the joy of bein' free---
TRUCK DRIVER TRAINING MEN STUDYING ENGINE	
CHICANO RADIO ANNOUNCER PARKING ATTENDANT	CHORUS: bein' free---
TWO WOMEN OUTSIDE STORE, FAMILY EATING HOTDOGS, GIRL SELLING FLOWERS IN THE STREET	SOLOIST: you and me.
CAB DRIVER OFFICE WORKERS (MEN & WOMEN) TRAFFIC COP STONE MASON GIRL ON BIKE CHILD IN DENTIST CHAIR WOMAN LOOKING AT PAPERS GIRL AT WORK SITE TELEPHONE CABLE MAN	CHORUS JOINS HIM IN REFRAIN: The joy of people workin' together. People determined to win. Building for tomorrow. Startin' to dream again. ANNCR: (VO): The Campaign for Human Development is all of us---together with hope---learning to care.
FREEZE FRAME: MAN WAVING	CHORUS: Learnin' how to care, Learnin' how to live and hope,
LOWER THIRD SUPER:	And learnin' how to share.
Campaign for Human Development U.S. Catholic Conference Washington, D.C. 20005	ANNCR: (VO): Campaign for Human Development. United States Catholic Conference

. . . .

Subgoal #3---Working Together

30-second radio spot

HARRY: (VO RATTLING OF DICE) All right, let's see if you can
          get past me on this turn, Joe.

JOE: All right, let's see, Harr, let's see. (DICE ROLL AND
          STOP) Oh, no, no, look at that!

HARRY:	Looks like you didn't make it, Joe, and is it going to cost you!
JOE:	Oh, I guess, but Harry, that's it. I'm wiped out.
HARRY:	Oh, too bad, old buddy, but that's life.
ANNOUNCER:	For too many people, that _is_ life. But we believe it shouldn't be. <u>The Campaign for Human Development.</u> <u>People Together---With Hope.</u> The United States Catholic Conference.

(All of the above courtesy of Francis P. Frost, Creative Services, U.S. Catholic Conference.)

For another example of strategic PSA campaign development, we turn to the work of the Lawler Ballard Agency. When the Commonwealth of Virginia raised its drinking age to twenty-one, the agency volunteered to communicate the change. The obvious target universe of the campaign was the teens who were no longer of legal age. But how to tell this target of the new legislation without antagonizing them?

Preaching or order-giving would be counterproductive, and a straight informative spot would do little to attract attention or promote compliance. Instead, Lawler Ballard copywriters turned to satire. As the youth appeal of *Mad Magazine*, "Saturday Night Live," and "Late Night with David Letterman" amply prove, teenagers enjoy satire that pokes fun at the adult establishment. But what to satirize in this case? Not Virginia lawmakers or law enforcement officials for this would impugn rather than publicize the regulation. Instead, the establishment chosen for parody was the whole institution of adult alcoholic beverage advertising. By lampooning these commercials, the PSAs were initially mistaken for them. Youthful viewers were lured into the public service pitch before they realized it, and thus, the humor-tinged announcement was accepted as a 'gotcha' rather than rejected as a boring or hostility-producing proclamation.

The objective of communicating the new drinking age to Virginia young people was achieved because the attitudes of the target audience were allowed to be a central factor in campaign formulation. Here are two of the spots from this public service effort:

Video	Audio
OPEN ON NEIGHBORHOOD TAVERN INTERIOR. YOUNG MAN STEPS UP TO BAR.	<u>MUSIC:</u> WHISTLING JINGLE THRUOUT <u>YOUNG MAN:</u> Gimme a light.

Continued

Video	Audio
BARTENDER CLICKS ON FLASHLIGHT IN YOUNG MAN'S FACE.	BARTENDER: Gimme some I. D.
YOUNG MAN SHUFFLES AROUND NERVOUSLY, THEN EXITS.	VO: Just a reminder,
DIZ TO ART CARD: 'Virginia has a new drinking age. 21 FOR EVERYONE. A message from the Virginia Department of Alcoholic Beverage Control.'	Virginia has a new drinking age.
. . . .	
OPEN ON FRANK BARTLES AND ED JAYMES LOOK-ALIKES SITTING ON FAMILIAR PORCH. THEY GET UP, WALK INSIDE,	SFX: LIVE ACTION
PULL DOWN WINDOW SHADE ON PORCH WINDOW	VO: In Virginia, if you're under 21, Frank and Ed don't want your support.
DIZ TO ART CARD: 'Virginia has a new drinking age. 21 FOR EVERYONE. A message from the Virginia Department of Alcoholic Beverage Control.'	

(Both the above courtesy of Marlene Passarelli, Lawler Ballard Advertising.)

What's in It for the Copywriter

With the substantial billings, media/production budgets, and on-air exposure that major commercial assignments offer, why do copywriters and their agencies (and outlets) voluntarily work on PSAs? Because, as Bozell group creative director Robert Osborn explains,

Creatives choosing PSAs as a way to showcase their talents come as close to agency heaven as possible: They choose whom they work for. Creative is in control of the end product. Clients are appreciative of the concern taken in their cause. Meanwhile, the agency is viewed as a socially active, moral member of the community. It all adds up to a situation ripe for good advertising.[6]

Industry reporter Cathy Madison observes further that "while providing legitimate contributions to worthy causes, high-quality, high-profile work also advertises the agency, helps recruit talented employees and boosts morale among staff plagued by down time or the creative shackles of regular clients."[7]

The most visible of this *pro bono* (donated) PSA work is coordinated by the Advertising Council. Founded in 1941 by the American Association of Advertising Agencies and the Association of National Advertisers, the Council is a matchmaker. It pairs member agencies with governmental and private nonprofit clients to service needy causes on a national basis. With a staff of 38 and an annual operating budget of $3 million, the Council limits its client roster to approximately thirty nonprofit organizations whose programs all possess significant, nationwide importance. Large volunteer agencies are then matched with these "accounts" and prepare the actual ads, which the Council then subsequently reviews and distributes. Council president Ruth Wooden admits that "in a sense it's impossible to avoid prioritizing. What happens is that we recognize advertising can really impact on some things more than others."[8]

Organizations whose needs cannot be serviced by the Ad Council are free to seek out *pro bono* help on their own, of course. And because the Council's roster of agencies is limited to the largest shops in the country, there is a great deal of *pro bono* work contributed outside its auspices by both station and agency copywriters.

Whether accomplished inside or outside the Ad Council, these voluntary creative efforts are examples of copywriter *enlightened self-interest* at its finest. As writer Daniel Clay Russ observes,

> *Pro bono* gets into award shows and helps recruiters and creative directors see who is out there who might want a higher paying job in a better city on great accounts. This is important if you remember that the creative portfolio isn't some self-congratulatory exercise. It is the writer's or art director's meal ticket. It is how they feed their families.[9].

"For most employees," concludes advertising journalist Stephen Battaglio, "*pro bono* assignments give them a chance to exercise a level of creative freedom not often permitted on an average packaged-goods account, as well as a personal satisfaction that comes from handling work for a good cause."[10]

PSA spots and campaigns, therefore, are likely to play an important role in your professional career—from both selfish and self*less* standpoints.

Endnotes

1. Joe Mandese, "PSAs: Too Many Issues, Not Enough Time," *ADWEEK* (May 18, 1987), 52.
2. Ibid.
3. Jim O'Donnell. Letter to the author, 12 June 1992.
4. "PSAs Should Demonstrate and Teach," *NAB RadioWeek* (October 31, 1988), 10.
5. Ibid.
6. Robert Osborn, "Viewpoint," *Winners* (May, 1988), 3.
7. Cathy Madison, "The City That Put 'Pro' in Pro Bono," *ADWEEK* (January 1, 1991), 17.
8. Robyn Griggs, "Matchmaking," *ADWEEK* (January 1, 1991), 18.
9. Daniel Clay Russ, "Oh, No, Pro Bono," *ADWEEK* (September 2, 1991), 17.
10. Stephen Battaglio, "Giving at the Office," *ADWEEK* (January 1, 1991), 15.

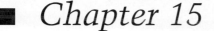

Chapter 15

Political, Controversy, and Crisis Campaigns

In this final chapter, we explore a more complex series of copywriter concerns—concerns that arise when the subject of your message is inherently contentious, frequently emotion-laden, and yet, frustratingly intangible. We are referring to radio/television campaigns designed to elect a political candidate, advance one side of a controversial issue, or mitigate a crisis of confidence in which an otherwise conventional advertiser suddenly finds itself embroiled. The principles of spot and campaign construction previously discussed also apply here but are complicated by the abrasive nature of the subject matter with which your messages must deal.

Political Advertising

Commercials designed to promote the candidacy of a particular individual for a public office are today known as *polispots*. Beginning with the 6,000 "Minute Men" who delivered identical Republican-promoting pitches over local radio stations in 1928, U.S. polispots have grown in prominence, sophistication, and perceived importance ever since. No longer limited to national or even statewide contests, candidate commercials are now a significant part of many local elections as well, with thousands and even millions of dollars being spent to influence voters in a single city or county. According to the Television Bureau of Advertising (TvB), campaign expenditures for broadcast television alone rose from $153.8 million in 1984 to $227.9 million in 1988.[1] Four years later, the total jumped to almost $310 million,[2] with an additional $3 million spent in cable.[3]

This ever-increasing use of electronic media paid advertising, together with greater candidate attention to such interactive opportunities as talk shows and televised town meetings, both reflect a fundamental fact about voter characteristics. As Professor Kathleen Jamieson points out, "For people who don't seek out other forms of political information—the very voters whose response to ads is greatest—the effect of political advertising is magnified. It may be even more important in state and local races where other forms of political information are less available."[4] Just prior to his election to the presidency, Bill Clinton predicted that when the campaign was dissected, "I think two-way communication between the candidate and the people will be the story."[5] In light of Clinton and Ross Perot success with such formats in 1992, both programs and *commercials* that manage to project a sense of dialogue are likely to grow in prominence.

What Polispots Are Not

Before going any further, it must be made clear that the comparative brevity of polispots as compared to full-length programs does not make the commercials inevitably superficial. In his landmark content analysis of the 1980 presidential campaign, Leonard Shyles scrutinized a large number of primary election spots. His findings concluded that "televised political spot advertisements are not merely frivolous diversions. Such commercials can accurately define the issues of a political campaign. . . . These data suggest that political commercials attend to contemporary issues and reflect the political concerns of the times, regardless of how entertaining and emotionally engaging such messages might also be."[6] In short, like any well-fashioned commercial, a professional polispot is based on a rational appeal while recognizing that emotional packaging is vital for any message transported by an entertainment medium.

Nevertheless, a political commercial *is* a much different animal from an agency pitch for soap or dog food. This difference extends to the way it is conceived and produced as well as to its eventual content. As a polispot copywriter, you must first recognize that the dynamics of an election campaign provide little lead time for spot development. Thus, polispot writing's abbreviated time line is more like that faced by the in-station copywriter than by an agency counterpart. Unexpected events and maneuverings by the other side can force literally overnight creations and execution changes.

Second, insofar as they feature the candidate, polispots are not usually dealing with professional talent but with media amateurs (the success of the Reagan exception thereby proving the rule). Demanding too much from the office-seeker's on-mike or on-camera performance can only result in an obviously staged portrayal that makes even the competent seem incompetent at best, or shifty at worst. In fact, given the time frame and talent limitations of the genre, political commercial creation is in some ways like producing local retail advertising in which the store owner insists he be a part of the message. Unlike the store owner, however, the candidate really *is* the product.

A third general difference between polispots and conventional commercials is that political messages, particularly for television, are often *postscripted*; they are written *after*, not before, they are shot. Footage of the candidate, supporters, and related events is gathered; the writer/producer's job then is to screen, select, and organize this material into a focused and meaningful message or series of messages. One cannot go back and reconstitute a rally, and a candidate's campaign schedule does not permit two or three days of prescripted shooting per commercial. Consequently, the political copywriter may spend a lot more time in an editing suite than at a typewriter.

Fourth, a campaign committee is not like a regular client where designated marketing vice-presidents and account executives do designated things in a clear chain of command. Instead, a political "coordinating" committee may be twenty people in a room telling you forty different things with no clear delineation of responsibilities or of who holds ultimate decision-making power. This is one reason most traditional advertising agencies avoid political accounts, leaving them to freelance specialists or to agency executives on temporary leave from their normal duties.

A fifth distinction between candidate and commercial commodity advertising is that most packaged goods and services constitute minor purchases. If the consumer makes an unhappy choice, it can be rectified on the next trip to the store. Whom to vote for, on the other hand, is an immutable decision that lasts for years and may impact all areas of the consumer's life. Most citizens sense this important attribute and are therefore much more wary of polispot claims. "Yet," observes political journalist Alan Baron, "people decide what to buy and how to vote on the same basis—what they perceive to be in their best interests. Presidents are a big ticket item, not an impulse buy, and there is a difference between 'instant gratification,' such as one might seek in a candy bar, and 'enlightened self-interest,' such as one might seek in buying a home—or in choosing a President."[7]

Sixth, a sloppy or amateurish *product* commercial is simply ignored by the audience. It does not impact prospects either positively or negatively. But such a 'null effect' safety valve is not built into candidate selling where viewers are always left with some sort of human impression. "If you see a bad spot for a commercial product, your mind turns it off," points out political consultant Dan Payne. "If you see a bad spot for a political candidate, you think 'what a jerk this guy is. He couldn't communicate in a 30-second commercial.' "[8]

A seventh dissimilarity relates to the share of market that a political candidate seeks as compared to what is acceptable to a product or service marketer. "A disinfectant spray manufacturer, for example, might be content with 20 percent of the $75 million market," explains professor George Comstock. "This allows him to be very specific in his appeals to a rather narrowly defined market. By contrast, the political candidate must obtain over 50 percent of the market or he will not be in business after election day. That means he must appeal to a much wider and more heterogeneous segment, and his advertising appeals cannot be too specific or information-laden or he will risk alienating a sizable portion of the market."[9]

Last, and as an outgrowth of the previous point, the personal stakes in a political campaign are much higher than those in product advertising. "Clients are different from candidates," cautions agency veteran Ed Buxton. "If their new campaign or new product bombs out, they can write it off and start over. The candidate—poor [guy]—is not so lucky. He is out on his lonesome, in the cold, and usually in debt."[10] We will not speculate here on the implications of this turn of events for that candidate's copywriter. Suffice it to say that a diversified account list is not an unwise precaution.

Polispot Types

Candidate commercials are usually grouped into three broad typologies: image spots, issue spots, and negative spots. Even though there is some overlap among this trio, the techniques they use tend to be quite distinct and their intended impacts much different.

1. Image Spots. These commercials focus on the personal characteristics of the candidate they are promoting. According to political scientist Richard Joslyn, "These characteristics most often tend to be personality traits. . . . Qualities that seem to be valued in the arena of political advertising are leadership, honesty, concern, responsiveness, strength, determination, perseverance, vigor and purpose."[11] Leonard Shyles adds that " 'image' is similar in meaning to a loose modern construction of Aristotle's 'ethos' concept, or the 'source credibility' of the candidate."[12] Image messages can *polish* a candidate's pre-existing aura but, because of their subtlety, are seldom able to change it radically.

Source credibility tends to go hand-in-hand with the title of incumbent, so image approaches are especially popular with current officeholders—at least those who have avoided any major misstep. In marketing terms, an incumbent is, as Stephen Battaglio puts it, "the established, maybe even the maturing brand."[13] So like any well-entrenched commodity, the incumbent or well-known front-runner prefers to reestablish comforting familiarity rather than raising issues or launching attacks that could prove disconcerting to parts of the constituency.

Ultimately, the image approach is designed to make the audience feel good about themselves by feeling good about their previous choices or current preferences. Thus, the following preconvention spot relies heavily on *we* to conjure up a sense of shared triumphs from the past. Along the way, it also stresses the need for the reassuredly calm and persevering incumbent to lead us in protecting shared values in the future.

Video	Audio
GRAPHIC: "We must not let our guard down."	BUSH (V/O): We have seen
DIZ CU OF BUSH IN WHITE SHIRT AGAINST LIGHT BLUE BG. RIGHT SIDE OF HIS FACE PARTIALLY SHADOWED	BUSH (OC): the demise of the communist system. We've seen the fall of the Berlin Wall. We've seen democracy and freedom come to Eastern Europe; and to all across South America---the same. We've made dramatic strides toward world peace. But we must not let our guard down. Who knows where the
DIZ GRAPHIC: "President Bush" and disclaimer	BUSH (V/O): next tyrant will come from.

(Courtesy of Alex Castellanos, National Media Inc.)

By its very nature, an image polispot should be low key and nonargumentative. "Image ads," Professor Anne Barton White found, "become the forum for the candidates' comments and vision to the viewers."[14] If they instead function as a flashpoint of contention, image spots cannot hope to accomplish their inspirational purpose.

Inspiration through nostalgia was clearly the hallmark of "The Man from Hope" centerpiece image ad in the 1992 Clinton presidential campaign:

Production Note: BC is the only voice; either VO or OC as determined by the visual

Video	Audio
FADE UP B&W PIC OF HOPE, ARK. TRAIN STATION, PAN LEFT	MUSIC: NOSTALGIC, GUITAR-LIKE THEME ESTABLISH AND UNDER

Continued

Video	Audio
	I was born in a little town called Hope, Arkansas. Three months after
DIZ B&W PIC OF LITTLE BC IN BOW TIE AND LIGHT SPORTCOAT	my father died. I remember
DIZ MS BC TALKING TO CAMERA, SITTING IN SOFTLY-LIT STUDY AND WEARING SPORTCOAT AND OPEN-COLLARED SHIRT	that old two-story house where I lived with my
DIZ B&W PIC OF GRANDFATHER	grandparents. They had very limited incomes.
DIZ B&W FOOTAGE OF JFK IN WHITE HOUSE GARDEN	It was in 1963,
B&W FOOTAGE OF BC AND OTHER BOYS NATION YOUNG MEN	that I went to Washington
BC TODAY IN STUDY	and met President Kennedy.
B&W FOOTAGE JFK AND BC SHAKING HANDS	At the Boy's Nation program.
ZOOM IN TO CU OF BC TODAY IN STUDY	And I remember just thinking what an incredible country this was. That someone like me,
DIZ, ZOOM OUT HANDSHAKE CU TO REVEAL JFK AND BC	who had no money or anything, would be given the opportunity to meet the President. That's when I decided that I could really
CU BC IN STUDY	do public service because I cared so much about people.
B&W PIC LAW STUDENT BC STUDYING	I worked my way through law school with part-time jobs. Anything I could find.

Continued

Video	Audio
DIZ MCU SHOT OF YOUNG LAWYER BC	And after I graduated, I really didn't care
DIZ B&W FOOTAGE PANNING STREET OF MODEST ARK. HOMES	about making a lot of money. I just wanted to go home and see if I could
B&W PIC BC BEING SWORN IN AS GOV.	make a difference.
DIZ BC TODAY WITH YOUNG SCHOOLGIRL AT COMPUTER	We've worked hard in education and
DIZ ELDERLY WOMAN KISSING BC	health care
DIZ BC SEATED WITH WORKING MEN IN DINER	and to create jobs.
DIZ SHIRT-SLEEVED BC WORKING AT GOV'S DESK BEHIND STACK OF PAPERS	And we've made real progress.
DIZ BC SHAKING BLACK CHILD'S HAND	Now it's exhilarating to me to think that, as President, I could
DIZ CU BC HOLDING LITTLE PONY-TAILED GIRL: SMILES INTO CAMERA	help to change all our people's lives
SUPER Clinton/Gore DISCLAIMER LOWER THIRD	for the better. And bring hope back to the American dream.
	MUSIC: HOLD CHORD TO TIME

(Courtesy of Linda Kaplan, Clinton/Gore Campaign.)

2. Issue Spots. According to Faber and Storey, an issue message "involves either the mention of a current *political* issue or a discussion of the candidate's stand on the issue."[15] For our purposes, issue ads are candidate-related whereas *controversy* spots (to be discussed later) deal with contentious topics not directly tied to a race for elective office. "Issue ads have become more like news packages," Anne Barton White points out, "appearing to deliver objective facts and information about the candidates and opponents. Sophisticated graphic techniques and anonymous, credible announcers deliver the messages."[16] The issue may be major or minor, but it should be one on which your candidate clearly holds the advantage. The most decisive issues are not always the most important but rather, those with which the audience can most readily identify. Thus, the constituency must be carefully assessed before any issue is targeted for exposition.

Intrinsically, issue polispots are more risky than image messages because of their potential for voter alienation. Issue ads also expose the candidate to opponent attacks on his or her position. For these reasons, front runners tend to avoid issue orientations whereas pursuing candidates tend to embrace them. Still, a leading candidate may want to mount at least one issue flight if it is an issue that can be dominated. In this way, leaders deflect criticism for "not taking stands" while publicizing a safe position on which they know they are not vulnerable.

Some strategists tend to divide issue polispots into "soft" and "hard" categories. A "soft issue" is one on which almost everyone can agree. By raising it, the office seeker can bolster his or her general image while reaping the additional benefits that come from an evidenced willingness to take a stand. Virtually no one but selfish spendthrifts, for example, could disagree with the basic posture that is struck by the Figure 15–1 voice-over crawl as it crusaded its way up the TV screen.

"Hard issue" commercials, in contrast, take a position on a subject about which there is more widespread disagreement. In scripting a hard issue approach, the copywriter at least must be certain that (1) the candidate's supporters are completely in tune with this stand, and (2) the candidate's position can be clearly and concisely articulated without any danger of public misperception. In this John Rauh polispot, the incumbent's wife addresses an issue that he has determined is fully consonant with the desires of his targeted voters. By making this position clear early in the campaign, Rauh solidifies support and makes it much more difficult for the opponent to preempt or distort the issue later.

Video	Audio
CU MARY RAUH	MARY: As past president of a family planning agency that serves sixteen thousand women in New Hampshire, I'm outraged when politicians try to interfere in women's private lives. That's why I'm supporting John Rauh for the

Continued on page 496

The national debt.

It is a massive storm that is clouding America's future,
an ill wind that is destroying jobs.

It is a debt so enormous that it will take
one-third of the federal income tax collected this year
just to pay the interest.

$199 billion in interest
that could be used
to create jobs,
but will only be lost in the storm.

When will it end?

When we choose a candidate who understands
that deficit spending is an irresponsible act of government,
not an uncontrollable act of nature.

A proven business leader who has the
know-how to balance the budget,
who will work with the free
enterprise system
rather than play politics.

The candidate is Ross Perot.

The issue is the national debt.

The choice is yours.

Paid for by Perot '92.

Figure 15-1

(Courtesy of Dennis McClain, Temerlin McClain.)

Video	Audio
	U.S. Senate. John's <u>always</u> been pro choice because he <u>trusts</u> women to make their own moral decisions. Why am I so sure we can count on John Rauh to fight for choice in the U.S. Senate?
SUPER ID: Mary Rauh	Because he's my husband!
ARTCARD: John Rauh. Democrat for U.S. Senate. Paid for by John Rauh for US Senate.	<u>ANNCR (VO):</u> Real change now. Vote for John Rauh.

(Courtesy of Michael P. Shea, Shea & Associates.)

3. *Negative Spots.* Negative messages are *direct* attacks on an opponent. Though perceived as a creation of television, negative advertising is at least as old as political handbills. Indeed, historian Henry Adams has called much of politics itself *the systematic organization of hatreds*—so it should be no surprise that direct attacks are the stuff of which a good deal of political advertising is made.

Certainly, the electronic media have given negative approaches a new, and perhaps tailormade form. "Our communications are now geared to quick takes," asserts New York Governor Mario Cuomo. "You call them bites in radio and television. That requires that you be simple and if you're going to be simple, negativism is one of the simplest of all emotions. Hate, I think, is easier to project than love. . . . Everybody responds to it. Everybody understands it. Quickly. And I think that's where the answer is. If you've got to communicate in 28 seconds, then negativism is probably a good bet."[18] "It is much easier to motivate people to be against something than to be for something," argues veteran campaign director Edward Rollins, "and there's not that much difference between most candidates because they aren't going to take strong stands on controversial issues."[18]

Nevertheless, clear front-runners seldom use negative polispots because they do not wish to be perceived as bullies. A long-shot candidate, conversely, can exploit negative advertising with much greater safety because he or she can play the role of underdog who is only trying to get a fair hearing. No matter who relies on them, negative attacks should almost never be made by the candidate; instead, they are assigned to other voices while the candidate profits from, but stays above, the fray.

The unrestricted growth of PACs (political action committees) in the United States has given additional impetus to negative advertising because PAC money is more likely to be used to defeat someone rather than specifically to support someone else who might then have to count PAC funds as political contributions. Yet, even without the independent advertising presence of such special interest groups, negative advertising would remain part of the radio/television landscape because the burden any challenger assumes is to demonstrate that the incumbent has done something *wrong*.

Negative advertising that is responsible, accurate, and relevant does make a contribution by informing the public of inconsistencies, failures, or abuses of which they should be aware. That this information is provided as part of an effort to elect the defendant's opponent does not, by itself, make the practice wrong, unprincipled, or misguided. As long as the criticism is office-relevant and verifiable, the copywriter should feel free to consider its use if campaign strategy thereby will be furthered. In the following above-board negative spot, the copywriter has stuck to the facts and exposed opponent vulnerability without resorting to personal vituperation.

Video	Audio
FADE UP ON SCENES FROM TIENAMEN MASSACRE. TROOPS. STUDENTS. TANKS. THE "GODDESS OF DEMOCRACY" STATUE BEING TOPPLED.	ANNCR (VO): When the Chinese Communist government cracked down on dissident students in Tienamen Square, many were killed on the spot by soldiers. Others were crushed by tanks.
SCENES OF STUDENTS BEING LED INTO COURTROOM.	Many of the protestors escaped, only to be caught later, dragged in front of kangaroo courts and sentenced to long prison terms or death.
SHOTS OF CAMERAS MOUNTED ON ROOFTOPS.	Many were caught by television surveillance cameras mounted all over China. After all this, Bob Lagomarsino intervened to permit a U.S.

Continued

Video	Audio
	firm to be allowed to sell more surveillance cameras to the Chinese Communist
PAN DOWN ARRESTED STUDENTS.	dictators. Lagomarsino later said:
SUPER QUOTE GRAPHIC	"I knew it was some kind of electronic equipment, but I didn't know what . . ."
SUPER LAGOMARSINO PICTURE	As one of the highest ranking members of the House Foreign Affairs Committee he should have.
DIZ TO CLASSIC SHOT OF LONE CHINESE MAN STEPPING IN FRONT OF TANK AND MAKING IT STOP.	In the fight for freedom it sometimes takes only one person to say "No."
DIZ SLOW ZOOM IN TO CAPITOL WITH LAGOMARSINO PICTURE.	Now's the time to say "No" to Lagomarsino and a Congress that admits it doesn't know what it's doing.
CUT TO HUFFINGTON LOGO, PIC, AND DISCLAIMER	Say "Yes" to freedom and to change. Michael Huffington, the choice for change in Congress.

(Courtesy of Don Ringe, Ringe Media, Inc.)

As mentioned earlier in this chapter, candidates themselves usually try to remain dignified by letting their surrogates or voice-overs articulate the attacks. In certain circumstances, however, candidates make points with the voters by showing they have the conviction to make the attack themselves. This is an especially appealing strategy for a challenger for whom name recognition is a vital goal:

Video	Audio
GRAPHIC: BLACK SCREEN WITH WHITE SCRIPT: Rick Lazio For A New Congress	LAZIO (VO): I want a better life for my family, so I'm gonna fight for a better Long Island.
SCREEN SEPARATES TO REVEAL LAZIO CU WITH LETTERBOX EFFECT.	Long Islanders can't afford higher taxes. That's why I voted against the sales tax increase this year. That's why I led the fight against deficit spending.
WHITE FLASH TRANSITIONS BETWEEN BITES.	In Washington, Tom Downey voted to increase taxes. He gave himself a 35-thousand dollar pay increase. Tom Downey bounced 151 checks over a three year period. That's over one a week.

SCREEN CLOSES TO ORIGINAL GRAPHIC SLATE:
    Rick Lazio
    For A New Congress
	I grew up on Long Island. I've lived here my whole life. I love Long Island. That's why I'm running for Congress, 'cause I think we can do better.

(Courtesy of Peter Pessel, National Republican Congressional Committee.)

Challengers who mount negative attacks must make certain, nonetheless, that the voters themselves don't feel criticized. As advertising authority Mark Dolliver warns, "Incautious attacks on the incumbent can seem to reproach the majority of the electorate that voted for him the last time around. It's as if Miller ads told you that you're a chump if you've ever bought a Budweiser."[19]

If your candidate has to *answer* a negative attack, researchers Brian Roddy and Gina Garramone indicate that there are two fundamental strategies that can be used: positive and negative. "In positive-response commercials," they say, "targeted candidates make no references to their opponents' attacks, but instead, present their own arguments about the topic of the attack commercial."[20] This avoids any intimation of mud-slinging while still helping to set the record straight. In the following Canadian spot, then Prime Minister Brian Mulroney's campaign answers his opponent's charge that Free Trade is a sellout by citing newspaper editorials that laud Mulroney's Free Trade efforts:

Video	Audio
PIC PARLIAMENT BUILDING/DAY	<u>VO</u>: With our economy strong, there could be no better time to
ADD <u>STAR</u> QUOTE AS LOWER-THIRD SUPER: 'Build on our strengths'	build on our strengths and take advantage of the trade deal, says the <u>Windsor Star.</u>
DIZ MULRONEY SHAKING HANDS WITH REFINERY WORKERS	Our country has take the biggest single step in its history
ADD <u>SUN</u> QUOTE AS LOWER-THIRD SUPER: 'Determining our own economic future'	toward determining our own economic future, says the <u>Edmonton Sun.</u>
DIZ MCU MULRONEY IN FRONT OF FLAGS	You have to thank Prime Minister Mulroney for having had
ADD <u>SUN</u> QUOTE AS LOWER-THIRD SUPER: 'The guts to negotiate'	the guts to negotiate the Free Trade deal with the United States.
DIZ MULRONEY STANDING WITH OTHER WORLD LEADERS	The <u>Globe and Mail</u> calls the trade agreement an
ADD <u>GLOBE AND MAIL</u> QUOTE AS LOWER-THIRD SUPER: 'Achievement envied by every other trading nation'	achievement envied by every other trading nation.
DIZ 'BUILDING A STRONGER CANADA PC' GRAPHIC	

(Courtesy of Shaun Masterson, Office of the Prime Minister.)

This is a positive attack response because John Turner, the perpetrator of those charges, is never mentioned nor, for that matter, are the charges themselves.

"In negative-response commercials," on the other hand, explain Roddy and Garramone, "targeted candidates call attention to their opponents' perversion of the truth and present their own arguments about the topic of the attack commercial. . . . This response strategy is labeled negative because, by claiming that opponents have distorted the truth, candidates are disparaging those opponents"[21] In the last half of their campaign, the Mulroney forces turned from the positive to the negative in an attempt to get unfavorable polls moving their way. Thus, in the spot below, we find John Turner and his charges both identified and assaulted:

Video	Audio
B/W MAP OF CANADA & U.S. COUNTRIES ARE LABELED BUT THERE IS NO BOUNDARY LINE	VO: John Turner says there's something in the Free Trade agreement that threatens Canada's sovereignty.
HAND WITH MARKER APPEARS	That's a lie.
DRAWS THE BOUNDARY ACROSS THE CONTINENT	And this is where we draw the line.
CU COVER OF FREE TRADE AGREEMENT	There is not one word in this agreement
ZOOM TO ECU HAND OPENING AGREEMENT TURNING PAGES TO REVEAL SECTION HEADINGS	that affects our independence, social programs, health care, pensions, or our culture. All those things we value that make us unique.
MCU SNARLING JOHN TURNER PIC	John Turner is misleading the Canadian people---that is the biggest threat of all.
DIZ 'BUILDING A STRONGER CANADA PC' GRAPHIC	

(Courtesy of Shaun Masterson, Office of the Prime Minister.)

In their study, in which subjects were exposed to *fictitious* polispots, Roddy and Garramone found that "Viewers evaluated the positive-reponse commercial more favorably than the negative-response commercial. It might be speculated that viewers prefer candidates to 'take the high road,' that is, ignore attacks and not indulge in mudslinging tactics. But the negative-response commercial was more effective in discouraging voting for the [original] attacking candidate."[22] As if to validate these findings, that is exactly what transpired in the Mulroney campaign, For the first half of the contest, the electorate responded unenthusiastically toward Mulroney as he reacted positively to Turner's attacks. But his prospects improved dramatically when he adopted a negative-response strategy. Voters may have "liked" his later ads less, but they were of much greater help in his ultimate victory. As researchers Michael Shapiro and Robert Rieger also discovered, "Compared to a positive issue ad, negative issue ads lead to some attitudinal backlash against the sponsor. But the sponsor of a negative ad still comes out ahead of the target. In many real-world political situations, that backlash may be worth it if it gives the sponsor a strategic advantage."[23]

Controversy Advertising

The International Advertising Association has defined controversy advertising as

> any kind of paid public communication or message, from an identified source and in a conventional medium of public advertising, which presents information or a point of view bearing on a publicly recognized controversial issue.[24]

Commercials that meet the terms of this definition are also known as *advocacy* spots. They can be divided into four categories: partisan, corporate image, corporate advocacy, and product legitimacy.

Partisan Spots

The bridge between controversy and political advertising is the partisan or political action announcement. Here, the disputation involves voting for or against the policy of a political party or coalition in general, rather than for or against any one candidate in particular. Unfortunately for the copywriter, the partisan spot thus overlays the amorphousness of a political organization atop the intangibility of an issue or belief. We must make doubly certain, therefore, that concrete implements are called on to define and register the controversy's essence and the correctness of our side's stand on it. In the following spot promoting endorsement of a new Canadian Constitution, a baseball analogy is recruited to stress the futility of voting "No" now in the vain hope of getting an "absolutely perfect" document later.

Video	Audio
OPEN ON TIGHT SHOT OF FASTBALL CATCHER BEHIND THE PLATE.	ANNCR (VO): We can wait for it to be absolutely perfect.
WE SEE UMPIRE BEHIND HIM.	
WE SEE MOTIONLESS BATTER IN FOREGROUND.	
BALL IS HURLED INTO CATCHER'S MITT.	UMPIRE: Strike.
CATCHER THROWS BALL BACK TO PITCHER.	ANNCR: With no compromises, no problems, everything just right.
BALL IS THEN CAUGHT AGAIN BY CATCHER.	UMPIRE: Strike.
CUT TO CLOSER SHOT AS CATCHER AWAITS NEXT PITCH.	ANNCR: You know, everyone happy about everything---all the time.
BALL LANDS IN MITT.	UMPIRE: You're out.
	ANNCR: Or we can say yes and really get on with it.
SUPER: YES/OUI (LOGO)	On October 26, say yes to Canada's future.
The foregoing is authorized by the Canada Committee.	

(Courtesy of Terrence J. O'Malley, Vickers & Benson Advertising Ltd.)

Corporate Image Spots

Like image polispots, *corporate* image messages strive to invest the sponsoring entity with a positive halo. It may be that even though this specific sponsor has not been singled out for attack, it is part of a generic category that is the subject of public debate or mistrust. Or perhaps the sponsor *is* well known and distrust is highly focused on it. Either way, it is the job of the corporate image message to defuse hostility without actually tackling the underlying issues that might be involved. At the same time, the corporate image controversy pitch strives to secure its client's legitimacy as a source of valid societal contributions.

The Dow Chemical Company, for instance, had developed a negative public profile—particularly among young people—because of its production of napalm and the Agent Orange defoliant during the Vietnam War. Even though these contracts amounted to a minuscule percentage of the firm's profits, the resulting protests gave this 70-year-old chemical manufacturer a sudden and decidedly repugnant notoriety. After two decades of cold and technical worded rebuttals had only made matters worse, Dow conducted a thorough review of its public communications methods. "It had taken us 20 years to develop a reputation as crusty, arrogant and single-minded," admitted Dow's Corporate Communication Manager Richard Long. "We clearly weren't going to change perceptions overnight"[25]

The most visible element in the new Dow approach became the company's long-range "Great Things" corporate image campaign. Through it, according to the firm's manager of public communications, Vicky Suazo, "We're concentrating on Dow products and services that help people, rather than trying to debate complex scientific issues via advertising. Our research to date suggests that we're moving neutral people to a more positive view of Dow; we're also nudging some of our critics into the neutral position."[26] One of the television spots from this image effort is presented as Figure 15–2.

Corporate Advocacy Spots

Because, by its very nature, overt advocacy is perceived as argumentative, most sponsors prefer the safer image course. Once a major public controversy that directly or indirectly involves that sponsor has been touched off, however, there is little choice but to meet the issue head on. Such a volatile situation presents an immediate need to encourage the audience to take a side—your client's side—before the public opinion battle is lost. At a time when a variety of governmental proposals threatened to alter the cable/broadcasting balance, several stations took to their own airwaves to stake out a beachhead for their case. The script on page 506 shows how WAFB sought to channel and influence public perception.

1. GRANDFATHER: So what are you doing at Dow these days, Peggy?

2. GRANDDAUGHTER: Well, right now, I'm working in agricultural research, Grandpa.

3. We're trying to help farmers find new ways to make every dollar work harder.

4. GRANDFATHER: We want to keep this farm in the family a few more generations.

5. GRANDDAUGHTER: Pretty tough, isn't it. GRANDFATHER: You bet.

6. GRANDFATHER: So your dad and brother are going to need all the help they can get.
SINGER: AND, YOU CAN MAKE A DIFFERENCE IN WHAT TOMORROW BRINGS.

7. GRANDDAUGHTER: I won't let you down.

8. SINGER: 'Cause DOW LETS YOU DO GREAT THINGS.

*Trademark of the Dow Chemical Company

Figure 15-2

(Photo courtesy of the Dow Chemical Company.)

Video	Audio
SHOT FROM BEHIND 6-YR-OLD GIRL AS SHE'S SEATED ON FLOOR, WATCHING "THE MUPPETS" ON CONSOLE TELEVISION	SOT FROM "The Muppet Babies" CARTOON
CU OF GIRL SMILING	
BACK TO ORIGINAL SHOT AS SCREEN GOES TO SNOW	SFX: HISSING OF "SNOW" ON SCREEN
CU GIRL'S SMILE DISAPPEARS	
ORIGINAL SHOT AS GIRL LEANS FORWARD SLIGHTLY	
CU HAND REACHING INTO CLEAR ASHTRAY AS SHE PICKS UP A FEW COINS	SFX: COINS JINGLING IN GLASS DISH
SHOT FROM BEHIND TV AS LITTLE GIRL WALKS TOWARD IT ON HER KNEES	
CU HAND PUTTING COINS INTO A COIN SLOT	SFX: COINS CLUNKING IN
BACK TO ORIGINAL SHOT LOCATION AS GIRL WALKS BACK TO POSITION ON KNEES. SCREEN GOES FROM SNOW TO CARTOON. GIRL SETTLES DOWN TO ORIGINAL POSITION, SCRATCHES HER BACK	"SNOW" AUDIO OUT. "Muppet" DIALOGUE BACK IN.
CAM ZOOMS OUT. <u>FREE TV</u> LOGO, STATION CALL LETTERS AND PHONE NUMBER APPEAR IN LOWER RIGHT SCREEN	<u>VO:</u> The time's coming when none of it will be free anymore. Call WAFB for details.

(Courtesy of Andrée Boyd, WAFB Television.)

Product Legitimacy Spots

Sometimes the issue is the product itself—whether and/or how its sale should be promoted. In nudging a controversial commodity into the marketplace, the usual strategy is to try to champion the audience's right to choose, their right to know their options and make their decisions accordingly.

Choice is not just the strategy but the central theme of the Today commercial in Figure 15–3. As a means of accentuating the difference between "The Sixties" and "Today," the first two-thirds of the spot was shot in black and white. The visual transformed to contemporary color with the words "Until Today." Being in tune with the times is thereby added as a reinforcing subtheme without directly raising potentially argumentative statements of values about birth control practices.

The *ill*egitimacy of a product can also, of course, be argued by an advocacy commercial. In the Figure 15–4 photoboard, a single, simple, but highly retentive comparison is drawn between cold high fashion (fur coats) and warm humanity (the cloth-coat alternative). The viewer is still given the right to choose—but the spot's point of view is convincingly registered.

Six Controversy Campaign Objectives

The selection of one of the four controversy spot types is made with an eye toward accomplishing one or more of six possible client objectives to: (1) restore balance to the public discussion, (2) establish the client's right to be a party to issue resolution, (3) strive to influence the public agenda, (4) defend/extend a point of view, (5) rebut charges, and (6) improve sales.

1. Restore Balance to Public Discussion. At least in democratic countries, most of the citizenry believe in people's right to be heard. Though this belief is not *automatically* extended to corporations or organizations, appealing to the audience's sense of fairness or humanity will usually beget a willingness to listen—provided, of course, your message is presented in an interesting and involving manner. In seeking to refurbish its image, Dow's "Lets You Do Great Things" campaign (Figure 15–2) reveals a company making not just chemical profits, but a positive societal contribution as well.

Similarly, with the Figure 15–5 commercial, Waste Management, Inc., strives to demonstrate that its enterprise, too, is meritorious. "Essentially," explains Waste Management executive Donald O'Toole, "many people view the people in the industry as 'those guys out there,' faceless and thoughtless. [Consumers] have the idea that we don't know what to do with waste."[27] Thus, the firm's television campaign works to balance this impression by showing, among other things, that a well-managed landfill can actually assist in ecological preservation.

ANNCR: When you
think about all the

changes in the
last 24-years,

it's hard to
believe

that your choices
in birth control

haven't changed
at all.

Until Today.
Today. The 24-hour
contraceptive sponge.

The Today Sponge
is the best idea
since the Pill.

It's safe. It's easy
to use. And it's
effective.

Today is finally here.
After all, it's time you
had another choice.

Figure 15-3

(Courtesy of Patti Halpert, keye/donna/pearlstein.)

A Winter Fashion Show from your fancy furrier

Announcer V.O.:
A Winter Fashion Show
from your fancy furrier:

Warm body…

Wait —

Second Model:
Warm body…

Cold Heart!

A Winter Fashion Show From Friends of Animals

Announcer V.O.:
A Winter Fashion Show
from Friends of Animals:

Model:
Cold Heart!

Warm body…
Model:
Warm heart!

Warm body…

Second Model:
Warm heart!

Announcer V.O.:
Don't support an industry that destroys
beautiful animals. Don't wear fur.

Friends of Animals.
Because they need your time,
your warmth, your love.

1-800-USA-0006

Model:
I'm warm-hearted.
I don't wear fur!

Figure 15-4

(Courtesy of George Lois, Lois USA.)

509

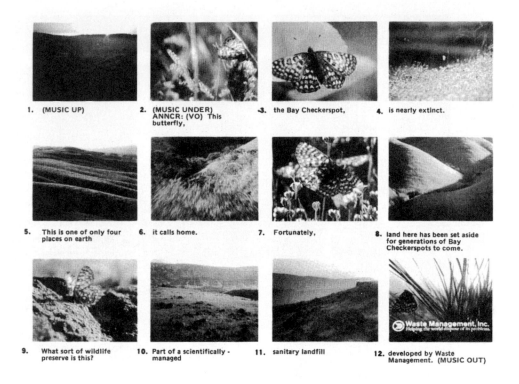

1. (MUSIC UP)

2. (MUSIC UNDER) ANNCR: (VO) This butterfly,

3. the Bay Checkerspot,

4. is nearly extinct.

5. This is one of only four places on earth

6. it calls home.

7. Fortunately,

8. land here has been set aside for generations of Bay Checkerspots to come.

9. What sort of wildlife preserve is this?

10. Part of a scientifically - managed

11. sanitary landfill

12. developed by Waste Management. (MUSIC OUT)

Figure 15-5

(Courtesy of Ronald Hawkins, Ogilvy & Mather Advertising.)

2. Establish the Client's Right to Be Party to Issue Resolution. A portion of any controversy—sometimes the major portion—swirls around "who can play," who has the credentials to participate in determining issue outcome and how we shall reach it. A "special interest group" for instance, must prove itself to be a *public* interest group (or, at least, a group with the public's interest in mind) before its advocacy will be accepted. Certainly, a firearm manufacturer's position on gun control faces an insurmountable task in showing it speaks with anything but pocketbook motivation. But the manufacturer could, however, provide the ammunition (no pun intended) that less vested interest spokes sources could articulate in support of its stand.

The following radio spot advocates women's rights—as asserted via the ballot box—to "have an impact" and "make a difference." It was produced by The Deciding Vote, a nonprofit committee of media executives, to assure all women that they have both the power and the responsibility to affect change.

ANNCR: This November, there is someone who has the power to
         change your life. Someone who will have an impact on
         the issues women care about, like healthcare,
         poverty, education and unemployment. Someone (pause)
         who can make a difference. It's you. (Pause) Yet,
         most politicians still think women should be seen
         and not heard. Make them listen. Vote.

         This was a non-profit, non-partisan message brought
         to you by The Deciding Vote, Women '92.

(Courtesy of Lisa Rosen, NW Ayer Incorporated.)

3. Strive to Influence the Public Agenda. Because there is no candidate to personify the target issue, the controversy commercial must bring it to the fore as a self-standing concern. WAFB did this in spotlighting the necessity for "Free TV" and so did the Friends of Animals message (in Figure 15–4) in terms of fur clothing.

As a further example of agenda-setting, Figure 15–6 illustrates the National Educational Association's endeavor to make school funding a major election-year topic. To symbolize that issue, their agency created "Tracy." This aspiring musician embodies the NEA concern and becomes the tangible vehicle for injecting support of education into the candidate races.

4. Defend/Extend a Point of View. Unlike the previous one, this objective need not concern itself with agenda influencing. Here, the issue is already squarely in the public eye, and the message can proceed directly to the task of championing the client's position on it. Many people, in fact, see this goal as being synonymous with controversy advertising *per se*. Though our discussion has identified additional goals with which advocacy advertising might be involved, there is no question that stark point-of-view espousal is the most salient task of most controversy campaigns.

The Canada Committee partisan spot at the beginning of our controversy discussion certainly mirrors this objective. Point-of-view extension is also achieved in the following message from the Michigan Committee to End Tax-Funded Abortions. Here, the issue is subtly shifted from a thorny debate over morality to a more clear-cut concern about money and fairness:

Video	Audio
RESTAURANT. SUBJECTS SITTING AROUND TABLE. CAMERA AT EYE-LEVEL, MOUNTED ON DOLLY TRACKS	SFX: AMBIENT RESTAURANT SOUNDS

Continued on page 513

NATIONAL EDUCATION ASSOCIATION
"MUSIC CLASS"
30 SECONDS

1. V.O.: Tracy's just learned her first songs.

2. V.O.: But next year, because of budget cuts, we won't offer music.

3. V.O.: Some may think music may not be as important as science ...

4. V.O.: ... But school shouldn't just be equations and formulas. Tracy was just about to master "London Bridge."

5. V.O.: I want to know why the people we elect can't do something. And so does she.

6. ANNCR: In this election year, what's more important than investing in our kids?

Figure 15-6

(Courtesy of Hank Goldberg, Beber Silverstein & Partners.)

512

Video	Audio
SWISH PAN TO 1ST GUY; START CAMERA ARC	1ST GUY: Hey, didya see the end of the game last night?
CAMERA ARC CONTINUES TO M2S	2ND GUY: Yeah, it was great. How about that news story on the election? 1ST GUY: Yeah---whadya think about this tax-paid abortion business?
ARC CONTINUES TO MCU OF 1ST WOMAN	1ST WOMAN: I'm against abortion. I just think it's wrong---
CUT TO CU 2ND WOMAN	2ND WOMAN: Carol, I know we don't agree on abortion, but this is a whole different thing---
CUT TO CU 1ST GUY	1ST GUY: Yup---this isn't about abortions. It's about who pays for them---
ARC CONTINUES TO MCU 3RD WOMAN; ARC STOPS, SHOT TIGHTENS	3RD WOMAN: Well, I'm not sure where I stand on abortion--- but I know it's not fair for taxpayers to pay for them---
DIZ MCU 1ST GUY	1ST GUY: You're right---it's not fair.
CROSSFADE TO GRAPHIC: Vote 'Yes' on Proposal 'A' End Tax-Funded Abortions.	SFX: POSITIVE LOUDENING TONE
DISCLAIMER	SFX: 'CHECK' SOUND AS PENCIL MARKS SQUARE ON GRAPHIC BALLOT

(Courtesy of Robert Bradsell, Ailes Communications Inc.)

5. Rebut Charges.   This is an objective a copywriter hates to face because it becomes a goal only when the other side has already put your client on the defensive. Under such circumstances, it is too late to strive to influence the public agenda and not enough just to extend a general point of view. Instead, your client has already been indicted in the public media, and you have little choice but to respond directly to the thrust or thrusts of that indictment. As mentioned in our analysis of the "Dissident" audience in Chapter 5, you cannot ignore or sidestep the main charge being leveled. That action will only confirm in people's minds that the allegation is true—and that you are "shifty" besides. Like the Tincanada spot below, your best strategy is to isolate the accusation and neutralize it by describing clearly extenuating circumstances (not excuses) while seeking to establish a common bond with your audience.

ANNCR: The recent rate hike in local telephone services has worried a lot of people. And it's making some of them angry. Angry at Tincanada Telephone. Like you, we're worried and angry too. Not just because we're area residents. But because we _are_ Tincanada. That's right. We're the folks being blamed for that added charge on your local phone bill.

VOICE: So what gives us the right to be angry or worried? Just the fact that the rate increase is beyond our control too. But we're taking the rap.

ANNCR: You see, recent government tariff regulations on long distance access charges have forced us to pay a lot more---a lot more to those long distance companies to get your calls in and out of our community. So to stay in business, we're forced to raise this revenue from local service customers. People like you. Whom Tincanada has valued as friends for 50 years.

VOICE: That's what worries and angers us the most. The fact that Tincanada's in danger of losing your friendship over new regulations created in Washington. Let's get mad together---but not at each other.

6. Improve Sales.   A controversy ad may seem an unlikely vehicle for product selling. But, as Jon Bond, president of Kirshenbaum & Bond, points out, "The essence of marketing is sacrifice. You make a strong statement to one group at the expense of appealing to other groups. You sell 20 percent of the population 100 percent of the way instead of vice versa. Only, with controversial advertising, the reaction of the peripheral groups is often a bit stronger than mere disinterest."[28] Bond's firm specializes in controversy marketing strategy and, out of its experiences, has evolved a list of four situations for which a controversial approach may be the most appropriate tactic:

1. When you have an awareness problem.
2. When you have a small budget or are being significantly outspent by the competition. Controversy causes consumers and media to talk, which creates a kind of multiplier effect on the budget.
3. When you don't need a large share to be successful (niche marketing), and don't need to appeal to a broad range of people. Controversy is a relative term; what offends some people may bore others.
4. When you can make the controversial statement relative to the product.[29]

Never mentioned over the air until the AIDS crisis, condoms remain a highly controversial product even though their role as an HIV-AIDS preventive has been endorsed by the medical community. So, rather than adopt the clinical and slightly ominous tone common to the category, LifeStyle's agency, Lois USA, decided to accept the fact that some people will never accept condom pitches. The creatives didn't worry, therefore, about offending this nonmarket but concentrated instead on a lighthearted campaign designed to make condom users less embarrassed about their purchase—and about asking for LifeStyles by name. The campaign's three-spot flight in Figure 15–7 "makes an assumption that there is some knowledge about AIDS and its prevention," reports agency head, George Lois. "I did the spots to change the fear of dying to the love of living."[30]

Such a strategy works given LifeStyle's market situation, but it will not work for every product or in every product category. As Jon Bond cautions, the worst condition for controversial advertising would be "when you are the market leader with a large share to protect. Advertising for a market leader must have a common denominator"[31]

Crisis Advertising

The journalistic Paul Reveres of today have an infinitely greater and more sustained influence than he did. An alarum raised by one of their stories can spread almost instantaneously across the country and impact the actions and beliefs of millions of people. As a result, when your client's product or service is the subject of this furor, a copywriter has little time to act before permanent corporate harm is inflicted. Because damage control is such a crucial advertising response in today's world of precipitate communication, we close with a special examination of crisis copywriting techniques.

Phantom of the Opera   15 sec. TV commercial

Announcer:
The Phantom of the Opera,
shopping for
LifeStyles Condoms!

Store Clerk:
Hi, Phantom. Taking a date to the
opera?
Phantom:
Yes, and I could use some LifeStyles.
Store Clerk:
Oh…but you didn't have to wear
that mask to ask for them!

Announcer:
LifeStyles.
It's a matter of condom sense!™

Azania of the Jungle   15 sec. TV commercial

Announcer:
The queen of the jungle,
shopping for
LifeStyles Condoms!

Azania:
I need sunscreen, hair mousse,
and a year's supply of LifeStyles.
Store Clerk:
Good thinking, Azania—
'cause it's a jungle out there!

Announcer:
LifeStyles.
It's a matter of condom sense!

Robin Hood   15 sec. TV commercial

Announcer:
Robin Hood,
shopping for LifeStyles Condoms!

Robin Hood:
Shampoo for the fair Marion,
and LifeStyles for all my merry men!
Store Clerk:
Oh, you use the same brand
as the Sheriff of Nottingham!

Announcer:
LifeStyles.
It's a matter of condom sense!

Figure 15-7

(Courtesy of George Lois, Lois USA.)

As *ADWEEK's* Christy Marshall points out, when a public crisis hits a company, there are basically only five possible courses of action:

Stop advertising.
Kill the product or dump the celebrity (if the crisis involved your spokesperson).
Pull the product, reformulate it, repackage it, replace it on the shelves.
Break a campaign to set the record straight.
Ignore it and pray it will go away soon.[32]

Four of these five options are company actions that will not employ the copywriter. Therefore, we need not concern ourselves with them here. The remaining choice, "breaking a campaign to set the record set," is, on the other hand, a copywriter-centered task that demands all the skill a wordsmith can muster.

The best strategy for dealing with a crisis is to anticipate it via what experts in the field call *pro-active communication.* "Before a crisis strikes, image advertising, issue advertising and pr can build a reservoir of good will," explains public relations firm president Steven Fink. "Then, when the crisis hits, the public will trust you more, forgive you faster. You can say: 'Give us your proxy, buy our product.' "[33]

Certainly, if pro-active communication has been running all along, the copywriter's crisis management task will be easier—but by no means minimal. You still must address the crisis directly and immediately. "If the corporation doesn't communicate effectively and quickly," warns John Burke of Burson-Marsteller, "it will have to play catch-up ball for six to nine months, and it may never catch up"[34] "Crisis," adds Phillips Petroleum spokesman George Minter, "abhors a vacuum."[35]

Quickness, however, should not be confused with *impulsiveness.* Never disseminate copy that 'tells the truth' before you have taken the time to cast that truth in a lucid, concise package. "You can over-explain and get yourself in trouble," Burke advises. "You can, for example, send a biochemist to talk about a chemical; he will tell the truth, and he'll over-tell the truth. He may create unfounded concerns about other issues."[36]

The choice of a spokesperson for your crisis commercial is crucial to its success. Public relations executive Richard Edelman asserts that "In a crisis, people are impressed by leaders, not products."[37] From this leader, the public expects "not absolute knowledge but absolute concern,"[38] declares Burke. You can write concern into the copy, but it will do no good if the spokesperson can't convey it. Thus, in selecting your 'leader' from among the client hierarchy, keep in mind that the spokesperson's voice quality (for radio) and physical mannerisms (for television) make a big difference. "People never remember what you specifically said," asserts Burke, "but they take away an impression. The nonverbal is as important as the verbal."[39]

In the case of its March 1989, tanker oil spill in Alaska, Exxon ignored these fundamental principles. First, the company delayed making any definitive pronouncement. Then, it relied on local, on-site managers to release public statements without coordination or the authority to be straightforward. Corporation chairman Lawrence Rawl did not make his first public comments about the *Exxon Valdez* disaster until nearly a week after the spill. As president of the American Association of Advertising Agencies John O'Toole observed at the time, "Silence is the crime Exxon is paying for. And that's a helluva price to pay for not running an ad the very next day."[40] By the time Rawl did speak up, "public perception was fast solidifying that the oil titan was unconcerned and stonewalling," reported trade publication editor Stephen Barr. "And rather than appearing contrite, Rawl blasted the state of Alaska and the Coast Guard for stalling Exxon's clean-up efforts."[41] Rawl may not have been the best top executive to handle the crisis communication task. But his failure to immediately activate an official who possessed these skills—with the copy support necessary to convey the truth crisply and contritely—created an immense image problem that continues long after the physical clean-up.

In contrast to the Exxon debacle, we now present four case studies in which effective crisis communication procedures and copy strategies *were* employed.

The Tylenol Crisis

In October 1982, a number of people in the Chicago area died after taking poison-tainted Extra-Strength Tylenol capsules. Though it was soon determined unequivocally that the poison had been introduced by someone after the capsules had been distributed, this fact had to be communicated promptly and in a way calculated to *preserve* the brand's good name. The term *preserve* is important, because it is more feasible to bolster a subject still perceived somewhat positively than to wait and face the uphill battle of restoring credibility to a term that, in the public's mind, has already been thoroughly polluted.

Working closely with the client, executives from Compton Advertising decided to take their case to the airwaves with an unvarnished report designed to set the record straight. For credibility's sake, use of any outside talent was ruled out. Instead, the agency screentested a number of top executives from Johnson & Johnson's McNeil Consumer Products subsidiary (the actual manufacturer of Tylenol) and selected Dr. Thomas Gates, McNeil's medical director, as the on-camera spokesman. The resulting Gates commercial (Figure 15–8) ran more than a dozen times in network primetime.

As the grainy Tylenol photoboard evidences, what had to be communicated—and communicated quickly—was a sense of urgent concern rather

COMPTON ADVERTISING, INC.

625 Madison Avenue, New York, N.Y. 10022

Telephone: PLaza 4-1100

CLIENT: MCNEIL CONSUMER PRODUCTS CO.
PRODUCT: TYLENOL
TITLE: "CORPORATE STATEMENT"
COMML. # JJCX 2046   TIMING: 60 SECONDS
DATE: 10/21/82

1. ANNCR: (VO) An important message from the makers of Tylenol.

2. DR. GATES: You are all aware of recent tragic events,

3. in which Extra-Strength Tylenol capsules were criminally tampered with...

4. in limited areas...after they left our factory.

5. This act damages all of us.

6. You, the American public, because you have made Tylenol a trusted part of your health care.

7. And we who make Tylenol, because we've worked hard to earn that trust.

8. We will now work even harder to keep it.

9. We have voluntarily withdrawn all Tylenol capsules from the shelf.

10. We will reintroduce capsules in tamper-resistant containers, as quickly as possible.

11. Until then, we would urge all Tylenol capsule users to use the tablet form.

12. And, we have offered to replace your capsules with tablets.

13. Tylenol has had the trust of the medical profession and a hundred million Americans for over 20 years.

14. We value that trust too much to let any individual tamper with it.

15. We want you to continue to trust Tylenol.

Figure 15-8

Courtesy of F. Robert Kniffen, Johnson & Johnson.)

than premeditated slickness. Production values were necessarily underplayed as a consequence. After explaining the facts of the situation, Dr. Gates's message offered the twin alternatives of (1) switching from Tylenol capsules to the much-harder-to-tamper-with tablets via (2) the company's offer to "replace your capsules with tablets." The precautionary action of withdrawing all capsules from the stores was justified as necessary to maintain consumer trust and characterized as a temporary measure until "capsules in tamper-resistant containers" could be developed. The spot also associated the company with the consumer by observing that "this act damages all of us" and made it clear that the company, like the people poisoned, was an innocent victim of a criminal act by an outsider.

This no-nonsense trust strategy was extended some two months later when the now triple-sealed capsule packages had reached store shelves. The reintroduction was heralded in a 45/15 commercial. The 45-second portion was devoted to a testimonial by San Diego housewife Paige Nagle, who affirmed that "Tylenol is worthy of my trust" and that the product's "more than just a pain reliever, it's something we can count on." As a trust/confidence builder, the testimonial avoided any mention of capsules, poisoning, or packaging. The 15-second announcer voice-over then explained the three safety seals as they were shown and warned against the purchase of open packages. Rather than reawaken memories of the disaster, the announcer's copy concentrated on the fact that Tylenol capsules were being "reintroduced" and thus fulfilled the promise that Dr. Gates had made in the previous spot.

Six months after the tragedy, Tylenol had recaptured 80 percent of its previous market share,"[42] a tribute both to product quality and a level-headed copy reaction to what might have been a panic-inducing situation.

The Hygrade Crisis

About the same time as the Tylenol episode, the Hygrade Corporation was rocked by a charge that a consumer had found a metal object in one of the Hygrade-manufactured Ball Park Franks. Three other complaints about hot-dog-encased nails and razor blades soon followed. The company immediately halted shipments, issued a voluntary product recall, and quickly obtained metal detectors to examine one million hot dogs. Hygrade's agency, W. B. Doner & Company, marshalled its forces and prepared to launch creative work as soon as (but not before) all the facts were available. Looking back, agency executive vice-president Skip Roberts emphasized:

> All the God and motherhood advertising appeals in the world would not give us one edge up forward if our customers were not convinced that the premium product, although they had enjoyed it for years, was still fit for human consumption.[43]

Only a few days later, polygraph tests on two of the complainants failed to support their "metallic" charges and a third failed to appear for the test. With examinations of both the meat and its accusers thus completed, the crisis advertising strategy was launched. "We recommended," recalled Roberts, "that our advertising be based on simple truths—we had a problem; the problem had been solved; and we were ready to go back on the market."[44] Within a day, the following TV spot was created. For speed, stark truthfulness, and audiovisual fact registration, the commercial was nothing more than a graphic crawl replication of a simultaneously running newspaper layout:

Video	Audio
WHITE-ON-BLACK ROLL OF VO-READ COPY AT EASILY DIGESTIBLE SPEED	VO: To our Ball Park customers: Thank you for bearing with us. We at Hygrade Food Products Corporation, along with the United States Department of Agriculture, have just completed an exhaustive investigation of Hygrade's Livonia, Michigan, plant, and over 600,,000 pounds of our products. The results: All facilities are operating according to the highest standards, and all products leaving our plant have been verified 100 percent safe--- just as it's always been. Our withdrawal of Ball Park Franks from the marketplace was entirely voluntary. U.S.D.A. inspectors have agreed that such action is no longer necessary, and normal distribution is now being resumed in all areas.

Continued

Video	Audio
	There is no evidence that any individual was ever in any danger. Nonetheless, we have taken the precaution of installing permanent ultra-sensitive metal detection systems in our plant. We want to maintain your trust in us and provide every possible measure of protection and safety.
	We wish to thank our many employees who so willingly volunteered their own time to assist in this inspection. And we thank you, our customers, for your support and understanding.
SLOW FADE OUT	Hygrade Food Products Corporation

(Courtesy of Debbie Cragin, W. B. Doner & Company Advertising.)

To avoid prolonging the sense of crisis, the print ad ran only once in sixteen newspapers in Detroit, outstate Michigan, Ohio, Chicago, and Pittsburgh.[45] The television commercial aired on the three major Detroit television stations for only one day. Despite such brief exposure, the credibility of the print-on-TV device plus what Doner account executive Debbie Cragin labeled "the timeliness and directness of the message"[46] combined to bring the potentially disastrous episode to a positive conclusion for Hygrade. And like the Tylenol response, the creative work in this case also exploited an amalgam of controversy copywriting techniques. The company justified its action in product removals as well as its subsequent quick return to "normal distribution" by citing the safety verification that was sought and obtained through "an exhaustive investigation and inspection."

The company's cooperation with the U.S.D.A. and that governmental agency's positive findings invested the commercial with additional legitimacy. Finally, though it did not make it a major issue, the fact that Hygrade examined "over 600,000 pounds of our products" and that this was accomplished through "employees who so willingly volunteered their own time" demonstrated that the company and its people were the episode's only real victims and should not be victimized further by unwarranted consumer avoidance of the Hygrade product.

The Market Crash Crisis

Without warning, on October 19, 1987, the Dow Jones Industrial Average fell $22\frac{1}{2}$ percent. To stave off panic or acute lack of confidence in the market, leading brokerage house Merrill Lynch directed its advertising agency to prepare print and television copy for public dissemination. Within forty-eight hours, Merrill Lynch Chairman William Schreyer was on the air 'restoring balance to public discussion.' Schreyer's pitch assured stockholders that Merrill Lynch was, with them, remaining active in the markets and that this was the reasonable course of action for all concerned:

Video	Audio
GRAPHIC: 'A Message From Merrill Lynch'	
DIZ SCHREYER; SUPER HIS NAME AND 'Chairman and CEO'	SCHREYER: I'm here for some straight talk about the stock market. It's important to everyone, it provides capital that creates jobs to make America grow. Emotions could run high during market turbulence, just when reason should prevail.
TIGHTEN SLIGHTLY	We're confident in the markets. We've stayed active in them for all investors. America's economy is the strongest in the world with great ability to bounce back. At Merrill Lynch
SUPER MERRILL LYNCH LOGO	we're still bullish on America.

(Courtesy of Betty Brody, Bozell, Jacobs, Kenyon & Eckhardt.)

Together with spots voiced by the firm's chief market analyst and director of research and economics, the Schreyer message stabilized stockholder confidence in the market in general and in Merrill Lynch in particular. The selection of these believable and top echelon spokespersons by the Bozell, Jacobs, Kenyon & Eckhardt agency "was the strongest message of all," maintains BJK&E account executive Gerald Sherwin.[47] Again illustrating that people are impressed by concerned leaders, Merrill Lynch's chosen spokespersons, and the BJK&E copy they articulated, achieved the firm's short-term reassurance goal while also enhancing its long-term credibility.

What made the success of the campaign even more striking was the fact that, at the time, the brokerage house had no crisis management plan in place. "We joke about it now," reflects Merrill Lynch's director of corporate advertising, Charles Mangano. "We didn't know we'd have to face the biggest crisis in our careers without a plan."[48]

The Eastern Airlines Bankruptcy Crisis

Our previous three case studies all deal with sudden, unexpected events. Conversely, after years of negative press coverage, Eastern Airlines' 1990 descent into bankruptcy was all too predictable. Nevertheless, once bankruptcy was declared and a trustee appointed by the court, an attempt had to be made to maintain public and employee faith in the carrier's viability. For Eastern to have any hope of survival, it had to be quickly established that survival was possible.

Accepting the challenge, Ogilvy & Mather/New York took to the airwaves with a series of spots built around Martin Shugrue—the court-appointed trustee. As the person clearly in the top position of leadership, and one who could not be blamed for Eastern's previous failures, Shugrue presented the only viable symbol and hope for corporate change. Labeled, "100 Days," the campaign featured the trustee in a series of print ads and black-and-white spots in which he talked forcefully to the public and to Eastern employees. "We're not going to promise you the moon," he admits in one commercial, "because we can't deliver it. What we can promise is that for the next 100 days Eastern is going to get a little better every day."

These ads, asserted advertising critic Barbara Lippert, succeeding in establishing "the bias in favor of a guy who's open, caring, and says all the right things. Technoproof that the company is flawed but trying, it's perhaps the most sophisticated visual form of damage control ever practiced on television outside of Bush's press conferences."[49] Shugrue's appearances in these quasi-documentary, black-and-white scenes project the feeling of crisis—but also of a crisis being actively managed by a candid, take-charge executive. In the

Ogilvy & Mather
Worldwide Plaza
309 West 49th Street • New York, New York • 10019-7399
Telephone: (212) 237-4000 • Telex: 12279 • Facsimile: (212) 237-5123

CLIENT: EASTERN AIRLINES
PRODUCT: CORPORATE
TITLE: "GROWTH W/ OPENING TITLE REV."
COMML NO.: EACO 0103 :30

MAN: The question was the 5% promise. Yes,

right here.

WOMAN: Is it true, uh, will I be here 50 years from now...

(LAUGHS) with Eastern?

MAN: Can I guarantee another 50 years of history for Eastern Airlines?

No, I cannot.

All I can tell you is

we're not just thinkin' survival, friends, we're thinkin' growth.

And airline economics

only works with growth.

I don't think you cut yourself back to profitability; I think you build yourself to profitability

and I think we can do that. And that's the plan.

Figure 15-9

(Courtesy of Yvonne Rivera, Ogilvy & Mather.)

Figure 15–9 spot, for instance, he makes no employee "guarantees," but promises assertive leadership rather than further dismal dismantling. Consumers eavesdropping on this staff meeting thereby seem to get "inside information" about renewed Eastern growth. They can purchase tickets with confidence because the airline is actually expanding rather than boarding up the store.

Ultimately, Eastern did fold. Years of fiscal and managerial setbacks could not be undone in "100 Days." Nevertheless, the Shugrue spots did serve to keep the airline flying longer than most analysts expected. Employees drew paychecks and passengers were accommodated for an additional period of time. As the Eastern episode demonstrated, crisis communication can't resolve corporate inadequacies. It can, however, help stabilize public perceptions while renovations are attempted.

As copywriters, we should not shy away from crisis assignments but rather should see them as rare opportunities to enhance our own skills and professional behaviors. As public relations executive and crisis management expert David Wachsman reminds us:

> In ancient Chinese the symbol for 'crisis' was a combination of two pictograms—one meaning 'danger' and the other meaning 'opportunity.' That's significant. A crisis is horrible by definition, but don't forget that by the way you deal with it you are going to be judged and defined for a long time. If you do the right things and do them when they should be done and are forthcoming and act prudently—with emotional soundness and understanding—then people are going to look at you differently. . . . You act first to save, stabilize, reopen and build the business up again. And second, you must behave in such a way that throughout the crisis . . . people look back and say, 'Those people really performed well. It was an awful thing that happened, but they did their jobs well.' "[50]

A Final Word from the Soda Bar

By this juncture, you've been acclimated to the overall dimensions of broadcast/cable copywriting, have suffered the rigors of scribbling for radio, and been exposed to the discipline of creating for video. Finally, you have endured at least a small measure of the struggle that occurs between market conditions and creative inclinations; grappling that is the necessary prologue to a well-fashioned electronic campaign—whether in the service of product, public cause, or politician. As agency president Malcolm MacDougall observes: "The words that appear in advertising today are the most expensive words ever written. Each and every one should be agonized over, crunched into a ball and tossed into the wastebasket, until just the right word is found—the word that perfectly fits the selling message, the word that has that special power to arrest, to penetrate, to persuade, to create customers."[51]

If you are utterly frustrated by all of this—great. Most creative people are. But since all art is ultimately a delicate balance between the discipline of form and the discipline of content, promising copywriters also find a stimulating encounter in the whole rule-clogged mess. Just don't become so intense in winning the encounter that you burn yourself out, like the kid who used up all his July 4th sparklers before it got dark enough to see them.

Instead, try to follow the long-trusted advice of veteran copywriter and creative director Don Cowlbeck and—

> Listen very carefully for the sound of your *own* soda-straw starting to suck bottom. When you hear it, go fishing.
>
> We are in a pressurized profession. "I need that next Tuesday." "We have to do something about our marketing situation in Phoenix." "I don't know what—that's what I pay you people for." "It's no big problem; how's about we discuss it tomorrow at a breakfast meeting. Say, 4 A.M.?"
>
> What fun! What a challenge! How much better than the hum-drum, ho-hum, another-day-another-dollar existence of others less fortunate than we.
>
> But there comes a time when each of us, under pressure, becomes cranky, finds his energies dissipated, himself unproductive and unhappy. My final secret—and perhaps most valuable one—is when your personal straw starts to suck bottom—go fishing.[52]

As your author and guide through the world of broadcast/cable copywriting, let me wish you every success as a wordsmith and leave you with one final and (after fifteen arduous chapters) heartfelt word—

S-S-S-SSLURP!
(I hope the bluegills are biting.)

Endnotes

1. "Political TV Ad Revenues Up Sharply in Campaign '88," *NAB TV Today* (February 20, 1989), 2.
2. "Political Spending Hits $300 Million Mark," *ADWEEK* (November 16, 1992), 8B.
3. Lisa Marie Peterson, "Cable TV Enters Presidential Race," *ADWEEK* (October 12, 1992), 12.
4. Kathleen Jamieson, "The Paradox of Political Ads," *Media & Values* (Spring 1992), 14.
5. Barry Golson and Peter Range, "Clinton on TV," *TV Guide* (November 21, 1992), 15.
6. Leonard Shyles, "Defining the Issues of a Presidential Election," *Journal of Broadcasting* (Fall 1983), 342–343.

7. Alan Baron, "Marketer of the Year," *ADWEEK* (May 1985), M.M. 4.

8. Stephen Battaglio, "Dukakis Ad Team Wasn't Ready for Political Hardball," *ADWEEK* (November 14, 1988), 4.

9. George Comstock et al., *Television and Human Behavior* (New York: Columbia University Press, 1978), 364–365.

10. Ed Buxton, "Adman, Pass By," *ADWEEK* (May 7, 1984), 26.

11. Richard Joslyn, "The Content of Political Spot Ads," *Journalism Quarterly* (Spring 1980), 94.

12. Leonard Shyles, "The Relationships of Images, Issues and Presentational Methods in Televised Spot Advertisements for 1980's Presidential Primaries," *Journal of Broadcasting* (Fall 1984), 406.

13. Stephen Battaglio, "Honing 'Brand' Images," *ADWEEK* (September 12, 1988), F.P. 38.

14. Anne Barton White, "Issue and Image Distinctions and Their Relationships to Structure and Content of Political Advertisements for 1988 Presidential Candidates Bush and Dukakis." Paper presented at the Association for Education in Journalism and Mass Communication Convention, August 1990 (Minneapolis), 29.

15. Ronald Faber and M. Claire Storey, "Recall of Information from Political Advertising," *Journal of Advertising* 13 (1984), 39.

16. White, 28–29.

17. "Campaigning According to Cuomo," *Broadcasting* (November 10, 1986), 121.

18. Randy Sukow, "Negative Political Ads Will Be Back in '92," *Broadcasting* (November 25, 1991), 56.

19. Mark Dolliver, "Political Campaign Ads Need to Be Energized," *ADWEEK* (October 22, 1990), 27.

20. Brian Roddy and Gina Garramone, "Appeals and Strategies of Negative Political Advertising," *Journal of Broadcasting & Electronic Media* (Fall 1988), 418.

21. Ibid.

22. Ibid., 425.

23. Michael Shapiro and Robert Rieger, "Comparing Positive and Negative Political Advertising on Radio," *Journalism Quarterly* (Spring 1992), 142–144.

24. International Advertising Association, *Controversy Advertising* (New York: Hastings House, 1977), 18.

25. Richard Long, "Controversy and Dow Chemical: Can a Leopard Change Its Spots?" Speech presented at The Center for Communication Seminar, 9 October 1986 (New York).

26. Vicky Suazo, "Controversy and Dow Chemical: Can a Leopard Change Its Spots?" Speech presented at The Center for Communication Seminar, 9 October 1986 (New York).

27. Fran Brock, "Waste Management Keeps Clean," *ADWEEK* (February 24, 1986), 2.

28. Jon Bond, writing in "Viewpoint," *Winners* (March 1988), 3.

29. Ibid.

30. Stephen Battaglio, "Nets Don't Find Condom Ads Funny," *ADWEEK* (August 15, 1988), 38.

31. Bond, 3.

32. Christy Marshall, "Crisis Advertising: What's an Agency to Do?" *ADWEEK* (August 13, 1984), 25.

33. Teresa Tritch, "Crisis Ads: When All Hell Breaks Loose," *ADWEEK* (October 17, 1988), 48.
34. John Burke, "Crisis Public Relations: Tylenol and Other Headaches." Speech presented at The Center for Communication Seminar, 13 November 1986 (New York).
35. "Marketers's Report Card, 1989," *ADWEEK* (November 27, 1989), M.R.C. 38.
36. Burke, "Crisis Public Relations."
37. Tritch, 62.
38. Burke, "Crisis Public Relations."
39. Ibid.
40. Richard Morgan, "Exxon Learns the Hard Way: Goodwill Is More Than a Balance Sheet," *ADWEEK* (April 24, 1989), 3.
41. Stephen Barr, "Sullied Waters, Tarnished Reputation: The Exxon Mess," *Corporate Video Decisions* (May 1990), 29.
42. Maria Fisher, "Tylenol Makes Extra-Strong Comeback," *ADWEEK* (March 21, 1983), 20.
43. Eileen Courter, "Reputation, PR Helped Hygrade Survive Hot Dog Hoax," *ADWEEK* (April 4, 1983), 43.
44. Ibid.
45. Emmet Curme, "Hygrade Counters Ball Park Rhubarb with Safety, 'Thank-You' Campaign," *ADWEEK* (November 15, 1982), 57.
46. Debbie Cragin. Letter to the author, 30 January 1985.
47. Tritch, 62.
48. Ibid.
49. Barbara Lippert, " '100 Days' Gives Psychological Lift to Ailing Eastern," *ADWEEK* (July 9, 1990), 19.
50. "Death Meets the Public Relations Business," *ASAP* (January/February 1990), 10.
51. Malcolm MacDougall, "The Advertising Cliché Code," *ADWEEK* (April 22, 1985), 52.
52. Don Cowlbeck, writing in "Monday Memo," *Broadcasting* (March 20, 1972), 19.

INDEX